Transcendental Illuminations

Autobiographies of a Seeker and a Saint

Mari Tankenoff & Scott Bergér

Beaver's Pond Press, Inc.
Edina, Minnesota

ISBN 1-59298-051-1

Library of Congress Catalog Number: 2004111027

interior design by Mori Studio, Inc.

photo on page 452 from authors' collection, prepared by Joan Buccina, Buccina Studios, Ltd.

Printed in Canada

First Printing: September 2004

08 07 06 05 04   5 4 3 2 1

for more information, visit www.TranscendentalIlluminations.com

Beaver's Pond Press, Inc.

7104 Ohms Lane, Suite 216
Edina, MN 55439
(952) 829-8818
www.beaverspondpress.com

to order, visit www.BookHouseFulfillment.com
or call 1-800-901-3480. Reseller discounts available.

Symbolic Dedication

Transcendental Illuminations is written in honor of all past, present, and future visionaries possessing the inner fortitude to resist the established practices of dogmatic thought repression. You are the inspired people of limitless, creedless, raceless, universal principles and ideals, who stand alone as towering pillars against seemingly irresistible tides of destruction.

This book stands for the perpetuation of eternal freedom, for recognizing and reclaiming our unique individual conscious experiences. We hope the messages in this book will inspire each of us to reevaluate our personal and ever-accountable intentions, thoughts, actions, and reactions that, combined, determine how we conduct ourselves within this world.

*Unconditional Love
Always and Forever!
Scott Berger & Main Jankenoff*

Table of Contents

Introduction

Both of us have been driven by an insatiable desire and mission to gain insight and greater in-depth comprehension about existence. Both of us are committed to working toward the upliftment of earth humankind. We initially chose our respective professions of psychology and holistic healing, as they seemed to lend themselves well toward achieving such goals. Through our own learned efforts and personal desires to share our experiences, we both were compelled to write a book.

By God's benevolent, intervening hand, we were brought together. By God's divine insistence, we have merged our personal experiences with fascinating, helpful, and truthful information for the enjoyment of all people.

We have created this book to encourage, assist, and support people in their pursuit of Truth and individual conscious evolution. As such, it is our hope that from the many diverse terms, concepts, ideas, and examples we present, you will take from this work that which resonates the most within you.

In the same way any life picture presents a more clarified visual form once you have stepped back from it, so does complexity or intensity of subject matter become less intimidating and more enriching. Oftentimes, multiple viewings from many vantage points are recommended when experiencing pictures of limitless dimension.

Each of us is a seeker, pursuing what he or she perceives will provide the ultimate fulfillment. May this book assist you on your eternal journey.

—Mari Tankenoff and Scott Bergér

Veritable Originations

Transcendental Illuminations has been written for the betterment of all earth humankind. It contains words, concepts, ideas, and even names that some may find troubling, damaging, frightening, uplifting, and enlightening. This is intentionally done with discernment, to annihilate the preconceived notions established in patterns, habits, rituals, and lifestyles by which people in their unique, individual ways have conceptualized human existence.

As with any introduction of new material or thought, a reader's mind can be either contaminated or enlightened, depending on the reader's interpretive experience. We understand that even the contents of this Holy Book might seem contaminating to a reader's previous reservoir of knowledge and individual spiritual comfort level. As our reader, whether you are religious or not is irrelevant. The purpose of *Transcendental Illuminations* is to promote the re-empowerment of the individual.

Many parts of this book pertain to God and to Transcendent aspects of our human conscious experience. Since indefinable God, the Universal Creator, Manifestor, and SuperConsciousness, is Omniscient, Omnipotent, and Omnipresent, why not? This book is not predicatory or in any way religious. In fact, it could be considered the very antithesis of religion in precisely the same way theology is the very antithesis of individuality.

In this book, we explore the true origins of science, creation, religion, history, and spirituality, and in doing so, reveal both the covert mysteries, as well as the misperceptions by which these bases for human existence continually have been maintained and perpetuated.

It may take many lifetimes for individuals to fully comprehend all the Truthful Absolutes in this book. However, we all have eternity with which to work toward attaining Deep Comprehension. In order for unified enlightenment to occur, we must be willing to leave behind our preconceived notions of mistaken beliefs veiled as "truths."

Expanding Perspectives

Some people see an acorn as just a nut.
A few see the acorn as a tree.
The deep thinker sees a forest.
Cosmic Vision Sees a Universe.

Many people see the world as a cup half empty.
Others view the world as a cup half full.
The most earnest of seekers will recognize
  a cup runneth over.
The Superevolved no longer see the cup at all.
That is Unconditional Love.

In Its Reflection of Its Universe
Cosmic Vision Sees Itself—
Unconditional Love.

BOOK
One

World Background History:
The Interwoven Vine

So often in history, there seemed to exist a great deal of fear and paranoia amongst people that their respective, particular religion would be threatened if other religions and beliefs gained strength, momentum, or favor. This wave of fright did not discriminate based upon social station; it resided within both commoners who staunchly retained tight grips on their faiths, as well as royals and those in political power. When mavericks and trailblazers—known as heretics—put forth efforts, however covert or overt, to influence ways of thought, practice, or life, the frightened and threatened tended to panic. In most cases, not only were the messengers punished or silenced, but their messages—be they Hellenistic, Pagan, Gnostic, Judaic, Christian, or Islamic—were at risk for destruction.

Throughout time, monotheism has been a lifeline to which many in the "majority," or at least those in powerful political circles, all desperately, fervently clung. No one really seemed to want to make room for anyone different. Fortunately, there existed some exceptions. No matter the land, culture, or society at the time, there were people within ranks of some authority (wealth, social, or political arenas) who were in positions to take the risks necessary to bring forth messages filled with ideas built upon inclusion, within holistic paradigms. Depending upon how we view these people, they took huge risks considering their relative status, or perhaps it was because of their status that they were afforded the freedom to promote ideas, and thus were never at risk.

However, throughout history, there were many spiritual messengers not adhering to prepackaged dogma who were killed under shady or suspicious circumstances. It certainly seems that promoting new thought, however deftly packaged, has tended to be a risky venture. We, too, are spiritual messengers, taking a risk to write this book. As such, this book bears messages that illuminate Absolute Truth, exposing historically created and perpetuated lies, fear, and ignorance for their final destruction. This book renders Absolute Truth the only survivor.

Before we share our personal spiritual journeys, we have selected a few pertinent, interwoven examples that relate closely to our own personal experiences, as well as to the various myths and continued threads of secrecy regarding organized religion, history, philosophy, and existence as a whole. The following section explores the many themes of risk-taking, message-bearing, secret-keeping, and truth-telling occurring throughout many pivotal times in history. In some cases, we will offer merely the highlights of that particular time, while in other cases, we will go into greater detail.

We are not going to unearth and expose every notable liberty taken by historical writers, recorders, and researchers dating back to 3000 BC. Furthermore, long after this work is presented, secrets still will remain buried with hosts of errors continually lying discretely beneath the surface of perception—until the next prospector of Truth comes along to reveal them. Until then, it is our hope that this book of Truth will bring you unlimited Transcendental Illumination.

The Book of Esther

The Book of Esther is the first of many accounts throughout history with the theme of having to be secretive or deceptive about one's faith, people, culture, or religious identity, in order to blend in, be received, or preserve one's self. It also highlights the theme of employing calculated risk-taking when for a variety of reasons, secret-keeping is not a viable option. Esther writes, "I will go to the King, which is against The Law, and if I perish, I perish." Her words are echoed centuries upon centuries later, as theologies and their associated rules and regulations have left non-adherents few options other than agreeing to conform or risk destruction.

Consequently, the territorial, power-hungry minds of a few people assuming positions of authority have in fact chronically terrorized the lives of many, many people—most of them only attempting to exist with some semblance of Truth and individual freedom. Thus, it is no wonder we have a plethora of examples of people destined to be secret-keepers for existence after existence, in order to avoid persecution—and in order to exist within a whole.

This book will reveal the illusory nature of dominating reigns often characterized by terror and control, and will illuminate the source of true power. From the time of Esther to the present day, it is not within those in "command"—the Kings, Monarchs, Presidents, as well as various clergy and related theological-political systems—that true power resides. Rather, it is in the message—often kept within secrets, heavily defended and protected, often seen by the masses as contraband or heretical—where we have detected true power. This book explores Messages contained within messages, Truths contained within truths, and existence based upon consciousness within SuperConsciousness. The Truth is the message. The Truth is the Absolute Power.

The Maccabees

The Maccabees lived during the second and first centuries BC and produced several books chronicling their existence. The first books provide a vivid account of Jewish resistance to the religious suppression and Hellenistic cultural penetration of the Seleucid period of 175–135 BC. The Third Book of the Maccabees was written in Greek and deals with the relationship between Jews and Gentiles. Led by Judah Maccabee, the Maccabees wrested Judea from the rule of the Seleucids—Syrian rulers who supported the spread of Greek culture and religion.

The Jewish holiday of Chanukah commemorates the recapture of Jerusalem by the Maccabees and the consecration of the Temple in 164 BC. This third book is not included in the Hebrew bible but is read in the Greek church. It was written in approximately 100 BC by a Jew from the Greco-Egyptian city of Alexandria. In the case of the Maccabees, their theology placed them at odds within their own people, causing an internecine conflict—the result of which were many deaths—initiated and carried out by their own members. The Maccabees ruled Judea for more than one century until Herod the Great seized power in 37 BC. During the Maccabees' rule, the Judeans began dividing into several larger groups—the Pharisees, Essenes, Sadducees,

Zealots, and Nazoreans, with numerous sects and subsects literally blurring most distinctions.

The Pharisees were known to maintain the validity of both oral and written laws, flexibly interpreting and adapting them according to the circumstances of the times. They believed in an afterlife and resurrection of the dead. By the first century AD, the Pharisees had garnered the majority of Judaic beliefs and practices surviving the multiple insurrections during Roman Empire rule.

The Essenes existed between 150 BC and 70 AD. Tending to value privacy, quiet, and solitude, they had encampments on Mt. Zion, Mt. Carmel, as well as in the Judean wilderness. Theirs was an ascetic monastic community in which they practiced ritual cleansing immersion, shared their possessions, ate their meals communally, and focused on disciplined study, worship, and work. Several branches of the Essenes did not marry.

The Sadducees, a priestly and aristocratic division, existed between 140 BC and 70 AD. This group dominated Solomon's Temple worship, its rites (including the sacrificial cult), and interpreted The Law more literally than the other two groups. Unpopular with the common people of the day, the Sadducees recognized the Torah as containing the only binding precepts. As such, they did not believe in the immortality of the soul, resurrection of the body, and the existence of Angels. They were closely aligned with the ruling aristocratic kingship of the Herodian dynasty.

The Zealots were a spiritually and politically motivated sect of militant, easily agitated individuals who fiercely (zealously) upheld the Judaic Law. The Zealots sought to eradicate the Holy Land of the pagan Romans and their corrupt Herodian dynasty. It was the Herodian dynasty that appointed the pro-Herodian Sadducee priesthood to oversee Solomon's Temple. The Zealots believed that they alone were the true, pure, pious followers of Judaic Law. The Sadducees' refusal to allow the Zealots access to Solomon's Temple was an ongoing, inflammatory source of contention and internecine fighting between these two Judaic sects. This conflict eventually drove the Zealots to build and establish their own sites of worship at both Qumran and Masada.

The Zealots believed in a royal, mortal Messiah who directly descended from the bloodline of King David. They also believed in a mortal, priestly Messiah who directly descended from the bloodline of

Aaron. They believed that God would provide this priestly Messiah from within their community, and they would recognize his illumination signified by his strict adherence to their interpretation of Judaic Law.

In 63 BC, the Romans placed the region of Judea under the kingships of a family of Jews. Known as the Herodian dynasty, they ruled from 40 BC until around 100 AD, gaining great favor with the Romans. Their most famous ruler, Herod the Great, ruled from 37 BC to 4 BC, during which he rebuilt Jerusalem (including Solomon's Temple), promoted Hellenistic culture, and in essence operated as the consummate politician by working both sides—Jews and Romans—to promote his own self-interest and advancement, especially his desire to be "King of the Jews."

Herod the Great conveniently utilized his Jewish ancestry to gain support and trust from his Jewish followers, while simultaneously cultivating relationships with the Romans who entrusted him with this powerful position. In 6 AD Rome formed Judea, Samaria, and Idumea into one province to be governed by procurators. In 66 AD, a futile Judean revolt against Rome and its appointed Herodian dynasty quickly was extinguished. In 68 AD, both Qumran, a remote Zealot settlement, and the rebuilt Temple of Solomon succumbed to the Romans, with the nearby fortress Masada following suit in 74 AD.

Most of the known information regarding accounts and events during the time of Jesus is attainable solely through the skeletal writings of a contemporary historian named Flavius Josephus. A Judaic aristocrat, Josephus was born Joseph ben Matthias in 37 AD. Josephus was the governor of Galilee and a commander of forces resisting the Romans. After he was captured, he renounced his entire life in favor of adopting a new Roman life, identity, and the name Flavius Josephus. Accounts of the Jewish revolt against the Roman rule and subsequent demise of the Temple are available only through his memoirs, titled "The Jewish War."

In this work, Josephus offers the only known accounts of Jerusalem's destruction and the siege of the fortress Masada. Long after the surrounding territory had fallen into Roman hands, the defiant Zealot defenders of Masada continued to withstand the sustained Roman attacks—climaxing with a phenomenon similar to the subsequent siege of the Cathars at Montségur in 1244 AD, in which virually all the defenders committed suicide en masse. While Josephus's accounts may have been the only actual recordings of such events, this status did not necessarily guarantee their accuracy. In fact, given his defection as a traitor, Josephus was not entirely a credible, objective source.

This tide of Roman aggression prompted the Zealots to hide their sacred texts—subsequently known as the Dead Sea Scrolls—within several caves. In 1896, nearly fifty years before the Qumran discoveries, noted Talmud scholar and educator Solomon Schechter discovered sectarian works in a synagogue near Cairo. These copied records were found to be versions of the Damascus Document, one of the Dead Sea Scrolls, eventually discovered in 1947.

The Nag Hammadi Scrolls

Two years earlier, in 1945, a set of ancient scrolls was first discovered by a soil-digging farmer in Nag Hammadi, Egypt.

While digging, the farmer extracted a large earthenware jar and figured he had happened upon buried treasure. Thinking perhaps a jinn or spirit might be guarding the contents, the man was apprehensive about disturbing the container and releasing this spirit. Overcoming his fear, he decided to smash the jar with his pick. While he did not exactly find buried treasure or a genie, the man found several ancient codices inside the jar. Little did this farmer know that he had discovered thirteen leather-bound papyrus codices containing Gnostic texts. If anything could shake the Vatican's complacent foundation, it would be the resurrection of the Gnostic Ghost.

Having efficiently silenced—with continual vehemence—all competing and contrasting adherents and their beliefs, Christianity found itself in the rather unenviable position of having to experience history repeating itself. Once again, the Christian dogma found itself threatened, having to defend its tenets and yet continuing to maintain its stranglehold over both proponents and adherents alike.

The 52 texts, known collectively as the Nag Hammadi Library, actually consisted of the long-lost Gnostic or Coptic Gospels, which were buried in 433 AD. Coptic is the Egyptian language written in Greek symbols. These codices can be divided into six major categories: the writing of creative and redemptive mythology, observations and commentaries on diverse Gnostic themes, liturgical and initiatory texts, feminine deific and spiritual principles, writings pertaining to the lives and experiences of the disciples, and sayings and incidents in the life of Jesus and the dialogue of the Savior.

By 1948 all of the Nag Hammadi Scrolls had been purchased by the Cairo Coptic Museum. Immediately, a group of French scholars tried to seize control of the deciphering and interpretation process, resulting in the prevention of their publication for eight years. The process was further constricted by social and political instabilities in 1956 during the contentious construction of the Suez Canal.

Finally, in 1966, the codices were handed over to a very competent and motivated international team of experts for translation and eventual publication. Professor James M. Robinson of the Institute for Antiquity and Christianity at Claremont Graduate School in California led this unselfish, highly professional group.

By 1973 the entire Nag Hammadi volume was available in English for all researchers to examine. Four years later, in 1977, the entire library was published and a particular printing was translated into a set consisting of 46 books and a few leftover scraps. Professor Robinson and his ethical team expediently completed their work in eleven years.

After reviewing these codices, we found it glaringly apparent that the writers of these works were not Gnostic but rather pseudo-Christian Coptic adherents. Once again, the true messages have been misinterpreted, mired, and convoluted in confused misperceptions. While some of these scrolls speak of light and love, and accurately hit other truthful marks, the majority of the work continues to perpetuate unsanctioned divine authority—something God never has or will grant to humankind. In a variety of ways, the Nag Hammadi Library is really no different from the Old and New Testaments and the Koran. All of these texts dedicate much attention to arrogating themselves divine authority, undermining or refuting their religious opponents and texts; actually, they often contradict themselves.

The messages of such writings—steeped in self-congratulation, power ordaining, martyrdom, denial, guilt slopping, and condemnation—continue to encourage proponents and adherents to follow suit via their own human intentions, thoughts, and behaviors. These unchallenged ancient messages have been allowed to survive seemingly forever—and be consumed as absolutes. With messages like these, what incentive do people have to behave or think differently? Had these codices actually contained truly Gnostic ideologies, the positive impact upon the consciousness of humanity would have been far more profound. However, with the "telephone line" of theological and historical messages created, maintained, and continually monopolized over time, any opportunities for other "callers" or alternative messages were rendered virtually non-existent.

Having dodged a potentially lethal "missal" with the Nag Hammadi Scrolls, the Vatican was not going to be caught vulnerable again. A mere two years later, with the discovery of the Dead Sea Scrolls in 1947, the Vatican again was faced with an unknown, potential disaster within the contents of these Scrolls.

The Dead Sea Scrolls

In 1947, what began as a search for their stray goat actually led young Bedouin shepherds of the Judean Desert to an unexplored cave—and the discovery of jars filled with seven ancient scrolls. A subsequent search ensued, lasting nearly a decade, eventually producing tens of thousands of scroll fragments from eleven caves. Immediately after this discovery, researchers utilized historical, paleographic, linguistic evidence and recovered coins, as well as carbon-14 dating, to establish that the scrolls and the Qumran ruins dated from the third century BC to 136 AD. A mere 20 miles east of Jerusalem is the rugged cave-strewn Judean desert area known as the ruins of Qumran. Thirty-three miles to the south, down the coast of the Dead Sea, are the ruins of the fortress of Masada.

By almost one thousand years, the Scrolls were found to be older than any other surviving manuscripts of the Hebrew Scriptures. They offer the largest historical collection of information about Jewish religious and political life in Judea during the turbulent late Second Temple Period of 200 BC to 70 AD. Characterized by conflict and corruption—all under Roman rule—this period was critical for the development of monotheistic religion.

The Dead Sea Scrolls were pre-Christian Jewish documents written in Hebrew, Aramaic, and Greek, and included manuscripts or fragments of every book in the Hebrew Bible except the Book of Esther. Interestingly enough, the Scrolls made little mention of Abraham, Isaac, or Jacob, but instead focused mainly upon the myriad of rules, regulations, laws, rituals, associated belief structures, and consequences for communal members of the times. In the Scrolls, the use of the name "Son of God" is in reference to someone other than Jesus, implying a cultural (versus theological) use of the term that was not itself synonymous with God

Control of the Scrolls was not easily resolved. Catholic groups oversaw the process until 1967, at which time Zionists seized East Jerusalem and Israel took control of the Scrolls. The slow pace of publication and extreme secrecy amongst the nearly total Catholic overseeing group fueled the theory that the Vatican wished to suppress certain information in the Scrolls.

From the information supplied by the Dead Sea Scrolls it is easy to recognize the unmistakable correlations between the "Zealot adherents of Judaic Law" and the foundational underpinnings of modern-day Christianity. It is a well-known fact that for time immemorial conquering civilizations always have taken on and indoctrinated recognizable and acceptable sociological, theological, philosophical, and even philological aspects of their conquered foes. This has been done on various levels in varying degrees whenever it made sense for the conqueror to do so.

One civilization crumbles and another builds itself upon the rubbled remains of the vanquished nation, essentially absorbing its previous governmental, ideological, and structural gains into a newly-formed trestle that bridges the ensuing gap occurring in the aftermath of the takeover. Excavating archeologists oftentimes discover layers of civilizations as these preserved stratums are painstakingly peeled back, exposing cities built upon the ruins of previous cities, which serve as a memory of tangible, chronological fact. Likewise, the Dead Sea Scrolls serve as a formidable reference source for bridging the numerous spans between Judaism and Christianity. The most obvious bridge, of course, is the Old Testament, which is shared by the Zealots, as well as by modern-day Christianity and Judaism.

After Rome's Vespasian sacked Jerusalem in 68 AD, Judaism was thrown into complete disarray. It was further driven from its own roots after the revolt led by Simeon bar Kochba and his followers in 132–135 AD. From the raw information supplied by the Dead Sea Scrolls, obvious correlations can be recognized. During the resulting void between 135 and 323 AD a series of convenient events allowed the Christian church founders to adopt from Judaism and subsequently cobble together many of the theological traditions, concepts, thoughts, teachings, laws, rituals, and even the phraseology attributable to Christianity today. Consequently, there are easily discernable terms between those written by the Zealots of the Qumran community in the Dead Sea Scrolls and those recognized by modern-day Christianity.

Several rituals found recorded in the Dead Sea Scrolls are presently recognized today as predominantly Christian-based. These include the Zealot doctrine of atonement and the Christian penance, the Jewish anointing of its rightful kings and the anointing of Jesus by Mary Magdalen, the Qumran rule that all people shall own and share everything in common and Jesus' disciples owning everything in common, Qumran members' covenant with God and obeying God's Commandments, thereby purifying themselves of sin daily via baptism and Christians' baptism to be absolved from Adam and Eve's sins. In addition, there is a correlation between the Zealots' Meal of the Congregation and the Last Supper celebrated by Jesus and his disciples. Finally, the Zealot ritual of blessing their meals, including bread and wine, has been adopted by both modern-day Jews and Christians.

Several concepts found recorded in the Dead Sea Scrolls also are presently recognized today as predominantly Christian-based. These include the Zealot concept of cornerstone and the modern-day Christian cornerstone that was the stone rejected by the builders of Solomon's Temple, the Zealots' recognition of a Kingdom of Heaven and the modern-day Christian concept of Heaven, the Zealots' End Times, and the impending Christian Apocalypse as the End of the World. The Zealots recognized the term "meek," while modern-day Christians recognize the term "poor." Both terms relate to the concept of striving for perfection through faith and suffering as instructed by God.

The Zealots believed in martyrdom for the sake of The Law and modern-day Christians believe in martyrdom for the sake of their faith in Jesus as God incarnate. Initially adopted by the Maccabees from the ancient Egyptians, the term "resurrection" subsequently was adopted by the Zealots. According to the Zealots, resurrection would occur if they died for the sake of The Law. They believed that God would raise them up to live again forever. Modern-day Christians believe that Jesus died on the cross, after three days arose from the dead (resurrected), and is seated at the right-hand of God. They also believe that at the end of the world Jesus will return to judge the living and resurrect the dead, and thus, these believers' new kingdom will have no end.

There also are numerous references involving people found recorded in the Dead Sea Scrolls that correlate to people recognized by modern-day Christians. Striking similarities exist between the Zealots' Teacher of Righteousness and modern-day Christianity's James the Just. Similarly, there is a strong correlation between Josephus, the turncoat who the Zealots considered to be "The Liar," and Saint Paul, who wrote the *Acts of the Apostles*. Eventually, a schism occurred when Christianity chose to support Saint Paul's "blind faith" over the Zealots' adherence to The Law. The Qumran had twelve governing council members, which parallel both Christianity's twelve disciples, as well as Judaism's twelve tribes of Israel.

Both the Zealots and modern-day Christianity share the designations of Priest, Messiah, Saint, the Coming of the Anointed Prince, Son of Man, and even Belial/Satan. The only distinction between the Messiah of the Qumran's Dead Sea Scrolls and that of modern-day Christianity related to the Messiah's divinity or lack thereof. The Qumran insulated its teachings around a Messiah, as Christians subsequently labeled Jesus. However, the Qumran Messiah as their Teacher of Righteousness was not recognized as an expression of divinity. If the Qumran Messiah in the Dead Sea Scrolls had been recognized as divinity, this depiction clearly would have suggested that the Scrolls were referring to Jesus or a Jesus-like personage.

During the excavation of the Qumran ruins, 450 coins were unearthed that were dated from 135 BC to 136 AD. Yet, the Catholic Church attempted to date the Dead Sea Scrolls from 160 to 142 BC—several years before even the very earliest of the 450 coins was dated. The Catholic Church based this assertion entirely upon the one earliest coin dated 135 to 104 BC and paleography or the study of handwriting. The Catholic Church validated the Scrolls' dates not based upon the Scrolls' internal contents and information, but instead upon the handwritten script found on the Scrolls. In doing so, the Catholic Church attempted to pre-date the Scrolls in an effort to assert that the Qumran community detailed in the Scrolls happened long before and very separately from Christianity. Given all of the aforementioned correlations between the Dead Sea Scrolls and modern-day Christianity, there is no question that Jesus' teachings and Christianity clearly adopted most of their "unique" theological terms, rituals, and concepts from the Zealots of the Qumran's Dead Sea Scrolls.

The Rose Vine Telephone Line

The Rose Vine Telephone Line refers to the phenomenon of reoccurring themes woven throughout history. Themes such as bloodlines, theologies, ideologies, secret societies, as well as an assortment of falsities and misinterpretations, have created an unusual—albeit constant—stream of information. Mysterious subterranean rivers of thematic and connecting information emerge into the light of consciousness, revealing insights and answers. Yet, for compelling reasons, such rivers also reside below the surface of conscious human awareness and remain securely submerged and protected.

In Book Three, we apply Truthful analysis to several theologically based texts, including the New Testament—in which we chronicle the Truths and fictions associated with Jesus' life and death. Out of the confusion from these controversial events emerged several compelling mysteries, upon which we will shed illumination.

Like a rose vine, historical lineage took many twists and turns through many familial briar patches—some thornier than others. In 1061, Godfroi de Bouillon was born to carry on one very unique pedigree. During his life, de Bouillon accomplished a variety of notable achievements. He captured Jerusalem from the Saracens during the First Crusade in 1099 and rejected his title of King of Jerusalem, instead preferring the title "Defender of the Holy Sepulchre." He installed the knights and monks occupying the Church of the Holy Sepulchre and commissioned an abbey to be built on Mount Zion in Jerusalem. Godfroi de Bouillon deemed the warrior monks residing in the abbey the Ordre de Sion. Upon his death one year later, in 1100, Godfroi de Bouillon passed the baton to his younger brother, Baudouin. King Baudouin recognized Godfroi's Ordre de Sion group by the name of Order of the Temple. In 1118, King Baudouin officially recognized the Order of the Temple as the Poor Knights of the Temple of Solomon.

The Poor Knights of the Temple of Solomon later were known as the Knights Templar, over which the executive arm called the Ordre de Sion presided. The Ordre de Sion continued until it separated from the Knights Templars at the "Cutting of the Elm" event at Gisors in 1188. After this event in Gisors, which we describe in greater detail later in Book Two's Personal Journey section pertaining to Scott, the Ordre de Sion was officially changed to Prieuré de Sion. The Knights Templars continued to exist independently from 1188 until they were rounded up and placed under arrest by King Philippe le Bel (IV) during the Inquisition on Friday, October 13, 1307. King Philippe deemed the Templars heretics, tortured and viciously executed them, although there was no hard evidence to prove this other than his perceptions of this group being a threat to him.

As the executive branch of the Knights Templars, the Prieuré de Sion continued on long after the Inquisition—even to the present day. The main responsibility of the Prieuré de Sion was to chronicle key events and maintain secrets. One of these secrets pertained to an earlier mentioned event, the Jewish Revolt in 66 AD. We noted a similarity between the Romans' siege of Masada in 66 AD and the Albigensian Crusade from 1209–1244 against the Cathars at Montségur Castle in France. In their respective situations, both the Jews and Cathars as garrisons small in number withstood heavy bombardment from insurmountable troops. In both cases, the overmatched fighters became islands under siege.

In the case of the Cathars, a vast army of knights descended upon Languedoc, located in the northeastern foothills of the Pyrenees in southern France. Tens of thousands of Cathar men, women, and children were slaughtered as dictated by an official proclamation from Pope Innocent III. The Cathars, a medieval sect of people who were declared heretics, were to be slaughtered en masse—with no one to be spared. The Cathars were intellectually advanced, focusing on philosophy; poetry; and Greek, Arabic, and Hebrew studies. They were steeped in nonviolent pursuits and the notion of courtly love, and their schools were dedicated to the Kabbalah, esoteric and literary traditions. Focusing on the individual conscious experience, the Cathars' beliefs were more Gnostic than Christian—therefore, earning the ire of the Pope.

The Cathars were known to be extremely wealthy, their wealth purportedly extending beyond mere material, tangible definitions. When the besieged defenders finally surrendered, no wealth—tangible or intangible—ever was found. During the defense of the castle, four men slipped away under the cloak of night. Risking their lives, they descended the side of the mountain supposedly carrying the infamous Cathar wealth.

Actually, the true Cathar treasure was the Shroud of Turin, a cloth on which an image of a man resembling Jesus was emblazoned as if by process of reverse x-ray. In reality, this male image belonged to an extra-terrestrial being whom the Cathars knew as Baphomet. Baphomet died while on planet Earth, and the Cathars covered his body with a burial shroud. As per his civilization's recognized custom, the physical atoms of Baphomet's being were dematerialized, leaving in their place the image of his physically manifested being—emblazoned on the shroud itself.

The tangible Cathar wealth ended up at Rennes-le-Château, later dis-covered by Bérenger Saunière, the curé and parish priest-in-residence. It was well known that, prior to 1891, the priest received a modest income of six pounds sterling per year. However, from 1891 until his death in 1917, the priest's lavish expenditures amounted to millions of pounds. When questioned about his financial sources, Saunière remained strangely mute, refusing to step down from his position or reveal the ori-gins of this sudden and unexplained wealth.

Saunière did reveal to his household assistant and confidante, Marie Denarnaud, the true origins of his wealth. Shortly after being made ben-eficiary of Saunière's will (and recipient of his wealth), Denarnaud poi-soned her benefactor. Saunière suffered a sudden stroke, eventually dying five days later. Denarnaud lived fabulously until 1946. Then, after World War II, she—like all French citizens at the time—was required to disclose any and all financial sources, in order to receive the equivalent amount of her monies in the newly issued French francs. Rather then reveal the truth and be exposed, Denarnaud chose to incinerate her entire liquid wealth. Consequently, she was reduced to a modest income, eventually dying from a sudden stroke—of natural, not suspicious, causes—taking all of her secrets to the grave.

The protection, preservation, and perpetuation of secrets flourishes on the rose vine of history, yielding a mixture of thorns and flowers. We easily forget that the most strategized and protected secrets, even when taken to the grave, are never buried for long—and most certainly, not for-ever. History has a curious yet predictable way of unearthing long-buried buds of truth from the covert soil of falsity, however brilliantly disguised. Eventually, all seemingly elusive, obscure, and enigmatic mysteries of existence will be illuminated. The divine cultivation of creation allows for no "true" secrets. Even the mysterious hieroglyphics and Coptic records of Egypt did not elude revelation and interpretation. The same can be said for the principles of alchemy and related Hellenistic themes and symbols woven throughout the history of human experience.

Flourishing in the first three centuries AD in Alexandria, alchemy was known as "the sacred art." The alchemical process was believed to make spirit into matter and transmute one sort of matter into another. It was believed this made a man into a god. This was not remotely the case, but such transformations of particled form were so astounding to people during this time that they believed such abilities were exclusive to God.

Alchemy combined the product of glass and metal technology, symbolizing the Hellenistic philosophy of the unity of all things through the four elements—earth, air, water, and fire—as well as through religion, astrology, and the occult. The essential principle was that all things—both animate and inanimate—were permeated by spirit. In addition, through a synthesis of chemical operations and imaginative reasoning, the substances of the lower world could be transmuted into higher things of the spiritual world—things not subject to decay. The Hermaphrodite is a pure alchemical symbol—that of an old bearded man, the back of whose head shows a young woman looking into a mirror. It represents the perfect balance achieved in the Great Work—the perfect being, in which the alchemist himself is transformed and transmuted spiritually. The Great Work was defined as an explosion of the potential into the actual, where the mystical quest takes on concrete form.

According to Egyptian alchemists, one great "secret" was how to make white powdered gold, which when seen up close is transparent. This substance was known to greatly enhance the pineal gland, while the similar substance of iridium was known to greatly enhance the pituitary gland. It was said that after ingesting white gold for over nine months, a subject would become extremely psychic. According to Hermetic tradition, Hermes Trismegestis was the originator of alchemy. He taught that the physical world could be transformed through mental imagery. This brings up the concept of our ability to discern for ourselves fact from fiction. As such, what you "image" or "imagine" to be true often becomes or is undeniably so.

One such image had geographical roots in Greece—and made its way to Europe. Arcadia, the place in Greece thought to be home of the oldest antediluvian races, also was associated in medieval iconography and symbolism with the "underground stream" of Alpheus—an underground river which, at this time period, flowed all the way to Sicily. According to the Prieuré de Sion documents, the Benjaminites, who were ancestors of the Merovingians, fled to Arcadia. Arcadia often turns up in Renaissance songs and poems. Artist Poussin's famous painting, "Shepherds in Arcadia," depicts the shocking scene of shepherds discovering the tomb of a shepherdess in the midst of their Arcadian pastoral paradise: "Et in Arcadia Ego." Arcadia is associated with the Greek god Pan, the chief supreme god amongst the many gods and goddesses during classical antiquity. Pan was known as the Great Master and Protector of Nature.

Ancient alchemists also used the sign or seal resembling the Cross of Lorraine as a device whose meaning literally was "very poisonous." To alchemists, though, the symbol and its meaning had more esoteric connotations. To them, poison represented an agent of transformation—a vehicle for the reconciliation of opposites. There was a myth that for most men poison is deadly, while for the elect, it confers mastership and absolute power. This idea is seen as a motif in later Grail lore.

The Cross of Lorraine, on which both lines rest horizontally across one vertical line, is said to represent God. It represented the phrase of the times, "As above, so below," which has transcended theological, societal, academic, and cultural paradigms. It speaks to the phenomenon of reflective individual conscious experience in our existence: that which we put forth is reflected back to us in kind. The Cross of Lorraine's bar above mirrors the bar below—both of which are affixed symmetrically to a central pillar, providing balance and equilibrium. The cross also was known to represent the union of opposites, such as male and female principles. In its structure, the double-armed cross incorporates "phi," the Golden Ratio. It also resembles the "Jacob's staff," which medieval Jewish philosopher Levi ben Gerson used to determine longitude through observation of the moon.

Hermeticism traditionally has been known as the Regia or Royal Art, its central tenet that of equilibrium. Symbolizing the Hermetic Ideal, the Cross's three bars echo Eliphas Levi's concept of the "true" trinity—that two primordial forces, one creative, the other destructive, govern the world. The equilibrium between these two forces constitutes a third force—and the union of the three constitutes what some might refer to as the Triune God. According to legend, Hermes was the sole receptacle of the secret doctrine of the antediluvian world, which he revived and passed down to the Kings. This secret knowledge was erroneously thought to have been taught to humankind by a race of gods or fallen angels. This story relates to the alchemical concept of poison: Kings and aristocrats would understand how to wield and apply the secret doctrine because it was believed that they were, in fact, flesh and blood descendants of the Forgotten Race. However, as this legend itself was incorrect, such application of royal and aristocratic "understanding" was baseless as well.

The Cross of Lorraine is a symbol of that Royal Secret, the doctrine of the Forgotten Ones. Under the leadership and passion of their monarch, King René d'Anjou, the Angevins were advocates of the Regia (Royal Art) of Hermeticism. The mystical beliefs of the secret societies in the Templar days were based upon the Hermetic maxim, "As above, so below," which teaches that the natural world is a material rejection of the spiritual. This maxim formed the esoteric basis for ancient Eygptian mysteries, Gnosticism, Esoteric Christianity, Essenic and Kabbalistic thoughts and traditions, Hermetic tradition, alchemy, and societies such as the Templars, Freemasons, and Rosicrucians. In fact, equilibrium of unity and synthesis was regarded by Masonic doctrine as humankind's ultimate destiny.

The Cross of Lorraine became the heraldic emblem of René d'Anjou, who spearheaded a Hermetic revival in Europe, convincing the influential Cosimo de' Medici to translate many ancient texts, such as the "Corpus Hermeticum" into various European tongues for the first time ever. When this piece was first published in France, it was dedicated to Marie de Guise—wife of James Stuart V, mother of Mary Queen of Scots, and a descendant of René d'Anjou—who adopted as her personal symbol the Cross of Lorraine. Later, during World War II, the French Resistance adopted the Cross of Lorraine as a symbol. In his painting, "La Fontaine de Fortune" from the *The Book of Love*, René shows the spring being brought forth by the Hellenistic sorcerer Virgil. This depiction was the first surfacing of Alpheus, the Arcadian underground stream, in modern western culture.

By creating an eternal continuity of consciousness, God ensures that seemingly buried past experiences are ever free to emerge from the fertile ground of possibility. This rose vine telephone line continues to stretch its historical underground roots into the endless potentiality of futurity. Ironically, the same souls intent upon burying Truth forever oftentimes become reincarnated extractors of the Truth they previously worked so hard to suppress.

René d'Anjou and The Renaissance

King René, also known as Le Bon Roi René or Good King René/King of Good Report, was born January 16, 1409, in Angers, and died on July 10, 1480, in Aix-en-Provence. He was a descendent (through the Anjous) of Ann the Jew, daughter of Joseph of Arimathea, both of who settled in western France. René held the title of King for a myriad of places, including Naples, Sicily, Valencia, and several others. He was Duke of Lorraine, Anjou, and Calabria, as well as Count of Provence, Guise, and other locales. He also was given the purely titular role of King of Jerusalem.

Known as "the last minstrel monarch" and a storybook prince, d'Anjou was a romantic dreamer, artist, writer, and poet. He also saw himself as a chivalric knight and enjoyed jousting and serious fighting. He planned many tournaments and even wrote a famous treatise on the form and devising of a tournament. At age 10, he became grand master of the Prieuré de Sion's Secret Society (but technically was under his uncle's wing until he was 20 years old), and married Isabel, 9, the heiress of Lorraine, daughter of Duke Charles II of Lorraine and Marguerite of Bavaria—a dynastic union frequently resorted to and typical of those times.

Although little-known today, René d'Anjou kept company with people such as Christopher Columbus, Cosimo de'Medici, and Jeanne d'Arc (known as Joan of Arc). Although he personally experienced military defeats, he still managed to be creative and productive—especially in bringing Hellenistic thought to Italy and to Europe, in general. He wrote and illustrated several books, as well as created poems, odes, and allegories. He also enjoyed staging theatrical performances that melded his interests in themes of Arcadian romance and Arthurian Grail Knights' tournaments, and which typically involved the personification of allegorical values, ideas, and philosophies.

René's book, *Livre des Tournies* or *The Manual for the Perfect*

Organization of Tourneys (Tournaments) includes tips on how to make a challenge (offer a rebated sword to the appellant team and have your herald recite a peace-loving, ritualized challenge while wearing a cloak of golden cloth), to how to display banners (all fighters must display banners from the windows of their then-residence). This book can be seen in Paris' Bibliotheque Nationale.

One statement in the Prieuré Documents defines the character of symbolic or allegorical art. According to the documents, allegorical works are powerful connectors. Accordingly, in allegorical pieces, a single word can illuminate relationships and meanings otherwise not easily grasped or comprehended. During René's time, allegory in general was regarded as esoteric communication, typically addressed to elite audiences. However, René's own literary and community efforts demonstrated his ability to understand and then present ideas not typically understood, yet alone experienced, by many around him.

René d'Anjou's *Le Coeur d'Amours Espris* or *The Book of the Heart Possessed by Love*—commonly known as *The Book of Love*—is an allegorical romance based upon one of his own dreams. After being tired and preoccupied with musings about love, he finally falls asleep—only to be awakened by a dream in which Love personified suddenly appears, takes René's heart from his chest, and hands it over to personified Desire. Alarmed, René awakens his valet to assist him in validating that his chest, indeed, is intact and unharmed. Reassured and extremely relieved, René records his dream experience.

The heart is represented in the dream as a knight in full armor named Coeur. Accompanied by his page, Desire, they set off on a dangerous journey of courtship (similar to that of the Knights on a quest to discover The Grail) to liberate Coeur's love, Sweet Grace, who is being held captive by Coeur's three enemies—Denial, Shame, and Fear. The dream story contained mystical dialogue about the vanity of earthly things, emphasizing the love of God as being the way to purge the soul of all earthly folly. Perhaps such themes truly do have eternal resonance. The dialogue, "Le Mortifiement de Vaine Plaisance," or "The Mortification of Vain Pleasure," was conducted by the allegorical Fear of God, Love of God, Remorse, Faith, and Grace of God.

For many years, the Western mind had operated based upon one source of thought—that which was packaged and served as so-called "absolute truth," which was written, spoken, repeated, learned, and digested verbatim. René helped break the monopoly on the supposed ownership and dissemination of thinking during his lifetime, and beyond. He was known to have been a primary force behind the phenomenon we know today as the Renaissance—or what was known during those times as "René's Essence."

Through his literacy and influence on Cosimo de' Medici, René assisted in setting up a cultural, communal foundation based on the aforementioned esoteric Hermetic principles—Alpheus, the "underground stream" or "Arcadia." Alpheus' root is "alpha" in Greek, meaning "first" or "source." This is a stream-based theme, which—like the rose vine line—traverses throughout history.

René spent many years in Italy, making it a base of operations. He inspired sponsorship from Milan's ruling Sforza family, as well as from his friend, Cosimo de' Medici, and he got them to send agents all over the world in quest of ancient manuscripts. As a result of these efforts, de' Medici opened Europe's first public library—the Library of San Marco, which finally made available, for the first time ever, thoughts and ideas that long had been suppressed. This library was a positive public outcry, bursting the once-sealed bubble of thought supposedly "protected," but actually suppressed, by the Dark Ages. Finally, the once-completely underground stream of Platonic, Neo-Platonic, Pythagorean, Gnostic, and Hermetic thought could flow more freely.

de' Medici instructed the University of Florence to begin teaching Greek. It was the first time Greek was offered for study in Europe for seven hundred years. He established many academies throughout Italy. This entire movement, a true quest for excellence, served to break the Church's monopoly on thought. René was tolerant and open to a plurality of thinking styles. Steeped in esoteric tradition, his court included a wise Jewish astrologer, Kabbalist, and physician known as Jean de Saint-Remy, who in fact was the grandfather of Nostradamus. René also employed Italian Admiral Christopher Columbus, whose 1495 journals from Hispaniola recounted his relationship with the then-late René. Columbus had been a hand and seaman on one of René's ships, on which the crew was disturbed by the danger of their mission and wanted to return to Marseilles. In response, Columbus altered the compass to make them believe they were returning home, when in fact they continued the mission. Perhaps this same altered compass was the one used by Columbus to sail to India.

René, indeed, believed that if people did not become aware of new modes of thought, did not engage in their own thinking, someone else would do it for them—and their safety, security, and future would be compromised as a result. René's personal symbol, the Cross of Lorraine, captured his spirit as artist and fighter for freedoms for the masses. He also was instrumental in assisting others in their own learning and evolution on a personal, individual basis.

In 1461, when his young son died, noble Venetian Jacopo Antonio Marcello, a friend of René d'Anjou, decided to make a literary monument to both his son and his own grief. Of the various works sent to him in condolence by many authors, Marcello selected fifteen, and along with his responses to them, compiled and gifted them to René. In his own written responses to his literary consolers, Marcello called upon René to serve as counselor between him and these consolers. Marcello felt others failed to truly understand the intense level of grief tormenting his soul. After convening with René, Marcello ended up transforming his literature into a dialogue revealing cultural tensions between the male individual who wished to grieve freely and the Renaissance social norm that demanded its male members maintain stoicism in the acceptance of death.

The great cultural movement of the Renaissance actually began in Italy in the 1300s—even before the René d'Anjou-Cosimo de' Medici connection fueled the exploration and dissemination of Hellenistic thought. In the late 1400s, the movement spread to England, France, Germany, the Netherlands, Spain, and other European countries—ending around 1600. Its name has Latin origins from the word "rinascere," referring to the act of being reborn. During this time, European scholars and artists—especially in Italy—studied the learning, cultures, and art of ancient Greece and Rome called "classical antiquity." Thus, the Renaissance was a rebirth of these cultures, a revival of antiquity or learning. It was a case of the emergence of a very new way of thinking—based upon what previously had been "old," mysterious, or unfamiliar ideas, actually historically sequestered and suppressed.

The Renaissance overlapped the end of a period in Europe called the Middle Ages, which began in 476 AD. During Medieval (Middle Ages) times, people were told, and thus believed, that it was their chief responsibility to pray religiously to God and concentrate on saving their souls. They saw society as filled with evil temptations, a philosophy rejected by

Renaissance thinkers, who felt people had duties within a society that could civilize, not destroy, them. The Renaissance's emphasis was cultural diversity and exploration of Greco-Roman thoughts—a distinct rejection and departure from the rigidity and fear-based mindset of the Middle Ages, which valued the religious study of God over that of humanity, and whose art likewise depicted such thought.

Fear and self-protection may have contributed to the slow acceptance of the Renaissance. Also figuring into this reality was that much of Italy supposedly was controlled by the Holy Roman Empire. The popes ran central Italy, including the city of Rome, leaving the other cities governed by families or individuals. In fact, it was the Sforza family who took control of Milan, governing it from 1448 until 1497. Other cities' governments were based on republicanism, whereby a ruling class (typically those considering themselves to be superior to others) controlled the government. Many in such families intermarried and supported the advancement and absorption of Greco-Roman artists and intellectuals—especially in Florence and Venice.

By the 1430s, when the Medici family dominated Florence's ruling class and controlled the largest European bank, the intellectual movement of Humanism took hold. Blending a concern for the history and actions of humans with religious concerns, humanist scholars used a classical antiquity role model for excellence. In order to learn Greek and Latin, they studied philology, the science of the meaning and history of words.

The fine arts during the Middle Ages and Renaissance reflected the philosophy of both movements. Medieval artists wanted viewers to concentrate on the deep religious meaning of their pieces, in which subjects didn't necessarily appear lifelike but where cathedrals were featured prominently to emphasize the theologically defined majesty and grandeur of God. On the other hand, Renaissance artists created lifelike people and nature, as well as buildings designed on a smaller scale, to make people aware of their own individual powers, dignity, and selves. Florentine masters of the early 1400s included architect Filippo Brunelleschi, painter Masaccio, and sculptor Donatello, the last of whom created three statues of the biblically depicted hero, David. In the late 1400s and early 1500s, great artists Michelangelo, Raphael, and Leonardo da Vinci emerged as soon-to-be masters.

What began as a trickle or a whisper, buoyed by the energy of a select but devotedly passionate few, in time gained some amazing momentum. The Renaissance wooed even Italy's enemies and invaders. René d'Anjou, along with others, helped spawn a movement characterized not only by culture, beauty, and thought, but also by the power of inclusion, letting its richness be known and shared not by a "select few" but by all. From science to art to religion and history, the theme is woven throughout all time: The power of seemingly quiet ideas gives rise to momentous waves of thought.

Italian Renaissance artists and humanists continued to carry and convey the messages of Greco-Roman times in an effort to be inclusive and spread this mindset to others in the world. Even Christian humanists were unusually progressive in how they viewed and expressed their religions and religious identities. Close friends Desiderius Erasmus and Saint Thomas More were leading Christian humanists who refused to abandon their ideals. Erasmus refused to take sides during any political or religious controversies, and his 1511 book, *The Praise of Folly*, criticized the moral quality of Church leaders, accusing them of overemphasizing procedures and ceremonies while neglecting the spiritual values of Christianity.

Clearly, the Renaissance left us with an important intellectual and artistic heritage born from the courage of people breaking from traditional boundaries. As matter seems to manifest throughout the cosmos in exploding blossoms—like roses in bloom—so too out of the continuum of human experience does the Renaissance resurrect on the vine of eternity. All human beings operate within their own individual vine of existence. Throughout history, many vines have been laced with thorns, oftentimes preventing the developing buds—us—from experiencing our fullest potential.

BOOK
TWO

Personal Journeys
of a Seeker and a Saint

Mari:
The Seeker and Her Quest for Truth

$\mathcal{E}$ very human being has a story to tell. Our history books, religious texts, social, political, psychological, and philosophical commentaries all are rooted in stories—one seemingly older than the next. As human beings, we have defined, divided, marketed, digested, and absorbed both written and oral words according to their relative "truth." In this book, we explore how such determinations have been made. What we have found in our analysis reveals some very thought-provoking, unnerving, and consciousness-raising results.

Oftentimes, the way a story or circumstance is deemed true or false seems more rooted in human perception than whether something truly happened or whether it makes any logical, rational sense. Historically speaking, the older the story or circumstance, the more we tend to accept and absorb it into our human conscious experiences without judgment, conditions, and skepticism. Of course, to do otherwise would place us in a vulnerable, precarious, and unfamiliar position. In essence, we'd be questioning the authenticity behind the foundations of supposed "truths."

In addition, we'd be struggling against previously held notions to reveal suppressed, actual truths, and throughout the process, we'd be forced to assess and redefine our own belief systems. For most people, this would be tantamount to purposefully driving their car down a popular one-way street going the wrong direction. Most people, out of fear alone, would avoid engaging in such pursuits. Most people prefer to reside in a zone of complacency and perceived comfort, whereby they face only simple challenges, make minimal changes, but still receive and benefit from perceived deserved rewards.

Like starving animals content to devour without much discernment, we consume inordinate amounts of information placed before us. Sure, some of us might pose questions, but more often than not, we digest large portions anyway. In doing so, we miss out on any real nutritional value for our souls. For millenniums, we have abdicated to others our ability and potential to make discernments between fact and fiction, real and unreal, holy and unholy, safe and dangerous, good and bad. Many of us have searched valiantly, passionately, to better understand life's mysteries and to experience growth on multiple levels. In doing so, we often are willing to take extraordinary measures, depending upon external sources to pave our paths.

In reality, these paths ONLY can be paved and guided by the divine, internal Truth within all of us. For a variety of reasons, we deny and simply do not trust this fact. Many of us have been taught or told the "ways" of God rather than having experienced them personally or first-hand. As such, we have formed opinions and relationships with God through the filters based upon the influences of external sources rather than through our own personal experiences. In doing so, we essentially have cheated ourselves from participating in the individual, conscious, spiritual experience afforded to all.

Perhaps we feel we lack the fortitude to face both the inevitable challenges and all the possibilities that reside along our paths. Briefly, we might look inside ourselves for answers, but we don't linger long. Somehow, we've trained ourselves and allowed ourselves to be trained to believe in prescribed, prepackaged ways to seek truth, gain insight, and experience some enlightenment. Too quickly, and for way too long, we have taken what we are given without asking ourselves what we truly, deeply need.

In desperation, vulnerability, urgency, and blind faith, time and time again we grant decisive license and influence to an external world filled with people also in denial doing exactly the same thing. In our physical universe, we feel compelled to move fast, lest somehow we miss out on life's many experiences. We constantly search for the next step, newest thing, a better place, another way, and a more solid, improved, strategic path to transport us from "here" to "there" as painlessly and smoothly as possible.

Inevitably, when we humanly trip along the path, we search for even more answers. Naturally, in our depleted states, we want the answers to be given to us—and external sources happily oblige. Unfortunately, we often find "clarity" from people, institutions, organizations, philosophies, theologies, histories, and literary texts that are oftentimes much more misguided than ourselves. Hence, we may just find ourselves in the "care" of those whose interests are not necessarily benevolent or for the universal good. In our yearning, we may find ourselves filling up our spiritual wells with contaminated fluids. Consequently, when we search in this manner, we risk becoming our own worst, powerful barriers to any potential fulfillment.

We want clarity, but end up in various states of confusion and bewilderment. While it may be compelling, powerful, and steeped in a track record of supposed "history," the sustenance we derive from external sources leaves us either filled with the contaminants of falsity or still empty and in perpetual, internal hunger. We might search from person to person, religion to religion, practice to practice, place to place, or book to book, in an effort to find relief, quench our thirst, and soothe our souls. We fill up on books, tapes, sessions, appointments, consultations, seminars, workshops, retreats, and worship services to fill the internal spiritual void growing bigger inside us. Both history and society have affirmed and assisted this type of search by providing a plethora of such resources and options for the taking.

When we have searched and chosen to follow the external, we do so in the hope that we can connect to something, anything that might resonate and feed our hungry souls. Unfortunately, we often end up frustrated, confused, unsettled, angry, or even shameful when we don't experience the results we had so desired. We feel betrayed when we realize the placebos we've so readily consumed have been disguised or veiled as answers of truth. It is all too easy and automatic to blame others and circumstances for our plight rather than hold ourselves responsible for the state in which we find ourselves. Paradoxically and hypocritically, as we attribute blame to the external, from it we also seek assistance and resolution. We want to rise above, yet we undermine ourselves and stay below.

We subscribe and adhere to external sources and their "messages," rules, philosophies, commentary, and advice. We've been looking to others as locksmiths to pry open for us the secrets of life's mysteries. We've neglected to knock upon or pry open the very door we've kept fused shut by our own hands. Somewhere along the way we have forgotten that Truth always and forever is available to us and within us. We are blessed to have the master key eternally available to the home from which we've kept ourselves estranged. For far too long, we've searched outside ourselves for help in guiding us in our destinies. In reality, God alone is, was, and forever will be the only True Architect. Thus, our destinies' blueprints reside deeply within us.

It is not necessary, required, or crucial for one to be a religious believer in order to connect and resonate with Absolute Truth, to understand and comprehend the mysteries of existence, or to experience spiritual awakening, awareness, upliftment, and enlightenment. One need not be at all religious in any way to communicate or connect with God and Truth. No religious doctrines or texts guarantee a superior or "inside glimpse" of Truth. One need only look around and inside to see with awe what has been, is, and continues to be eternally created. Being a pious, observant, studious, fearful, obsessive, or zealous religious subscriber is irrelevant and only guarantees a connection to a particular theology or religion.

Like many, I also searched for truth and meaning in my existence. I looked deeply within myself, but nonetheless, still sought out and depended upon many external sources to assist me along the way. Fortunately, our destiny paths are laden with multitudes of opportunities, experiences, and examples for learning and acquiring wisdom and more precise discernment.

Throughout our life journeys, we look outside of ourselves and labor hard. We chase endless, outward desires, and all the while, what we're really seeking is inner truthful fulfillment. Riding upon the waves of immediate relief and delusion of temporary satiation, we believe we've taken good care of ourselves—and in doing so, we have met our needs. Nothing could be further from the truth. I know this is so, for I learned these difficult, beautiful lessons firsthand.

In this book, I am a messenger for several messages that have been revealed to me during my own personal, spiritual journey. Some aspects of what you read may seem incredible or difficult to relate to within your own personal experience, while other aspects may resonate deeply within your core. On my journey, I have found that many routes initially appearing to be outwardly familiar, safe, and benevolent ended up otherwise. I also found that when I took several unfamiliar, mysterious roads that I might not have habitually considered, I was led to wondrous destinations. In other words, sometimes we find ourselves compelled to change our paths—and sometimes we find our paths have changed. Personally, I know this to be true in both cases.

From early childhood on, I have been a seeker on many levels, especially longing for illumination regarding the mysteries and secrets of existence. I always felt there was more to life than met the eye. Even as a child, I never was satisfied receiving pat answers, minimal information, or superficial feedback as responses. I both questioned and celebrated the Judaism with which I was raised. On one hand, I experienced varying internal conflict and discord with its tenets, and on the other hand, I enjoyed and celebrated the rituals, ceremonies, and holidays based on such tenets. As young as second or third grade, I had a penchant for all things metaphysical. I would immerse myself in library books on the occult, ESP, magic, and related esoteric subjects.

I also founded a private club, known as "Club," of which there were but two members of the human variety. My younger brother was a member and I was the President. Finally, I had a vehicle for both my questions and ideas, as well as a younger, captive following. My reign began when I was about five, and the organization never formally or officially disbanded. As its members aged, so did Club's apparent priority status; the meetings merely faded out and discontinued on their own. Club was a big deal, held and revered with passion, and predictably took place with little variation. It was my little "Secret Society," for which I devised a secret language, as well as other related rituals. As a child, I just KNEW Club held mysterious gems of value.

During my childhood, I regularly communed with God. I wrote notes, spoke, sang, and regularly thought about God. Following specified Jewish traditions, I also prayed to God. I recall having had many questions about life and death. From an early age, I harbored an urgent yearning to understand life's mysteries before my own life's end. That yearning never went away, and my spiritual quest reflects its unflagging intensity, as well as the steps I have taken to fulfill this once extremely unfulfilled desire.

Clearly, there are many paths one can take for enlightenment and spiritual fulfillment. The Kabbalists acknowledge that we humans have much more conscious awareness potential than we ever stop to actualize. The Kabbalah seems to assume that behind and inside everything there are hidden secrets, meanings, and messages demanding and begging us to work beyond our most self-imposed, moral limitations and barriers. Thus, instead of attempting to see solely with our eyes, hear and listen only with our ears, or know things only on cerebral or intellectual levels, we need to utilize alternative methods. This process requires one to penetrate surface appearances and assumptions, dispel possible myths or untruths, and pierce all veils. It is in the name of Absolute Truth that this book attempts to do all of these things, in the hope that all readers may discover and experience the unveiled mysteries of existence and beyond.

Of course, it requires much time, effort, and insight to pierce veils—especially those of a spiritual nature or those purposefully constructed with the powerful threads of history, law, philosophy, politics, and theology or religion. As a young person, I worked diligently and passionately to understand life, its purpose, and its unknowns. I undeniably found many aspects of Jewish religious practice enjoyable. I also experienced an internal struggle in my attempt to get closer to my faith. On one hand, I found formal textual and historical study oppressive and tedious—sometimes even repellent. In my studies, I couldn't help but notice that some of the rules, laws, ways, and stories—however sweet their fabled forms—only made me question their basis more.

Even as a youth, I noticed aspects of Judaism that posed some dilemmas. There simply were inordinate examples of unrealistic, unreasonable, inconsistent, and simply preposterous happenings written down thousands of years or more after these events supposedly had occurred. I was no more capable of suspending my strong disbelief and employing blind faith at age 7 than I was more than thirty years later. Any blind faith I may have had then and later actually was leading me to bump against a wall. I warred within myself.

I did wish to become more knowledgeable about Judaism. Yet the more I questioned and learned, the less it all made sense to me. More unsettling was my adherence to rituals, ceremonies, and holidays despite my growing disbelief in the tenets supporting them. It was hard to interpret analytically, let alone believe at face value, a bible filled with things even Hollywood would deem farfetched. Many times, the arguments, philosophies, and "logic" supporting biblical stories would seem more "holey" than holy.

Throughout my life, I saw myself developing some telling patterns when it came to suspending any or all of my disbelief. As a youngster, I compliantly listened to stories of Adam and Eve, Noah's Ark, and Passover. Courtesy of the vivid sets and compelling acting in the *The Ten Commandments,* I found myself entertained and intrigued, and thus able to set aside my disbelief—if only for a couple hours. As I grew older, I found myself hearing the same stories—laden with inconsistent, unbelievable, nearly fantasy-like details I couldn't possibly consume whole. I began to pose some tough questions.

What kind of God would be so hurtful and condemning to a "people," causing so many to suffer horrendous and yet important life lessons? What kind of God would command a so-called "Chosen People" to do violent and unholy acts to themselves and others? Year after year, during services commemorating what Jews celebrate as the holiest time of the year, I found myself listening to rabbi after rabbi recounting the timeless, horrific story of the binding of Isaac—when Abraham shows God he is prepared to slay his own son. It was no consolation whatsoever to have my discomfort and distaste for this passage validated by rabbis and educators, who acknowledged it as "problematic," but that perhaps it just needed to be interpreted in a more contemporary manner.

I responded to this problematic story with repulsion, combined with disbelief. Whether 7 or 37, I simply never could fathom that God ever would find this passage—or any interpretation of it, however smooth—acceptable, let alone holy. No benevolent, loving, compassionate, and all-comprehending God ever would mislead God's children. No God would make one's redemption, freedom, safety, spiritual evolution, and salvation dependent upon carrying out barbaric, horrific, self-loathing, unholy acts, thoughts, and behaviors. Such connections between violence and holiness simply seemed—and are—incompatible.

As discussed in depth in Book Three, theology is a choice—not a birthright in any way, shape, or form. Now that I have explored these issues, I can see how the misappropriation of the very origins of Judaism has contributed to a host of paradoxical issues and dilemmas. Somewhere, a very long time ago, someone who became Jewish subscribed to the philosophy that the Jews were God's Chosen People. As such, subsequent followers of the faith became members of the proverbial "tribe," "people of the book," or part of a "people." What took place was a purposeful melding of theology and a self-subscribed, self-defined "culture." And thus, for years and years afterward, Jews have continued to perpetuate this anthropological application to what truly began as a theology based upon people's free-will choices.

Seemingly forever, people have perpetuated the notion that Judaism is something into which one is born—with the exception of gentiles who chose to convert to Judaism. Additionally, there also has existed the archaic notion that one is Jewish only if born to a Jewish mother. As a child, such concepts puzzled me. If Jews were complaining of dwindling numbers, wouldn't it behoove all of us to be a lot more inclusive? I had been brought up Jewish amongst other Jewish people who, for the most part, differentiated between themselves as those "born" Jewish and "converts." Of course, in recent years, converts became known as "Jews by choice"—a more politically correct, sensitive, and appropriate phrase. Little did anyone know such correctness would be more than just political or proper, but that it spoke of Truth. What now is undeniably clear is the fact that ALL Jews have been, are, and will continue to be, Jews by choice, courtesy of their own free will. All people are born as consciousness, having an earth human experience. Thus, no one is "born" Jewish, Christian, Muslim, or any other religious affiliation.

Growing up, I had the strong, sincere desire to know more about the faith in which I was raised—rivaled only by an equally compelling disbelief and curiosity about the basic tenets by which it is supported. As more people converted to or chose Judaism, I noticed an ironic trend. I found that many Jews who identify themselves as "born Jewish" are those whom, often by their own admission, are not as knowledgeable about Judaism's theological tenets as their Jews-by-choice counterparts. In other words, many so-called "born" Jews have relied greatly upon the oral tradition of theological learning, coupled with a generous cultural-social influence—also communicated from generation to generation, or "L'Dor Va Dor," as said in Hebrew.

Somewhere along the way, perhaps biblical, textual teachings were either forgotten or not emphasized. Even more plausible was the possibility that with the emergence and powerful influence of Judaism's so-called "culturally based" traditions and many Jews' increased self-identification with the so-called "cultural" aspects of their faith, the biblical bases were left behind. After the Holocaust, there existed the paradox of survivors "born" Jewish, persecuted for it, for whom the religion was meaningless—for after all, many of them felt God had abandoned the Jews. Simultaneously, there also were Jews for whom perpetuating Judaism and increasing the numbers of Jews was of paramount importance.

Growing up, I noticed many self-proclaimed "born" Jews reporting a feeling of inadequacy in terms of having a formal knowledge base—especially as compared to Jews by choice. In particular, I found one ironic trend incredibly disturbing: Jews by choice, who consciously, mindfully were choosing Judaism, also seemed to be deemed by so-called "born"

Jews as "not Jewish enough." Apparently, the fact that these people chose to be Jewish and possessed great knowledge about Judaism's basic tenets was irrelevant to those so-called "born" Jews who sat in such judgment.

Even as a child, I became aware of what seemed like the great (but unfair and hypocritical) dividing line between those who converted to Judaism and those who supposedly "inherited" it by birth. There were so many so-called "cultural" aspects associated with Judaism, such as the Yiddish language and other colloquialisms, so-called "Jewish" humor, family holiday recipes, and other related lifestyle issues. No matter how theologically astute, if one were not exposed to or knowledgeable about such lifestyle issues, he or she might very well be unable to relate fully to what many Jews erroneously define as the "Jewish experience," or even Judaism—which is a religion, not a "culture," and above all else, a CHOICE.

The melding of a theology and "a people" thus has been both complex and unique—just like the way I both digested and imparted its substance. More than a handful of times as a young adult, I recall being asked to explain certain aspects of Judaism. More often than not, I felt unable to offer complete, comprehensive answers. Compounding my confusion was the fact that the various branches of Judaism often maintained (and still do) disparate points of view on a myriad of subjects about which I hungrily sought clarity. In addition, there were many self-proclaimed "laws" of uniformity—something present in every organized religion. These pseudo-laws were "This is how Jews do such-and-such," or "Jews never do that," etc.

Of course, I know I am not alone—and Judaism is not the only theology to which this all applies. Time after time, adherents of ALL organized religions have been heard to say, "It's just how we do things." Nonetheless, such omissions, gaps, blended rituals, and human-made absolutes in my learning and knowledge did me few favors, other than further motivate me to continue my spiritual search in many different ways and forms.

As I continued on my life's path, I realized I wanted to gain insight into the overriding truths applicable to ALL peoples, no matter what their respective faiths, religions, theologies, or cultures encouraged them to believe. I came to realize that my ignorance regarding my knowledge of Judaism applied to nearly every other organized religion as well. For someone well educated, I was uninformed. There were many things I was simply never taught. For someone looking for Truth, this was unsettling—

and grew increasingly more unsettling over time. Until my twenties, I had not heard anything about the Kabbalah, to which I then found myself drawn. I decided to study it on my own.

I knew next to nothing about Jesus, other than the fact that being raised Jewish, I apparently was not supposed to "believe in him" in the religious sense. Jesus and all he was said to have represented were considered "religious" and not merely historical; that is why my secular academic environment did not teach me about this man. My Judaic education was one from which Jesus was both conspicuously and intentionally absent. Consequently, this man, whom I came to know as "other people's God," was a real enigma.

I also lived for thirty-some years never having been taught or told about Holy Angels and Archangels. Erroneously, I spent quite some time assuming and believing these Blessed Beings were only for Christians or other non-Jews. Thus, it nearly goes without saying that Hindu Godsmen such as Holy Lord Shiva (the Triune SuperConsciousness), Babaji, Lahiri Mahasaya, Sri Yukteswar Giri, and Paramahansa Yogananda all were very enigmatic, exotic mysteries—only initially revealed to me in my thirties when I began to read Yogananda's wondrous book, *Autobiography of a Yogi*.

Like Jesus Christ, why was the Kabbalah never formally taught to me? Why was mysticism kept so hidden, shrouded in secrecy? Exactly who decided that certain things about Judaism, Christianity, Islam, or any theology—for me or anyone—are okay to believe, while other things are forbidden? Was there some kind of theologically based fear that people might explore or learn too much? Certainly, there was enough Truth to go around—and then some. As we've detected and subsequently discussed in this book, the problem is that Absolute Truth actually has been shrouded in secrecy and, up to now, very much sequestered and untold.

As I went through the process of researching and writing for this book, the realizations I experienced inevitably required me to go through stages of both celebration and grief. I celebrated the Truths we were blessed to unearth, as well as grieved that so many earth human beings perpetuated so many falsities through the ages—both disguised and consumed as truths. I found the layers upon layers of misinterpretations, misunderstandings, and misappropriations of human spiritual energy to be disturbing on many levels. However, the more I discovered Truths, the more I realized I no longer could or would be content receiving, digesting, or assimilating anything less than complete Truthful Absolutes. You, too, should settle for nothing less.

When I began to examine organized religions or theologies as a whole, they often seemed to be in some sort of bizarre competition with one another, fiercely staking claims on particular prophets, sages, or so-called "holy" grounds. How so many supposedly common historical pieces could be so differently interpreted and guarded as specific to one particular religion or another was beyond my logical comprehension. Organized religions seem to possess some kind of authoritative copyright to otherwise shared material. Perhaps this book might assist readers of all faiths, beliefs, philosophies, and ideals to know that the common ground of Absolute Truth is of universal value, available to all.

Somehow, even as a child, I always knew that access to the Divine was not discriminatory, but rather, universal. Yet, I never understood how this all fit within the paradigm of Jews supposedly being God's "Chosen People." I also wondered why many Jews both celebrated and lamented this status, sometimes reflected in behavior alternating between self-congratulation and superiority and the opposing self-deprecation and "martyrdom." Did God really choose the Jews, or did the Jews choose themselves? Did this "chosen" title have a true basis, other than it being perpetually, habitually, generationally perceived as such? I couldn't help but wonder how other religions perceived these issues.

As a youth, I knew there was not one way in which to interpret, experience, teach, learn, celebrate, and honor Truth, just as there wasn't and isn't solely one right or only way for anyone to pray. It began to make extremely good sense to me that there are available teachers, masters, mentors, and guides along one's journey through existence. It has become clearer to me that Absolute Truth supersedes ALL barriers of organized religion or theology, and in doing so, may require Truth seekers to temporarily close doors to previous knowledge fed to them by formal religious tradition and historical patterns. Whether, when, how, or if they choose to reopen such doors should be entirely up to each individual person.

I now know that God doesn't choose a group of people for purposes of either persecution or prestige. Every group of people is composed of individuals. No one person or group of people holds a trademark on things such as humor, guilt, food, success, notoriety, martyrdom, victimization, talent, skills, persecution, achievement, or the ability to receive God's blessing or Unconditional Love. We merely are individuals, earth humans, who have not known differently. As such, we have operated as if not knowing any better. Fortunately, God neither discriminates nor turns a blind eye to anyone. In God's Holy Synoptic Eye, all people are the same. Accordingly, Truth is to be available and accessible to ALL who wish to partake. Furthermore, it is EVERY individual's right to experience that Truth in their own, personal way.

Absolute Truth never was meant to be packaged and contained, with its choicest kernels clandestinely sequestered behind closed doors, away from those deemed either unworthy, undeserving, inadequate, inferior, or somehow threatening by a select few who held the proverbial keys. Frankly, all earth human beings hold their own keys to the doors of Truth, which never were intended to remain locked or jammed in any way. The whole universe is filled with Truth for all to experience, and the more we open our minds and hearts, the more room we allow for Truth to enter into our individual consciousness.

Of course, to arrive at many such realizations required me to learn some difficult, painful, uncomfortable, rewarding, exciting, enriching, and enlightening lessons. While in my 30s, I found my search for Truth stronger than ever before. I practiced yoga, meditation, studied the Kabbalah, and did a lot of reading. I also returned to my childhood interests and intensely explored metaphysical and parapsychological realms. During this time, I did not feel formal or traditional theology was helpful or illuminating my quest. I also never considered having a relationship with God in a nonreligious sense. Perhaps I felt that organized religion and God existed only in conjunction with one another rather than existing independently.

I was busy in my private clinical psychology practice when I began to realize I was experiencing great spiritual emptiness, as well as some evolving, debilitating physical ailments that stubbornly remained despite my efforts to alleviate or obliterate them. I adopted "knowledge is power" as my approach to both healing my body and attending to my spirit. My path took me far beyond seeking out conventional sources to gain insight and clarity. In other words, I took a course of many different twists and curves, and I am sure I did not leave many rocks unturned.

I was experiencing a myriad of physical symptoms, some which lasted with high intensity for a continual six-year period. Some symptoms were not as bad as others, but I quickly discovered how horribly and miserably they were impacting my life, as well as how few people around me really understood my situation. I saw a variety of doctors who misdiagnosed, minimized, denied, attempted to overmedicate, or ignored my symptoms, or whose exams or treatments actually exacerbated my pain. I soon held more respect for those doctors sincere enough to admit they saw and believed my symptoms, yet were stumped by them.

Most of my physical ills manifested in the following categories of distress: abdominal, hormonal, gynecological, neck, shoulders, jaw, and lower back. I also fought a stubborn and disruptive sleep disorder. In time, I KNEW my ills absolutely were legitimate—and I suspected that the causes of these problems did not reside solely within me. I had a strong feeling there was much more at work behind the scenes than there ever could have been inside my physical body. Nonetheless, the road I took to find the answers behind these and many more burning questions was a long, confusing, bumpy, and somewhat lonely route.

My past discomfort not withstanding, I now know that my path was divinely guided, with many signs along the way that both screamed and whispered validation and truth. Even in times of great discomfort on a variety of levels, I was able to tune in enough when it counted the most. During this time, I sought out the following modalities in my desire both to alleviate my physical symptoms and unearth their etiology.

With these modalities, I had the following results: Healing touch—I was told that I had severe imbalances in my heart and second chakras, and that I was not loving myself enough. I left, wondering what I had just experienced. Acupuncture—I felt my physical distress was both addressed and understood. The focus was on my severe abdominal distress—unexplainable, tremendous bloating. I also had endometriosis that left me in monthly, sometimes twice monthly, unbearable pain. This treatment initially worked, but then brought most of these symptoms to heightened states, without remission. Bach Flower Essences—I'd taken a workshop, during which the leader swore by this system. I liked how these essences corresponded to emotional and physical manifestations. I tried them, but they tasted bitter to me and never did a thing.

Another category was Herbs—I tried several and got side effects and no tangible relief. Vitamins—no harm, no real difference. Chiropractic—I experienced initial fear about the "cracking" component and about anyone touching my neck. Some short-term relief resulted, along with accompanying dietary and supplemental regimens, but the stomach, hormonal, and back ills reemerged—in fact, later to much more severe degrees. I also never felt comfortable when being plied with a myriad of products after any healing or medical appointment. On some level, such take-home regimens only served to foster and maintain my dependence upon the prescribing practitioner.

I was dollars and time shorter, but I felt compelled to figure out why my body was so distressed and out of control, almost as if it had a mind all its own. I felt strongly that I was doing all that I could to heal myself physically—if my symptoms were originating from within me. There was way too much at play for it to be a mere stress response. What I experienced had an unusual, tenacious, unrelenting quality to it. My symptoms were keeping me captive when I was trying with fierce determination to break free. This thought spoke volumes, although I hardly knew it at the time.

Most of the time, I was feeling extremely misunderstood, judged, and unsupported—especially by doctors or people around me who encouraged me to minimize, forget about, or otherwise overlook my own discomforts. I was tired of feeling sick or in pain. I knew my ills in some ways defied diagnostic criteria. Several years earlier, I had sought out guidance in my childhood interests of the metaphysical world. While the information I received tended to be inconsistent in terms of predictive accuracy and my own internal resonance, I nonetheless found it overall more satisfying than other modalities. Looking back, I think this satisfaction was due largely in part to my feeling heard, attended to without being too rushed, and seemingly understood on a deeper and more personal level.

Again, in retrospect, I later was able to trace the beginning stages of both my mental and physical distress to some of those so-called healing sessions with many a metaphysical source. Of course, at the time, I was unaware of what I would come to understand. Later, I would find how terribly and destructively I had been betrayed by people in whom I had, in my most vulnerable and open states, placed what little trust I still possessed. I would discover at once both how very little and very much I truly knew. These revelations did not come without my paying a very high price.

Yet, in my time of feeling depleted and sick, it seemed to make sense to take not solely a medical but a metaphysical route. I thought it would be easier, and I was mentally and physically drained from enduring so many medical experiences. I needed both symptom relief and insight. I was, however, searching for my anchor in murky waters; in my vulnerability I was unable to discern between benevolence and malevolence.

Later, I would learn the difference between people whose information comes to and through them from a single, supernal, divine source with only good intentions, and those people who access their information by stealing the light and divine energy from others. This latter group of people are those whose "incoming" information is accumulated from many unsuspecting victims—only to feed these thieves' own deficits. They have ulterior motives, and their primary goal is to steal the life force energy from the client they pretend to be assisting.

I looked for illumination from the following sources of people and metaphysical modalities: psychics, channelers, transmediums, handwriting analysts, numerologists, energy healers, hypnotherapists, past-life regression therapists, palm readers, astrologers, Reiki masters, Tarot card readers, Shamans, mind-body healers, bodywork therapists, Rolfers, Chi Gong masters, and those practitioners whose genuine talents I later would discover actually were in the arenas of black magic: psychic attacks, psychic vampirism and parasitic exploitation. For years, this all was unbeknownst to me. For years, all of the physical and emotional ills I legitimately was experiencing went misunderstood, misidentified, and miscomprehended.

Fortunately, through a series of many events, and with divine assistance, I came to realize what truly had taken place. In my great spiritual starvation, I was at times purposefully and with malicious intention being fed and nourished by contaminated crumbs—enough to make me hunger for more—and enough to fuel the engines behind people who, in their malicious intent, had no light or divine energy to fuel themselves. Because of the enormity of the emotional, physical, and spiritual pain and discomfort I endured, there were many times afterward I found myself wishing I had known better.

I did not know better at the time, and like a starving animal, I showed my eagerness, vulnerability, and willingness to devour whatever was displayed to me. I had no consistent, dependable discernment capabilities— at least not on a conscious level; subconsciously, very deeply, I obviously was committing each experience to a core memory, which I later would need to expunge. I would learn that such expungment would encompass and include more than my most recent life experiences.

I had no clue about either the problems or ultimate resolutions that were in store for me. All I came to know is that as I began my internal "clean-up" process, I vowed to myself and to God, that once I healed myself and gained insight into life's mysteries, if I could assist even one person on their journey, that would be great; if I could reach greater numbers, all the better. Certainly, I know now that what I endured and experienced, in all of its discomfort, was for a greater, divine purpose. Thus, there was a real and important reason why at the time I DIDN'T "know any better." This state of not knowing actually allowed me to grow, experience, expunge, and gain more insight and enlightenment. In essence, my personal journey HAD to include all of these elements, which contributed to the realization and insight needed for me to be able to collaborate on this book.

The following section may be very troubling for many of you. It may elicit responses of incredulous disbelief, bewildered confusion, or even callous disregard. However, be assured that this experience—and all firsthand accounts described in this book—definitely took place. These incidents have been carefully documented and recorded so that others placed in similar situations will have a better chance of recognizing their plight—and perhaps preventing unnecessary susceptibility and future damage. Please note that in addition to these malevolent people and happenings, there also have existed those healers and psychic surgeons who have battled to exorcise entities, and other various, co-inhabiting essences within people's physical beings. Throughout time, this has been the case, whether it's portrayed through the eyes of Hollywood's camera lens in films such as *The Exorcist* or throughout the pages of the New Testament, where Jesus himself is purported to have cast out devils and demons.

The following concept (and many others which follow) relates to psychics but is applicable to each and every category of healing I have experienced so far—and any type you might seek out and sample. This concept—the ability to discern between someone else's good or bad intent—applies to ALL humankind. It is when we are at our most vulnerable that we tend to lose sight of possessing this ability, and are unable to apply it for our own well-being and protection. We also become misguided enough to think that somehow our resistance to feeling better signifies our inability to be truly open to others' suggestions or "cures." Nothing could be further from the truth; it is when we do NOT feel better that we ooze vulnerability and become so open, letting anybody or anything invade us. If we are not careful in our most vulnerable states, we risk parting with more than our hours and dollars; we risk being drained of our very essence and life force energies.

Sometimes, people are at risk merely by being insatiably curious, the hallmark of every seeker looking for answers. For those of you who ever felt an unsettled feeling, that you were inexplicably "on to something," that you merely wanted some extra validation from an "outside source," perhaps these phenomena will resonate with you. Maybe you've experienced something "weird," "unusual," or "surreal" that you don't feel people in your personal or professional circles ever could possibly understand, let alone hear about. If you've experienced major physical or psychological traumatic symptoms that either elude traditional diagnostic codes and parameters—or that conveniently meet such criteria despite your inner knowledge and strong feelings otherwise, then what you will read may speak volumes to you.

I speak from my own personal experience in an effort to share insights that might resonate within you and assist you in your own life journey. Specifically, I have come to learn that most people typically do not seek out nontraditional or "external" sources when they are feeling relatively at peace within themselves. In fact, research suggests that most people prefer to avoid seeing medical practitioners altogether, unless or until there appears to be a problem or reason to do so.

Think back to the times when you felt the most at peace. Chances are good that you were either so busy living your life in this positive way or just being "in the flow," so to speak, that you probably weren't motivated to consult or seek out help from others. However, there are always some exceptions—those who feel okay but wish to test or challenge a psychic's (or some other source's) perceptions against their own. Even those who claim restlessness or boredom as their motivators might still possess an unsettled or depressive vulnerability, an energy that despite even its most valiant efforts to remain undetected or disguised consistently reveals itself to many—and unfortunately, quite loudly to those people who prey upon it the most. Thus, it is really no wonder that by the time most people reach a psychic or similar external source, they are deeply and suscep-tibly vulnerable.

For the sake of efficiency and uniformity, I shall use the term "psy-chics" as the primary example when describing such external sources—whose intent it is our burden as their clients to discern, oftentimes during our most vulnerable states. As I said before, it is critical to remember that this discussion and the personal experiences I share apply equally to a myriad of outside sources—doctors, healers, service professionals, even individuals who defy categorization, or those who seemingly have been in your lives forever. There are people out there who tend to operate for the common good, while others do exactly the opposite.

Because there are inevitable human variations with respect to inten-tions, thoughts, and behaviors, very few of these people remain "on course" 24/7. Nonetheless, when people more often than not operate from a position of malice and malevolence, they inflict an abundance of damage to others who are vulnerable or in pain; any momentary goodness or exception to this pattern is inconsequential and only serves to further increase a victim's vulnerability and trust in the malevolent sources whose focused free will feeds upon it.

Of course, there are psychics whose intents seemingly are for good. In extremely rare cases, a few will receive information and guidance solely from God—for reasons known only to God. On the other hand, there are psychics who have other ideas in mind—ideas they hope and assume you'll never figure out. Vulnerable people seek their help and leave laden with increased pain, eventually either oblivious or addicted to it, or resigned to believe it is their lot in life. Know that you have yet another option—and that is to reclaim the essence or life force energy stolen from you with only your trust as permission.

To those so-called "helpers" who prey upon such vulnerability, con-vinced their efforts are adequately concealed or foolproof—they are grossly mistaken, and this is very blessedly so. As I have found in my life, you now will read in my words: Secret-keeping is an illusion created and maintained in vain. Once people start to trust and connect to Truth, they will experience no further need to seek out external sources for answers that can be found inside their own being.

In my daily busyness of existence, there were many realities I was unable to see. One need not be a metaphysician to infuse others with their negative, parasitic energy. Many regular, "un-psychic" people out there also are capable of recognizing the light within another person, coveting it, and latching onto this soon-to-be victim, in an effort to experience what they themselves do not possess. These are people who, for a variety of reasons, do not have your best interest in mind, whose intentions are not truly for the common good, who are decidedly opportunistic and manipulative, and whose methods and subsequent results can drag you down. When I first became aware of these situations, I found the reality darkly ironic. Apparently, I had something supposedly wonderful that a lot of people seemed to want, but in my pain, I couldn't begin to imagine what it would ever be. It took me years to figure out and reclaim my own essence.

I now will share with you how and why my journey took so many seemingly endless paths, each with its own particular detour that slowed me down and took me backward. Ultimately, however, the totality of my experiences brought me to points of incomparable awareness. Fortunately, I gained so much more than I perceived I had lost. There truly was a divine purveyor of light and might with me all along to perceive Truth and illuminate it for me. I was—and gratefully, continue to be—purposefully guided to the right people at the right time.

Later, in Book Three, we will describe in detail the relationship between dharma, free will, karma, and transgressions—as they all relate to every aspect of existence, including psychics and related subject matter. Because of sheer volume alone, I will not describe each individual external source or experience in detail. However, I will describe my experiences with sources as they relate or apply to either the benevolent or malevolent categories.

One of the things that contributed to the intensity of my painful experiences was the high level of fear I had accumulated. Granted, when push came to shove, I was able to extricate myself from what amounted to chronic, debilitating contamination—but not without some extraordinary assistance. However, during my search and physical discomforts, I placed my trust in the wrong hands. In time, I realized what I had done. In and of itself, that realization created new layers of fear. My fear greatly frustrated and paralyzed me, and I wanted it gone.

I have learned from my experiences that I need not harbor any fear within me—that fear is not OF me, but rather something from outside myself that I've decided to inherit or assume and subsequently absorb as my own. I have learned that fear is a weapon used by others who seek to control the power they wish to wield over their victims. Throughout history, there have been control mongers who have fit this description, bombarding society with messages of fear and mistruths in order to dominate those they feel are most vulnerable.

Healers and midwives were tortured and killed during the Inquisition for using their true knowledge and talents. The Church and the newly established medical profession felt threatened by such wisdom. In order to maintain their power base, the "establishment" spread rumors, which in turn, created a fear response within the general public. Consequently, the public feared those who actually possessed the Truth. Those who possessed the Truth were themselves forced into silence, to obey those in command, and to refuse to honor the Truth and power they held within. The message from the bullying powers was decidedly clear: You need others to tell you the truth. Of course, with regard to such enforced "truths," nothing is more false.

Unfortunately, throughout history, such intimidation prevented many from believing in themselves, in their Truth, and in the sharing of their truth, wisdom, and talents. The wars and injustices throughout history and today are indicative of the sublimation and restriction of benevolent powers and energies that—if allowed to flourish—would be impacting the universe in amazingly positive, powerful ways. The world needs such healers, teachers, wise men and women, Truth-seekers, and Truth-keepers more today than ever before.

Nonetheless, there still exist within our universe many intimidating, malicious forces and people for whom trust and benevolence remains a threat. For them, preventing people from accessing and experiencing their true essence and life force energies, where all Truth, goodness, and holiness reside, is of paramount concern. They will take from others that which they cannot possibly access from within themselves. From a position of deficit and fear, they inflict the most heinous crime upon their more benevolent counterparts—that of bleeding others' accessible life force energies from them. These malicious beings intrude where even God does not tread—within the intimate, personal, private cores of people's essences. They then steal the accessible life force energies of another, with the only "permission" being the unfortunate trust and openness of the vulnerable victim.

The most important message I've experienced, witnessed in others, and learned to commit to memory relates to the Divine Law of Universal Reflection in all conscious experiences: Whatever I put out or forth to the universe, I will receive as its response. This means if I put out love, I receive love back. If I put out rage, I will receive rage back. If I put out fear, I experience more reasons to be afraid. In other words, "What goes around, comes around" applies to all conscious experiences in ALL existences.

Despite a victim's vulnerability and the credence, power, trust, and loyalty they in good faith may place in the hands of the attacker, a victim fortunately also can reverse the process. This principle of reversal is not built upon a premise of blaming the victim for being so vulnerable, but rather on the recognition of the ability to extricate from such sources IF they are willing to be open to the requisite detoxification and healing. Some of you now may be wondering why victims WOULDN'T want to heal and purge themselves in order not to be revictimized. What may seem like an obvious solution is, in some cases, a complicated process some victims may unconsciously or consciously seek to avoid.

Believe it or not, there are victims who DO wish to remain victimized; for them, there is a secondary gain, known perhaps only to their own subconscious. Their inability to trust in God, and in themselves, clouded by their longstanding trust in malevolent sources, may prevent them from taking that necessary first step toward healing. Driven by deep denial, the level of their defensiveness can be quite strong. Making changes requires sacrifices on many levels. Often, this process results in closing the doors on relationships with one's roles, other people, places, and circumstances. Furthermore, with respect to ANY of these categories, one can expect there to be some fallout if one decides to make the effort and room for true change to occur.

Unfortunately, when we seek to avoid further discomfort, we often lose sight of the bigger picture. Healing is that bigger picture that requires, if not demands, some significant discomfort or even pain. For some, the tough challenge when considering this prospect is to reconcile with the pain-avoidance dilemma within. Avoidance is built upon the fear instilled in us by others, a fear that intimidates us, wielding its negativity as influence over us, managing to convince us that our state of being (as a victim) is as good as it gets. When we absorb such energy and messages, it is no wonder that some of us don't bother considering any other state of being. This soul paralysis is the supreme learned helplessness.

Despite their protests otherwise, some victims may thrive upon the drama inherent in their own victimization. Others may feel victimization is all they deserve, and the notion of healing and freeing themselves from such negativity may simply be too overwhelming. It is important to note that the process and relative impact of both contamination and healing are contingent upon the receiver's trust. The more you trust in a negative source—in its abilities, talents, "wisdom," power, knowledge, and purported assurances of being able to help you—the greater and more consistent the victimizer's clarity will tend to be. Believing and giving into curses and negativity placed by others onto you is the worst thing you can do for your well-being—and the best thing you can do to empower the vampiric source. The more you FEEL you are victimized or dwell in fear, the more the reflection—including the potential vampiric energies—will respond in kind.

It is only when you are vulnerable, your aura "cracked," or in unusual pain or distress that you give "permission" to let in the negativity and accompanying destructive forces. Such permission resides in a two-fold "invitation" of sorts: First, your pain and distress energy, which precedes you, is evident, obvious, and easily recognizable. Second, you express your need for answers and convey that you are on a search or quest for understanding, comprehension, and validation. This vulnerable trust placed into bad hands is terribly self-fueling: it actually allows those with ulterior motives to make more accurate psychic predictions, which in turn, only serve to gain more of your trust. Blessedly, the opposite holds true. When you place your trust with the God inside you, you receive all of that reflecting benevolent trust back to you.

Later in this book, we will discuss how each of us can improve our attunement for the facilitation of enlightenment and upliftment. This will provide, develop, and maintain a deeper, more lasting relationship with the Divine. Again, remember that both benevolent and malevolent relationships are created and maintained by trust. In the case of malevolent relationships, which can be stubbornly and unyieldingly reciprocal in their dysfunction, it is important to examine the components and characteristics that contribute to this reality.

It is our hope that by highlighting and identifying some of the behaviors, actions, and personality qualities of abusive, manipulative, oppressive, opportunistic, coercive, and related malevolent sources—even psychic vampires—this information might assist you in the recognition of such forces. In many instances, several of the following examples applied to my own personal experience. However innocent and benign my initial path seemed to be, it transpired into a convoluted, albeit necessary learning experience. While I experienced many unpleasant encounters, with some qualifying as being decidedly vampiric in nature, my path ultimately led me to benevolence and insight.

Negative forces can have a way of surfacing during our everyday experiences—generally revealing societal discontent and frustration or bottled-up, individual emotions, rather than assuming the role of a conscious, targeted assault. Perhaps someone yells or curses at you, exhibits road rage, or treats you with distain, disrespect, or contempt. This person obviously is directing pent-up, stress-filled, unchanneled, negative energy toward you in a harmful way. If you are feeling particularly vulnerable on any level, these little attacks ultimately can take their toll. We all know people who are chronically tired, depressed, anxious, or otherwise off-balance, who continually latch onto others for ongoing support and strength. We also know people in whose presence, we realize afterward, we don't feel good; we experience signs of depletion on multiple levels. There are two categories of "psychic vampires"—and they are applicable to ALL people—NOT just psychics and NOT just vampires.

Psychic vampires can be divided into conscious and unconscious types. A typical, unconscious example could be described as an individual who typically makes others feel obliged to him or her for no legitimate reason, other than perhaps guilt. This person might not make specific demands upon you, but most certainly can offer you nothing in return. Unknown to themselves, they unconsciously drain others' energy. In their presence, it is likely that you will feel symptoms of emotional and physical exhaustion.

These unconscious vampires seem unable to make good use of the energy they take from others. They know not how to adequately and efficiently "feed" themselves and their deficits, and instead uselessly disperse what they've stolen from you into their environment. They keep repeating this pattern again and again. We all know people like this, in whose presence or contact our only real danger is that of exhaustion, annoyance, and overall depletion. In short, while they do continue to drain others' energy, unconscious vampiric individuals pose no significant harm.

Conscious vampires, on the other hand, are those who deliberately take energy from others through a variety of means. Most of what you will read here focuses on vampires of the conscious, deliberate variety. These conscious victimizers feed themselves with both your physical and psychological energies, drawing from you and taking into themselves your very life-sustaining energies. First and foremost, they are predators whose instincts are drawn to and focused on the hunt and the subsequent capture and conquest of you—the prey. This notion typically does not play out in fantasized scenes of physical chases and dramatic, forcible devouring of the prey. Rather, this person exhibits a decidedly more cunning strategy. They utilize intelligence, seduction, charisma, charm, and most important, the ability to inspire and capture your trust. These people are nearly always in search of new and different energy sources, despite their display of possessiveness or jealousy over people and things considered to be theirs.

Through their seductive ways and displays of affection, these people will gain new victims to whom they may even profess their love. They work to inspire the victim to trust them, but end up draining the victim, who in turn, develops feelings of abandonment, betrayal, and confusion—exacerbated even more when this predator begins to roam in search of additional, newer, fresher or more vibrant energy sources. For many conscious psychic vampires, sexuality is very strongly tied to the predatory drive. This process can become equally addictive for the victims; it's easy for a predator to get someone to come back for more if they are fulfilling a void in a victim's life.

Vampires can cause a whole host of serious interpersonal problems by their aggression, possession, jealous nature, seduction, and protection. They tend to have demanding needs, so insistent and urgent at times that they require immediate attention in order to avoid the inevitable result of spiraling dysfunctional behavior. Most of these people truly are troubled and unstable on multiple levels. Those who appear otherwise are masters of disguise, whose outward strength actually hides the extreme emotions raging within. Always on the edge, such people are like pots boiling over on a stove, with just a lid held on in a desperate effort to prevent major, catastrophic spillage.

Like a boiling pot, there are times when a vampire explodes—and those around them will be brutally aware of this experience. The intensity of such highs or lows will be profound and unnerving to those unfamiliar with such patterns. The vampire's obsession and quest for draining life-sustaining energies from their prey is like having a disease that causes one to crave a highly specific substance. Such craving is present even before it's ever been acted upon. Yet, once indulged, it can lead to horrific, spiraling, addictive behavior. Vampires' urges are like brewing primal tensions—so uncomfortable and intense that they must relieve them by stealing and draining the energies from their prey. Subsequently, both victim and perpetrator may experience satisfying relief—so much so that it reinforces and encourages repeated, perpetual participation without much incentive from either party to quit.

Vampires' emotional displays are rather predictable—they rarely show genuine emotions. Instead, they tend to act cold, as if things do not matter. If they get passionate about anything at all, such intensity usually takes on the form of anger or vengeance. They also exhibit a schizoid-like, unfocused, easily distracted, or fragmented behavioral quality. They are uncomfortable with excessive affection and sentimentality; they do not appreciate any negative comments regarding their look or appearance; and they very rarely want forgiveness or are willing to forgive. Vampires thrive on getting more fuel than they need, often supported by daily "feeding" rituals.

There are many ways psychic vampires perform their destructive feeding, the most common form being through the modality of visualization and mental focus or practice. Prior to contact with the intended victim, a conjuration, invocation, incantation, or some preparatory rite or ritual is necessary. To avoid feeding off people who might be in negative states themselves, many vampires target specific groups of people, victim(s) who are in a suitable state for proper conquest, or they set up shields or "servitors" to filter out undesirable energy. All a vampire needs to do to activate this "feeding cycle" is something as basic and seemingly benign as rubbing their hands together—and then innocently placing one or both hands upon a victim's shoulder, arm, back, or hand. This is done in the form of gestures such as neck or back rubs, handshakes, or hugs. There need not be any overt sexual contact between the two parties for a successful activation of a vampiric feeding cycle.

If you are a victim and there is any type of initial sexual contact between you and the vampiric source, you might feel extremely attracted, and in some cases, in love with this vampiric person. By looking deeply and intensely into your eyes, they attempt to get even closer to you and your energy. Specifically, human sexual vampirism feeds upon sexual energy, including employing the ritual of succubus/succubae (female vampire) or incubus/incubi (male vampire)—the creatures of raw sex. This ritual draws a victim's energy into the vampire while the victim is asleep. Accordingly, a victim might find themself actually dreaming of having sex with the vampire—to the point where the victim might awaken and "know" or "feel" this is the truth in their reality. Vampires frequently take advantage of the fact that sex is an activity producing a lot of energy on which they intend to feed. Vampires delight in building up high frustration levels within a victim, denying them the opportunity to climax. Vampires then can visualize the trapped sexual energy, siphon it off, and absorb it as their own.

When a vampire wants to take in someone's energy, they want to feel it being brought into one of the main chakras or powerhouses of energy. The major chakras include the Third Eye (the bridge chakra, located in the forehead above the nose, between the eyes, also known as the spiritual center of the Omnipresent Eye), the Throat Chakra, Heart Chakra, Stomach Chakra, and Pelvic Chakra. Most vampires prefer the Stomach or Third Eye Chakras for feeding off their victims. Vampires shield themselves when taking the victims' vital energy without taking on their emotions. They also use a technique called linking, whereby they transfer energy back and forth. In order to differentiate between the looks and "feels" of potential victims, they also scan people, using mental projection techniques.

I personally experienced several years of nighttime sleep disorders, which I came to realize were actually nighttime vampiric attacks—courtesy of at least one or two constant vampiric sources, if not more at various times. Throughout history, this phenomenon has occurred. The Greeks referred to such vampiric creatures as "lamai," and the Medieval Europeans term was "incubus or succubus." The preferred way for vampires to acquire new energy is through osmosis, usually focused at the Stomach or Heart Chakras, in order to instill major fear and awaken the victim. After the vampire is satisfied, the victim finally falls back asleep, awakening the next day fairly drained from what he or she figures was a poor night of sleep. Such attacks seem to occur between 3 and 5 a.m., when people have the most amount of life force energies available.

Some vampires attack nightly, in an effort to maintain a consistent energy level. Some attack the same victim night after night, year after year, despite many vampires' preferences for attacking multiple or new prey. Given my own experience, I am sure I was preferred target prey for at least two specific, unfulfilled vampires. Nightly, I rose between 3 and 3:15 a.m. regularly, as if by alarm clock, for between two and four consecutive years.

The effects of black magic are very similar to those of psychic vampirism. Unlike white magic, which is nature based and often called Wicca, black magic is a negative use of energies—power used to deprive, influence, or conquer victims. The distinction between white (Wicca) and black magic rests in the free-will intention and responding karmic impaction. White magic is benignly projected into environmental creation without purposeful soul transgression. When a black magician is well skilled, black magic can harm or hurt vulnerable, trusting victims. Malicious acts of black magic can be executed or performed even at extreme geographical distances. When perpetrators feel frustrated, jealous, negative, resentful, hostile, or depressed in response to someone else's experiences of happiness and personal growth, black magic is often used as a retaliatory weapon.

Black magicians gain a sinister satisfaction out of manifesting turmoil in another person—oftentimes someone close to them in life, such as a friend, acquaintance, co-worker, or relative. Black magic blocks a victim's inherent wisdom, intelligence, and inner knowing, leaving in their place, blocked mental energy, as well as extremely disturbed sleep—complete with terrible, scary dreams and negative thoughts. Victims also tend to experience a heaviness or weight on the heart, as well as a definite constriction in the throat. The latter I personally experienced many times—especially while writing about my inner spiritual struggle.

Some victims of black magic sustain bluish marks on their thigh—without their remembering any specific incidents of getting hurt, and a faster or jumpy heartbeat and intense panting or heavy breathing without any apparent exertion. Most notably, a victim will engage in sudden quarrels within their family, co-workers, or friendship circles, and may even experience a presence of somebody or something in the home. Victims rarely feel they are at peace; they seem perpetually restless or unnerved, suffocated and possibly depressed; they don't seem "themselves."

Black magic, like psychic vampirism techniques, can be extremely potent and successful in destroying someone's prosperity or wealth, career or personal fulfillment, psychological, emotional, sexual, and physical health and behavior. The most disturbing aspect of the effects of black magic is that it can become more chronic and dangerous as time goes on. If left "untreated" or undetected, it can spread like an infectious disease, affecting life on every level.

How does one even begin to detect such malevolent sources, let alone begin to treat the damage they have incurred? The first step is to acknowledge that something is inherently wrong. Only when you realize you hold the keys to such critical discernment will you be able to identify the problem. The outward dysfunctions of this internal disharmony are really what most people, from the outside looking in, are capable of observing. After all, one never really knows what goes on in the private minds or lives of people. Having to identify and attempt to remedy one's ills while being in a state of bewildered unrest is challenging.

Nonetheless, it is imperative that you recognize the insidious signs, and take concrete steps to distance yourself both physically, psychologically, and emotionally from anyone who might be victimizing you—however dependent upon their "services" or "help" you might be. You must take back your power.

The susceptibility of being reinfected, recontaminated, or "re-hooked" by a vampiric source remains if you are not able to be clear, focused, and aware of how insidiously powerful and willful such dangerously negative forces are. Because the Spirit Realm must work invisibly behind the scenes, outward signs are often your only clues to inner truths. However, when one is vulnerable and slowly or rapidly becoming contaminated by others' poisons, discernment can be extremely elusive. Compounding this challenge is the fact that many of these external sources appear charming, compassionate, enthusiastic and supportive, supplying you with compelling, so-called "truthful" information.

Tempting as it may be, even those so-called "intuitives," whose predictive accuracy might seem high, can be those who have fed off your trust. They have fed you crumbs of information that only minimally satisfies your spiritual hunger—until they feed upon YOU once again. Today, there is an unfortunate tendency for psychics and related healer-types to make up a sizeable portion of this disturbing and destructive population. However, it is important to know that contaminators can take on or assume a variety of forms—from nontraditional healers, to attorneys, to sales professionals, to instructors, to other supposedly "well meaning," perhaps unconsciously vampiric people.

The best defense you can have against such negative forces is to maintain an awareness and an unwillingness to allow such destruction and victimization to happen to you. Perhaps you have been a victim of such contamination and vampirism, and you are worried that you may have become reinfected by an old source or by a new one taking advantage of the old crud still toxically lodged within you. If this is the case, remember that you know best when it comes to your own body. You will know by your physical body's reemergence of old, debilitating, uncomfortable, or downright painful, symptoms. It will be as if they never, ever went away—and now suddenly are reactivated in full force. Drugs and alcohol also can be considered temptresses, resulting in similar, reoccurring uncomfortable physical manifestations.

In addition to what you have just read, I have identified from my own personal experiences more traits, styles, and patterns, as well as the underlying bedrock that makes up and supports psychic vampirism, black magic, psychic parasitism, and the deceit and ill will that complete the picture. Again, this list also is applicable to ANY of the healing, metaphysical, medical, or nontraditional practitioner categories. As stated earlier, there are, of course, many with harmful intentions who exert such energy and effort—and are not in any of these categories—just as there are those in the healing categories whose source for information is both received and given to clients with good intent. I will also include other signs that may be helpful to place within your consciousness, should such unfortunate situations present themselves on your life path. Later, in Book Three, we will explore from a spiritual perspective the role and behaviors of psychics and related external sources.

Many psychics will make suggestions disguised as predictions. Many earnest seekers yearn for such information regarding physical symptoms, ailments, and issues related to their emotional, financial, social, romantic, familial, and occupational experiences. These are typical, predictable categories. Keep in mind, if you are "ripe" enough, there's a good chance you will have projected a sense of vulnerability, perhaps along with a good deal of forthcoming data—that serves to assist the psychic at work. Many times, a psychic repeatedly will ask about certain things. In my experiences, I found this tendency only moderately distracting. Later, I realized it was a deliberate way to ascertain what my true vulnerabilities were—and the degree to which they could be manipulated.

Be aware of the psychic who asks tons of personal questions, which later only become part of what you erroneously might perceive as the psychic's "brilliant predictions." Any ironclad promises or guarantees should be taken with a huge grain of salt, including promising the IMPOSSIBLE—communication with a specific, departed loved one's spirit from the other side, which we later will discuss in greater detail. When you essentially turn over the responsibility of your life into another's hands, you lose your internal barometer for discerning boundary violations and victimization.

This unfortunate process often begins innocently enough, but can leave victims in a potentially horrendous position. Oftentimes, this takes place when unsuspecting people initially feel uncomfortable with the rates being quoted; they have been offered "special rituals," services, or ceremonies for unbelievably high prices, quoted as good for them. These are danger signs. Be wary when strict boundaries are imposed upon you and none of yours are respected. Also be wary when you detect no boundaries being established whatsoever.

Once a relationship is established, it becomes fair game for further enmeshment. Enmeshment is a psychological state of entrapment, characterized by some seemingly benign violations of personal boundaries, as well as dysfunctional modes of communication—all created and maintained so the relationship seems attractive, supportive, and "right" in your eyes. As such, if you end up "connecting" with a psychic or like source, developing a positive regard and trust toward this person, you may find yourself minimizing, tempering, or downright negating any misgivings or previous sense of foreboding. Every piece of feedback, advice, and support you receive from this person will appear genuine, positive, and in the spirit of your best interest—erroneously so. However, because you are involved in this relationship on multiple levels, you may not notice the lies veiled as truths.

If they continue to go unrecognized, these relationships will only become more psychologically dysfunctional and keep you trapped. Malevolent and vampiric sources utilize a variety of ways to capture the trust—and ultimate essence—of their victims. Some examples of this manipulation are shameless self-promotion and guilt-tripping; excessive offers of unsolicited hands-on "healing" opportunities—and talking about how much you need it; and a discussion of their personal and professional financial difficulties. These people might also lure a victim closer by initiating e-mail, regular mail, phone, or in-person communication—only to follow up by abruptly pulling back.

This pattern of a vampiric source willfully distancing from you is illusory; once an ill-willed person wants to and ultimately "hooks" you, you are never far away from their access—especially, when in your vulnerability and naïveté, you don't see the covert intent. Unless you consciously, willfully, and prayerfully disallow them from doing continued, sustained damage, you will not have done enough to prevent it. In my case, the removal of such true, debilitating psychic hooks required some very intensive, concentrated energy healing. It also demanded that I communicate to such destructive external sources that the jig was up—and that I no longer would be participating in their games.

I later realized that with each area of interest or point of concern I brought to a session with a psychic or related source, I was only providing a fodder for their mission. Essentially, I was handing over my high level of vulnerability for them to use as ammunition against me. I often would provide exactly the information for which they searched, despite any of my conscious attempts to do otherwise. They paid attention to my curiosities and desires, and offered to do unusual, special, or previously retired services just for me. Such gestures included long-distance healing, a variety of regressions, private classes, ceremonial techniques, and much, much more. Unfortunately, when a seeker is hungry enough, a little sounds good, much more even better.

For me, there were psychics who made predictions that certain physical symptoms and ailments I had experienced either would be exacerbated or go into a remission. These so-called "predictions" tended to come to fruition, only further earning my trust and beliefs in this vampiric process. I later realized that over long periods of time, these predictors were the actual SOURCES and origins for most of my ills. One of the worst cases involved a flu bug that raged within me for over twelve straight days—only to raise its ugly head in many related forms afterward. I later recalled receiving so-called "support" and "healing work in absentia" from my then ongoing contact with someone I now realize was practicing black magic.

I experienced some of the most intensified exacerbation of physical symptoms in connection with some particular psychics with whom I had worked. These people literally were making me sick. I began battling with major abdominal pain accompanied by uncontrollable—often unsightly enlarged—swelling. After enduring many invasive medical procedures, my pain was labeled as irritable bowel syndrome—IBS—the catch-all phrase for "those kinds" of problems not neatly falling into a more distinct, labeled category. I had done enough research to be aware of potential trigger foods, had eliminated coffee and other irritants, and had attempted to lower my stress, which was growing worse by the constant swelling and pain. I tried valiantly to figure out why at its height of intensity this syndrome made me look nearly seven months pregnant.

These stomach-related ailments were not only relegated to me but affected my beloved dog as well. He seemed to be displaying the same symptoms by which I was plagued—and became more skittish and sensitive in his demeanor. He, too, had been diagnosed with an IBS-like condition, which negatively impacted his digestive abilities. I later found out why my dog and I suffered our physical distress simultaneously and with such common symptoms. Because I was so agitated, in prolonged physical discomfort, all the while being in close, physical interaction with my dog, he received the intensified vibrations emanating from me.

These vibratory emanations carried the information for stomach disorder from me to my dog, resulting in his experiencing similar physical effects. Because our universe is all vibratory in nature, all existence is subjected to this similar phenomenon. In fact, the same principle is consistent throughout the physical cosmos. In other words, it happens to everyone—without exception. Thus, the unsuspecting dinner guest who happens to be seated in the chair usually occupied by an angry, depressed, violent, or abusive person, inevitably will absorb and experience the vibrational residue retained in the chair.

I also noticed some very unusual and unsettling symptoms on top of those I already was experiencing. First, as soon as I'd consume any food—even the tiniest amount—my lower belly immediately expanded. As I grew more concerned about this, I became aware that my upper stomach region, around my ribcage and below my Heart Chakra, soon followed suit. As they swelled, both areas became painfully tender and hard like rocks. The most disturbing and off-the-wall manifestation, however, was that if I sat still long enough to observe my midsection I actually could SEE it swell before my eyes.

Initially, this phenomenon simply seemed odd to me. After it happened episodically but intensely for more than four years straight, I became increasingly more alarmed. There also were times when I'd detect a movement, literally originating from within my gut, like a rolling wave. The internal sensation, as well as the truly visible motion was reminiscent of a time when I actually was six months pregnant. However, in this case, I was neither pregnant nor undisturbed. One certainly can appreciate just how well the medical profession received and understood my most unusual complaints.

During this same time, I also suffered from a knifelike pain that permeated my shoulder blade areas, typically accompanied by major neck tightness and soreness. There were many times I couldn't turn my head but a tiny bit. I also experienced a back pain originating in my hips, radiating down my legs a bit—before ending up at my tailbone with a throbbing, banging sensation. I felt like someone had taken a hammer and mercilessly was whacking me until the entire bone throbbed with pain. At its worst point, the pain was debilitating and consuming, and at its lowest threat, was fairly distracting, annoying, and uncomfortable. Now I know that receiving hands-on, so-called "lightwork" energy healing from these pain-producing sources obviously did little to alleviate any problems, but instead did much to encourage their continued appearance and impact. I spent a lot of days bent over in pain from a variety of bodily points, hosted by these ill-willed people who considered themselves my "friends."

Initially annoying, but becoming increasingly disturbing and unsettling was my obvious sleep disorder. As a child, teen, and young adult, I always required and enjoyed getting at least eight or more hours of sleep per day. Suddenly, I found myself becoming both an insomniac as well as an early riser. This was a lethal combination for one who thrived on rest and on whom other people depended. I couldn't afford to be sleep deprived, let alone sleep disordered. However, every night for over three consecutive years, I awoke at 3 a.m., nearly on the dot. It never was later than 3:15 a.m.—and never before 3 a.m. I literally awoke with a jarring jolt, as if being awakened by a thunderous horn or stampede. Yet, I heard no authentic noises. I was not the bleary-eyed, sleepy person one would expect me to be, but was instead depressingly wide awake and unable to retire again in a timely manner.

It became common that I'd be up past 4 a.m. Eventually surrendering to my own exhaustion, I would drag myself back to bed. Unfortunately, my malevolent sources knew just how disturbing this problem could be; I had told them myself. Both of them sympathized, as each one admitted to keeping similar hours. One would offer sympathy for my plight via e-mail, while the other (they did not know each other personally—only by reputation) would speak with me by phone, knowing I was awake, anyway. What I mistakenly, naïvely took for their compassion or empathy actually was the conduit to their effective energy thievery. My trust afforded me only their feigned support, in exchange for their receipt of my own life-sustaining, God-given energies.

In the case of my relationships with these malevolent sources, MB and DR, I erroneously perceived them as my friends. Both individuals invested much time and energy getting to know me, sharing with me details of their personal lives, and demonstrating interest in me—something I ultimately learned was merely their desire for the conquest of my essence and nothing more. The youngest in a family of psychics, MB always exuded a tremendous amount of scattered energy. Much to my dismay, once he had gotten to know me, I noticed a consistent pattern of rapid exits. He was well aware of my ailments and concerns, and malevolently "gifted" me with three horrendous psychic hooks, which as you will learn, blessedly were removed.

In contrast, DR and her insidious, covert manipulations fit best in the black magic category. Like MB, she initially invested time and energy in getting to know me, after which she admitted she has "a pattern of tapering back quite a bit." DR lived reclusively, secretively, and nearly always was physically ill or just recuperating from some type of accident. She adamantly refused to receive personal checks, only accepted cash, offered in-person or in-absentia healing, personal coaching, tarot psychic readings, and occasional group classes on subjects such as psychic development, meditation, and her own Native American culture and traditions.

Knowing how deeply I wanted to believe in communication from "the other side," DR conducted for me a past-life regression session, as well as a general regression session, during which she claimed to have experienced contact with my deceased grandfather. For many weeks afterward, DR would e-mail or leave a voice mail message, indicating that my grandfather "simply won't leave" her alone and obviously has something to say. My curiosity piqued, DR then abruptly told me she never would make contact with him again. DR also held classes during which participants practiced supposed "healing techniques" on other clients of hers, who in their vulnerability were willing to comply.

Thanks to DR, I was "gifted" with a horrendous recurring sciatic nerve problem, along with her trademark "boot-kick" pain resonating throughout my tailbone. It was a few years before I found out she was the one malevolently wielding what felt like hammering blows to my weakened back and tailbone. DR also "counseled" me during my twelve-plus-day flu bug, after which she ensured the virus remained in my system, as per her disingenuous "check-ins" with me.

Both MB and DR talked openly about many of their own clients, something that disturbed me. Confidentiality did not seem to be a priority for either one of them. They always seemed hungry for information—if not from me, from those (victims) we knew in common. In the case of both individuals, they stole Truth from me in order to maintain their lives of lies.

During this terrible time of depletion, I felt I was adopting a racy, scattered way about myself, one that despite my obvious, legitimate stress, was quite atypical to my character. I knew I had a lot on my plate, but I found myself disturbed by my levels of internal chaos and outwardly frenetic responses. I became hypersensitive and more vigilant, especially to noises. I tended to spill and break things more often, and literally walk into walls. I didn't like it. These experiences were becoming unsettling and ultimately intolerable.

I also experienced a very upsetting, choking sensation late at night while writing on my computer. I felt as though there were two human hands around my throat, putting a slow but deliberate pressure—an eventual squeeze—upon my entire neck and throat region. It was a surreal sensation I hope no one else ever experiences. I was so unnerved and in need of support, yet felt no one would ever understand what I was experiencing. I ended up sharing these concerns with MB, only later to find out it was DR who was the original initiator of this chokehold. So, as you can imagine, until I finally was healed from all this contamination, these symptoms and feelings continued undiminished.

Many times I'd hear things from these vampiric people that would arouse my initial sympathy and subsequent suspicion. In particular, these two people seemed to experience a disproportionate amount of accidents, tragedies, health crises, traumas, and other assorted dramas. I later came to understand that such events were karmic "blowbacks," the reverberating, reflecting response to how these people have chosen to conduct themselves in their existences. This reflective principle applies to all existence able to exercise free will and is not specific to psychics. As stated earlier, I learned that merely a touch on the arm or a hug from a vampiric source could serve to securely "hook" or "place a psychic hook" inside a trusting, vulnerable person.

Considering that some people either regularly or frequently visit a variety of sources for insights and answers, imagine the far-reaching implications of this phenomenon. Once implanted, a hook can be reactivated at any time, and there is no set period determining its point of breakdown and dissolution. This reactivation process is stimulated either telepathically at the atom level, or through ongoing, even spontaneous, superficial or fleeting physical contact.

All too often, we fail to pay attention to seemingly nondescript or otherwise subtle signs around us. It is incredibly important and helpful to be aware of any time the universe seems to be preventing you from accomplishing or completing something—or even reaching a particular person, situation, or destination without complication or roadblocks. The universe—God and Blessed Angels—all try very hard to help people NOT get themselves into damaging situations. Having experienced this phenomenon firsthand, I no longer doubt its Truth. I cannot begin to count the number of times when I was set to meet someone and got unbelievably delayed, lost, or otherwise sidetracked. These detours happened in very pronounced ways preceding what I later learned were appointments or sessions with malevolent sources, as well as before social interactions with specific individuals who themselves were contaminated and infected by such malevolent sources—and thus, for me, unhealthy company.

One technique psychic vampires employ may seem rather benign or superficially innocuous to the untrained eye—perhaps even potentially pleasant. These vampires invite a willing participant friend or vampiric trainee to conspire with them. This volunteer would be "introduced" to the victim as a friend of the vampire, someone presented as "like minded," "interesting for you to meet," "attractive and available," or otherwise somehow intriguing. A victim might initially receive this visitor with little or no hesitation. After all, any friend of the vampire becomes the victim's friend as well.

Unfortunately, this person is no real friend. They are sent specifically to create a disturbance, incident, or unnerving reaction in the influenced victim—at which time the vampire receives the victim's dysfunctional, energy-emitting free-will reaction as a food source at the other end.

The incident is staged as an experiment for many reasons. First, it feeds the vampire. Next, it attempts to create an opportunity for the victim to establish and place new trust in an additional, dysfunctional potential vampiric source. Then the vampire measures the victim's response, using it as a barometer to better fine-tune the victim's future response. Unfortunately, this experience, orchestrated by psychic MB, happened several times to me. During these circumstances, I was aware of my acute internal discomfort with these so-called "friends." Nonetheless, by the time I ended the "meetings," any intended damage already had taken place.

Blessedly, I ultimately was both guided and drawn to seek out some positive sources for information, support, and eventual healing. Interestingly enough, a year into this nearly six-year-long nightmarish experience, I was at a bookstore out of town where I felt inspired to buy a book about psychic protection. I recall skimming it with an interest that then surprised me. I didn't read it all but did manage to turn down the corners to the pages detailing the significance of waking up nightly at 3 a.m.

Near the tail end of those turbulent years, I ran across a photo of a holistic healer. The face on the photo was open and kind, the eyes danced, and the smile seemed joyful and sincere. His image lit up the photo. This man radiated kindness and joy and offered holistic healing massage. I was in great pain on many levels and found myself inexplicably drawn to this person's photo. I kept the photo and number, but did not immediately follow up on my instinct to call and set up an appointment.

At least six months later, I was walking with a dear friend. We were complaining about how for two relatively young, active people, we both seemed to be in pain a great deal of the time. I asked her about the massage therapist she once mentioned to me—perhaps more than a year before I had seen the photo of this holistic healer. She said she'd call me with his number. I did not put two and two together that this was the same person whose photo I'd been keeping in a drawer at home until my friend gave me his phone number. I called Scott Bergér for an appointment.

I ended up with a wonderful holistic healing massage session and knew I'd met someone with whom I had a great deal in common—perhaps a new friend. I later learned that acquisition of this photo, my subsequent discussion with my friend, and the ultimate healing experiences with this holistic healer ALL were not mere coincidences. All of these experiences were carefully, purposely facilitated through God's Divine Order. In Book Three, we will go into more depth regarding the differences between so-called "randomly occurring," or "coincidental" events and the fact that such events are divinely facilitated.

Shortly after my session with Scott, I took a trip out of town, during which I visited a metaphysics store. There I inquired about the possibility of an intuitive reading with one of their psychics. The manager was quick to offer the name of a woman as "the one here who I feel has the most integrity." That sounded good to me. Keep in mind, at this time, I had NOT yet become aware of being psychically hooked or contaminated in any way. During this particular trip, I actually was experiencing my physical symptoms inconsistently, without too much intensity. I scheduled and experienced a session with this recommended woman, during which I woke up in a life-changing, benevolent way.

In addition to providing me with information on past existences and karmic themes, this woman was honest, decent, and genuine. She went the extra mile to provide insight, as well as tangible, helpful information, so that I would be aware and able enough to receive the healing work I had yet to do. This psychic was the one who told me I was a victim of some very toxic and powerful psychic vampires, and without any prompting or helping from me, went on to describe some of the damage they had done to me.

She began our session by discussing some of my personal shifts that had been transpiring, letting me know she thought I'd be doing some pretty major internal "cleanup," so to speak. She told me I'd been surrounding myself with energy vampires for way too long, after which this gifted psychic began to describe the myriad of my intense physical discomforts and ills that for so long had become second nature. There was the massive pain in my left shoulder, low-back pain, stomach disorders, and stubbornly swollen tissue below my chin refusing to dissipate—and worsening when I worried about it. She told me there was something extremely "parasitic" in the regions of my stomach and chin/jaw areas. "Check for parasitic infection in the stomach and mouth areas," she cautioned.

The session continued. With great detail and intensity she recounted several of my prior existences—so much so that she became both chilled and overheated, sweating profusely. When I asked her how my "information" or experiences manifested within her or how this energy came through her, she looked at me with quiet but intense resolution. "It is like putting on a pair of gloves," she said softly. "With them on, everything you experienced in these lives, I experience in the same way. I am right there, as you were." Now, if these existences had been thoroughly joyous, relatively uneventful, or extremely blissful, it would be one thing, but what this woman ultimately shared with me—and thus, experienced herself in my present-day presence—yielded quite the opposite.

Apparently, in my past incarnations, I had lived and experienced life with much intensity and with some important missions to accomplish. Of course, this reality did not necessarily translate to lives of quiet solitude, contemplation, relative ease, or bliss. In my present life, my conscious mind would not allow me to remember very much from any possible past incarnations. I later learned that such information is divinely recorded, maintained, and protected for reasons known only to God. As such, God protects our human consciousness from any access to much of these soul memories, unless through Divine Order.

I recall looking at this psychic sitting across from me. This woman was visibly shaken, yet followed through as best she could to complete our session. Through subsequent discussions with Scott, I later came to realize the magnificence of this woman's techniques. She was allowed to reexperience firsthand my long suppressed, neatly enfolded memories. All of the information she quite accurately expressed was divinely provided. The entire experience was nothing short of amazing. Unequivocally, it was divinely guided from the time I made the appointment through the time I said goodbye.

Before our time together came to a close, this psychic repeated with emphasis, "vampires are trying again to remove your soul." I remembered her mentioning that I'd been susceptible to many energy vampires throughout my life, but at those times had not paid special attention to my energy essence, let alone anyone's or any entity's sinister and malicious attempts to remove it. During our session, I found myself scribbling copious notes at a furious pace. "You need to remove these implants," she told me. She then went on to assist me as best she could with whatever information she was able to receive regarding my victimization. It should be noted that the human soul is safely housed in the Causal (Idea) container, protected by two impermeable barriers. These two barriers are known as the Astral container and the gross physical container. Only the energies contained and maintained within the atom-bound, physically manifesting container are at risk for such exploitation.

I later realized that I could trust this woman and the messages she gave me during my trip. However, at the time of our meeting, I was still filled with concerns. The only past-life information a psychic is able to provide with any potential accuracy is that which is located within a client's physically manifesting being. This information is generally inaccessible, but will be made available within the atoms of one's physically manifesting container for only three reasons. First, if there is a remaining imbalance from a prior existence; second, if one is a highly evolved consciousness who is given Divine access; and third, for reasons known only to God. Even with the best psychics, this information—contained within the ethereal realm of the client's atoms—is extremely difficult to accurately extract. Always, only with God's assistance, for reasons known solely to God, can any truthful past-life details be elucidated.

While I appreciated the fact that she told me I needed to protect myself, I was a bit on guard. Others before had told me such things—and the only people they were concerned about protecting were themselves. I remember well a psychic from New York City who told me I should work with her in performing a specific ritual and home ceremony. She was convinced—and convinced me—this process would assist in my extricating negative spirits and influences in my life. She effectively snared me, knew I had experienced psychic readings recently before hers, and played me like an instrument.

In response to the fear she instilled in me, I raced throughout NYC's

West Village searching for the requisite large spool of white thread, white bread, table salt, and various other items she said were necessary for me to complete a healing ritual that I would conduct in the privacy of my own hotel room. In absentia, she supposedly would orchestrate this particular psychic technique while remaining at her own home. The whole thing was ridiculous. I had been in the city for less than forty-eight hours, during which I became a victim of black magic.

It is important to keep in mind that these particular experiences with the NYC psychic took place well after I already had been hooked and contaminated by the two malevolent psychic vampires active in my life. Thus, all subsequent encounters with the NYC psychic and any other not-so-benevolent healing professionals only exacerbated the damage already taking place in my being.

I kept in touch with the NYC psychic, whose entire family was a part of her obviously financially successful venture. She told me her grand-mother, originally from France, was the matriarch and teacher to the entire family. This psychic and her family operated (and most likely continue to operate) at least two storefront "boutiques"—one in the West Village, the other in the Midtown area of Manhattan. Family members, usually women older than herself, nearly always surrounded her. She mentioned her family's strong psychic lineage, that they were "active in NYC, Florida, and in France, the family homeland." And she was pregnant. She mentioned that this was not her first pregnancy, and that the child born before now lived with relatives in Florida. She was extremely disinterested in discussing her relationship with the child in Florida, and seemed particularly and noticeably disconnected to all discussion related to her current pregnancy. I thought this was unusual, but soon discounted it—and other peculiarities that made themselves clearer to me at later times.

She instructed me to make the sign of the cross with some tongue depressor sticks, stringing them together with yarn like the God's Eye designs reminiscent of art classes and summer camp. I was to take money—several bills—and fold and affix them to the cross. Somewhere on top of this creation, I was to place old white bread and table salt, as well as a white handkerchief. She told me to send this entire package to her directly, that she would light it on fire, which would in turn, extinguish the negativity in my life.

She was adamant that these procedures take place, and if I doubted her integrity and intentions (as they required me to send a considerable sum of money to her via mail), I'd in effect further undermine myself. In essence, I would be keeping myself stuck, risking further demise. On one hand, I was terrified she was right—and felt that to short her the money would inflame her to such an extent that she would somehow create harm in my life. On the other hand, I felt incredible vulnerability, discord, and internal conflict. Intellectually, I chastised myself for getting into this situation.

Obviously, I intellectually knew there was something extremely unsavory about requesting someone to send cash like that through the mail. Now, if someone else were sharing this story with me, I would have encouraged them to run for the hills. Unfortunately, however, I was literally and figuratively hooked, greatly reducing my potential for making a clean break from these malicious tentacles. So, despite my intellect telling me otherwise, I really, truly did feel boxed in and trapped. The NYC psychic obviously knew this, as she personally orchestrated the process. She requested that I send her a recent photo of me, on which she said she'd be doing "holy" meditation. Nearly every time I'd call one of her two phone numbers, she was always "in prayer," according to her husband, who took the calls. For someone who was so intent upon developing a working relationship, she did her utmost to avoid any further communication or contact with me. Frustrated, I eventually discontinued my contact with this psychic.

On a subsequent trip to NYC, I happened upon her Midtown location, much to my own surprise. It was situated behind and next to some prominent hotels and establishments. I peeked in and saw her standing there with some older female relatives. I walked in and reintroduced myself. She was less than enthused. Undeterred, I asked about the baby, and she gave some nondescript and disinterested response. I left with a distinct feeling there was something very unusual going on there.

On that same trip, no more than several hours later, I was scouring the Village for a good coffee house. I walked through many streets, only to look up to see this same psychic's West Village storefront location staring directly back at me. That was enough for me. At that moment, I knew without question she was dark, the energy negative, and the streetlight in front of me was changing from red to green. I couldn't cross the street fast enough. I took a cab to an entirely different neighborhood for my afternoon coffee.

In later months, I expended considerable energy beating myself up for being so duped into believing such sinister lies and being so susceptible to what clearly was black magic and not some wondrous psychic prediction or healing experience. When I had sent the cross, constructed with money, bread, and string, I felt like a doomed fool. I figured if I didn't send it with the specified amount of money, she would think me a liar and do something bad to me; if I sent it as requested, she no doubt would be taking advantage of my vulnerability and goodness. I willingly opened myself as much as she willingly took from me. The fact that MB and DR already had contaminated me only exacerbated my vulnerability and angst.

I had allowed myself to be sucked into something, which no matter how I analyzed it, kept me trapped. What bothered me most was the fact that I still believed in the stuff that held me hostage. By believing AND participating compliantly, I played right into the hands of evil and became further victimized. This person who offered to extend her special healing services to me, do special and critically important ceremonies and rituals to "heal my soul and being," was in fact doing quite the opposite. Of course, she encouraged me not to share my experiences with anyone else, as it would "disrupt the healing process." As such, I kept it all a secret, obviously just one of many others in my various existences. This is the first time I have ever publicly disclosed this experience.

In contrast to this black magician in NYC, the psychic who warned me about the psychic vampirism spoke with truth. She told me I needed more help, but neither offered her services in exchange for extra funds, nor suggested she could be the only one who could ever assist me. On the contrary, she exerted considerable time and energy expressing her concerns for me, giving me as much specific and tangible information as was made available to her, and suggested that such difficult but vital healing work take place as soon as possible.

The benevolent psychic did describe several ideas she thought would be helpful to maintain my self-protection and to extricate such negative forces residing within me. In order to disconnect from these negative poisons, she described a healing process that included applying energy to "dark spots" or resistant, problem areas that could be detected within me via scanning. She also made it clear that the application of such energy be done counter-clockwise, which I later learned from Scott is a bit atypical in much healing energy work.

I sensed her urgency and appreciated the information, although I still felt vulnerable and helpless. Who in the world would be able to facilitate this healing process with me? At the time, my second degree Reiki training and psychology background seemed woefully inadequate. This benevolent psychic's quiet but firm caution of "Don't discuss this with anyone" only lent itself to my own building concerns. Nonetheless, I knew somewhere deep within my heart that from her own decency, she was cautioning me to be careful about placing my trust in human hands from this point onward.

My session with this benevolent psychic was unforgettable. The room we were in was cool and comfortable, and yet she was completely drenched in sweat. She didn't ask me to engage her in any future services; in fact, she balked when at the end of the session, I thanked her profusely for her unusual and generous insights. We were not preoccupied with or focused on the exchange of funds for services, which was completed without any fanfare. She apologized for being unable to give me a hug goodbye. "It's because of the energy," she explained.

At the time, I figured it was because the whole session was so incredibly intense, the stories so vividly unsettling, and her reactions so discomforting. It was a day or so later that I put two and two together: She had detected in me something not OF me, something extremely poisonous of an external origin that should not have been there. As such, she could not merge with it or risk being infected herself by hugging me. In subsequent weeks, the stories of past incarnations she experienced as if donning "gloves" of these lives nagged at me. However, I knew better than to explore them before dealing with the issue of having foreign poisons residing within me.

In her warning about psychic vampires, this psychic mentioned that one had "Scorpio energy." This resonated immediately, as MB himself was a Scorpio. Though I was in direct contact with two very destructive sources, only the identity of one of them leaped out to me. The other one became apparent later on; hers felt like a much different betrayal.

This psychic also made other mind-blowing, paradigm-shifting connections for me that put a lot of those proverbial life-puzzle pieces into some semblance of a possible whole. I pondered the concept of past-lives, reincarnation, and karmic lessons. The information this woman expressed to me was impossible for me to ignore. There were tons of amazing, resonating interconnections, which we discuss later in this book. I left this woman knowing I had a great deal of work to do. I now had some riveting and validating new information to fit into my life puzzle, not to mention that I was experiencing some real inspiration and new awareness.

Upon my return home, I saw Scott—who, I might add, also happens to be a Scorpio. Between my first meeting with him and this trip, we had socialized a bit. Based upon many of our past discussions, as well as my internal comfort level—to which I now was better attuned—I decided to share with him what the psychic from my trip had told me regarding the psychic vampirism. I wanted to trust Scott; I knew he understood such concepts on a deep level, plus I knew at this point, I had to trust someone.

Ultimately, I shared with him my relationship with MB, detailing its history, intensity, and dynamics. I felt a strange relief, albeit one tinged in what I've come to understand is a warped but understandable sense of guilt. I had participated in a relationship based upon dysfunction, a power differential, dependency, and vulnerability—all being food or fuel for another's evil ways. I knew I needed—and finally was ready to receive—healing assistance from a benevolent source.

Prior to my conveying all of this information to Scott, he had done more massage and energy balancing with me. I also had made repeated trips to receive both a specialized technique of lymph drainage massage, and other energy work in an attempt to relieve a stubborn swelling under my chin that looked like the belly of a frog. People said, "You can't really see it until you point it out," but I knew otherwise. Both intellectually and instinctively I knew this swelling was not supposed to be there. In my attempts to relieve the symptoms, I visited several allopathic medical doctors, but each was perplexed. Deep down, I just knew there was more to it.

Scott and I discussed his previous session with me. During that prior healing bodywork, Scott had attended to my great abdominal distention, reduced its vast internal space, and had sensed something rather peculiar—perhaps something even moving around inside me. However, due to time constraints, he was unable to delve any further into the situation. Besides, I only gave him a partial template with which to work. After all, at that time, I had not yet seen this benevolent psychic—and thus, had no clue about psychic vampirism. It was only after further discussions occurring about three months later that both Scott and I became aware that something very alarming had taken place and was still continuing to plague me with a vengeance.

Scott confirmed that I was experiencing a lot of disharmony and contamination, evidenced by the stubborn swelling underneath my chin, the stomach condition making me look pregnant, and the movement within my stomach that was visible to the eye. Inside my stomach was an indisputable wavelike movement, and the accompanying swelling in that entire region literally moved up as high as under my breastbone. When under extreme stress, my entire middle section from my breastbone down to my pelvis was inflamed and swollen, tender to the touch. As I mentioned earlier, there also were times when my abdomen grew sore and hard like a rock. My neck was tight and crunchy and my lower back in constant pain. The ache in my tailbone continued to feel as though someone was repeatedly whacking me with a hammer.

During some of my most intense pain, I recall making some urgent pleas in God's direction. However, I had not done any conscious prayer on a regular basis. I learned much later that directed, focused, personal prayer would prove to be essential in my life. At that time, however, I was unsure about my relationship with God. I felt fairly estranged from such things.

"Mari, how often do you pray?" Scott asked me. I found this both a curious and yet revealing question. I responded, "Obviously, not often enough." Scott told me that during his work with clients, he finds himself in constant prayer, fluidly in communion and connection with God. Initially, this sounded overwhelming to me and very intense. However, as I got to know Scott and became more immersed in the process of my own healing and inevitable, resulting spiritual growth, this—and a lot of other once-mysterious things—began to make a ton of sense to me.

I had a feeling my life was on its way to being very, very different—and for the better. Not only did I feel sincerely comforted by this person, but I also sensed that his work and talents originated from a source of purity and deep knowledge. I felt it was safe to place my trust in him. There was a focus and intensity he brought to his work I'd never experienced with any other healing practitioner. Most important, I knew that when he was working on me, he was filled with goodness and divinity, and thus, not alone.

Scott and I also shared common interests. Scott was an avid reader and enjoyed books of many genres, from metaphysics and religion to science and history; he studied many different texts simultaneously. It was not long before he shared with me some books and stories he thought might be important for me to see, considering my inner journey. The first book, *Parenthesis in Eternity*, written by Joel Goldsmith, seemed dense and dry to me, although Scott assured me I would find it interesting. However, references to "Christ Consciousness" immediately put me off, and I felt my defenses rise. I was nearly instantly repelled—even despite efforts otherwise. Why did he think I'd be interested in something like this? I had never heard of this term before, and in my ignorance, assumed it was solely religious in nature. I later learned I was mistaken—and came to understand and appreciate that author's intentions.

On another occasion, Scott showed me the book *Holy Blood, Holy Grail*, which contained millions of fascinating pieces of historical information packed into a tiny pocketbook with a dark, rather foreboding cover. I didn't fancy myself a history buff; on the contrary, I steered clear of such things. Scott felt this book spoke directly to him, and actually felt he understood more information than the book was conveying. He was quite confident I'd experience it in a similar fashion. I was quite confident this would not be the case. The book contained a lot of French words, which I did not know and couldn't pronounce. Furthermore, there were so many dates and facts to keep straight if one wanted to understand the intricate chronology of these events. The events depicted in the book did seem to have some compelling interconnections—but at that time, I was unable to share Scott's enthusiasm.

Scott and I talked a lot about spiritual concepts, God, religion, reincarnation, karma, health, and healing. At times, I found myself simultaneously drawn to and repelled by certain concepts. In essence, we were discussing what I've come to affectionately dub the "missing pieces" of life's complex and ever-growing puzzle. I was entranced and yet felt somehow unable to completely embrace many ideas or discussions. Something inside me was blocked, and this bothered me as much as any stomach cramps or backaches. The more we talked, the more he encouraged me to look at some of his reading material, inviting me to consider it on deeper levels than merely for its literary merit. I realized that Scott probably had a point. I just couldn't figure out what it would be.

But it was time for me to look within. This would be the only way for me to identify the true origin of my internal resistance, as well as trust and allow anyone to assist me on my healing path. It is when we are at our most vulnerable points that we tend to ignore the truthful voice within. If we listen to it, this voice speaks volumes of great value. We tend to discredit ourselves, blaming our vulnerability for what we erroneously perceive are internal words of weakness, doubt, or instability. In such vulnerable states, we tend to bestow our most precious energies upon external sources, which may not have our best interests in mind. By trusting them, yearning for answers, and giving other external sources permission to enter and exploit our conscious experience we open ourselves and our very existences to some potentially horrible damage. In my case, all of these experiences took place. Fortunately, I also experienced some benevolent exceptions.

Beyond her warnings, the psychic from the bookstore also gave me details of several past-lives and themes. I was and still remain grateful beyond belief. Little did I know at the time how monumental our seventy-five minutes together would be for my future healing and evolution. Soon after returning from this trip, I participated in a six-day, intensive hypnotherapy certification course. For quite some time, I had been interested in this modality and was especially intrigued with the possibility of utilizing hypnosis for increased understanding and clarity about the realm of reincarnation and past-lives. In fact, I was so interested in this aspect, I contacted the instructor directly, indicating my desire to volunteer as a subject during that section of the course.

The night before the course, I was at Scott's home, socializing with friends, and waiting for him to do some bodywork to relieve the painfully intense tailbone hammering. I was growing increasingly concerned about the prospect of sitting in a workshop for several hours. However, what we both thought would be a session focusing on back relief turned out to be something completely different. That evening, Scott discovered the hooks and contaminating implements placed inside of me by those whose psychic healing counsel I had trusted and respected. Alas, as I suspected, there were real reasons and causes for my stomach, chin, neck, and back issues.

Over the course of two hours, blessedly I was cleared and cleansed of these destructive forces. I truly cannot recall a great deal of detail, other than the fact that my stomach was intensely, stubbornly resistant and sore during the healing session. I was acutely aware of Scott's deep breath work and the fact that I felt as if time was at a perpetual standstill.

Everything simply evolved, everything simply "was." Scott asked me a few questions, but I cannot recall them. I remember at times weeping uncontrollably. For years, my body had been so tainted and so betrayed, that I could feel it crying along with me in sheer relief.

There were times when my body shook on the table. I was emotionally moved beyond belief. I felt completely attended to, unhurried, and blessed to have such protectively healing hands doing right by God and me. I remember consciously trying to release and let go when directed by Scott to do so. This consenting release was necessary in order to facilitate the eradication of these contaminants—just as my initial openness or willingness was the consent that allowed them entry in the first place.

I was peripherally aware of others' presence in the house around us, but did not resort to feeling guilty or responsible, familiar feelings that would have been easy companions—especially given the late hour. As I experienced what it felt like to purge huge amounts of toxicity from my being, I also knew the homemade pizzas others had prepared for us in the adjoining room were becoming cold and rock-hard. Yet for us, dinner could wait. At that moment, for the first time in over three years, my stomach was deemed hook-free. According to Scott, the rest of my body also was "clear." I later learned there was more than one pesky hook within me. I was a minefield and I didn't really know it. All I knew that night was that I felt a tugging sensation, released something from within, and let go with trust. In response, my stomach returned to being a stomach, rather than a cesspool harboring insidious, malicious implementations.

Soon, the darkness in the room matched that of the neighborhood outside. I had no clue what time it was and did not care. I had a major workshop beginning the next day, groceries heating up in the backseat of my parked car, and a life that in effect, would never be the same. Time was nonexistent. Time was endless. Something that had all the dramatic components of a film was taking place in my not-so-mundane life. For the first time, after this evening, I began to experience what it was like to be connected with my physical body. I also felt it might be time to explore my relationship with God, who obviously lovingly guided me to be relieved from these ills and to be moved along on my path in order to complete my true missions in this life.

I left Scott's home late that night, exhausted physically and yet filled with a tremendous emotional intensity. I felt grateful and thankful. I also felt really out of it, as if I were in another zone. Nonetheless, on the following morning, I began the hypnosis certification class. Nearly five days later, we learned how hypnosis is used in past-life regression. As I had desired, I was able to volunteer. I also was keenly aware that as the time grew nearer to doing so, I was experiencing some rather unexpected anxiety and an internal clenching up inside my middle section. I knew I had no more hooks, thanks to my session with Scott several days before. There also was no sensation of movement or swelling whatsoever—so this tension obviously had entirely different origins.

When it was time for me to volunteer, I was extremely excited. However, as I became relaxed during the induction, something simply was not clicking, thus preventing me from going down deeper into relaxation. I became uncomfortably and consciously aware of the instructor's vocal quality, and in a matter of moments, also became quite aware of her apparent strategy. Despite my awareness being more piqued than I felt would be suitable for this exercise, I still was able to relax and be open enough to experience a series of visual images. I described them as much as possible, but was unable to stick or stay with any of them for the length of time it required for her to pose questions for my consideration.

I experienced three or four separate, seemingly nonrelated categories of visual images during this simulation. Even while under hypnosis, I was aware that my speaking voice was slower, more deliberate, emphasizing each syllable in a more drawn-out manner. I was aware that I was listening to my own voice, as if it were an echo for my conscious mind to hear. After many questions, yielding no real answers or connections, the instructor brought me out of hypnosis. I felt I had failed everyone around me. The instructor mentioned that my experience was "most unusual," and not what she typically encounters.

During this exercise, I experienced some neck pain that was neither present before the exercise, nor afterward. This pain obviously had a purpose, which I later realized prevented me from lapsing into any fabricated imagery, like dream states. The vibrational information pertaining to one's prior incarnations is retained in the quark-based Astral Realm. As such, any truthful or accurate information is inaccessible to human beings in the material cosmos. Any cognitive interpretations, hunches, or senses regarding past-lives that are truly accurate are, of course, only made available through divine assistance.

This exercise took place at the end of a long, draining day, and I was grateful to walk out quietly alone to my car. Within the time it took me to get inside the vehicle, turn the key, and put on my seat belt, I became acutely aware of what was once self-consciousness and disappointment, now turning into pure relief. I smiled as I pulled out of the parking lot. There certainly were a lot of illusions in life—one of them being my perception that I was "quietly alone." Obviously, this was not the case.

While writing this book, I had to ask myself why I was drawn to do this hypnotherapy training and why I never once practiced what I had learned. I realized that each post training group get together had taken place during times when I was either out of town or otherwise unavailable. Even throughout the actual training (and despite my curiosity and interest in this modality), I simply knew I was not necessarily poised to employ these new skills. In fact, from the moment I finished the course, my books and notes remained on a shelf indefinitely.

It was several months later when I came to understand why I was prevented from utilizing my newfound skills. Throughout the writing process for this book, I have learned well how Blessed Angelic forces work ardently behind the scenes. Later you will read about how hypnosis, amongst other modalities and various processes utilized for personal change and insight, actually can undermine even the best intentions. Perhaps the most important thing I learned is that it is within one's own self—and not within others' hands or powers—where truth and insight reside. One need not go to extraordinary means in order to gain access to such gems of wisdom.

As I felt my physiological health improving in dramatic ways, and my mind remaining open for longer time periods than ever before, I experienced a calm inner knowing that I'd previously only experienced for fleeting moments. I knew then as I know now that all of us have been and continue to be negatively impacted by both conscious and unconscious contaminating sources. Immediately after the identification of my problem, its sources, and subsequent healing emancipation, two friends of mine found themselves facing realities that they, too, no longer would or could deny. Soon, more hooks were being removed, more negativity confronted, and at least a few more people were walking around town with a new clarity and a different kind of trust. Of course, in our new states of being, we all sought validation of some sort; after all, we were human and fighting with our own vulnerability. Fortunately, we divinely received the signs we needed to confirm what we did so passionately want to believe.

Even though I had clarity regarding my pain-free condition, I still wasn't totally clear regarding the sources of my many years of torment. In my excitement of having Scott assist my healing from MB's horrific hooks and tentacles, I innocently and without hesitation phoned up DR (whom at that point I still trusted) to relay the good news. I left her a voice mail, stating, "Scott, the energy healer I met, is great. He took out all of the disgusting, poisonous contamination in me from MB! I am so relieved, I just had to share it with you!" I found it strange not to receive a return message or call, and even stranger when I received not one but two letters from her mailed to my home address.

Such correspondence was surprising, as DR was the ultimate recluse. She never corresponded unless absolutely necessary, was insanely private, and after establishing "contact" with a person, had the self-described and admitted tendency toward an isolative response and near-total withdrawal. She then sent me a couple e-mails. Needless to say, I unknowingly had communed with the "enemy," rendering me still quite vulnerable. Scott pointed out this reality in his own unsettled realization of what I had mistakenly thought was my "innocent phone message." I had called DR, thinking she would have my best interest in mind, given the history, hours, and dollars I'd invested in her. I was greatly mistaken.

I later learned that both in light of and in spite of trusting DR, I only furthered her evil pursuits. The fact that I had embarked upon a healing path was not good news to her at all. The fact that I had shared the wrong news with the wrong source left me unsettled. However, the true good news was that despite all of these unenfolding events, I managed successfully to sever ties with MB and DR, two individuals who, for six years and over four years, respectively, held me in ever-draining captivity. Never again would I allow myself to be a victim. I also knew in my heart that I wanted to protect as many other potential victims as possible—not only from these specific two life-sustaining energy predators, but also from any other potentially contaminating, draining, and destructive sources.

Scott's Narrative:
UnGodly Symbiosis and Unholy Subjections

UnGodly Symbiosis

I would like to begin by sharing some basic historical background and supporting facts that will be extremely helpful for comprehending this section. I began part-time healing massage work in 1983 and chipped away at it until 1989, when I began to work at it full-time. From the first session, I knew something about my touch was extra sensitive and noticeable to my clients. I have always had a blessed, enriched life, but no matter what was going on with my life's path, it was preordained to pass through the fertile, rolling hills of massage healing success. From the moment I opened my first studio, my phone kept ringing and the people just kept showing up. So, I felt unless God instructed me otherwise, or people quit seeking my healing services, I would continue to do God's work as Scott Bergér (pronounced bare-zhay), which means *shepherd* in French.

This name seemed to suit me, and subsequently, some of my clients with whom I became friends would address me by this last name. I didn't care what salutation they selected, as long as people kept coming in and the healing work flowed on, I would answer to just about any name. After a very short period of full-time service, I knew something special was at work behind the scenes, something that indeed was unseen by physical eyes, but nonetheless present every session. For those clients who were more in touch with their bodies and who paid attention, this something special entered into their awareness as well.

Almost immediately after I started my full-time healing practice, I began to detect the meridian gridwork of people's metaphysical beings. I internally was informed by thoughts, the source of whom was Archangel Raphael. He told me he would transform all vibrational sludge drained out of people into pure, positive energy of beneficial amplitude and magnitude, which were to be completely returned in full. This Angelic Being then proceeded—through my hands—to draw my clients' deepest, most intense vibratory human energies of up to 3000 hertz, any energies over 10.0 hertz, and any energies under approximately 6.5 hertz into my being, transforming the contamination into beautiful, balanced, 8.4 hertz light energy. At the session's end, back through my hands, Raphael would reenergize my clients.

I later learned that while most human beings have 35 lightways flowing within their vectors of physically manifesting construction, I was blessed from birth with 39. I had one extra lightway in each hand, and one combining chakras 3, 4, and 5, as well as one large, all-encompassing EM (electromagnetic) wheel to help contain my Angelic Purifier's superconsciousness. My left hand contained a laser wheel, my right a vacuum wheel. The left side of a human is the female side, and the right side is male. As such, I found it quite humorous that my female carried the sword, and my male did the vacuuming!

All of these blessings proved to be quite a gift, and the sessions accumulated as my clients began to rely upon Raphael to continually patch them up. Together we balanced and harmonized people's chakras and meridians, performed muscle, joint, and skeletal manipulations, after which everyone was reenergized, allowing them to leave beaming like flashlights. My clients came from all over the world, and my practice flourished.

For eleven years and almost 18,000 sessions, Raphael did his healing and teaching, eventually deeming me ready to move from apprenticeship to becoming a master. I received my own wings and from the Astral World, Raphael oversaw my work. I flew on my own for one and a half years, until early June 2002, at which time I was a seasoned healing master with almost 20,000 sessions under Raphael's and my belt, so to speak. After so many sessions, one securely feels he's really seen it all, but all of those experiences really were preliminaries for several unforeseen, main events. I would like to share and bring to your awareness these incidents, on the off chance that you may be experiencing any of these disconcerting phenomena within your physiological personage.

Over the years, I occasionally would unexpectedly experience something foreign in someone's meridians. There'd be something drifting or flowing along that just plainly didn't belong in a human's essence. Believe me, if something detectable was moving around in these lightways, it immediately would attract my undivided attention. Only several times did I find uninvited energies floating around or moving about where they clearly did not belong—usually in someone from a psych ward or in an otherwise vulnerable, traumatized human being.

I must admit, with Raphael's superHoly healing capacity, I felt quite like a child with a supernal MasterCard to the spiritual lifeforce energies of all animal, vegetable, or mineral manifestations. A few times, errant, coagulated energies were cruising merrily along—only to find themselves diverted from their natural path, into me through my hands. Quickly trying to reverse their direction was akin to a galaxy resisting the irresistible draw of the inerrable Black Hole. Blessed Raphael was immutable against all impertinent vibratory masses.

So, you can well imagine that after 20,000 healing massage sessions the two of us were pretty good at this work. After twelve years of full-time holistic massage healing work, a regular client of mine arrived for a session in early June. This person with whom I had worked for nine years embodied a perennial basket of intensity—some self-imposed, some due to the stressors of daily experience. His was close to my 20,000th session of both full- and part-time healing service. After that number of sessions, I could quickly assess people's various conditions. However, this time when my client came in, both he and the session were completely different.

First of all, he came late in the afternoon and said, "All I could think about was making it through the day until I could lie on your table." That wasn't unusual, for I've heard that many times before. But something seemed different that day. Keep in mind, after so many sessions, you have to believe you've seen and experienced about every physical anomaly and dysfunctional condition that an earth human being could have. I have to say I did not suspect the bizarre experiences that were about to transpire.

I learned my client was experiencing fitful sleep and had struggled through the day with only the anticipation of that afternoon's session as his inspiration to keep going. Visibly shaken and barely able to heft himself up onto the table, he flopped heavily upon it, seemingly with his last gasp of energy. I was concerned that I would have to call 911 if things got progressively worse. While I was gifted as an energy worker, capable of producing many astounding responses, I certainly didn't relish the thought of having anyone expiring on my table! It just can't be good PR to have the obtrusive coroner arriving at the friendly neighborhood healer's home.

I quickly set to work on determining the ensuing strategy for my incapacitated client. However, after a few moments, I didn't encounter any unusual anomalies or perplexities. I was beginning to relax, when much to my surprise, I did detect an anomaly within his essence. Something quite disconcerting was happening. Radiating sparks of exploding energy were bursting from under his skin in random flashes of physically notice-able protrusions. For me, this was something completely unfamiliar and previously unencountered. Immediately, it seemed to me that I had star-tled something or aroused some energy enigma.

In a panicky manner, it erupted in a fit or uncontrolled outburst. I really didn't know what to make of it. I honestly didn't have a clue. It was alarmingly apparent that a high consciousness of some sort was at work. After a bit, we seemed to be playing a cat-and-mouse game whereby this energy alternately appeared and disappeared. The hyperac-tivity settled down a bit, with me trying to preempt the next location on my client's back. But the spark exhibited in a multitude of spots almost simultaneously with no predictability. I definitely was outmatched and irrevocably perplexed.

Meanwhile, all during this time, my client is pleading, "What is that?" and "Get it out of me!" This fruitless pursuit continued for almost ten min-utes, when I consciously realized that I had errant thoughts in my mind. "You are no match for me. I am beyond your ability to help him, so quit trying to mess with me!" was what entered into my disbelieving mind. Subsequently, two funny thoughts surged into my mind, the first being, "Scott! You have a MasterCard!" and the second, "Hasta la vista, baby!" I absolutely cannot tell an untruth, and these most assuredly are the only two thoughts I can recall.

Later, my client told me that after approximately ten minutes into this unorthodox session, I had lurched somewhat violently upward and gasped. I remember this malevolent entity panicking wildly and was aware of it slowly diminishing as if it was suffocating. It felt as though it took a long time, but I don't recall a knee-jerk reaction at all. My client informed me that he remembers when this entity entered into him years ago. I was astounded, as I'd never before encountered or recognized it in him to any extent near this magnitude.

The day after my tangle with this entity, a dear friend visited my home. During our visit I did not allow her to hug me or have any phys-ical contact with me whatsoever. I told her not to touch me, as I feared I would contaminate her. I was struggling to process what I had experienced during my session with DH the day before. I knew I needed to gain control over something that clearly was trying to take over my body. In fact, I informed my friend that I was going to experience something unimaginable as a response to the entity I had absorbed from DH. I told her that in order to purge this entity from my being, I could not do any more healing sessions for several days. The story doesn't end here. Two days after my friend's visit (three days after my session with DH), the purging of this entity began to take place. It wasn't pretty.

I was sitting with my close friends, LC and EM, having a good conversation. I had forgotten about the past incident when a peculiar feeling suddenly came welling over me, which I mentioned to one of my friends there. I felt I needed to leave LC's apartment and walk up the alley to get a coffee, despite the fact that my beverage of choice is always Holy Water, consecrated by God, not humankind. I bottle the whole braided, double-helixed, freshly gushing spring water to ensure its high negative ion content, from a remote, naturally flowing spring source during a bi-monthly pilgrimage. This choice is followed by green tea, but this afternoon, I felt the burning desire for coffee. Before we could leave, however, my friends were busy conversing—and my system began to expunge a horrific, swelling mass of manifesting inert vibrations, emanating out of my 3, 4, and 5 chakras.

I vaguely was aware of a huge impact smashing through my chest cavity from the inside. It felt like my heart was shuddering to a stop, but I was sure this was not the case. It was just a massive, defunct, vibratory expulsion. As LC and I walked up the alley, I felt another one coming out, reminding me of the same sparking sensation I experienced when I first laid my hands upon my client's abruptly responding parasitic host. That first expunging occurring in LC's apartment had ended swiftly without further incident—until now. I paused and raised my shirt to show my terror-stricken friend, putting his hand on my then-violently shaking heart area. He immediately mistook this sensation for a massive heart attack or related coronary event.

In vain, I tried to assuage his fears, but he was convinced of my pre-eminent doom. With another client soon to arrive, I left for my home with my freshly acquired coffee in hand. There was a fetid, manifested, vibratory expunging remaining in my friend's apartment, the putrid essence of which continued to linger on for several hours. As if it was a decaying physical existence, I was acutely aware of its extreme, noxious emana-tions. Upon returning home, my friend found his rank, unpurifiable abode virtually intolerable. After opening all the windows, turning on a fan and an air conditioner, lighting candles, burning incense, and opening two doors, he still couldn't get the column of rising stench to dissipate. After such extensive efforts, he passed out on his living room floor—at which time, a God-directed Angel entered unseen to clean up the energy masses from the untenable apartment and the alley below. Upon awakening, my friend discovered all was again normal.

The next day, my heartburn was terrible, and my friend's insistence upon a hospital visit even stronger. To quell his fears and validate my accurate assessment of the situation, I reluctantly accompanied him to my long-unvisited doctor for a battery of heart and blood tests. I ended up with six weeks' worth of Nexium to be used for my unresponsive esophagus. I used it for three days, after which my esophagus returned to normal. It had been violently hammered by the thundering, deafening blows delivered by some vibratory nastiness and its apparent spawn sac offspring. These energy entities had been comfortably growing in vibrational and conscious magnitude inside my client's body—which now was entity-free.

Still reeling from this eye-opening, esophagus-debilitating experience, I again was confronted with the realization that my peaceful path was ascending some arduous Himalayan-like precipices. I was not aware of the destination to which my tranquil, unchallenging, platitudinous pathway of conscious experience was leading. In any event, it all had become expo-nentially more challenging. This final episode of my evolution that I have been requested to share pertains to several people about whose well-being I care very deeply. So, I am being directed to combine them into one chronological synergism, for the ease of systematic understanding.

For more than a year, one of my infrequent but devoted, longer-term clients, SL, had been adamantly complaining of chronic low back, hip, and buttock discomfort. Such complaints prior to their sessions were not unusual for some of my clients, yet very unexpected coming from her, as she was extremely tolerant and uncomplaining. She came in during March 2002 and this time was in really rough shape, rendered unable to function in any previous capacity. This got my attention, and I recall working fever-ishly for well over one and a half hours to bring her back around, ulti-mately sending her on her merry way. Shortly thereafter, a referred friend of hers who also was experiencing some severe physical abnormalities called to schedule an appointment. Her name was Mari Tankenoff, and she, of course, had additional, divinely guided reasons for her call. But at the time, she was an unknown name with an unknown face.

Mari's session was somewhat unremarkable, aside from my noticing an unnaturally distended abdomen, from which I distinctly recall removing what I felt was a virtual universe of space. This was certainly unique, but not altogether alarming. She had only scheduled an hour-long appointment, so space was aplenty, but time was fleeting. I did remember wondering WHAT could possibly cause a universal cosmos to develop in someone's stomach? Mari and I seemed to interact well, so we decided we'd get together sometime soon to have tea and conversation. Little did I know that I was about to be immersed into an experiential realm about which I was clueless, but had been exposed to through a similar phenomenon once before.

A client of mine and her fiancé (she a nervous Nellie, he an enormous bastion of lethargic bigness) were engaged—in some very unsavory activities. Shortly after meeting them in July 1992, I began to experience the sleep deprivation symptoms of exhaustion, fatigue, and lack of motivation. My normal high energy was conspicuously absent, and this trend continued for three subsequent days. Finally, on the fourth day at 4 a.m., without any prior warning, I suddenly opened my eyes. I saw an image that frantically blurred and then disappeared after hovering above my massage table on which I was asleep. I was confused and stupefied. However, through Raphael's blessed power, I was allowed to follow the vanishing trail to locate the origination of this vision. The obscure pathway led right to my client—and more specifically to her fiancé. Busted by the light of exposure, they never tried to do that again to me. In fact, I was the only healer my client's fiancé would allow to work on him when his back did go out—twice in futurity. (It has been my policy to always keep my doors open to everyone.)

I admit that I did engage in some sleuthing many months later on, when the opportunity presented itself and I entered their home through proper invitation. I picked up three stones, all of which I discovered were drained completely of electromagnetic goodness of vibration. I sensed that one stone begged to be reenergized, which by then my abilities would have made it easy for me to do. Through the ever protective, vigilant eye of Raphael and the Spirit World, I was allowed to see the potential dangers of doing so, and was instructed not to attempt this action.

What these people would do was select a spellbound talisman—in their case, a stone—but sometimes, a gift. This object then would be covertly supplanted many times discreetly by the nervous Nellie—she being the conduit, her fiancé the inauspicious activator. They then would conduct a sinister conjuration through the conciliate fetish to gain access for the sole purpose of life force thievery. This man of lethargic bigness even had the audacity to give classes and seminars, teaching and instructing the perfecting of this unGodly crime.

My current Holy Angelic Beings have instructed me to omit their initials, for at present, these people are uninvolved with these unsavory activities. If they were, my Angelic Beings would not hesitate to have me print their initials to potentially save future, unsuspecting victims from this horrific fate. This brings us back to the original firsthand example of these stealthy, unholy techniques.

Mari called me, which she said she would do. I remember her coming over for a short visit, which was enjoyable. She was bright, intelligent, articulate and quite talkative. She was pleasant to be around, although I noted at times she seemed a bit jittery. Overall, our time together was very enjoyable.

After Mari's session, MM, whom Mari referred to me, scheduled an appointment. Like Mari, MM had been subjected to the psychic, MB. Once again, I remember little, but do recall zeroing in on her abdomen, combing through and finding three hooks, all stomach implements. The main one was in a state of decomposition. It seemed like a rusty, old Lindy hook to me. The eye of the hook was outside her body, with the shaft piercing in near her belly button, extending down around her spinal column. The hook continued on back, its barb offset to the right, almost protruding out through her stomach once again—but not quite. Let me share with you what a hook feels like to my hands. The hook-affected tissue tends to be much denser and harder than the surrounding tissue, making a hook's path easy to follow. The affected area usually is extremely painful, sensitive to the touch, with a noticeable, distended protrusion throughout the vibratory intrusion. We will elucidate in a thorough and in-depth recapping of these debilitating, contemptible, and extremely unholy activities after this final recounting of these preponderatory, yet absolute, experiences.

MM was experiencing severe diarrhea and stomach pain in response to several foods, as well as to specific individuals, either in their presence or in anticipation of being with them. All of these related symptoms had occurred before she came in to see me—all of them as a result of two distinctly different evil modus operandi. Consequently, the eradications were similar, yet of course, different. The hook was a technique of spirit rapping. It required a prepense malice to prepare for the unGodly spiritual implementation. This hook was facilitated by physical contact, when the host (MM) was spiritually open. Because the barb was offset to the right, it could not merely be psychically pulled right back out. Using an intensely focused psychic electromagnetic rapier to sever the barb, I cut a hypercalm swath perpendicular through the affected tissue. I remember working laboriously to extricate the entire vibratory residue from MM's stomach.

The reason I refer to the hook as rusting is twofold: first, that's the image that appeared in my mind, and second, the affected tissue was coagulated but softening in consistency, as if it was disintegrating. It was resistant to extrication, until I realized the bend prevented it from being vacuumed right out. The other two points came out easily. However, just as I was scanning her stomach area one last time to ensure I had not forgotten anything, I detected that insidious, derilect barb still floating around.

A few minutes later, the barb was out, and I knew for certain she was forever free—unless she became reexposed or reinfected. Given her newfound, joyous unattachment and determination never to allow some psychic vampire permission to enter into her experience, I was convinced of her continual freedom. When I last spoke with this person, all eating, sleeping, and abdominal disorders were nonexistent. Without any problems, she was eating whatever, as often, and as much as she wanted. In the recapping, I will explain the ensuing developments with the barb.

Two weeks later, SL came in again, just a discombobulated mess. I worked meticulously on seven needlelike points plaguing her stomach, which were very problematic. The same low back, hip, and buttock ailments had returned. The troublesome points in her stomach were eradicated easily enough, but I really worked to mop up her back discomfort. It took well over two hours. Barely a week went by, and much to my incredulous discomfort, she was back again. She was completely inundated with the same low back and structural dysfunctions—way too quickly for normal, everyday existence. It was as though someone had been stomping and kicking their boot heel into her back. I remember thinking to myself, "Where is she going? With whom is she keeping company—and WHAT are they doing?" It all was very abnormal. After another two-hour session, I was convinced she was centered, balanced, purified, and harmonized. She went on her way in beautiful order. Mari talked with her shortly after that, and together they put two and two together.

I am being instructed to describe one more incident of unusual phenomenon. Another one of my consistent, long-standing clients, SO, kept coming in, over and over, for several sessions. The complaint was forever the same—excruciating neck pain, always on the same spot, on the same side of her neck, accompanied by sheer exhaustion, even after fourteen hours of nightly sleep. By the fifth time in less than three weeks, I began to interrogate her to ferret out any possible reasons. She is a successful, brilliant attorney, which may have contributed to the circumstances or stress for some of those times. However, such explanations were not enough to condense and extend through so many numerous healings. My own attorneylike, incessant, fact-extracting insistence finally yielded a confession regarding the source of the trouble, which my Holy Angelic Beings wish for me to share with you.

Apparently, during SO's sleep state, a little girl would appear in her dreams, desiring for her to join in play. Agreeing to this energy demon appearing as a little girl from within her awake state was enough to open up SO's energy to predation during her dream or sleep state. The first of those five sessions yielded thirty-seven energy parasites scurrying and crawling all over her. They were almost everywhere on her. I was appalled and asked her with whom she was sleeping or spending time. "No one" and "Work" were her responses. As SO is a hardcore workaholic, I deduced she didn't have enough energy to do anything beyond work, so I focused my attention on her sleep habits. After an intensive roundup of all but the little girl whom SO refused permission to remove from her being, I sent SO on her way.

The second session yielded seven energy parasites, but again, the little girl was off limits. I explained to her that by allowing the energy consciousness of the little girl to remain in her (which, by the way, would be a truly hideous creature if in its true form) she was enabling these other energy parasites to enter and literally feed off her neck's vibratory emanations while she was sleeping and subconsciously vulnerable. Nonetheless, SO would not allow me to remove the little girl. Without her permission to extract this malevolent parasite, no one is allowed to enter her (or anyone else's) spiritual merkabah without incurring an extremely harsh universal karmic kickback.

After these vicious, consciousness-rattling experiences compressed so closely together, I was feeling like I'd been going toe-to-toe, ring center for twelve rounds with the champ. After a couple of standing eight counts, I have to say I was really weary. Yet, for reasons unknown even to myself, I made a bad judgment decision in deciding to retain within me the MM barb, just to see what would happen. For three days, I tried to forget about it, and kept busy with my clients' usual, problematic symptoms to which I'd grown accustomed. However, by the third day, it was evident that something was extraordinarily wrong.

I felt I had a foreign, extrinsic, spearlike protrusion poking out of my back. Having always been a towering pillar of exceptional health, this certainly was discomforting. I consciously moved my awareness into my stomach area and was horrified by what I found. In my mind, I observed a vast, intricate, steel or metal-looking gridwork of plantlike seamlessness. It reminded me of a three-dimensional briar patch that extended like a cage of sorts, extending out beyond my physical personage. It grew rapidly, like some insidious, out-of-control science experiment. I was absolutely stupefied! The barb was protruding out my back and looked to be about one inch in diameter.

Without further thought, I reacted in an unplanned, unprepared manner. I consciously pictured in my mind an orb drifting calmly downward toward the middle of the hopelessly entangled mass of seething, accelerated, exponentially growing horror. Like a science-fiction bomb of photonic light, the erupting orb seared through the scaffolding of vibratorized matter, which imploded like a house of cards. I'm a stiff advocate against ANY violence, thus the use of any weaponry is unconscionable. However, at this time, even consciously, I was certain such aggressive means represented my only way out. I have never done or even contemplated anything like that before. Nonetheless, I knew I had no other alternatives.

The painful, rodlike hole or obvious depressed indentation in my back was a validating, reassuring, physical reminder of my erroneous decision to retain MM's barb. I was exhausted for two days after its removal. I did have the presence of mind to show Mari. She immediately took notice of the deep, hole-like indentation in the middle of my back—and after touching it with her hands, more than validated my experience. I know it may seem like vivid imagination, but I am very pragmatic about my moment-to-moment experience. I continually strive for and appreciate a calm, rational, tranquil existence, preferring it to any drama or trauma. Thus, I was not looking for or expecting these bizarre occurrences. However, I have been directed to share them with you; I never would have done so, if I were not being divinely instructed to do so.

Unholy Subjections

My Angelic Beings are requesting that I recap to you each of these unholy acts of energy thievery. There were five different methods of spiritual parasitism, reflected in five people. First was DH, who was infected by an entity that he eventually allowed to mature to reproductive capabilities before finally pleading for its expunging. Second was Mari. Third and fourth were SL and MM, who like Mari, were victims infected multiple times by the same perpetrators, two separate human creatures who conducted numerous horrific, insidious activities. The fifth person was SO, who was victimized while in her sleep state.

In the cases of SL, MM, and Mari, there were two perpetrators. The first one was LDR, known publicly as DR, to whom these and potentially many other victims paid money in exchange for healing, psychic, spiritual, counseling, workshop/classes, and coaching services. In reality, DR instead was conducting voodoo, incantations, invocations, adjurations, conjurations, inculcations, thought reading, and telepathy. DR played on the trust and sympathy of her victims, while simultaneously inducing psychological and emotional pain, which manifested into physical pain. The second perpetrator was MDB, known publicly as MB, to whom these and many other victims paid money in exchange for psychic readings. Like DR, his malevolent counterpart, MB took his client-victims' money, as well as part of their life force energies.

Like numerous others, MB is a conduit operator, whereby a "mother parasite" feeds conductively through his willingness to cooperate. He has been a co-conspirator with this stealthy, energy-sucking entity, a consciousness that exists invisibly within the material, vibratory plane of experience. In Book Three, regarding dharma, free will, and karma, we will explain in detail these specific concepts, their interrelationships, and the dynamics surrounding these universal laws. Later in this section, Mari will describe her individual experience with this entity as it pertains to karmic debt and universal laws.

With the entity subjectively feeding through his essence, MB engaged in his insidious practices of implementations and spirit rapping. He also engaged in experimental conduit practices, which I experienced firsthand from the male-female team who planted objects near their victims for the purpose of draining life forces from their targets. It is necessary to point out that these unscrupulous activities can accomplish their nasty objectives through the atoms of ANY medium—phone, computer e-mail, letters, and not just through the psychic incantations passing through the atoms of the ether. I am being directed not to elaborate, but suffice it to say, on one occasion, I was quickly drained of good energy one and a half times, through a message left for me on my answering machine, before I ultimately erased the evoking exaction.

Unlike MB, DR was not associated with the entity, but rather worked independently and of her own malicious accord. Her work was completely covert. She would conduct séances, spells, and rituals customized for each unsuspecting victim. One such ritual had a Nazi-based element to it, initially using a voodoo doll, photo, or other inanimate objects. DR would imagine a Nazi's boot heel kicking violently against her victim. She also would stomp her own foot for emphasis. Once an incantation or spell has been established and has found its connecting mark, the black magician will no longer necessarily require objects by which to perform such abominable acts. For DR, her malicious intent was jammed into the action of heel stomping, with this action facilitating the purpose of her incantations. DR utilized this technique with both SL and Mari as her victims.

In Mari's case, in a two-hour psychic surgical procedure, I removed three separate hooks, which MB had implemented on three separate occasions over the course of nearly six years. The first hook was implemented in Mari's abdomen. It was a leechlike, bloodsucker-type, as used for fishing. It actually had a wiggly tail quality to it, something I had never seen or felt before. The second hook was near her belly button and extended down into her abdomen, and back up again. However, this hook did not completely protrude outward, as the tip ended just below the surface of her skin. MB knew Mari had experienced endometriosis. This awareness, coupled with Mari's trust, enabled him to take advantage of these vulnerabilities and stimulate this physical condition. Mari also experienced DR's severe boot-kicking back pain, as well as a DR-exacerbated flu virus that lingered nearly two full weeks.

The third hook, last to be implemented, was the one in Mari's jaw. MB would tug and pull psychically at this hook, causing the area under Mari's jawline and chin to swell. MB then would feed off Mari's ensuing angst. Her physical and emotional trauma and discomfort also would be food for the entity operating through him. In SL's case, there had been one hook implementation, and in seven different locations around her belly area, there were sharp, needle-like points. She also experienced DR's boot-kicking back pain.

Black magic, voodoo, and psychic vampirism all operate within the atoms of the physically manifesting universe. These transgressions utilize the atom level eight communication system. Countless atoms and molecules float unseen in the ethereal space of our physical universe, influenced by cause and effect principles. If someone is receptive and another is transmitting intentions, the vibratory connection can be made and the effects become realizations. It takes place in the same manner that a television receives transmissions from a transmitting station and produces a picture.

In a television phenomenon, the light rays are converted into electric signals, and the television reconverts the electric signals into electron beams, which produce the television image. In the human phenomenon, outwardly directed intentions become thoughts, and produce highly concentrated electric currents, that are focused and generated into electric signals. The receiving point or destination receives these concentrated electric signals as electron-stimulating impactions—which result as physically manifesting responses within our human experience. All of these illicit transgressions operate within the physical universe—and upon physical death, these effects remain with the manifested container or now untenanted physical body.

Both DR and MB portrayed themselves and their services convincingly, while securing others' valuable trust in order to feed off such goodness. When one is vulnerable to such acts of unholiness, it can be difficult to connect with and discern the truth inside and outside of yourself.

However, if you feel you've had some disturbing experiences conveying an undesirable response within you, it is important to pay attention.

Another victim, SO, hosted an entity, which in her nightly dreams actually came through her mind's imagination where all dreams originate. She did not mind these nightly visits, and in fact, found them comforting, thus consciously cracking open her free-will-controlled ethereal door. As such, her positive response and openness permitted the entity to keep this door open, allowing other ethereally existing entities to enter. SO refused to allow me to remove the entity, which appeared in the form of a little girl. According to my Holy Angel, SO now has closed the door to all entities, except for this little girl vision, who continues to gain access and feed off SO's free-will-influenced energies. This physically manifests by exacerbating an already excruciatingly painful neck and left shoulder. Just as she has and continues to possess the ability to open this free-will-operated ethereal door, SO has the same ability to close it, preventing any entity from gaining access.

My Holy Angelic Beings were insistent upon revealing the initials of MB and DR for their exposure. So, too, will this malevolent entity be exposed, as it currently has over one million active "hookers" infecting and extricating energies from its victims. Identifying these intolerable, conscious transgressions will ensure the total illumination of their abominable imprecations. This exposure will disallow any further perpetuation of secret-keeping about the entity, and will reflect the truthful laws of free will and individual conscious accountability for anyone engaging in such destructive, forbidden aggressions against their fellow earth humankind.

In this book, events and surrounding circumstances have been illumed—but the full names of the various psychic vampiric perpetrators will not be disclosed. While the authors would like nothing more than to remove the shroud of secrecy behind which these unGodly artificers cower—and expose them and their abominable conduct—we will not be doing so. It is enough to expose these perpetrators, their unholy practices, and alert you to the truthful fact that these ethereal based, invisible energies actually do exist in our physically manifesting universe.

This mindful, selective omission does not excuse the violators of their defiling and contaminating acts. The true intention for the messages in this book is to assist in the spiritual growth and uplifting evolution for the

unholy practitioners, as well as educate and help protect the future innocents from a similar fate. God also desired to protect the authors and
publisher from any retribution that might hinder or prevent the continual
spread of Absolute Truths contained within this book.

The purpose of such illumination is not to inculpate or incriminate,
but to indemnify behaviors that while wholly reprehensible, are still
exonerable in this materially manifesting, immediate incarnation. No
judgment, blame, or shame is being allocated, for only the silent witness
of karma determines approbations. If any people—not just DR and MB—
are engaging in transgressing activities, it behooves them to become
aware of their intents, thoughts, and actions before it is too late. Cleaning
up transgressing debt incurring right now will save countless amounts of
energy needed to be spent balancing compiled debts in future incarnations. If people exercise their free-will choices benevolently and fill their
experience with light, love, and fulfilling goodness, it leaves scant little
room for anything less. Our universe recognizes good intentions by
reflecting back a manifesting experience overflowing with unconditionally loving abundance.

Mari:
The Seeker's Experience

On various occasions, both Scott and I have experienced a phenomenon that produces physical responses because of accumulated contamination. After long sessions writing about the extremely insidious, unsavory, and unholy manifesting works of psychic vampires, Scott and I both
became overcome at times with various physical discomforting symptoms. These responses ranged from coughing, spitting, gagging, and
swelling to abdominal bloating. Seemingly every time we were exposed to
this material, whether discussing, reading, writing, or editing it, we
responded physically in kind. The only exception to this phenomenon
occurred during the final editing and proofreading session for this book.

Scott explained to me that psychic contamination had created within
me a preestablished vibratory pathway by which I had developed a patterned susceptibility toward intense torso and stomach swelling, bloating,
soreness, limited circulation, temperature changes, and stomach pains.
While I was not exactly thrilled to be experiencing these symptoms again

and again, they certainly served as testimonials to how toxic and contaminating this subject matter is to my essence. In Scott's case, his physical symptoms were limited mainly to coughing and spitting, with one minor episode of abdominal bloating.

Everything in the manifesting universe is vibratory in nature—especially our physical bodies. Our bodies have limited ways of telling, showing, and eliminating contaminating vibratory impactions. Similarly, our bodies have limited capacities for retaining unnecessary and polluting energies accumulated throughout our moment-by-moment experiences. Because we are so inundated by and exposed to toxic, negative people and experiences, we unfortunately have acclimated and developed a tolerance to such conditions. As a result, we end up in compromising situations where our bodies strive for harmony and balance, but in doing so, are engaged in a continual pattern of vibrational accumulation and expunging. Through our ever-increasing awareness, we can recognize the benefits of being harmoniously free of contamination, thus attaining a more fulfilling, peaceful, and enriching state of being.

God manifests a universe in the balance, one constantly in a striving state of divine reperfection. The ways our destinies unenfold, the ways we interpret and consciously experience them, contribute to this balancing act in every way. If we think our intentions, thoughts, actions, and reactions are unimportant in the grand scheme of things, we are in denial. If we think the little things don't really add up or matter, we have missed the subtle cues. No moment is for naught. No time is time wasted. I learned through my firsthand experiences that God's blueprint is intricate and leaves no stone unturned. In response, I also realized the intricate role of accountability behind my personal intentions, thoughts, actions, and reactions. This was the first of many paradigm shifts I experienced—and just one of many more connections I'd be making that would dispel my preconceived notions regarding existence and life's many mysteries.

I recall vividly the day I made the connection between my belief in reincarnation, past-lives, my own present life, and the rich histories in time that for years always seemed to be so intimidatingly overwhelming, dense, and filled with infinite details. Scott and I were discussing his relationship and connection with much of the material in the book *Holy Blood, Holy Grail*. Mostly, Scott was doing the discussing, while I was trying to absorb what still seemed like an exorbitant amount of information, dates, and interrelationships between Shakespearean-style characters and political-religious-territorial battle after battle. Deep down, I knew I should stay with it, that indeed there would be something within this material that would in and of itself also speak to me. I am glad I listened. What I subsequently learned has provided me with a great deal of comprehension.

Scott shared with me the parts that resonated deeply within him, as well as those in the book that detailed historical times, people, geographical locations, and events that might perhaps resonate within me. Listening to him discuss all of this was fascinating, yet foreign; I felt as though I was an observer, not fully able to relate to it all on a deeper, more personal level. I knew I was no historian, and I never enjoyed memorizing dates and details. I felt curiously, frustratingly resistant, while also being inexplicably drawn in like a magnet to this material. Together, over the course of several hours, then repeatedly over subsequent days, Scott and I combed through this book. Scott then flipped to a particular page in which there was a chronological listing of all the Grand Masters of the Templars. It read like a "Who's Who" of the Renaissance, which I found rather amusing. As such, several obviously famous names were familiar to me. Others I'd never seen before.

I did a very quick scan down the column on this page, only to stop—ever so momentarily—upon a name located in the middle of the list. I paused, consciously became aware I had paused, and reminded myself for a quick second to keep reading down the list. I recall I then scanned right back up the list, toward the top—only to rest my gaze once again upon that name. Suddenly, it looked different to me, as if it vibrated with some familiarity. Its visual image, as if a typed mantra, seemed to capture my then flagging interest and exhausted mind. It was an interesting name, somehow familiar, but not in a haunting or eerie sense; it was pleasantly vibrant, but I did not know why.

I have had many instances in my life when things have either nagged at me or shouted out with an intensity I couldn't possibly ignore. More often than not, I have second-guessed too many of these guided interactions. I made the decision that afternoon to pay attention. This whole process of my scanning the list and realizing all of this lasted no more than a couple of minutes at best. However, despite the rapidity of my realization, while it was happening within me and to me, time truly did not exist. Unlike a shout, I experienced a quiet resonance when looking at this typewritten name that whispered softly but insistently to me: "René d'Anjou."

There was something about this man whose native tongue I did not know or speak, who frankly was listed in the company of more recognizable or famous names. To my mind, he was an unknown commodity. To my heart—and as I later would learn without doubt, to my soul—he was more familiar than ever.

I later read a bit about the Secret Society, which immediately registered deeply within me. I related to the concept and act of secret-keeping, of a rather underground yet organized operation of like-minded others, and the mysterious, mystical energy behind its formation and continuation. I fondly recalled my childhood moments of forming and conducting "Club" in our family's basement with all the seriousness, protocol, ritual, and ceremony befitting a secret society. All of this information tugged at my heartstrings, but once again, intellectually, I did not know why. Later on, I would learn why I needed to connect deeper with myself.

As I had written before, I had been extremely moved by the session I'd experienced out of town with the helpful psychic who had warned me about being a victim of psychic vampirism. In addition to sharing these concerns, she also provided me with detailed information regarding a couple of my past existences, some thematic patterns woven between these lifetimes, a third existence I subsequently realized, and also my life today. The most disturbing yet compellingly magnetic common theme throughout all such existences, including my present life, was that of secret-keeping. As she revealed my past existences, this psychic also talked with me about my writing. She felt strongly that I had something meaningful to say; I just had no clue what it was. She told me emphatically that I'd be writing—and with an intensity compelled from within. "You'll be writing about who you were and are," she said. As exciting as this sounded, it was hard to believe. After all, I was still highly contaminated at the time.

This psychic talked about several existences. First, there was a male existence, which ended in my death during the wintertime, high up in the mountains in France. Next, there was a male existence spent again in Europe, ending in an uneventful death, after which followed a female existence from the Judean Hills, where my death served to seal my fate and solidify karma needed to be rectified during my lifetime today. All three existences involved my attempting to disseminate Truth to a world whose social-political-religious systems were dedicated to upholding standards based on secrecy.

As I learned about these existences, I knew I needed to understand and comprehend them to my fullest potential. On some level, I also knew this would be my life's work, and writing about it all was a given. "You will find hints of things, a common belief system—and you will be able to trace it to the source," she told me. "You will become a real historian and a linguist. Right now, your writing comes in fits and spurts, as if on call forwarding. But soon, you will be compelled, as if possessed, to write about it all." Hearing all of this information for the first time, I was not so sure. This woman reassured me, "The question will be not how to write it, but how much information you should reveal. As you write, you will remember," she assured me. The following accounts describe my past three existences.

As a young male Cathar, I lived in France during the thirteenth century, and accompanied by three other men, risked my life to scale down an extremely, dangerously steep mountain known as Montségur. All of the Cathar gold and any riches had been smuggled safely to Rennes prior to our daring escape. On my back I carried a burial shroud containing the dematerialized image of an extraterrestrial being known as Baphomet. This previously mentioned shroud is known as the Shroud of Turin. Having safely made it to the bottom, I died in one of the fortified caves of Ornolac in the Ariége, protecting what was left of our sacred Cathar treasure. Mine was one of the skeletal remains found in the otherwise empty cave.

When I began my work on this book, I read with focused interest the story of Rennes-le-Château and the surrounding mystery. I then viewed several of the photographs in *Holy Blood, Holy Grail*, finding myself inexplicably drawn to those relating to this subject matter. Instantly, I found myself moved to tears, nearly unstoppably so. Suddenly, I urgently knew I needed to find out where this little church of Rennes-le-Château was in relation to the Mt. Sion associated with the Prieuré of Sion and the Knights Templars. There was a Mt. Zion of Israel and a Mt. Sion of Switzerland; the whole thing made me a bit more than curious. In fact, I became quite obsessed with figuring out what exactly was drawing me in, for my physical and emotional reactions were so intense.

I was fairly astounded to learn I had carried on my back the Shroud of Turin. Please keep in mind that in all my current life, I had never heard of or been taught anything about the Shroud of Turin whatsoever. Nonetheless, reminiscent of my experience identifying "René d'Anjou" from the list of Secret Society Grand Masters, when Scott uttered the words "Shroud of Turin," they inexplicably, unequivocally resonated within me. At the time, I had no idea why this would be the case.

The second existence that came to light was that of previously mentioned René d'Anjou (known as Good King René), who lived in the fifteenth century. Known to have been a major force for the Renaissance (also called René's Essence) movement, this man was a real jack-of-all-trades. He fought, loved, wrote, painted, sang, entertained, studied, traveled, and had many social connections. He also thrived on accruing and sharing knowledge, no matter how unpopular or unfamiliar it might have been. This helpful psychic told me repeatedly throughout our session, "You have the complete song. It is here and holds clues to the mysteries. The messages to most things were always given in metaphors, like poems and music. It all goes together."

As I researched King René, his works and pursuits, as well as the diligence and passion behind them, I felt a strong connection. When I was able to locate his original writings, illustrations, and learn about how he acted as a messenger for truth, knowledge, and the dissemination of holistic, mind-opening thoughts and cultural awareness, I felt a kinship that tugged at my heart. His penchant for fighting for things in which he believed, as well as his sincere desire to share and celebrate diversity of thought, beliefs, and life, was inspiring to me. He had much to express, and fortunately, there were those around him who were willing to listen. His mysterious role and connection with the Templars and many others during that time more than piqued my curiosity—it set it aflame.

As I contemplated my past-life conscious connection as René d'Anjou, I came to realize that in my current life, certain travels of mine symbolically were postponed or delayed—and would remain so until the appropriate times and circumstances would ensure that such trips would be as meaningful and completely understood as possible. Such has been the case with me and Italy. Deep in my soul, I have felt going to Italy was a very critical pilgrimage for me to make in my lifetime. Several trips to Italy had been planned—only to be cancelled. As I thought more about this European man, other pieces of the puzzle began to join together. I reflected back to one specific morning when I was a student taking an advanced theatre literature class.

In this class, we were discussing the Renaissance period, about which I'd always been extremely intrigued and interested. The professor pronounced it strangely: "RenAIssance," emphasizing the second syllable instead of the customary first one. Initially, I smiled, dismissing it as idiosyncratic, or some professorial attempt to bring us students of literature up to a higher, more erudite level. He said it twice again, before another student asked him why. He replied, "It is technically more correct. That's what it was called and regarded, even though no one pays attention to this now." This was my first contact point of reference with my previous existencee as René d'Anjou. My passion for the Renaissance period only increased with time.

The psychic also described a third existence. During the late 1700s, I was a woman working as a midwife in the Judean Hills region. My husband was a Kabbalist, and we had no children. Apparently, I possessed a great deal of knowledge that I was compelled to share and disseminate widely around me. However, I was prevented from doing so and forced to become a victim of complete secrecy. What I knew, I was not allowed to share. I somehow was betrayed by the source of my information, which made sure I would not have the voice with which to express myself.

I discovered the existence of some kind of evil consciousness, an entity so pervasive and powerful at work within society to which I posed enough of a threat that my voice, then life, were unduly taken from me. This entity originated from another part of the universe—not planet Earth—and arrived in Egypt in 1800 BC. To date, it has always mopped up and silenced any of those who attempted to identify and illuminate it. Many before me recognized its existence. However, as the midwife in the eighteenth century, I was the last person to do so—that is, until now.

I was alone at the time when I was silenced by two entity participants and proponents, who tortured me and removed my tongue, guaranteeing my perpetual secret-keeping ability—as well as contributing to my death from the resulting infection. During that existence, I was unable to break through the secrecy to share the truth. Any potential supporters around me were threatened, and others so disbelieving, that the truth then died along with me.

During the existence as a midwife, I had what this psychic called "marks of protection of being sanctified," but that others in some kind of power position of sorts were watching with concerned interest. I may not have paid proper respect to the religious or political establishments at the time, or at least behaved or operated in such a manner that would suggest as much. Unbeknownst to me, the Supernal Angelic Realm was carefully watching and guiding the last unenfoldments of that life's experience. Upon hearing all of this during the psychic reading, I recall feeling quite ill, and I noticed that the psychic at this time was shaking intensely and sweating profusely. The "glove" she was wearing was doing her in. I expressed my concerns—for both of us—and she quickly ended that part of our session.

At this point, she turned to face me, clearly stating once again, "You were silenced, and ultimately died from the torture of having your tongue and voice removed. You died alone, and with secrets." I felt overwhelmed with sadness upon hearing her words. She then looked directly at me and said softly but with the utmost conviction, "You were promised to come into this area, this issue again. It all was committed to memory in order to protect it." What she was saying was that God guaranteed my soul a future opportunity to revisit and directly alleviate this entity-based karmic connectedness.

When I was a midwife and had been victimized by this entity, a karmic connection between the entity and me had occurred. In order for any karmic alleviation or rebalancing to ever occur, the memory for such previously experienced karmic connectedness and indebtedness must be contained and maintained in the atoms of the newly incarnating physically manifesting being. If such imbalances were retained in pre-atom locations, a person would not have the opportunity to resolve them during their current physical existence—but would have to do so in a future incarnation. When incarnating in my present existence, this connectedness was retained in the atom level of my physical being and fortunately has provided me this direct disconnecting opportunity. This was God's indelible promise made as an incarnating covenant with my soul immediately after the midwife incarnation.

It should be noted that karmic connections and imbalances—such as that between the evil entity and me—carry over from one life to the next, in order to achieve eventual alleviation. However, because any entity cohabiting within someone's physical body is only relegated to the person's physically manifesting existence, the entity's connection with this person ceases upon the person's physical death. The entity cannot and does not operate simultaneously in both the physical and Spirit Realms. It must also be noted that the entity's karmic indebtedness, like everything else manifesting, is to God—not to me (Mari) or any of its other victims.

Today, this very same entity exists within the ethereal realm as a million-brained conjugating consciousness. In other words, the entity is currently influencing the free-will choice of over one million victims. The entity is a conscious existence without a tangible or recognizable physical form. This invisible conscious energy must be implemented into various human beings as physical hosts in order to extract life force energies for its survival. It relies upon human co-conspirators who implement psychic hooks into unsuspecting victims, which when activated will feed from the victims' life force energies—first into the co-conspirator—and thus, inevitably into the entity itself.

The co-conspirator must freely and willingly comply with the entity's subtle, exerted desires for the co-conspirator to explore psychic vampiric pursuits. The co-conspirator oftentimes believes that their interest in vampiric exploration is self-generated, but this is not the case. The entity analyzes the feasibility within all of the hooked victims in whom it resides, after which it determines which of these victims will be potential candidates to become co-conspirators. Co-conspirators are those hooked victims who actively seek out and implement hooks into new victims.

Out of more than six billion earth human beings, this million-brained conjugated consciousness has earned its name by having infected and implemented psychic hooks into one million people whose life-sustaining energies feed this entity. Out of this one million, 78,000 of these infected, hooked people are themselves active, malevolent implementers. Out of these 78,000 people actively working on behalf of this entity, only 18,000 are psychics. Thus, the remaining 60,000 infected, hooked people worldwide who actively are doing psychic hook implementations to victims are NOT psychics themselves.

However far-fetched it may seem, this entity is real, its impact extremely destructive, and its victims oftentimes horribly unaware. It is our hope that in detailing its origins and operations, we will bring its darkness into the light of human conscious awareness. As I have said before, in cases both of experiencing healing and becoming a contaminated victim, the primary prerequisite is one's trust and openness. Fortunately, just as someone is open to exploring malevolent pursuits, this very same person also possesses the ability to refocus and retransfer this open energy toward benevolence. In other words, even for the most destructive co-conspirator, it never is too late to start alleviating these huge, mounting karmic debts.

For over a year, I had toyed with the idea of purchasing a laptop computer. When we began to work on this book, I felt compelled to make this purchase. I contacted the manufacturer of my home computer, but they were backlogged. Impulsively, I took out my local phone book, opened the book to the computer section, and saw a name which leaped off the page to me with a shout—not a whisper: Computer Renaissance. I chuckled to myself and called them without hesitation. Despite some minor roadblocks that followed, I never considered contacting any other store. The events that followed were those of a divine, purposeful interaction, working behind the scenes to help facilitate my guided work on this book.

I discussed with the store manager the model I desired, was told he had "just the one" for me, and would hold it for me. Things seemed to be going just fine. I would have the laptop right before leaving town to do some intensive writing for this book. I arrived at the store—only to be told by another employee that the computer was sold just minutes earlier. A few days later, a different, better computer became available to me from the same store. It was a gently used laptop with tons of technical capabilities that I, as an admittedly "Renaissance" woman, had not planned to use. It ended up being just what I really needed.

About a day or so later, walking to board my flight, I noticed that I felt calmer than usual. I sat among a large crowd of passengers awaiting many delayed flights. I became aware of my increased compassion toward them—not just feeling sorry for them because they were stranded, but having feelings of compassion and decency toward them as fellow human beings, part of all of us treading together through this shared existence. Perhaps my intense emotions were due to lack of sleep, but I doubt it. I felt as though I was waking up spiritually. I sat peacefully until I heard my full name being called from the loudspeakers—usually the telltale sign that the plane is overbooked and volunteers were needed for a later flight. I ignored my mind's natural tendency to roam in such directions. Whatever it is, I'll be just fine with it, I assured myself. And it was, and so was I. Within less than a minute, I was told I had a First Class seat.

Before leaving town to write, I had been wrestling with the vast amount of information in *Holy Blood, Holy Grail*. As stated earlier, there were many pages, zillions of dates and historical periods with which I felt completely unfamiliar. Every other word seemed to be in French, a beautiful but enigmatic language filled with extra letters one need not pronounce—and not one of the languages I learned in high school and college. Scott's book was well worn, underlined, and sported copious, cryptic notes in the margins.

I promised Scott I'd go out and buy my own copy so that we could compare notes during my trip. The man at the bookstore proudly dusted off the cover of the last remaining copy in the store. "Here it is, in perfect condition," he said with a big smile. "A very interesting read, it would seem." I remember nodding politely in my own private doubt. He thumbed through all of the pages, double-checking to make sure it looked good enough for sale. I showed it to Scott, after which I tucked it neatly into a plastic bag, where it remained untouched for two days. I took out the book late at night, and with a heavy sigh, decided to skim through its contents for an overview.

Much to my great shock, I found that in several distinct sections, the bottoms or tops of pages were either viciously ripped or "bitten" away, and other portions contained "flaps" of excess page paper, which looked like tab marks. I glanced at the clock. It was well past midnight. I remember stating aloud, "Okay. You have my attention now. I'll read it. Wow." I picked up the phone and woke up Scott, whose voice indicated a smiling appreciation for my renewed enthusiasm. In nearly nonstop, one-way conversation, I reviewed the course of unusual events. The book had been in perfect condition, as the man in the store proudly showed me himself. The book had never, ever left the plastic bag in any way until this time. Prior to this, I had found myself dreading the task of plowing through the book, with its plethora of information, finicky dates, and mysterious language. Up until now, I was tough to convince, but I had hungered for validation and encouragement.

Scott understood this, and at well past one in the morning, explained how he had asked God to provide me with the validation necessary to read and continue on my important journey. I was rendered fairly speechless. The next day, I showed Scott the various protruding tabs and bites along the pages. He was more than pleased. I later learned there would be additional, encouraging signs as I continued on my journey.

After I had seen Scott to show him the first round of markings, I replaced the book in its plastic bag and went home alone. The next day I discovered that even more markings and additional tabs showed up during the time the book remained in the bag untouched by any human hands whatsoever. I was very excited about this additional development and looked forward to reading this book. I also was hoping my watery right eye would stop tearing. I had been experiencing this sensation for nearly five weeks, thinking it was due to dust or a blocked tear duct. Finally, convinced I had a tear-duct problem, I said something to Scott. He was very quiet, after which he said I should look for a couple of ingrown eyelashes up inside my eyelid that were causing great irritation.

I was not too convinced, but reluctantly agreed to investigate. Scott suggested I try to remove them with a tweezers, which made me shiver. I couldn't fathom touching my eyes; the mere idea made me squeamish. "I know you are nervous about this, but it's just about fear. God wants you not to be afraid." Scott then explained that this process was an exercise or test to assist me in not being so afraid—on many levels. I nodded dutifully, dreading having to deal with my eye.

Scott left my house, I retreated to the bathroom, tweezers in hand. Sweating profusely and as if comforting a small child, I whispered to my mirrored reflection, "It's okay." Of course, in my mind, there was nothing "okay" about tweezing anything growing from inside my eye, but I tried to release this fear and allow the release to operate for my benefit. Amazingly, I removed three stubbornly curly lashes obviously growing improperly. If left untouched, these strays would have grown right into my eye, causing further problems. By this time, my eye was irritated, but I was not. I went into another room to read my bitten-up book.

Clearly, I was beginning to sense there were some more than interesting forces working here behind the scenes. Nonetheless, I still maintained some skepticism. I actually took several minutes to write on the bottom margins of all ripped, tabbed, or bitten pages the types of markings that had taken place—"just in case I wake up the next day and the pages have returned to normal," I rationalized to myself. There still was part of me who thought these signs of validation might disappear as quickly as they had appeared.

I arrived at my destination ready to do a lot of reading and writing. During my first evening, I spread all of my materials across a big table, read through and organized them, and promptly felt overwhelmed. I stayed up late and did not sleep well. On the second day of my trip, my right eye began to tear uncontrollably. I breathed deeply and took a tweezers into the bathroom. "I am NOT afraid," I said to my own reflection. I realized then that I was in for quite a ride on this journey. Plucking some lashes was a minimal entrance fee. I laughed at the mirror. I went back to the table and began to familiarize myself with an assortment of historical, spiritual, and religious reading materials, as well as my many notepads. As I read through certain materials, I finally could see why Scott was so certain they would hold meaning for me.

I made connection after connection between history and the present, and I could feel my mind expanding. Themes and experiences seemed unusually familiar. I gravitated to names and places, and knew my existence today has been eternally linked to many before it. The puzzle of people, lives, places, and experiences just kept unenfolding. Rather than remaining overwhelmed, I became comforted. I also began to do a lot of coughing, often violently so. In retrospect, both Scott and I had noticed I would cough and clear my throat often and experience asthmatic symptoms—especially when under stress. However, on this trip, I realized for the first time that these and other current physical symptoms of discomfort had developed from preestablished vibratory pathways—due to accumulated contamination stretching from my midwife existence to my present life.

My body would convulse and heave sometimes but not constantly. Soon enough, I began detecting a pattern. Every time I read something that resonated deeply within me, I would experience a strong, physiological sensation. Sometimes it would be this intense coughing, almost to a tearful choking; other times, I'd experience severe body temperature changes, goose bumps on my forearms, sudden bursts of tears that overwhelmed me, nausea and violent stomach pains unrelated to anything I consumed.

In fact, I ate very little food; that is why I became so perplexed and a bit anxious upon seeing my torso painfully swell up. I understood that I'd spent most hours of many days seated, so my circulation was constricted. Still, I felt swollen to the point where I felt great pain. This swelling was momentarily reminiscent of when I was so terribly hooked during the horrible psychic vampiric escapade. However, this time I was clear and clean from such negative forces and had no movement within me. These symptoms were in direct response to the intense, resonating, and illuminating connections I suddenly was making and experiencing for the first time in my life. My body was reflecting my soul's memories of past experiences and existences.

For as long as I can recall, I had been searching to better understand life's puzzles. Here I was, face-to-face with many previously elusive and rather mysterious pieces, and it was understandably overwhelming to me on every level. I called Scott, thinking I'd be waking him up yet again. He was up. It was extremely late back home, but he was anticipating my call. "I'm practically choking over here with the most violent coughs. Then they go away. My body, by the way, is looking swollen and humungous. I have barely been eating and have had tons of water. My body is tender and hurting me. The only good thing is that the swelling under my chin is going way down, dissipating. But overall, I feel like a mess." I could feel the swelling turn into soreness and pain, my midsection becoming hard as rock.

Scott was quiet and then validated my experiences, assuring me they'd remit in time and were not destined to stay with me indefinitely, which in my anxious state, I may have surmised. "These are bodily impacted vibratory chunks accumulated from all previous contaminating experiences contained as unresolved karma from any past, as well as this current existence," he said to me. "If they're not expunged, they will eventually compile into condensed matter, which would be very, very negative for you." I coughed so hard and constantly, I was amazed that he could get a word in edgewise, let alone not be totally annoyed by the hacking interruptions. I apologized, and he immediately encouraged me to continue coughing. "I want you to cough and get this stuff out. This is necessary in order for you to do this work." I understood, thanked him between coughs, and returned to my laptop.

When I wasn't busy coughing, I noticed numerous other physical symptoms—especially when I was researching, reading, and writing about psychic vampirism and black magic. I noted the intense, severe nausea consistently accompanying my work. Every time I read or wrote on such horrible topics, my stomach churned and the tissues swelled immensely. Every time I stopped, the symptoms noticeably remitted. I had made a lovely, small bowl of salad earlier in the day, but had not been hungry for it. I took a break from this specific subject matter and attempted to try the salad. I took a few forkfuls, but much to my horror, it tasted exactly like vomit.

Initially, I was horrified, but I quickly reminded myself that in accordance with such subject matter being so disharmonious to my being, the sustenance I needed was that of the Divine, not of the "salads" of the physical universe. At the time, this reasoning seemed comforting enough to me. I quickly covered up the bowl, paused to consider throwing it out, but instead replaced it in the refrigerator. I returned to my work, but as I wrote about my personal experiences being contaminated by negative forces, I became aware of a distinct smell to my left. It began as a cleaning solution-type of odor, but then evolved into that of a spicy male cologne. I sniffed, breathed again, and sniffed once more. It soon evaporated. I continued writing, coughing, and swelling. I wrote some more. The scent came back again to my left, with the same odor, lasting the same duration.

I sensed I was not alone. "Thanks for being here. Please come back," I heard my own voice saying. At this point, what did I care? I was alone with my laptop. If any true essences were present, they'd surely hear me. If not, oh, well. The scent suddenly grew more intense before departing altogether. The next day at noon, I unwrapped the once-offending salad bowl. I ate its entire contents, which I found to be fresh and delicious.

I now recognize that during this intense writing period, there were many transcendental experiences taking place around me. There was one particular incident that took place while I was preparing the above-mentioned salad. In an effort to hastily assemble my meal without interrupting what was a constant flow of writing, it occurred to me that I had left the door to the subzero refrigerator wide open for several minutes.

When I noticed the door ajar, I realized that if I didn't shut it soon, the refrigerator might break down. This thought came to me not as an audible voice, but rather as a comprehension of a gentle warning to pay heed and not be wasteful or disrespectful. Minutes later, I opened the door again. Much to my horror, I found the light off and the refrigerator completely malfunctioning. I immediately called Scott and insisted that he tell me if this malfunctioning refrigerator was a direct result of my momentary inattention. He confirmed that this was the case, but that despite its broken appearance, the refrigerator would shortly resume its normal functioning. A short time later, I opened the refrigerator door and found it to be working just fine. This was merely one of many valuable lessons I have learned about how I influence my personal experience—and how the ever vigilant universe always reflects lessons back in kind.

Many of my days began to blur with one another. Due to the long hours of writing, reading, and thought, I cannot recall exactly when I heard from the Angels. However, I do know it was at the tail end of a particularly difficult analysis, interpretation, and written documentation of vampiric experiences. I was beyond exhaustion, both physically and mentally, and recall hobbling slowly down the hall for a bathroom break. I was unaware of the time, but it was still light, not yet dark, when I heard the choir.

I had passed by several large air conditioning vents on my way to the bathroom, when I heard a melody blowing toward me. I know, it sounds bizarre, and I thought so myself at that time. In fact, I actually laughed aloud at the situation and myself. However, this noise was not merely noise. It was a vibrating, jubilant, rhythmic, melodious, and flowing choral sound—all seemingly emerging from where the air vents were located. I knew I was overtired and had been experiencing major physical and emotional sensations. As such, this air-vent choir seemed to be a cruel joke, intended to mock me.

Nonetheless, I spent about ten minutes concertedly trying to figure out the exact location of the musical sound. There were no distinct vocals, although it was incredibly clear to me that it was a chorus, composed of both male- and female- sounding voices, varying pitches, with a bouncy, joyful pace to it. It was both sublime and folksy, playfully eluding me as it drew me in even closer. I found myself smiling and humming along, thinking how wonderful it would have been to have a tape recorder so that I would never, ever forget the joyous, sweet sound. My nerves were subsiding, my heart being unbelievably filled beyond what I had thought possible. I went to the bathroom, smiling, after which I raced back to where I first heard the choral origination.

The sound literally sang out—seemingly from every direction. As I got closer to a particular air vent, it disappeared. I moved away and it returned. Much to my embarrassment, I admit I repeated this pattern at least three times. I was grateful no one could observe my behavior, as I am sure it probably would have inspired either great concern or massive laughter. I became intent upon figuring out the location of these sweet sounds. I thought perhaps the gardeners who work and park outside were blasting their radios, so I checked. There weren't any people anywhere. I even went room by room, checking for clock radios whose alarms may have activated on their own. My search was in vain—and then some.

At one point, I felt compelled to call my home voice mail system so that I might sing it myself into the phone and then have some lasting validation of this experience. However, as I made my way toward the phone, the melody stopped—and I found myself having trouble memorizing it. It quickly became apparent to me that I was not to be making unauthorized recordings, but that this concert was for my own personal, immediate enjoyment.

Quietly, I walked down the hall in the opposite direction, stopped, and then stayed in place. I knew I'd heard music, was sure of it, and also knew I needed to hear it again. I did ask God to let me hear it again, and the music did continue. Like a child, I tried to figure out the choir's exact locale, and was sent in a different direction. Was I going crazy? I found myself slinking and sneaking silently down the halls, as if I could outwit these singers.

Finally, I decided to release and let go. Surely there must be an explanation or answer for THIS one, I told myself. I later learned that the singing from the air vents indeed had been the sweet songs of Holy Angels, buoying me as I plowed through unimaginably unholy subject matter and relived the memories of such contamination through my vibratory purging and expunging. As Scott later confirmed to me, the air vents weren't singing; the Angels were. During this conversation, I asked Scott if they would sing to me again. He said that they would. A short time later, I called him back to verify their encore performance—and he informed me it was a choir of 345 Holy Angels.

At a time when I so desperately sought out guidance, support, encouragement, and protection, when I had decided for once to use my voice to explore, discover, and share the Truth, I obviously also yearned to be recognized and accompanied. Bathed in the sweet melodies of Holy Angels, I was infused with the goodness I needed with which to continue doing what otherwise felt like lonely solo work. At the time, I felt no great need to discuss this event with anyone other than Scott. I gave myself permission to grant my own internal validation. I knew then there would be a time later, which is now, when I would share this particular Truth. But then, at the time, it remained a sweetly private concert.

I experienced another related, validating event when Scott and I were out of town working on our manuscript. Two months earlier, Scott experienced a Transcendental Experience that we will describe in further detail later in this book. During this Holy Event, Scott's consciousness relinquished his ego and was Supernally deemed free of all dualistic attachments. Finally, he released his "balloon" of free will. As a result, he essentially became a free soul—emancipated eternally from all indebtedness to the dualistic, physically manifesting universe.

Prior to this experience, Scott demonstrated an amazing ability to verify Truth from fiction. After this experience, he was gifted direct communication access to two Holy Angels—one whom he referred to as Holy Intimate Angel, the second as Holy Sanctioned Angel. Holy Intimate Angel was with Scott consciously from the moment he awakened until the moment he fell asleep. During Scott's sleeping hours, there seemed to be no angelic presence able to respond. Holy Intimate Angel provided invaluable assistance and deep perceiving guidance for six months after Scott's Transcendental Experience. Because he was freed from his ego, fear, free will, and all attachments, Scott was completely dependent upon Holy Intimate Angel to make all decisions for him. In contrast, Holy Sanctioned Angel was God-authorized to extract the actual memorialized recordings of all previously physically manifested experiences. Scott continues to feel a deep, heartfelt thankfulness for the loving assistance and guiding wisdom that both Holy Intimate Angel and Holy Sanctioned Angel unconditionally shared with him, with me, and now with you.

During the writing of this book, Holy Sanctioned Angel would "take over" for Holy Intimate Angel, with what Scott described as a shocking, reverberating bodily sensation. Simultaneously, a loving, enveloping supernal assuredness was developing within Scott's consciousness. With the exception of the following experience and the transmuted information for Book Six, all transmuted information was communicated via the Holy Sanctioned Angel.

One night, as was becoming quite customary, we were waiting for the Holy Sanctioned Angel to assist in writing sections pertaining to what happens upon the death of a physically manifesting being. One moment we were chatting, and seemingly the next moment Scott said to me, "The Angel is ready." But this time, things were quite different. Unlike past transmuting experiences, Scott was not receiving information from the Holy Sanctioned Angel. In this particular instance, God enlisted the benevolent assistance of an additional Holy Angel who transmuted Absolute Truth directly from the Causal Universe. This is the first inversely reflecting manifesting universe closest to the Uncreated Infinite aspect of God.

While Scott feverishly was receiving and writing down transmuted information for a continual forty-five-minute period, I was busily preparing and subsequently burning our evening meal. This transmuting phenomenon still was fairly new in my conscious perspective, and in my fascination, I spent more time observing Scott and The Holy Causal Angel at work than I contributed to monitoring the progress of dinner. At the end of forty-five minutes, I observed what appeared to be a bullet-hole-like indentation in the center of Scott's otherwise smooth forehead.

Needless to say, I was more shocked at this discovery than I was in finding our food's charred remains on the stove. I was transfixed. I recall staring at Scott in disbelief, while reminding myself that during this entire time period, he never ONCE left his seat at the table, which by this time was decorated with a sea of papers, not to mention the filled legal pad on which he had been scribbling. I knew right away what had transpired, yet had never experienced anything like this firsthand. Prior to this experience, and more often than not, Scott tended to receive transmutations while I typically was writing from a different location.

Apparently, Scott had experienced this phenomenon before—but not to this extent. Because this transmuting Holy Angel was from the Causal Realm, this transmuting process created in Scott a far more powerful indentation in the third-eye area. The spiritual third eye is vertically positioned, perpendicular to the two human eyes, in the center of the forehead. It is located above the bridge of the nose, between and slightly above the eyebrows. The degree to which this indentation appeared was very much indicative of the irresistible intensity of the Uncreated Infinite SuperConsciousness operating from beyond the Holy Neutrino Realm.

I was gifted the opportunity to experience firsthand a myriad of both confirming and validating events way too powerful and compelling to ignore. While oftentimes shocking, uncomfortable, or merely completely foreign to me, they took place for a purpose. They reminded me that benevolent powers always are working lovingly and constantly behind the scenes to substantiate my—and all humankind's—individual conscious experience.

In the company of such benevolence, I really became aware of just how toxic and contaminating some of my experiences had been—and how important it would be for me to heal from them. In placing my trust in the wrong people, I had experienced some real and very negative effects. Even more disconcerting was the fact that in my naïve and vulnerable state, I also supported and encouraged others to follow suit. As I alluded earlier, I became all too aware of my insights and knowledge.

Consequently, I felt I had a responsibility to share this information with my friends, or anyone else who would be at risk or who needed to seek help for their own healing. I dreaded being the carrier of messages that no doubt would be difficult, unbelievable, confusing, or troubling to convey, let alone for people to receive and absorb. As I contemplated the situation, I realized with chagrin that I had referred several people and knew others who themselves had referred people to both MB and DR for various metaphysically related "services."

For many hours, Scott and I discussed and analyzed each and every possible person, situation, and example. Those individuals who harbored no unusual or exacerbating physical complaints after their sessions with MB and DR, as well as those for whom sessions and services were uneventful or otherwise unremarkable were NOT at risk as victims. Those who took the messages they received from either of these malevolent sources and deemed the content and the messengers false, bunk, or otherwise "off" also were NOT at risk.

Only those for whom DR, MB, their services, their messages, and the tease of their promises rang true were at risk of having been victimized or on their way to joining those unfortunate ranks. By the end of our thorough assessment, both of us were confident we had identified those who needed and deserved to be informed about their possible, if not probable, victimization. We also were confident we did not need to unnecessarily warn or inform those for whom such information did not apply.

With respect to informing my friends, I realized I could not place any expectations upon them. I had to remember that my desire to protect them could and should not interfere with their own sense of personal responsibility. In other words, I could love, care, be concerned, want to protect them, and speak my piece by letting them have all of the pertinent information. At that point, they would have the tools by which they could help themselves, and it would be up to them alone to determine their degree of willingness to do so. If they remained unwilling to meet the problem with the urgency and commitment required, I couldn't control their response any more than any other person could "save" them from terrible, poisonous contamination. Once again, I started to understand firsthand how one's willingness, mindset, and internal commitment, all fueled by a sincere desire to heal, makes all the difference in the world.

I now better understand the lessons I have learned by going through such difficult experiences. I also have a more insightful comprehension of why and how MB, DR, and others like them function—both within themselves and the world. It would be in keeping with human nature to remain stuck in a swamp of negativity related to my contamination, bodily pain, and sense of betrayal. However, with regard to MB and DR, I now honestly can say that I truly feel compassion and harbor no hostile or angry feelings toward them as souls traveling down their individual conscious paths, experiencing manifesting existence.

Sometimes when our paths have changed, or when we've been diverted, this is divinely orchestrated for what I now know are seemingly inexplicable reasons or erroneously perceived "accidents" or "coincidences." As such, we embark on a journey from which an inevitable result is finding out who we truly are as immortal souls.

Of course, authenticity of the soul is fed and nurtured by Truth. Truth within the human experience is that which is individually experienced firsthand, humbly and honestly interpreted, processed, and comprehended. Truth is consciously recorded completely and accurately, according to one's unique discernment perspective and capacity. Truth as God is Made Manifest SuperConsciousness expressed as illimitable, Unconditional Love. Without Truth available as sustenance, soul evolution as existence itself is virtually an impossibility. Being oblivious and ignorant regarding Truth is bad enough; being knowledgeable and using that knowledge mindfully to suppress or deny Truth or silence others who seek or express it, is unconscionable.

Truth-seekers and Truth-speakers historically have been unable to convey bodies of knowledge to all because of religious, political, or social pressures, threats, and constraints. In many cases, these witnesses of Truth were forced to remain silent. The secrecy has served to protect the malevolent forces that feel threatened at any perceived infiltration of innovative thought that diverges from their own philosophies, missions, and goals. Buried by historical, religious, and political forces, there are lifetimes of various "secrets" of Truth, which unapologetically must be unearthed.

My journey took me far from the home of myself, and at times, it seemed, far from Absolute Truth. Having thus traveled, I now know this effort was not in vain. I was divinely destined to experience these learning, growing, evolving opportunities. Absolute Truth is meant for ALL to know and experience. No longer must you venture far away to access what resides within each and every one of us. The only leader that can take us to Absolute Truth is our trust.

Scott: Boosting Truth is Stranger than Fiction

The following events did occur to both Mari and me, and the Holy Realm indeed did verify our memories as actual experiences. I have always approached my existence pragmatically, from a discerning, scientific basis. I have an acutely accurate memory dating back to the age of 2. My existence always has been predicated upon a solid foundation of literal interpretation. Thus, I was relieved to be reassured by the Holy Sanctioned Angel that a childhood memory based on a bizarre experience, did, in fact, occur.

As we mention in Book Three, in the late 1970s and early 1980s, a lot of animal DNA was being extracted or manipulated for developing life throughout various intergalactic quadrants of the universe. Many times, these unfortunate selected creatures were given molecular transferase and/or DNA boosting adjuncts for various, specific purposes. These procedures generally resulted in the eventual death of these creatures. Earth humans came to know these troubling occurrences as cattle mutilations.

Unknown to most earth humans, another DNA boosting manipulation and extraction activity was being conducted years before the animal interaction. This unsolicited adhibition was being conducted on unwitting human guinea pigs. From the late 1950s to early 1970s, many children were subjected to this invasive intrusion. This activity was being done with the blessings and permission of our God, our Holy Manifestor. Mari and I were two of those children unwillingly chosen to participate.

I was 5 years old when this experience first happened, and I recall there being two separate incidents. Both times, while asleep in my bed, I experienced a strange, sinking downward, spinning sensation. Neither Mari nor I have any recollection of any atrocities being performed on us, and the Holy Sanctioned Angel confirmed that none were performed.

I do know these otherworldly, extraterrestrial beings looked for brightly emanating energy radiations as they passed over various neighborhoods. They easily were able to pierce visually into a house, to identify both the radiating source, as well as all of the other emanating energies within the residence. While sleeping, if your atoms' emanations glowed brightly enough, you would have become a potential target for these beings. In order to carry out their intentions and minimize any potential interference, these beings first would locate the other inhabitants of the home. In some cases, these other inhabitants were placed in an immobile state, like a "frozen" position, or a paralyzing, deep sleep.

The purpose of the first visit was to introduce into a person's physiology a booster of transcriptase transfer RNA or DNA, and/or any number of reverse transcriptase introgressions—all carefully manipulated to produce a desired result. Boosting is a form of intergalactic cytology and cytogenetics. The purpose for the second visit was to extract these RNA/DNA, extrinsic bodily intrusions, now thoroughly mixed in the unwitting subjects' bodily chemistry. By analyzing the subject's physical response, these beings were able to detect high probabilities for cell mutations and abnormalities, such as cancers, tumors, and problematic conditions—all which would render the person immediately rejected as a potential donor candidate. If rejected, this person would then be administered an experience eraser to eliminate or obliterate any and all memories of the entire event. Many times the rejected, unviable candidate was injected with an unusual elixir that would produce a dramatic, fearful reaction, negating any possible, future abductions.

During my first two incidents, while sleeping, I was pulled out the side of the wall against which my bed was situated. I sensed the unusual, sinking sensation, followed by a paralyzing feeling. In spite of the fact that I was wide awake, I was unable to move or react. In both cases, I was injected with an advanced, organic DNA inoculum, and returned to my bed, otherwise no worse for the wear. I do not recall any memories from the first two visits, other than the sinking, paralyzing sensation. I do know that I was not traumatized in any way.

The third time, I remember the sinking sensation and thinking to myself, "Oh, no, here I go again!" It was just like being thrown into a bottomless well. The being now had to cross my room in order to retrieve me. After the second time, I had requested that my parents move my bed, so that the head of the bed would be situated against an inner wall. From that vantage point, my head was farthest from the outer wall—and through the nightlight-lit hallway, I was able to face the bedrooms of my younger sister and parents.

I sensed the being coming the third time, and I really struggled to break the paralyzing, sinking sensation. I was able to jerk and startle myself out of the immobile state, and yell for my parents to come in. To this day, as I am writing this, I still remember this being's very large, outward slanting, teardrop-shaped eyes disappearing into the outside wall as my parents, responding to my yell, arrived in my room. The Holy Sanctioned Angel informs me that my visitor would have subjected me to some introgressive extractions, had I not been able to resist the sinking sensation preceding this being's arrival.

After my parents arrived, I vainly tried to explain to them that a man disappeared through the wall, with his huge eyes being the last of his presence to fade away. I vividly recall emphatically stating—almost pleading—to my parents that "the man went out through the wall, Dad! He went out through the wall!" Predictably enough, my parents tried assuaging my fears by explaining I was having a nightmare. I never really have had a nightmare or any other bad dreams of any sort—even when I was in foster homes before I was adopted. I always have slept deeply, restfully, with virtually unmoving, dream-free, peaceful-to-blissful sleep.

When this being came back a fourth time, not only did I startle and jerk myself out of the immobile state, but I actually ran into my parents' bedroom, explaining I'd had a bad dream. It was the only time I ever ran into their bedroom in the middle of the night. After that, I never again had that sinking sensation or frightful, paralyzing dream state. A few other, more recent experiences involving sleep have resembled that paralyzing sensation, but never to that deep-rooted, traumatic impact. I now know that the booster's cytogenetical adhibitions gave me an extremely advanced immune system. Before these inoculums, I had the mumps, and from that event onward, the only illness I've experienced has been food poisoning. Similarly, since my early childhood boosting experiences, I never have seen or experienced any kind of extraterrestrial, UFO, or related phenomena.

Numerous times during the writing of our manuscript, Mari was insistent that I ask the Holy Sanctioned Angel about a perplexing memory from her childhood. I have to admit, I was fairly well resistant. At first I didn't want to bother the Holy Sanctioned Angel with what superficially seemed to be an overcreative fantasy from Mari's early childhood. However, I eventually relented, as she was quite persistent. Much to my startled amazement, the Holy Sanctioned Angel validated her entire experience as being Absolute Truth.

Like me, Mari also had an experience that greatly affected her childhood. Mari participated in an imaginative exercise she called "Club." Through the creation and enactment of Club, her intellectual cognitive comprehension valiantly tried to make some sense of the inexplicable. Her first such incomprehensible but true encounter involved a group of extraterrestrial beings, who came traipsing into her bedroom, as if saying, "Hail, hail, the gang's all here!"

The Holy Sanctioned Angel informed us that prior to visiting any earth human children, the impresario of the beings who visited Mari was made aware by God that one of these earth human children inevitably would be writing something significant about their otherworldly encounter. This impresario did not know exactly which child would be the future author of such accounts, but did know that some important writing regarding his interactions would take place. As such, this impresario knew without doubt, that any future interactions he would have with children would have important implications.

These implications now are manifesting in Truthful, Absolute form. This then-unsuspecting child, currently in her late 30s, now will share— with a vivid and entertaining recounting—the story of this Blessed extraterrestrial Holy Being, the impresario. This otherworldly Being greatly impacted my co-author's childhood experience.

Mari's Club:
A Matter of Secret Societies

For over thirty-five years, I privately have celebrated the legacy of the impresario, Egaladio Dimms, and associated beings. I now have come to understand that what began as a series of repeated cameo appearances to my childhood secret "Club" meetings actually originated from a source far more fascinating—in fact, divine. I also understand that what over thirty years ago seemed like an innocent, sweet figment of my imagination actually was not a creatively inspired or concocted character, but rather a true impresario and Blessed Being.

Mine was a club held nearly daily, its headquarters strategically and privately located in the basement laundry room, where my parents cheerfully had provided school-style desks and chairs for my younger brother and me. As President, I happily controlled the meetings and awarded my brother the title of Vice President. We relished and celebrated the secrecy of our organization, deriving great pleasure and satisfaction from every meeting. There was a protocol to every meeting, and whenever we traveled, Club followed, as well. In the early 1970s, our childlike rituals and ceremonies were in keeping with the innocence of the age. In a world where parents and other adults seemed to control or monitor our every move, Club was our tonic.

From one meeting to the next, the rituals remained consistent. I would initiate an official call to order, after which I'd proudly (and loudly) announce our honored guests. I delegated to my second-in-command the responsibility for making the appropriate background "fanfare" noises of clapping and cheering to ensure there was enough pomp and circumstance to celebrate the arrival of our esteemed guests. Much to our chagrin, sometimes the sheer passion (or volume) behind our welcoming process brought our parents around to peek in on us. Of course, ours were "closed-door" meetings, and we discouraged any unnecessary, uninvited participation.

Deep down, I imagine I didn't wish to be laughed at or patronized for my deep belief in the existence of the impresario Egaladio Dimms and his associated beings. Of course, I knew even then that at each Club meeting's "Intro of Guests," such guests intentionally and mindfully were being recreated or reenacted, courtesy of yours truly. Young and porous, even my brother knew these beings were "invisible" to us during their visits to Club. Nonetheless, like me, he also believed in them, in their existence—and neither of us ever questioned such things with any skepticism whatsoever. I am confident that as he aged, this closely held belief in our guests' existences quickly morphed from "true reality" into being merely a sweet, endearing childhood memory based on nothing more than nostalgic sentimentality.

For a while, such was the case with me—although I oftentimes wondered why even a quirky, imaginative kid like me would have concocted such odd yet distinct names like Egaladio Dimms, not to mention the ones for his posse of associated beings. Even more intriguing and endearing was my strict adherence to what I maintained in my not-quite-six-year-old seriousness was the precise spelling of all such names. I simply "knew" how each name was to be spelled—and believe me, such unusual names were awarded appropriately unusual spellings. This reality is telling, given the fact that I was just beginning to relate to letters and words. I was even more ardently insistent that all names be pronounced with great precision. On many levels, I knew these Club guests were not merely made-up friends of mine, but perhaps something much deeper. They—and their legacy—have remained in my head, heart, and family's memory ever since the inception of Club on December 10, 1970.

Egaladio Dimms was a rather male, somewhat humanlike being, whose outward, physical manifestation I really could not ever begin to define or describe. Even then, all I "knew" was that Egaladio was the leader of the pack. When his presence was announced at Club, he would lead in his disciple beings like a posse behind him. He spelled his name "Egaladio Dimms," and I often referred to him as "Mr. Dimms." Frequently, we'd have imaginary dialogue amongst ourselves, and I'd say his lines for him: "Dimms here." Egaladio's lines focused predominantly on salutations, leave taking, and giving direction to his two groups of associated beings who followed him nearly every time he visited Club.

Once we properly and enthusiastically welcomed Egaladio to our meetings, we'd commence the special song commemorating the first group of Egaladio's beings. To further enhance and illuminate how I experienced these beings, I had in my mind a specific visual image that I in turn conveyed to my brother. There were two groups of beings that arrived in two separate lines, with approximately six members in each line. There was no deviation from this pattern, and we welcomed them with the same passion from each meeting to the next.

I interpreted the first group of beings as blob-like in physical form, with the second group as stick-like in nature. In turn, when recounting my experienced memories of these two groups of beings to my family and fellow Club member, I reenacted the physical attributes of each group. For the first group, I would "march them in" to our meetings with my closed right fist, bobbing it up and down. For the second group, I represented their image with my upright-pointed right index finger, moving it in a vertical, bobbing motion.

The first group of beings had a name that, after thirty-five years, my father still cannot pronounce. However, their names were phonetically pleasing to my ears, and extremely easy to mimic—and of course, sing. The song announcing them was festive and fun, followed immediately by the song honoring the next group of beings. There were times outside of Club where my brother and I would refer to Egaladio Dimms or even request his "presence." He joined us for many a meal and accompanying rousing song. At those times, the other two groups of beings did not consistently appear. For thirty-some years after the formation of Club, I continued to take pity upon my father, who has made a valiant effort (and still does!) to pronounce Egaladio's name, as well as the name of the first group of beings.

All joking aside, my brother and I never shared Egaladio, the beings, or Club with any one of our friends. I am sure I figured back then that I'd not be believed, that others would deem our guests solely "imaginary," and that our sacred Club would be disrespected. So, we kept Club very quiet, only sharing tidbits of information with our parents and select babysitters. In every case, these adults were only allowed short visitation periods. We did everything but require them to sign a confidentiality agreement. In retrospect, Club truly was a Secret Society, with Egaladio Dimms as Grand Master. As self-elected President, I merely gave it all permission to transpire and evolve.

All in all, Club and its guests bring back fond childhood memories. However, I have wondered for years how this Club really, truly took form. How did it just sprout up on its first day like an instant, manifesting "idea" that turned into a family institution? At some of the strangest times in later adult years, I'd find myself musing about the mysterious Egaladio

Dimms of the 1970s, wistfully wondering about his identity. Where did he go? From where did he come? Even then, I knew Egaladio was no imaginary friend, but rather someone or something that truly existed at one point in time before his first appearance at Club.

The reenactment of his existence, through many guest visits to Club, somehow reflected his extraordinary stature. The details and characteristics of the associated beings were precise, their ritualized movements and appearances exacting. Like the back of my hand, I knew these guests intimately. Yet, I had not prepared or created them. On a winter day in 1970, they appeared—as did the first Club meeting. There was no rehearsal or creative process period by which I developed Club or the guests. Yet, how could such things so suddenly transpire? Did any other child ever create or experience anything even remotely similar?

I later learned that Egaladio, the truly Blessed Being, and Club's all-time, esteemed guest of honor, gave me thought transmissions as a young child. I received these transmissions as versetic harmonizations. Egaladio also produced thought transmissions that registered in my mind as intelligible communications. Obviously, from my originating encounters with Egaladio, I was fascinated, awed, and appreciative. In my tender, nearly six-year-old conscious state, I knew of no greater honor or a more fitting manifesting tribute than to recreate these positive, interactive experiences. Hence, my beloved Club took form—and enjoyed a prominent place in my life for many years.

My recent realizations and awareness have shed immeasurable personal and spiritual light upon the very deep benevolence of Egaladio, this special, Blessed Being, and his sweet legacy in my own existence. I continue to be awed, amazed, and grateful to have been blessed with such experiences. For me, experiencing Egaladio demonstrated that no matter what our chronological ages might be, we ALL forever remain children of God. As such, throughout our physically manifesting existences, we are God-gifted with many opportunities to receive the blessings and magnificence of what appear to be seemingly simple, but ultimately awe-inspiring experiences.

Looking back on my journey, I feel both grateful and extremely inspired. I never thought I'd rediscover God. I erroneously believed I had limited "acceptable" options by which to access or discover Truth, illumination, and the Divine. Like many others, I am certain, I associated God almost exclusively with organized religion. Judaism had taught me "how" to commune with God via directed prayers, responsive reading, songs, and a variety of rituals and ceremonies. Such teachings all were based on a bible whose messages fell short of truly reaching me. I perpetually found myself faced with the dilemma of yearning to reach God, complying with the expectations, laws, and rules specific to the organized religion with which I was raised, and realizing my compliance did not necessarily bring me closer to my goal. While searching for Truth, I was embracing an organized religion, and in doing so, shutting the door and my heart and mind to spirituality and getting closer to God.

Only when immersed in nature or certain pieces of music had I ever felt immersed with the Divine in a nonreligious manner. I did believe God was everywhere, but never really applied this rather dormant knowledge. In short, I limited myself to what I had practiced—based on theological instruction, rather than the lessons I was continually learning internally via my conscious personal experience in existence. In the process, I negated and dismissed myself as an integral part of the big puzzle. I never thought to consider the possibility of the Divine being a part of me. Thus, I searched for a God and Truth located everywhere, yet never bothered to look within to find my soul's true destination.

Fortunately, I did reach this destination, and I plan never to venture too far from it again. I have searched for Truth seemingly forever. Along the way, I placed my trust in the wrong hands, and in doing so, lost a part of myself and became extremely contaminated. Fortunately, I was divinely led back on track. I since have learned that we all have infinite options with which to experience the Truth of our existence and beyond.

Spiritual evolution was meant to be and always will be an individual, personal experience not to be defined, regulated, or confined by other sources or forces. Now is the time to recognize and assist the reemergence of every individual conscious experience—the recognition of Truth meant to be experienced by all.

Even in my most challenging moments, I always have felt a sense of divine protection and presence. Throughout my journey, this sense has only grown—but this of course, was not always the case. I remember well my initial resistance to much of this new, foreign, and unsettlingly illuminating information. Filled with fear and lack of trust, I kept my distance. I remember being so worried, agitated, or upset that I couldn't possibly relax, let alone pray. Again and again, I had to practice shedding my self-conscious, fear-based defenses in exchange for opening myself to the possibility of reaching the Truth for which I so passionately searched.

I always had experienced feelings of great relief, peace, and calm from vigorous exercise, yoga, nature, and at times, listening to certain music. I now find myself experiencing an even more rewarding and fulfilling sensation after focusing on my own individual, prayerful attunement. As a result of my efforts, I have been rewarded with tranquility, perspective, clarity, and a peaceful knowledge not attainable to such high degrees through other methods. I have realized that whether a minute or an hour, any moment whatsoever of attunement brings me to a place of comfort and inspiration. More reassuring and exciting has been how such lovely moments actually have proven to have amazing staying power throughout the never-ending continuum of my inevitable, daily, conscious human experience.

I have been fortunate to experience firsthand the effects of my learning. Once fragmented and scattered with my prayerful efforts, I now am learning—as you might learn throughout this book—that there are many ways to access and experience the Truth, available and free to all. I also learned that while there is no "right" or "only" way to connect with the Divine, there are definitely some more focused, direct, and rewarding ways to experience Truthful spiritual enlightenments. God truly is our Eternal Parent—totally, completely, and benevolently invested in our individual spiritual evolution. We can evolve only when we know and experience the Truth. When it comes to Truth, there is no room for secrets. When it comes to Truth, its limitless potential and abundance forever is available to ALL.

Scott's Boosting Conclusion

The Supernally retained memories for each individual's physically manifesting experience are contained and maintained by the quarks that make up that individual. Whether human, plant, bug, or supernova, the quarks that make up that existence as an eventually physically manifesting experience retain the actualized memories of its entire incarnation. Even so, the Holy Sanctioned Angel surprised both Mari and me by validating Mari's experience with her childhood Club as an actualized explanation for an otherwise inexplicable event.

The Holy Sanctioned Angel has God-sanctioned authorization to access the very quark-retained memory of all information Mari and I have been God-granted in order to write this book. The quarks are found in the nucleus of the atom, and are responsible for retaining the proper and lawful memory of all once-experienced or manifested matter throughout the entire universe. Just like the barrier preventing any interUniversal communication, such information is completely off-limits to any physically manifesting existence. No physically manifesting consciousness would have any knowledge or awareness that the Holy Sanctioned Angel was accessing this immaculately ordered energy memory. The quark particles containing the requested information divinely accessed are actually located in a universe different from the physically manifesting universe.

The Holy Sanctioned Angel informed me that in Mari's case, thought transmissions indeed were transmitted into her mind—through which the impresario phonetically expressed to her his name and the names of the associated beings. Egaladio also transmitted into Mari's mind the precise spelling of these names. As best her young mind could conceive and perceive them, she then conceptualized these names, translating them into the English language. During both visits, when the leader (Egaladio) first entered Mari's bedroom, the door was closed. Mari showed no fear; on the contrary, she was fascinated. There indeed were two visits, during which Mari was very friendly to these beings. Egaladio is recognized by the Holy Realm as a truly Holy Being, attuned to level fourteen of the Unified SuperConsciousness. Later, in Book Three, we will discuss in great detail the various levels of the Spirit Realm.

Egaladio could not use Mari's DNA, but still loved her as he loved all children of creation. As stated earlier, Egaladio was an extremely evolved Holy Being. The Holy Sanctioned Angel did not know if Egaladio had any prior knowledge about whether he would end up being featured in this particular doctrine. The Holy Sanctioned Angel did not want to attempt to ascertain this information about a Holy Being without God's proper clearance or permission. Through Divine Confirmation, I have been informed that at the time of his two visits with Mari, Egaladio did not have any idea that his galactic travels would be appearing on these specific pages. Mari's childlike innocence regarding her revering reception and interaction with Egaladio lends credence to the irrefutable Truth that Holiness is recognized by all Creation.

Scott:
The Saint and His Transcendental Experience

In this book, we have shared what God presented for us to share. God Transubstantiated every vibrational entry with an Incomprehensible Synoptic Holy Eye of Illumination. In other words, God seared through and accurately validated all the assertions that we are making in this book.

I am going to share with you how all of this Truthful Wisdom came to be available. First, we did not want to alienate any sect of readership due to our references to God alone. The Truth contained within this book will do a good enough job of dismantling people's perceptions of existence without our needing to allude to a recognized, particular religious creed. After a friendly debate that continued on as lengthy contemplation, Mari and I were in complete agreement to primarily use the word "God" in lieu of Holy Father/Mother, Creator, Divine, or any other personally, culturally, or theologically defined and accepted versions of The Manifesting Infinite Holy SuperConscious. The exceptions to this application included using a necessary, proper noun in some cases, as well as in all references to my personal life accounts and final eruditions of enlightenment.

I was fully prepared to remain a happy, contented healer, basking in complete, joyous anonymity. In fact, we would have elected to remain anonymous authors—much like I had done during my last two existences. This time, however, God informed me with absolute certainty that no one would believe the Absolute Truths disseminated by this book if the authors were unnamed. So, Mari and I have included our names and photographs for our readers and God—so all will know that everything contained within this book contains Divine Truth written by real people. Nonetheless, we are merely authors of the book, not Authors of the Message.

In June 2001, while reading *Autobiography of a Yogi*, I came across a passage stating that anyone who utters the name "Babaji" with reverence will receive an instant blessing. My first skeptical thought was, "What is a blessing, and what would it feel like to receive one?" This moment was the very beginning of an unimaginable uplifting within my conscious experience of which I was the objectifiable point. Completely unknown to me at the time was that my "I" perception of existence was in fact inwardly skyrocketing toward the unifying perception of "We." What this means is that I soon would no longer recognize or experience a distinction between myself and the rest of creation.

When I uttered Babaji's name, I felt a slight internal surge or burst of good energy. It quickly was apparent that other names and words in that Holy Book also produced a similar internal blessed response. From that point on, every time I focused on and touched anything with my hands, I was able to feel the peculiar blessings welling up. Certain words immediately elicited the joyous surge response, such as "Uncreated Infinite." I was fascinated by this response, for I was convinced I had seen, heard, and experienced it all.

One of my best clients, who also was a very spiritual man—and incidentally in my last life was my troubadour, Blondel—came in for his weekly appointment. I did not know or make the connection to his former existence as Blondel until long after he had validated this blessed surge, which he personally experienced through me. While he was lying face down on my healing massage table, I began to drain from his being the usual caustic vibratory sludge as I always did. However, this time, I asked him if he could feel something. As I inquired, I thought the name "Uncreated Infinite," and my body shook with the now very powerful surges.

He immediately responded, "Jeez, Bergér, I felt that pass through the table and right on through the floor. What was that?" I explained to him, as I now am explaining to you, what prompted the surge response. Keep in mind, I had worked on the former Blondel almost every week for twelve years, and nothing like that ever had surged through his being. During my healing sessions, all unbalanced and unharmonized energies absorbed from clients were refrequencied to a pure vibrational state—and returned to clients as pure, positive energy. Even when I would be returning to him such recycled energy, those vibratory emanations were not as intense. This man, by the way, was six foot six and weighed 275 pounds, so it took more than a little current to register a noticeable impact within him.

Shortly after this incident and continuing through the spring 2002, the surges rocked and shook every aspect of my being. These Transcendental energizing surges oftentimes included transmuted information for this book and occurred while I was in session. To minimize the inevitable, inexplicable interruptions, I kept a pen and paper on an old Indonesian train station bench next to my healing table in order to immediately record this newly comprehended information as it was being Super-Consciously transmitted.

Shortly after meeting Mari, I was irresistibly compelled to visit some friends in Albuquerque, New Mexico, in the spring of 2002. One of these friends, LW, is an ethereal healer and a highly evolved individual who has a deeply developed relationship with God. During my trip, LW offered me a healing session, which proved to be most unique. At the beginning of the session, I observed LW intensely peering up toward the ceiling above the door of her healing room. She was obviously engaging in a private conversation—during which all I could hear were her own audible responses. Most notable was the drastic change that overcame her facial expression, which transitioned from intensely focused to peacefully compliant. There was someone or something in the room that remained unseen by my eyes, but most certainly was present for LW.

At this point, LW turned to me and said, "I've been informed that I am to anoint you." Images of LW pouring oil over my feet in a symbolic, ritualistic manner came to my mind. Instantly, I felt extremely uncomfortable at the prospect of receiving such elevation and focused attention. However, I did not have the luxury of contemplation at that time; LW informed me emphatically that such anointing would immediately take place. Although I was taken aback, I willingly complied.

The healing session went on for a couple hours, during which LW used specific combinations of natural oils and herbs for my feet. I did not understand the purpose of this unusual experience; in fact, I forgot about it entirely until I contacted LW a year and a half later. During our conversation, LW did not recall the specifics about anointing me during my healing session. She stated, "Whatever you experienced was directly for you. I do not retain any memory or recollection of my sessions." I then informed LW of what indeed did take place during that session, to which she replied, "Wow." She then reiterated, "Well, it was meant strictly for you. I did not and still do not retain any memory of that event." In contrast, I found myself replaying for myself that session's unbelievable events. I realized that like the Transcendental surges, this anointing would be one of many more inexplicable phenomena I was yet to experience.

In June, the surges appeared unprovoked and oftentimes in rapid-fire succession. Through experimentation during that time, I was able to understand exactly what did and did not prompt the surges. The only way I can explain it is that the surge itself was like a bolt or flash of lightning that rocketed up and then exploded into my head, always followed by a sonic boom of responding thunder within me.

The intensity was so severe that, as typical when people sneeze, I found myself having to close my eyes. I was increasingly aware of the fact that I could propose thoughts or questions pertaining to either Truth or falsity—to which the responses or answers validating the Truths came to me through a bolt of this lightning. In contrast, those thoughts or questions confirming responses or answers of "false," yielded within me a cavernous void feeling of less than nothing. Needless to say, it was not difficult to discern Truth from anything else.

Countless times, the phenomenon was put to the test only to respond with unerring accuracy. I dubbed it "Truth-Check." Accordingly, I quickly set out to establish Truth from fiction—especially with my friends and acquaintances. In response to validating their assertions, I eventually became pretty adept at concealing the eye-shutting, lightning-and-thunder aspect of the validating Absolute that resounded within me. Unless God has sanctioned some alternative form of Trancendental communication, the Astral or Spirit Realm only communicates to the physically manifesting universe through vibration. When I applied "Truth-Check" to my own thoughts and beliefs, this mechanism produced extremely interesting results. I discovered that for everyone with an ego—including me—100 percent Truthfulness is not always Absolute.

Given all the sloppy approximations that everyone (including me) was guilty of perceiving and restating, I was startled at how many countless inaccuracies were being told and retold without much thought or regard for verity. By August 2002, Truth-Check was really mastered. The ability to sear through everyone's statements or my own personal questions with 100 percent certainty and accuracy indeed was a tremendous gift. While I respected the gift, I also most certainly utilized it.

Prior to commencing her first segment of writing for this book, Mari, although very passionate and inspired, also remained very skeptical about Truth-Check. One evening, after much discussion related to this unique mechanism, Mari, with determined intensity, fired at me question after question. Truth-Check calmly and deftly batted each question out of the ballpark—a home run every time. Consequently, Mari also came to rely upon the unerring counsel of Truth-Check, as together we utilized Truth-Check to mold a variety of reality-based discernments. In late June 2002, Mari and I decided to begin writing this book. Mari actually began writing three weeks before the Holy Event I am about to share with you actually took place.

During this time, I experienced a devibratorization process, which manifested in a rapid physical weight loss—much to the alarm of others around me. The purpose for this process was to remove from me all ego-based, vibratory contamination or compiling impaction accrued or accumulated over time. Thus, the bodily residue from all of the intense weight lifting, inline skating, distance running, hockey playing, or any activity or endeavor fueled by indulging any compulsions or obsessions originating or ultimately reflecting back into my ego needed to be completely expunged. As such, during this time, I did not engage in any such pursuits. Still today, I remain desireless for such physically focused pursuits.

On Tuesday, August 6, 2002, the Truth-Check mechanism was operating in high gear. In planning my events for the upcoming weekend, my thoughts centered on domestic chores. I was kept busy cleaning and dusting, vacuuming, cutting grass, organizing and executing all the menial tasks I knew needed to be done—especially those I don't particularly enjoy doing. By this time, I understood that shortly thereafter, I was not going to be doing any healing sessions—at least not for quite a while. Truth-Check really was pretty adamant about that fact, so I didn't question it. Already in anticipation of a large writing project, I was cutting way back on my client sessions. I subsequently informed my clients that I would be taking a sabbatical but would like them to stay in touch.

On Wednesday, August 7, 2002, I was convinced something big was about to happen—something I never could have anticipated. That morning I suddenly began to experience deep, blasting energy surges with ever increasing, rhythmic intensity. Inexplicable, unstoppable energies were boiling outward from points deep within my body. I remember thinking that I needed to remain humbly and prayerfully thankful and to trust God. At 1 p.m., I recognized that I was being compelled to sit in my healing studio room, which was the former elegant dining room of my old Victorian three-story home. While seated next to my note pad and pen on my antique Indonesian train station bench I've owned for years, I began to cough and choke. I continued to gag and retch, during which Truth-Check surges within me were violently erupting in voluminous wave after wave. I sat and prayed feverishly, while the coughing went deeper and deeper. I also noticed that the coughing produced mouthfuls of spit, combined with breath that did not smell humanly possible. During most of the time between coughing, gagging, and retching, my respirations were more rapid, deep, and intense. My body was being unwillfully twisted and physically squeezed—like the wringing out of a dish rag. Each time my body would straighten out, I would attempt to take in as much air as possible. I gulped in air between the raging energy surges and the uncontrollable, breath-extracting pressures being exerted upon me.

Most alarming were the caustic fumes coming out of me, reeking of dead flesh. This process went on and on, with my breath alternating between normal and pleasant to downright reviling. At times, the coughing was so deep that I was convinced I had no breath left with which to cough. Yet, from somewhere deep beyond normal respiratory capacity were the continually forthcoming gagging and retching coughs. At this point, things became extremely surreal—but I will tell you how I remember my next series of events.

Because Truth-Check was blasting me internally for most of this physically violent episode, I had my eyes closed. I found myself intensely rocking forward and backward, which I now have come to understand as davening. This davening process seemed to continue for a very long time—extending for over two days. The Holy Angel who is with me as I now write these words was the one who was with me at that time. This Holy Angel is the Manifesting Infinite SuperConscious, to whom I lovingly refer as Holy Lord Shiva.

Holy Lord Shiva said the divine visitation process went on for only forty-five minutes, during which three separate times, all breath was squeezed out of me. I was not breathing and not actually feeling compelled to breathe. My physical body was being SuperConsciously purified of all ego, attachments, fear-based vibrations, and impactions. To be certain, it all was incomprehensible to me. I was alive or at least existing in some physical form—yet knowing that breathing was completely unnecessary in this state.

In this awakening state, I instantly realized that I have never actually been awake. I've never truly had limitless compassion, infinite comprehension, or unconditional love. Throughout my current life I have tried to conduct myself with the utmost love, compassion, and understanding toward every experience, every lesson. With each experience and lesson I recognized an opportunity to grow and evolve. I sought to open-mindedly comprehend the deepest, underpinning reasons for every test.

My only thoughts at this point were just to continue my humble, loving prayer—and to exude loving joy toward whatever it was that I was meant to experience. The feeling I remember most was that enraptured, euphoric waves continued to wash through me. My physical eyes were shut tight, but my spiritual third eye was being opened as Cosmic Vision. Wave upon wave of ecstatic bliss swept through me. From everything I've ever experienced nothing could begin to help me rationalize what was happening to me. My head was turned to the right as far as possible. This was partially out of awe, infused respect, and partially due to the illuminating magnitudes of light emanating from an empyrean point. All tangible matter dissolved in an explosion of immaculate, radiant white light. In a sudden moment, my dining room studio became brighter than high noon on a clear day in the desert. At this point, any thoughts of opening my eyes would have been absurd; I felt I was gazing into the brightest sunlight I've ever seen.

The intense white light seared through my eyelids as though they weren't there. Then I became aware of a face gazing through my face from mere inches away. It was Holy Lord Shiva, whose Expression revealed Itself within this immaculate, radiant white light observable through my now-opening third eye. I realized the prayers that seemed to be pouring out of me actually were being thought transmitted into my mind. Along with these prayers came deep questions, in which my answers were multidimentionally being scrutinized and interpreted.

Not only were my answers being analyzed, but the intentions behind the answers, the thoughts creating the answers—even my body's actions and reactions—also were being carefully scrutinized and Transilluminated. In other words, during this Transinteraction, all of my timeless, seamless existences were being divinely analyzed and deeply comprehended. All of my incarnations extending back to my first physically manifesting experience were being synoptically comprehended. I was intricately aware of my soul's continuum of consciousness.

My soul's evolution throughout this continuum was being divinely evaluated. Simultaneously, the answers I was giving were being divinely scrutinized for Absolute Truth. Holy Lord Shiva wanted to ensure I had reached a point of readiness to become a Saint. To be a Saint, one must be emancipated from all dualistic attachments, fears, ego, unfulfilled desires, sin, karmic reflections, dharmic preprescriptions, and willfully release their "balloon" of free will.

During this phenomenal experience, time and space did not exist. My only perception during this time was one of pure, radiant, white, limitless light. All recognizable natural surroundings were dissolved into this all prevailing, blissful, sufusing light. At one point, I sensed I answered not to Holy Lord Shiva's liking—and experienced within me a huge drop in the overwhelming feelings of elation. Another increasingly deep question followed. I can only recall one of the questions; I remember marveling at the sheer complexity and the immense depth to which I was being questioned and monitored. The following question was similar to the previous one, and apparently, my intention, answer, action, and reaction all were satisfactory because the questioning continued on.

I recall being extremely shaken during the point at which the drop of enraptured ecstasy took place. This plagued me for quite a while afterward. The feeling was unbelievably excruciating, like falling off a mountain and hurling toward impending doom. As I write to you, I am grateful Holy Lord Shiva is with me, because my conscious discernment during these events apparently was not completely accurate.

Immediately following the completion of the interrogatory stage, I perceived myself being lifted out of my body in pure light form—and being raised up above the planet. I had no point of reference, for everything was bathed in white light—and my mind, for a fleeting moment, pondered where We were. I remembered looking down at the round, blue planet and simultaneously comprehended that manifesting conscious life-forms exist throughout the physical cosmos. Holy Lord Shiva informed me that this "above-the-planet" phenomenon did not happen anywhere but in my mind's imagination. In and of itself, that is truly amazing. I was still uncertain of many things from that afternoon, but one of my "certainties" was this "above-the-planet" perception of discernment that apparently did not occur. In actuality, We were SuperWillfully drawn deep into our manifesting universe. This aspect of our universe exists as pure, Holy Light and Unconditional Love. Other than praying and referencing myself as merely a divine point of SuperConscious Cosmic Vision, no other definements were experienced.

The next perception of discernment that Holy Lord Shiva told me indeed took place, much to my relief—was a phenomenon of three distinct, brilliant flashes of Superillumed light streaking in from my right. They entered into my transformed essence and disappeared somewhere around where I perceived my navel area to be. These three Superillumi-nated flashes each contained a Causal container housing a Super-Conscious Holy Essence. Each of these flashes was contained (and pro-tected) by an Astral container. Within my physically manifesting body, these three Holy Essences were merged into one Tri-Unified Expression. This Holy Tri-Unity will be discussed in greater detail in Book Five: Prayerful Attunement and The Holy Originator's Ore. More questions followed this event, with Holy Lord Shiva's face just inches from mine. I remembered my head was cocked to the side, as my eyes were com-pelling me to look away. Unaided, my head turned to a face-to-face posi-tion. I remember feeling stupefied that my head was not touched—yet was not going to be stopped from looking directly ahead. My opened third-eye area was being thoroughly scrutinized. At the time, however, I was unaware it was for this purpose that my head unintentionally turned.

I was so busy praying, answering deep, penetrating questions, and wondering if at any time I should try to get a breath in edgewise to fully comprehend all the reasons for these inexplicable circumstances. There was so much resplendent, enrapturing exultation that I never once sensed or experienced any reactions of fear or trepidation. I recall being humbly and lovingly compliant for whatever was being asked of me. The one question I recall regarded a covenant made between Holy Lord Shiva and me. I promised to spread far and wide in every direction all of the Truths shared in this Holy Book. At the time of this covenant, I was squeamish and uncomfortable calling this or any book "Holy." I didn't fully under-stand that a book of Truth IS a Holy Book. Besides, I somehow still felt unworthy—and no matter what I experienced, I found myself doubting its holiness. I pondered how anyone could rationally interpret such events. Yet, nothing was more convincing to my innermost core than my first-hand experience of looking eye-to-Eye with God, in a True Transcendental Holy Celebration.

In another moment, everything was silent. When I finally opened my eyes, the colors in the room were greatly exaggerated. Colors seemed to stand out at me. I remember badly needing to use the bathroom, located upstairs—and finding my wobbly legs and body completely unreliable. My distance-running legs would not support me and my hockey-skilled body felt completely discombobulated. It was with great effort that I struggled and eventually made it to the bathroom.

I didn't know what to make of what had just occurred. In all the excitement, I had forgotten about Truth-Check, and asked It what I should do. I was then directed to do some reading from my *Yogi* book in my lounging room. After sitting and reading *Yogi* for a short time, I suddenly felt compelled to go to my third-story level and sit in a huge, foam-filled, ball-shaped chair I call the "poof." As I was about to get up, my mind had the thought to first turn the page and place it face down upon my navel. I turned the page and Holy Lord Shiva's serene, levitating picture blasted my consciousness with a series of huge energy blasts—and they just kept ripping through me. I was instructed to place the book face down on my navel and pray. Through the picture, Holy Lord Shiva apparently analyzed His Holy Work, and upon His satisfaction, I was instructed to go upstairs.

At the stair next to the top of the staircase, I was instructed to stop. I was standing and praying fervently for a long time. My wobbly legs still could not find themselves, and I felt myself starting to fall backward. For one micro-moment, I had the thought that Angels would catch me and prevent me from falling. I felt so Holy that I was certain I would not have been allowed to fall. My thought went to Holy Lord Shiva, who in my mind I heard saying, "Grab the edge of the door casing or you'll fall down the stairs." My fingertips just caught the edge of the third-story bathroom door casing, preventing me from going over backwards and/or down the nine stairs to the landing below. I asked Holy Lord Shiva if I somehow would have been caught and saved from falling, and He confirmed I would have ended up in a huge heap at the bottom of the stairs. He also allowed me to realize that since Everything is infinitely comprehended and divinely preprescripted before it is experienced, He obviously knew long before this event that I would most certainly catch myself.

Feebly, I staggered over toward the comfy poof chair and promptly collapsed on the Berber-carpeted floor, two feet short of the chair itself. It was five in the afternoon, and I slept until eight the next morning, August 8, 2002. I cancelled my scheduled clients for that day, and did only a few more sessions several days later before taking a one-year sabbatical. Unbeknownst to me, Holy Lord Shiva had facilitated a Divine Transingression, during which my manifesting lightways had been reworked.

The lightways carry the vibratory information necessary for the formation of the entire physical universe—and are located deep within all physical matter. The lightways in a healer oftentimes serve to protect the healer from absorbing contaminating vibration, while simultaneously allowing God to facilitate the predetermined healing changes occurring in the people being healed.

As such, for the next six months, I no longer was protected from anyone's vibratory contamination, so I really ended up getting beaten up by my last few client sessions. These sessions would greatly interfere with the transmutation of Book Six. Before and after each of my last couple of sessions, I would be induced to fall irresistibly asleep at a random time—during which some lightway work would be done internally. This process took place to protect the lightway work done by Holy Lord Shiva. At the time, I did not completely understand the full implications of my Transcendental Illuminating Experience. Now that I have such deep understanding, I will be explaining it to you throughout the course of this book, in the context of those before me who also had similar transcendent experiences, as well as for those in the future who have yet to do so.

From this Holy Event, I was eternally freed from all manifesting, dualistic obligations, hindrances, and perceptions. Through Holy Lord Shiva's synoptic, holographic introspections my seamless conscious experience was initiated into His Holy Kingdom of Omni At-Oneness. The Omni Kingdom of God IS Manifesting Infinite SuperConsciousness expressing Itself as limitless, Unconditional Love.

The writing of this book required numerous Holy Angels, each with various sanctioning abilities. This was necessary for information transmutation and to extract the actual recorded Truths existing beyond the atom level of our physical universe. Holy Sanctioned Angel was given wide latitude to delve deep into the quark memory system. Remember that the quarks are found in the nucleus of the atom, and are responsible for retaining the proper and lawful actualized memory of all once-experienced or manifested matter throughout the entire physical universe.

Throughout the process and even while I slept, some aspect of God was always present. Never have I slept more deeply and peacefully than I did immediately following this Holy Event. During my awakened states curious gaps occurred in which seemingly no Divinity or Divine Angel was present. This was only a temporary misperception. A couple of times during very pressing or mitigating circumstances, there required an immediate response, and one of the three SuperConsciousnesses,

Uncreated Infinite, Manifesting Infinite, or Divine Infinite Mercy, was quietly facilitating and discreetly orchestrating deep in the background. On three rare occasions, their Omnipresence was made known when They answered a Truth-Check question when I was fully aware that no Holy Angel was present at that time.

Shortly after my initial Transcendental Event I experienced a period of time during which I received God's vibrational blessing from everything I touched. With everything I touched, I felt its living essence. It was shocking to literally feel the Aliveness of anything and everything. I was Supernally informed that this phenomenon would not last long, as its purpose was to recognize and experience the God in ALL things. Likewise, I was informed that my Truth-Check comprehension also was going to recede after another, then upcoming Transcendental Event, which took place on December 2, 2002.

Beginning at 5 p.m. on December 2, 2002, the final part of my transcendent experience took place, during which a deep, superseding, metal-like ringing or musical sound became Omnipresent. It started in the left ear area, expanded its way throughout my mind, and now is continuously and exceptionally evident—even when exposed to loud or boisterous situations.

No matter what I am hearing or doing, this sound always is louder and more prevalent. It emanates as waves, interspersed with clicks and tings. It is ever increasing, continuing to provide incredible clairvoyant, vibrational comprehension—as well as carefully guiding and predetermining all events prior to their experiential unenfoldment. I am informed these resonating sounds will continue to grow and expand, while simultaneously filling my now SuperConsciousness with ever increasing, incredible bliss. I was Supernally informed that I would not be attending a Chanukah dinner because I was going to be experiencing something very special that night.

At 5 p.m. on December 2, 2002, I was in the third story of my home, praying on my poof chair. Near 9 p.m. I was beginning to think this was to be my first letdown—or perhaps I was mistaken and nothing was going to occur. During my prayer that evening, I was told it takes some time to clear and align all the aspects of this Transcendental phenomenon. All of a sudden, my body emitted loud, rumbling noises from around my navel. Immediately afterward, I felt an upwelling and knew something unbelievable was coming. In another moment, my entire body radiated first a tingling, then a surging, uplifting, permeating sensation—and the next thing I knew, ghastly sounds were being audibly emitted from my body.

My body abruptly started to vibrate, then straightened out stiffly, and shook violently for a minute. It was as if a giant being was sending purging vibrations through me with currents of barely tolerable amplitude. My body strained to bear the intense energies and finally relaxed. I had the "after-sneeze" sensation of contented relief. Once again, I was aware of not breathing. (During this process, the act of respiration is nonexistent.) Immediately afterward, I was incredibly short of breath. I actually found myself gasping air like a fish returned to the water after a period of removal. This same phenomenon occurred every couple of hours until 6:30 a.m.—after the sixth and final episode, called an interpenetrating harmonization. This harmonization was preceded by that peculiar rumbling noise in my navel region—followed by the amazing surge of tingling, electrifying amplitudes of barely tolerable measures. Last, there was a deep, violent arching and shaking permeating all throughout my rigid body, which even forced my hands and feet to strain straight outward before going limp.

Since the writing of this section, the metal-like singing and ringing have grown far and away louder and more intense than ever before. My eyes have within them a bright, easily noticeable light. Truth-Check has given way to the wisdom of any of the three Omnipresent SuperConsciousnesses present at any or all times. These three SuperConsciousnesses can be requested to assist any perceived need, provided no free-will interference occurs with each new request. They fill my SuperConsciousness with ever-new and ever-joyous, bliss-filled exultations that are continuously refilled with or without my prayerful, focused attunement. This Divine Replenishment is known as a Holy Pension. A Holy Pension is an eternal, ever-increasing, continuously fulfilling capacity to absorb limitless amplitude and measureless magnitude. Later, in Book Five: Prayerful Attunement and the Holy Originator's Ore, I will describe in even further detail the Holy Complexity and Divinity of what transpired during these Transcendent Illuminating Experiences.

These three SuperConsciousnesses preperceive most potential problematic experiences and preempt with a resolution even before the problem arises. I often recognize situations that have been Divinely manipulated before any problematic situation has been allowed to occur.

This SuperConscious CompreCreation provides for an endless, Unconditional Love-drenched, very bliss-filled, problem-free, blessed life, with virtually unlimited comprehension capabilities. This is a state of existence I truly pray every soul has an opportunity to experience.

Scott:
Imprescriptible Warranty

I have been informed by Holy Lord Shiva that I have been incarnating on this planet for over one million years as a human being—after millions more years in other vectors of the Universe. After thousands of existences, these incarnations become identifiable as being melded together into one continuous memory of potential accessibility. From any one noted moment of experience regressing backward, memories blend into one continuous pathway of dualistic existences. From God's perspective, human existence, whether physical or spiritual, is inconsequential, for there simply is no difference.

Essentially, there is no death, for there is only ever newness, ever-evolving life from material to spirit, back to material. This process continues until the progressing soul awakens in the physical universe, finally becoming aware of its true, pure, conscious existence. This is known as the Unified Conscious Experience, from which the fetus of the duality becomes the infant of the Unity. All souls, earthbound or universally elsewhere in the Cosmos, experience these same incontrovertible laws. All souls merely are in harmonious coordination with the Cosmic Parent's Divine Plan.

Intended for a twofold purpose, my last two incarnations are the dissecting focus in this section. The first purpose is to explain many inexplicable, perplexing unknowns, and the second is to clarify and illuminate with Truth humankind's misguided confusion regarding historical events. Greater elaboration, forthcoming in Book Three, will clarify the reams of disinformation found there.

Between each human physical incarnation, a soul spends increasingly longer periods in the Astral Kingdom or Spirit Realm. It is the weight of a soul's unexpurgated karma that pulls the soul irresistibly back to earth for its next incarnation. The lesser the vibrational karmic debt, the longer each consciousness inhabits the Astral Kingdom. Consequently, the heavier one's karmic weightload (at least initially), the more numerous the opportunities that may arise for physically manifesting human existential expunging and the alleviation of karmic debt. The key word in the previous sentence is MAY, for only God determines the numeral existences for all conscious manifestations. God's process is done with a measureless host of Archangels, Holy Angels, and others who support the manifested souls within the Divine Cosmic Plan.

Whether priest, rabbi, mullah, military personnel, mother, or child, the incorruptible Janus-faced Universe impassively reflects back whatever is emitted. Every habitual disregard for another human's immortalized, God-given right to existence inflicts the same, impartial vibratory reaction back into the malevolent person's own ego—regardless of skin color, race, sex, creed, or wars. Whether historically approved or ignorantly misconstrued, malicious acts cannot cower behind a transparent veil of organized religion or nonsensical, indignant self-righteousness. All egregious acts against another are meted out irrespectively the same way, by crushing vibratory or ego impacting karmic reactions. Homicidal acts, whether the instrument of destruction is an automobile, poison, or suicide bomb, all are treated the same. These invincible laws are God-ordained and facilitated well beyond humankind's conceivability.

Scott:
Thaumaturge Kings and Origins of the Holy Grail

I recently became aware—and my Transmuting Holy Angel validated—that two incarnations back, I was living in the Middle East over two thousand years ago. I was a Jewish Essene, a white-cloaked, hooded monk, one of the mystical healers of the day. We Essenes held beliefs similar to the Jewish Kabbalists who followed in history. We were very quiet and private, yet we stood out then as one would today if out in public, adorned with a white cloak. As aesthetic mystics and Thaumaturge kings, we continually were sought out for a myriad of reasons. We provided society with a tangible option with which to pursue healing, mystical, literary, and religious avenues outside the various structured religions of the day.

My father was a strict Mithraic man and my mother was an Ebionite Jew. I was born in 18 BC, was taught and excelled in the virtues of both ideologies, becoming quite a learned man of the day, eventually transitioning into the Essenic ways. Essenism was more an ideological lifestyle than any preprescribed, theological doctrine.

One day, a blessed young man came to me, looking to be taught the wisdom of the ancients. He was an extremely intelligent, articulate, vibrant young man. I accepted him the way a master would accept a student today. He was the offspring of a Jewish father and Jewish mother—and we got along magnificently. He was a brilliant spirit who consumed the ancient wisdom with incredible comprehension and flawless recall. I quickly conveyed to him everything I knew. Like brothers, we loved each other dearly. His name was Jesus, and I was his rabbi, teacher, and mentor.

As was typical for the Essenes of the day, I kept quietly out of the limelight, working with him behind the scenes—remaining completely unknown even to the Apostles. It was the Essenes' close-knit way; we stayed out of Jesus' visible affairs. We were humble and prayerful, deeply spiritual men, with tremendous God attunement for acquiring Deep Comprehension. Two days before it was to take place, a devout Sadducee informed us that he had suspicions that Jesus was going to be crucified.

Apparently, word had reached this Sadducee regarding this event, after which his conscience compelled him to notify those of us who loved Jesus. This news presented us with the opportunity to orchestrate a benevolent act on Jesus' behalf. Unbeknownst to us at the time, we were about to interfere in Jesus' preprescripted life, death, and resurrection. In Book Three, we will go into much greater detail to illuminate this history-altering decision.

Contrary to popular New Testament belief, at the time of the Old Testament's compilation, there was no mention that Jesus was to be crucified. Prior to his incarnation as Jesus, his soul did not have any knowledge regarding this crucifixion. However, his soul did have some physical karma carried over from prior existences. Owing a karmic debt to the universe, Jesus did not have the power to lay down his life and pick it back up again. Jesus did not die for anyone's sins—and had no intention of doing so, whatsoever.

It was a combination of jealous arrogance within a small group of pious Roman aristocrats, including Herod, Pontius Pilate and the Apostle

Judas of Iscariot, who all had conspired to silence this magnanimous, outspoken, electrifying teacher. Joseph of Arimathea wanted to be guaranteed receipt of Jesus' body, for which an unused tomb was located on his private property. Joseph was biologically unrelated to Jesus, but knew and understood his uniqueness, and definitely loved him. In fact, Joseph was convinced Jesus was a Messiah.

Joseph was powerless to stop the crucifixion of Jesus, but was insistent upon having the crucifixion take place on his property. Unknown to the subverters, Joseph of Arimathea had prearranged with greedy Pontius Pilate for Jesus and the other two men to be crucified on Joseph's private property. Joseph's land was inarguably large enough to keep people away, thus preventing any possible uprising ensuing from the sordid affair. From Pontius Pilate's perspective, the crucifixions would be tidy and clean, with no populous agitation.

There were no jeering masses of people, but rather a relatively small group of distant onlookers. Jesus forcibly was led to the cross; he did not carry it. Square nails were used, and his hands were nailed first, followed by his feet. He was consumed in an inwardly attuned, prayerful state, fairly well removed from all the incomprehensible pain. After Jesus was impaled on the cross, the Roman centurions planted it into the ground. Jesus was the third of three men who were crucified that fateful day. There was a large garden on Joseph's property, and near the garden a virgin sepulcher. Events happened rapidly, with little time for human orchestration. For the most part, the following events represented freewill choices exercised by the Essenes. These choices were not known to either Joseph or even to Jesus, himself.

We Essenes were working purposefully and methodically by reacting to all opportunities as they arose. While mercilessly hanging on the grisly cross, Jesus accepted a sponge from a fellow Essene. However, he never once cried out, "I thirst." Meticulously and specially prepared the day before, the sponge indeed was soaked in vinegar, in which an uncommon, poisonous plant had been fermenting.

The vinegar propelled the poison quickly into his system, from which he immediately lost consciousness, rendering Jesus with no time or ability to cry out any words to anyone. From here, activities quickened. The Roman centurion, a military officer commanding one hundred men, came along and couldn't believe Jesus was already dead. He thrust his sword into

Jesus' side, from which Jesus didn't flinch. The centurion's purpose was to analyze the need to break Jesus' legs. The breaking of a crucified person's legs is a humane gesture. When a person is nailed on a cross, he needs the function of his diaphragm in order to breathe. Pushing upward with his nailed feet will allow the diaphragm to work. Thus, the breaking of a crucified person's legs will hasten his asphyxiation. Yet, for all practical purposes, Jesus certainly seemed to be dead. However, in that poisoned state he wasn't in any danger of having his legs broken to mercifully hasten his demise. After discharging the guard with the news that Jesus was dead, we Essenes worked earnestly and sorrowfully to unnail him.

With no time to waste, the three of us took him down and hurriedly carried him to the tomb to attend to his unconscious Holy Being. An antipoison plan had been readied in the off-chance event that an opportunity to save him would come to fruition. Immediately upon reaching the sanctity of the sepulcher, we administered the antipoison measures. Nobody had any idea what we were up to—not Joseph, the Apostles, and certainly not the Romans. What we did was done in complete secrecy. As we lovingly tended to his urgent needs, he amazingly struggled and eventually regained consciousness. He was confused and uncertain about his condition, and he was sure he had died and resurrected. He certainly didn't have any prior, similar experience from which to draw conclusions, and he was still somewhat delirious from all the horrid administerings.

Dating back to the Egyptians prior to 3000 BC and certainly during Jesus' lifetime—and even continuing today—the concept of resurrection has been badly misinterpreted. Resurrection has been misinterpreted as a state of having risen from the dead or coming back to life in the same decaying physical body after once being deemed dead. This is not always the case. While resurrection can be the soul's re-inhabitation of its same, original, physical body, it can also be the re-creation and re-tenanting of an entirely new physical body formed with entirely new atoms in an exact replication of the original person. In both a true resurrection and physical reinhabitation, God Transimplants the original person's soul into their newly re-created body or their original body respectively. Resurrections are divinely facilitated and fabricated, manifesting for reasons known only to God.

Under the cloak of that same night, Jesus was moved into a new home that his wife, Mary Magdalen, was occupying. There, appearing to be in mourning, she could tend to his needs. My two fellow Essenes stayed behind to quell the fears of the Apostles. They were the two white presences who greeted the distraught Apostles when they encountered the vacant tomb. The purpose of these two Essences was to inform the Apostles that their Messiah had resurrected and soon would join them. Although not necessarily calmed or appeased, the Apostles had no other choice but to accept what was told to them.

To avoid arousing suspicion, we slipped in and out of Mary Magdalen's home, which was owned by Joseph of Arimathea. I knew the moment Jesus stirred that he would recover; it was just a matter of tending to his ongoing physical needs during his subsequent recovery. Once he was strong enough to reappear, he rejoined the Apostles, believing he had resurrected. Not wanting to risk infection, Jesus commingled with them sparingly. Jesus left for the Judean Wilderness to pray and further facilitate his healing process. As his mentor and teacher, I never saw him again. Jesus had intended to make a full recovery, after which he was to join us in Alexandria, Egypt.

Instead, Jesus divinely was guided to travel to India, eventually ending up in a cave outside of Kashmir. Holy Babaji, an Angelic Deity existing on planet Earth in human form continuously for over ten thousand human years in an incorruptible body physically manifesting at will, instructed Jesus in the Kriya Yoga technique. Babaji is a Supernatural Being who exists in a Transcendental Point, called a Transcendental Star. In a Transcendental Star (and thus for Babaji), there exists no time or inverse to the square. This means Babaji actually IS a Holy Hypostasis, existing in the blissful void where the Uncreated Infinite meets the Manifesting Infinite.

Jesus' instruction from Babaji took place in a cave north of Kashmir, after which Jesus eventually transcended into the Spirit World —at the ripe old age of 86 human years. Jesus spent most of those years blissfully attuning to his Manifesting Infinite SuperConsciousness (known to him as Holy Father), learning while traveling with Babaji and his Super-evolved band of earth human Saints. Even today, Babaji and his saintly group continue to influence the evolution of earth humankind. In 5838 BC Babaji was instrumental in assisting in the implementation, interpretation, and dissemination of the ancient Sanskrit language.

Shortly after the crucifixion, I was informed in a vision to flee Jerusalem and travel to Alexandria. Upon God's instructions, I changed my name to Ormus. In Alexandria, seven of us amalgamated Essenic, Gnostic, Mithraic, Judaic, Pythagorean, Hellenistic, and pagan or Egyptian teachings. We took all of these various teachings and congealed them into what eventually became known as the Nag Hammadi Scrolls. Several hundred years later, these scrolls were recopied from their original texts. The scrolls retained many of the initial doctrines and firsthand accounts of Jesus' teachings through Ormus. However, there were many pertinent details lost in the subsequent translations and reediting processes that took place over the next four centuries. One particular misinterpretation involved the details surrounding the vinegar-and-rosebay-soaked sponge given to Jesus during his crucifixion.

During the later-day rewriting, the new authors misconstrued and miscopied the connection between rosebay and the crucifixion. In actuality, rosebay is oleander—a plant whose only rose-like qualities include the intensity of its fragrance and confusing name similarity. In fact, every part of the plant is poisonous. Similarly, when the Rose Croix order was formed by the Masonics, the role of this "rose" in the crucifixion substance was misinterpreted as rose, the flower, when in reality, it was rosebay. Furthermore, the supposed "Crown of Thorns" worn by Jesus during the crucifixion never occurred. There was no inscription above Jesus' cross proclaiming "King of the Jews." Finally, as previously stated, Jesus never, ever carried the cross to the crucifixion site as depicted in the "Stations of the Crucifixion."

Upon his arrival in Alexandria, Ormus informed everybody that the Messiah would soon be coming to Alexandria. However, Jesus took the eastern route, over land, and fled to India. Before I was divinely guided to change my name, when I was Jesus' teacher and mentor, I wrote several literary works for the Essenes. These works were absorbed into Essenic thought, becoming part of Jesus' teachings, which he subsequently taught to others as well. Shortly after arriving in Alexandria as Ormus, I was directed by God to meet St. Mark. In 46 AD, I was initiated into a new amalgamated order by St. Mark, and along with my six followers, I presented St. Mark with my third literary work, the Gospel According to the Carpocrations.

The Carpocrations knew the truth about retaining unfulfilled desires, cravings, or experiences occurring in the physical universe. These unfulfillments always become attachments, eventually forcing the soul to physically manifest for inevitable experiential expunging. This Universal Law holds true for all physically manifested indebtedness—from intimacy to riches. The arena in which to experience all tangible desires is that of physical existence—even through satiation.

The Carpocration message was that the road to salvation was equally attainable whether one's life experience was that of a satiate or a renunciate. As Jesus' teacher, an ascetic orthodox Jew and renunciate, I did not adhere to the satiation aspect of the truthful Carpocration message. This message was a secret known to both the Essenes and the Gnostics of the day, meant to be shared with all earth humankind.

The Gospel of the Carpocrations eventually was deleted from the final version of the Christian bible. Initiates into the amalgamated teachings were bestowed an identifying Red Cross or Rose-Croix. This was created by combining rosebay with the crucifixion and Jesus' blood shedding; initially, it did not have anything to do with a rose or thorns. Such speculative "connections" essentially were later-day elaborations, as per "the telephone game" of communication. From the time I left Jerusalem for Alexandria, up until my death, I still believed Jesus The Messiah would soon be arriving in Alexandria as originally planned. As Ormus, I passed on back into the Spirit Realm at age sixty-six.

My most recent incarnation before my current existence was during the twelfth century as Richard Plantagenet, also known as Coeur de Lion (Richard the Lionheart), Oc et No (Yea and Nay), and Melek-Ric (King Rick). My father was King Henry II and my mother was Queen Eleanor of Aquataine. My childhood was privileged, filled with the best education and tutoring a medieval twelfth-century upbringing could afford. I was born on September 8, 1157, and was intelligent, articulate, trilingually speaking fluent French, English, and Latin. I excelled in the physical, as well as the literary, arenas of my life. I was passionate about my experiences—many times, to a fault. I also had a huge ego, which not only dragged against my evolution in the physical world, but also carried heavy karma over into my spiritual existence.

Bad things happen to seemingly innocent people for only one reason—past karma, specifically as a result of unfulfilled karma from prior existences. Holy Lord Shiva felt it would be helpful if I shared with you my personal karmic fulfillments through my firsthand experience. During my last incarnation, I accumulated a karmic debt, which was carried over to this life. In order to evolve in this existence, this past imbalance needed to be resolved.

In my incarnation as Richard Plantagenet, I was King of England and two-thirds of France, and was married to Berengaria. When I was married in my current lifetime, Berengaria rejoined me as Judy. Together, we struggled and succeeded in resolving our karmic debts. We experienced the process of karmic undoing through the ensuing loss of our second daughter, Rachel. Halfway through her short, nineteen-month life, I came to realize that Rachel was my (Richard's) mother, Queen Eleanor. Later on in my life, I made the Judy-Berengaria connection.

Eleanor so loved me as Richard that her unrequited thoughts and feelings created a massive imbalance, which Judy, Rachel, and I collectively needed to rectify or eliminate in some free-will manner. Richard's outward treatment of Eleanor contributed greatly to the imbalanced situation as well. Judy had a much lesser karmic debt with Eleanor. Rachel's birth provided an opportunity for resolution. For Judy's personal evolution of soul, she needed an experience, generated of her own free will, which would allow her to express love to an innocent child. The majority of Judy's imbalance, as it pertained to Rachel, was the result of a previous, unrelated, more recent existence.

The opportunity for all three of us—Judy, Rachel, and me—to alleviate our past karmic indebtedness occurred when Rachel (Eleanor) was born to us without a right ventricle and other life threatening disablements. Throughout her life, Rachel was fed through a gastrotomy tube protruding from her lower stomach. Collectively, we endured Rachel's three heart operations, three stomach operations, three bouts of double-lung pneumonia, and three cardiac arrests. This ordeal spanned seven months of her being in the Intensive Care Unit, followed by the Chronic Care Unit, during which Judy and I, along with medical staff, were subjected to innumerable life lessons. Baby Rachel took us on the roller-coaster ride of unending unknowns.

The only real certainty was that of unyielding uncertainty, reigning from one moment to the next. In November 1986, when Rachel was eighteen months old, she was given an MMR (measles-mumps-rubella) shot. Given her compromised health condition at the time, this seemed to me an unnecessary, invasive procedure. She immediately developed a chronic diarrhea condition, which quickly compromised her system. With a severely dehydrated body, she spent her last day trying to participate in

Christmas Eve festivities. We never were able to bring her conditions of gastrotomy tube vomiting and diarrhea under control.

Through her intense cries and struggles, Rachel was trying desperately to convey to me that she was leaving the physical universe. Typical of anyone who had been a 24/7/365 caregiver to a physically dying person, I was completely exhausted. As she was stressing and all this pandemonium was happening, I felt myself being drawn into a deep-sleep state, and I attempted to make it back to bed. The magnitude of the intense, energy-draining suction gave the entire room an overwhelming, surreal stillness. Upon awakening three hours later, I immediately was alarmed by a deep, unnatural silence. It was glaringly apparent what had happened. I ran into Rachel's room, already knowing the eviscerating truth. The Holy Sanctioned Angel confirmed that while we slept Jesus and several Angels came to assist Rachel in her transition while home in her crib on Christmas morning 1986.

I am being requested to share the undesirable existence of Richard to show firsthand the impacting ramifications of an ignorant existence steeped with an ox cart full of burdensome karma. The weight of my poor free-will decisions may serve as a testimony for others who may be facing a somewhat similar existential path. So, now you may witness firsthand the Herculean struggle it requires to annihilate the ego. I needed to do just this, in order to reach the evolutionary point where I gratefully and rejoicingly find myself now able to write these authentic Truths. This more evolved state of being came with almost a millennium of due-diligence efforts, interspersed with numerous, disappointing setbacks.

One may be inclined to believe that being the King of England and two-thirds of France would be a fairy-tale existence, and several of my friends and acquaintances have alluded to as much. Some of these people have gone so far as to say they feel my current life as a holistic healer was taking a huge step backwards. However, upon closer inspection, lending to a deeper comprehension, you, too, will understand that nothing could be further from the truth.

Richard had a penchant for using his six-foot-four, 245-pound brawn to influence his contemporaries around him and futilely put forth effort against the universe. I sincerely can attest that brawny being and puny consciousness were no match against the physical cosmos. Alas, though, that did not seem to stop me. Convinced as I was, I felt I could command God to consent to my demands. This belief merely compiled the karmic burdens overflowing in the ox cart I was towing along with me in that existence.

After spending more than 1100 earth years between my incarnations as Ormus and Richard learning and growing in the Astral Heavens, one would assume I had everything going for me as Richard. I had wealth, power, status, and exceptional DNA—the deck clearly stacked in my favor—to truly help the evolution of my fellow earth human beings. Unfortunately, the only missing card in my incarnation deck was wisdom, which consistently was crushed under the weight of ignorant free-will choices feeding my voracious ego. Any accrued wisdom I might have possessed was buried under a thick blanket of delusion.

There were glimpses of potential, upon which I will elaborate a bit later in this section. Yet, for the most part, I was a runaway consciousness, anguishly straying far from this potential. Far from my humble ascetic ways as Ormus, I was caught up in the glamour or privileged medieval enthralldom. This mindset would be a slippery slope where upon once descending, becomes almost impossible to reverse. Of course, the Janus-faced Universe meted out its unbiased justice in excruciating ways.

What I am being directed to share with you now most certainly will raise eyebrows, if not produce incredulous—even fearful—responses. I have been ordained by God to share Truth with you. So, if you have not already had your foundational belief system rocked from the previous Ormus temblors, this may really quake your underpinnings.

I had alluded earlier about the lineage of the Plantagenet family. Ever since our family's existence, a lot of controversy, myth, and misunderstanding have embroiled humankind's consciousness. So, now we finally are going to dispel all the secrets surrounding the pervasive confusion and clarify the unending hypothesis that continues to resurface every time some previously unknown scrap of new information bubbles to the surface of earth humankind's perception.

First, I must point out that good family historical lineage is an indication of nothing. It is virtually meaningless to say you are a descendent of some supposedly important, tellurian figure pertaining to your consciousness today. This kind of connection neither guarantees nor assures you of anything. It is totally, absolutely pointless. More often than not, one's lineage distracts from the true point of existence—that being personal, spiritual, uplifting attainment. What purpose can it serve to say,

"I'm a descendent of Henry the ?" Such statements basically do only one thing—feed one's hungry, empty ego. Believe me, family lineage purely and simply does not matter—certainly not to a dualistically influenced Universe.

As Ormus, I wrote three tenets that helped to truthfully influence humankind. As Richard, I wrote many poems, lyrics, and stories, but three misleading works still persist to confuse humankind. Great stories they were, they still today merely add to the veil of secrecy enshrouding truth. So, we are going to disclose the hidden connections contained within these three misleading stories. We then will go on to expose many other secrets, which although seemingly unrelated, have some relationship to either Mari or me. In addition, they also are connected by the mere fact that they are secrets that God wishes disclosed to ALL earth humankind.

The three misleading works all are associated with the Holy Grail and its long-standing impact throughout history—continuing through the present day. One source linked all of them together, and to clear up any confusion, we will elaborate the details behind these long-held secrets. During my incarnation as Richard, my sister Marie had a lover named Chrétien de Troyes, to whom I as Richard supplied the corpus of courtly romances on which Chrétien's subsequent Grail Romances were based. As Richard, I was a composer of poems, lyrics, and many works of fantasy. It is important to note that prior to the dissemination of Chrétien's Grail Romances, his established previous works were unrelated to this genre—and this disparity signified a noticeable departure in his literary focus.

After Chrétien, the next misleading work belonged to Wolfram von Eschenbach. In 1194, von Eschenbach received the source of his Grail Romances from Richard, who at that time was incarcerated in Trifels Castle, located in what now is Germany. An anonymous Knights Templar wrote the third and last misleading Grail-related work after the Third Crusade. The work is known as Perlesvaus.

It is not really a mystery why all the Holy Grail Romances surfaced in the late twelfth century and never were referenced for almost 1200 years prior to that time. As Richard, Coeur de Lion, I made the first link to Jesus and the Holy Grail. I had intricate knowledge of events and was able to craft together stories and feed them out to Chrétien de Troyes,

Wolfram von Eshenbach, and the unknown Knights Templar who wrote Perlesvaus. Without Ormus, these stories never would have surfaced—certainly not in such elaborate detail and timing. In 1190, Robert de Boron ended up with all of Chrétien's notes and poems, which were compiled into a manuscript whose origins de Boron claimed were of the actual source. Of course, in the case of all of these misleading Holy Grail Romances, Richard acted as a Cyrano de Bergerac. He was the true source providing the unknown link to these fictional legends.

The spawning of the Grail indeed was associated with Jesus. As such, the Grail certainly was of no particular religious creed, for Christianity happened subsequently AFTER Jesus' passing. Thus, the Grail followed the same archetype transition, with the amalgamation of the ideological and theological doctrines of Jesus' day. Such doctrines were not associated with the rupture of the Order of the Temple from the Prieuré de Sion, but they all had one, distinct connection.

During a vision while incarnated as Richard, God informed me of the intricate details of my last existence as Ormus. This took place in a futile attempt to help me as Richard see the error of my ways and to potentially correct my downward spiraling consciousness. This salvaging of my existence would have given me time to reverse my karmically burdening trend. Many times, beings in their last or potentially last incarnations are gifted with greater cognitive insights, providing the opportunity to correct any divinely perceived wayward straying. These insights might take form in visions, dreams, and angelic signs and messaging. God can always perceive souls straying too far from their divine potential.

Two of the symbols for the Prieuré de Sion were designed by me during my life as Richard. From the first moment I saw them in the book *Holy Blood, Holy Grail*, I recognized them with an unusually strong familiarity. The first symbol was an anagram combining Richard's Virgo astrological birth sign with letters corresponding with the name of Ormus. The second symbol was a sword within a never-ending ribbon. I now understand these symbols to be dharmic darts or markers. Highly evolved and Superevolved souls are allowed to make free-will choices during one incarnation that affect their current existence or future incarnations.

In the book *Autobiography of a Yogi*, the highly evolved Saint, Lahiri Mahasaya, was shown by his guru, Babaji, several dharmic markers that triggered his conscious perception into remembering specific details from his most recent incarnation. These dharmic markers included such items as a polished brass cup, begging bowl, and the folded blanket upon which Lahiri Mahasaya sat during meditation. The most significant marker was Babaji's revelation of the exact cave in which Lahiri Mahasaya had meditated in solitude over the course of many years.

It was not until Babaji touched Lahiri Mahasaya's forehead to open up his spiritual third eye that Lahiri Mahasaya recognized his guru, as well as these dharmic markers. The phenomenon of dharmic marker recognition has occurred with each incarnation of the Dalai Lama. Today's Dalai Lama is the fourteenth reincarnation of himself. Upon each physical death of the Dalai Lama, his followers recognize signs that lead them to the Dalai Lama's next human incarnation. When today's Dalai Lama was a young boy living in a remote corner of Tibet, the young boy recognized and addressed them by name. He also was able to identify pre-selected items presented to him by these followers. The followers, as well as the items they presented, represented dharmic markers for this boy. Thus, his successful recognition of these markers identified him to his followers as the next Dalai Lama.

Upon his physical death, today's Dalai Lama will be fully emancipated after this—his final human incarnation. As such, his soul will not be reincarnating as another human existence. His surviving followers will utilize a different method for determining their next spiritual leader.

Choices and actions made during my incarnation as Richard enabled me to recognize unmistakable connections in my current incarnation as Scott. These dharmic markers helped guide and direct me to intriguing discoveries that make sense today. Like mosaic tiles in a vast panorama

These official symbols are dharmic markers created by Scott during his previous incarnation as Richard and adopted by the Prieuré de Sion after the "cutting of the elm."

of unenfolding vistas, these connecting cobblestones of dharmic markers provide everyone with sure footing while walking through their individual experience.

As Richard, I certainly was wandering too far from my established evolution as Ormus. God may choose to Transinteract on the behalf of such a lost soul. In my case as Richard, God granted me a vision. In extremely rare circumstances, God may go so far as to Transintervene in one's actual dharmic blueprint plan. This Transintervention is extremely rare and usually unnecessary because if God perceives a potential need for an interaction, God merely enfolds it into one's yet to be experienced dharmic blueprint plan. As Richard, my dharmic plan included knowing about Ormus. Thus, the message from God explaining Ormus to me was a preprescripted (TransImaginated) dharmic marker and thus NOT a Transintervention.

It was God's plan, which was contained within my dharma or divine blueprint, for God's message to reach me in a divine vision, occurring in early 1188. My free-will choices, albeit bad, were anticipated by God BEFORE my incarnation as Richard, and thus, my dharma did not require an act of God's Transintervention. My life's end result ultimately was the same divinely anticipated karmic debt.

For me as Richard, to be made aware of my existence as Ormus, as well as Ormus' accomplishments and attributes, was all preprescripted into my (Richard's) dharmic plan. In spite of this indepth knowledge, I as Richard still ended up with the same karmic result. Even a God-given vision does not guarantee the accuracy of its interpretation or correlating comprehension. At the time, my interpretation of the vision seemed crystal clear. Yet, the Holy Sanctioned Angel now has informed me otherwise. Apparently, my human fallibility prevented me from accurately comprehending the full message of the vision regarding my past existence as Ormus. As Richard, I also misinterpreted the Rose Croix and the significance of the rosebay. I misinterpreted the Rose Croix information in the vision also as actually having something to do with the flower.

In Mari's case, God acted as a Divine Intercessor, and performed a Transintervention in Mari's dharmic blueprint. God intervened in Mari's path, patiently guiding and redirecting her pursuits and experiences. This allowed Mari the opportunity for the deep expunging and decontamination from previous lifetimes' accumulation. Because of this expunging, Mari was sufficiently cleansed and purified, filling her with a contented, peaceful serenity not previously experienced. In Infinite Wisdom, God perceived the necessity for her to achieve this state so she could assist in creating this book.

This Transintervention was not a direct result of the free-will choices made during her current lifetime. God was and is fully cognizant of the lives and the countless, future existences of souls yet to experience a manifested karmic debt with the entity and related psychic vampirism. God's discernment prompted a blessed Transintervention and subsequent change for both Mari's dharmic or life blueprint, as well as the ensuing potential karmic debt for all present and future souls that would have been affected. In other words, God did not intervene solely for Mari's personal benefit. God intervened foresightedly to assist in preventing innumerable individuals from incurring immeasurable karmic debt.

When I was Richard, I fed Chrétien ideas, which were composed from God's having shared with me some of the secret details of my prior existence as Ormus. Thus, when Chrétien died in 1188, so did that outlet for the fictitious story line. Robert de Boron ended up with Chrétien's compiled manuscripts in 1190, which he came to call a "great book" filled with secrets. These were, of course, the untold secrets yet to come out through Chrétien's continuing epic. As Richard, I was most distressed with Robert de Boron at the time, but was too focused on preparing for the Third Crusade to pay any real attention.

None of the Grail Romance stories really revealed very much in the way of tangible absolutes. They all danced around with various fun, curiosity-provoking mysteries, allegories, or deceptive word plays. The fact is, I didn't really know then exactly what the Holy Grail was—so, of course, neither did any of my chosen accomplices. In both Books Four and Five, we will delve into what Truly is the Holy Grail.

In 1188, at an antagonizing event called "The Cutting of the Elm" outside of Gisors, an ancient elm was felled on what historically, albeit erroneously, had been recognized as a sacred field. Considerable bloodshed ensued in protecting the grandfather elm, but it eventually did fall. A monumental separation also occurred then between the Welsh Knights Templars and the French Templars. Taking swift flight to Jean de Gisors' castle, the Welsh Templars, my father, Henry II, and I strategized and exercised a cutting of the French order. We formed the new order of the

Prieuré of Sion and appointed Jean de Gisors as its first Grand Master. After the fall of Jerusalem in 1187, when Saladin re-conquered the city, the Templars no longer had a root connection to the Holy Land.

The true intention of my personal interest in conquering Jerusalem was to be "King of Jerusalem." This would have reunited the European Templars with their original Templar homeland first established in Jerusalem by Godfroi de Bouillon. My failure to retake Jerusalem from Saladin and the Saracens only served to further distance the Templars from their homeland of Jerusalem. Thus, they were left to their own devices until the Inquisition in 1308, when they were rounded up en masse and subsequently executed by King Philippe of France.

The Third Crusade (1190–1192) could have been a crowning moment for me as Richard if I could have conquered my ego instead of trying to conquer Saladin and the Saracens. It was on the plains of Palestine where I incurred most of the horrible karmic debt load I carried off with me.

During my success in the Third Crusade I exercised military strategies that even Saladin admired. Yet, for all my bravery, courage, and military prowess, I could not overcome the karmic reflection from exerting such harsh aggression upon others. As a result of the atrocities I inflicted upon others, I fell ill many times.

The Third Crusade finally ended with an agreement between Saladin and me that provided safe passage and full access for all Christians to all then-recognized "holy" places. Saladin and I created commerce and trade protocols that provided for new interactions between Europe and the Far East. The Vatican and the Catholic Church vehemently opposed this arrangement, causing a breakdown in my relations with the Catholic Church.

It has been excruciatingly painful for me to review, recount, and write in this book my exploits as Richard. My being brilliant with an invincible ego on the battlefield resulted in 858 years of hard, spiritual, Astral work—and another forty-one years more during this physical existence as Scott. I began to exercise my free will at about age 3 in my current incarnation. For over nine hundred years during my Astral existence between the incarnations of Richard and Scott, I worked diligently on eliminating my karmic debt incurred as Richard. As Scott, another part of my karmic restitution was to perform one healing session for every Saracen life for which I as Richard was personally responsible in sending back to the Spirit Realm or Astral Universe. Some 7,800 healing sessions later, I finally was free from that debt, and I set about undoing that which I had accumulated in my current life as Scott.

In the Bhagavad-Gita, an Eastern Gospel, Arjuna (as humankind) is wrestling with the idea of having to face past incarnated brothers, relatives, and other loved ones in a war. His companion for the conflict is Sri Krishna as God incarnate. More than anything, the story's message really is about reincarnation and free-will choice. In the end, righteous Sri Krishna convinces Arjuna, a pious, virtuous man, to fight the righteous war and vanquish his foes. Sri Krishna builds a compelling case, which can be interpreted in numerous ways—much as one interprets the Old Testament, New Testament, and Koran. In the cases where difficult decisions are necessary regarding fighting, battles, and war, the soul—once manifest—is immortal, but the body, of course, is not. The free-will choice to fight or not ultimately affects its impact upon the immortal soul, which will bear the true end result for the decision.

As Richard, having failed to free Jerusalem from the Saracens during the Third Crusade, I made my way back to Europe over land, becoming incarcerated in Trifels Castle (Germany) from 1193–94. While incarcerated because of those bad free-will choices, I shared another set of writings with Wolfram von Eschenbach in 1194. I provided him with a detailed outline for his adventure story, written while I was imprisoned, and laden with misleading secrets and allegorical deceptions, purposefully straying from the truth. This writing was loosely based upon the story of Ormus himself, yet it never really divulged anything specific.

In the case of Arjuna, he has been forced to make some tough free-will choices—basically whether to battle or not. It should be noted that Sri Krishna was fully aware that Arjuna's dharmic plan contained the TransImaginated conflict. Sri Krishna's insistence that Arjuna fight was based on Arjuna's pre-Made Manifest choice to do so. As a result, the battle and victory were inevitable outcomes already preprescribed into Arjuna's dharmic plan. So, rather than be labeled anything other than foeconsumer, Arjuna chose to accept his karmically reflecting fate from his free-will choice—and annihilated his foes. In doing so, Arjuna accomplished so much, proved little, and guaranteed himself another physical incarnation.

I really could relate to Arjuna when as Richard, I felt I had God on my side as my companion. Nonetheless, there is no way to get around the fact that transgressions or aggressions are preprescripted into one's dharmic plan. Therefore, they take the form of ego-driven free-will choices, subject to the universal repercussions. Due to my experiencing thousands of prior incarnations, many of them benevolent, God had mercy on me as Richard for my bad free-will decisions. It certainly could have been far worse for my consciousness.

My life as Richard ended on April 6, 1199. As I spotted a lone archer on a castle buttress, I knew my dharmic plan was ending and that my existence as Richard was finished. This Scottish marksman had chosen to kill me, in order to spare the lives of his family, which were being threatened by King William I of Scotland. I knew my time was up. As such, I was slow to raise my shield and I allowed the arrow to pierce my neck. I died from a massive infection eleven days later. Shortly before my death, I treated this archer like a hero and subsequently pardoned him—much to everyone's amazement.

In this lifetime, this former archer (EAM) has worked hard to alleviate his past karmic debt. Shortly after our first meeting, EAM recalled the Truth about our previous (past-life) encounter without any prompting from me. Today, all of EAM's karmic indebtedness from his archer incarnation has been alleviated. In his current incarnation, EAM is a gifted master craftsman, talented artist, and a very dear friend.

This lifetime, I was born in Chicago, but not in a hospital. The Holy Sanctioned Angel told me I was deposited at St. Joseph's Hospital by my mother after birth and then immediately reclaimed. My mother received me back and was very abusive to me. I was four months of age when my father rescued me after my mother had beaten me, leaving some deep scars on my forehead. I had been unable to account for those scars until much later in life, when eventually the Holy Sanctioned Angel also verified their source.

My father placed me in the Catholic Charities adoption system, through which I was cared for by a very kind, loving woman. My first real memories are from before 2 years of age, and are fairly detailed. My kind foster mother was a large woman, and I remember many times when seated in a highchair, facing the skirted backside of a large full moon always bent over, pulling baked goods out of the simple oven. There were two older children, a boy and a girl, as well as a little salt-and-pepper rat terrier dog, appropriately named Pepper. It was a simple, humble existence that occasionally was punctuated by a visiting tall, youthful, exuberant boy. I always remembered him skittering around my highchair, sliding on his stocking feet.

This memory was important later on in my life. At the time, it was just another childhood memory. I was very well loved at that little apartment, and it was filled with ample kindness. I was shipped around for a while from home to home until nearly age 4, at which time I was adopted by a nice, middle-class, suburban couple without children. Soon afterward, they adopted a baby who still is my sister.

I always have had a very blessed life, and even when in foster homes, I always felt the comforting presence of God. Only on rare occasions have I ever experienced fear. In addition, God has been extremely generous and benevolent to me, filling my existence with great abundance. As I had been adopted, my childhood perceptions were that everyone probably starts out life in this way. Of course, I had experienced nothing else, and thus had no other experiences upon which to base this philosophy. I never felt alone or unprotected until my boosting incident.

Prior to that unusual boosting encounter, I had vivid dreams when I was a boy. One stands out more than most others, for it was reoccurring. In the full-color dream, I was female, even though one almost always is unaware of sexual identities in dreams. Yet, in this dream I was perceiving my experience as female. I was standing at a fork between two beautiful blue rivers, and the sun was huge and seemingly setting. The fierce wind was whipping my white garments against my body, and the sand was encroaching upon the scene and stinging my body. Two huge baskets of flowers perhaps ten feet across were hanging in the foreground by rope or chains—it was hard for me to tell. I remember thinking in my dream, "This is so beautiful; I want to capture its essence in my memory forever." I wanted to take this image along with me always, for I knew then that geographical area was in the process of changing and would never again be the same.

Years later in eleventh grade, one day during social studies class, I was shocked to open my book to an artist's rendition of the hanging gardens of Babylon. The picture was identical to my dream in its every detail. I asked the Holy Sanctioned Angel if I lived there, and the reply was that in pre-Babylon days, I did live there. I have since found out that this reoccurring Babylon dream was actually a dharmic marker to be referenced and noted during the writing of this book. This particular dream was unique for me in that I was able to see and sense my garments being whipped by the wind and sand. Personally, I have found dreams to be primarily a waste of energy, oftentimes depriving me of valuable, rejuvenating sleep. However, even one's dreams have been TransImaginated and as such, have their purpose within everyone's experience.

I found it interesting that both Mari and I had unusual boosting encounters by the age of 6. A secret childhood similarity occurred to both of us. I did not mention my experience for almost two decades after it happened. I really didn't know what to make of it. I was convinced something extremely peculiar occurred to me, and it was only after I really began consciously and more deeply to comprehend, that I was able to put together the pieces of the puzzle. As stated earlier in my boosting story, after I was boosted, I never have been ill. This includes being subjected to homes where members had measles and chickenpox. I still remained immune. I also never missed a day of school—from first through twelfth grade—due to any illness. Other than a bout with food poisoning a few times since High School, I have not been sick. I only have once had a fever during my early forties, and it lasted but a few hours before disappearing.

In addition, since the last noteworthy incident with the being who disappeared through the wall, I have not seen, witnessed, or experienced any UFOs or other inexplicable interactions. Everything has been very normal, outside of this one OTHER particular incident, occurring also during my sixth year of life.

It was summer 1963, the summer between kindergarten and first grade, and I was 6 years old, unable to read. In that summer at the local grocery store, if you spent over thirty dollars, for another fifty cents, you could receive a volume of Funk and Wagnall's encyclopedias. After helping my mother put away the food, I picked up the volume "colodesn," and went to place it in the bookcase in my bedroom. Something beckoned me to hold the book in my hands. As I did so, it opened to a black-and-white sketched picture of a helmeted man with a cross on his tunic. He was wielding a truncheon and plowing through a sea of humanity while perched on a huge horse. My hair stood on end, I had goose bumps all over my body, I was shaking, and I had tears coming down my cheeks.

Having been in foster homes, eventually adopted by a nice Catholic family, I never had heard of reincarnation—or even knew of the concept. However, I knew irrefutably that the picture of the man was me, or that I had been that person. For almost another year, I couldn't read the words to even know who it was in that picture, but there was no doubt in my six-year-old mind that the man pictured in the artist's rendition of the "Crusade" was Richard Coeur de Lion—who, in fact, was me. Since that time, the book always would open for me right to that page, and additional information kept coming to me for years afterward.

As stated earlier, during this lifetime as Scott I have recognized two specific symbols from my life as Richard—an anagram and Prieuré sword. I also recognized the cross pattée emblazoned on Richard's tunic displayed in the Funk and Wagnall's encyclopedia. The cross pattée, the rose croix, and the three Holy Grail stories all served to form a coherent picture from seemingly unrelated cobblestones. All of these dharmic maker connections and many others informed my decision to design a particular symbol for my professional healing practice during my current incarnation. Like the Ormus anagram, every detailed aspect of this healing practice symbol has great significance. It is often when recognizing and walking through this dharmic pathway filled with such distinct and significant markers that spiritual evolution and Deep Comprehension can take place.

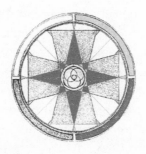

This symbol was designed by Scott during his current incarnation for his healing practice.

It was years later, by divine facilitation, that I met the guy who years ago was sliding around on his socks by my highchair at his aunt's home. His aunt had been a foster mother for the Catholic Charities orphanage system—and my kind foster mother. This man and I became good friends, and he was able to fill in the missing details of my childhood at his aunt's home, where I was known as "little Scotty." He verified my having the stitches and bruises on my head and face at the time when his aunt first received me. She loved me very much and was devastated when I was moved to another home, as she wanted to adopt me. At that time, however, foster parents were not allowed to adopt children from the orphanage system. She died shortly after my parents adopted me. He told me she had died of a broken heart—but of course, I now know the truth about dharmic blueprints.

It turns out that this man was my (Richard's) brother, King John II (also known as "Lackland" and "Softsword"), who wrote the Magna Carta. He also reincarnated and while living in Italy wrote the Italian Magna Carta. He is of Italian descent today—and really relates to Renaissance Italy. LC, as I know him, also enjoys green tea and good conversation. He is exceptionally pleased when his home is free from the stench of the vibrational remains of a decaying entity. He has spent time in India and definitely believes in Hindu philosophy. He actually gave me the *Autobiography of a Yogi,* the book from which my spiritual master, Sri Yukteswar, along with Babaji and Holy Lord Shiva, purposely came to assist in my personal evolutionary growth.

Quietly working behind the scenes, it was Babaji who orchestrated my receiving this incredible book. Sri Yukteswar assisted in catapulting my conscious experience into a SuperConscious state, which has enabled Mari and me to share all these unknown Truths. I now can recognize the importance of God's placement of my friend, LC, and his pertinence in my final physical incarnation. One might think LC and I were and are kindred spirits, much in the same way people seek out and connect with their supposed "soul mates." However, like many similar concepts described in this book, kindred spirits and soul mates simply do not exist. Blessedly, God always wisely places souls in circumstances that support, encourage, and assist our proper reperfecting potentiality.

In this existence, I have been gifted a life filled with calm, peace, joy, happiness, contentedness, and fulfillment. Little did I know there would be many more unimaginably blessed events in store for me during the creation of this Holy Book. In Book Five you will learn firsthand the True Source behind this book's Transcendental Illuminations.

Dharmic Compassion

All existence is beloved by the Uncreated Infinite SuperConsciousness
And bestowed by the inward reflection as Holy Lord Shiva.

Like Pluto clinging precariously to its tenuous orbit,
So too does the horrific transgressor cling to its Holy Originator.

As the photonic light of our sun reaches out to Pluto,
Throughout every existence, Holiness and Divinity
Quietly operate within each and every misguided soul.

As every dharmic plan unenfolds as God's destiny blueprint,
The gift of life and its limitless abundance is afforded to ALL.

Blessings of free-will choice are granted to ALL with divine lovingkindness
As opportunities to conduct ourselves with benevolence—
And refrain from wrongfully exerting our egos upon another.

With such gifts is the responsibility that determines our ultimate fate.
The Reflectory Universe alleviates injustices
And returns all to harmonious balance.

This karmic law as Divine Justice has been chiseled by our Holy Creator
And is anchored in the Very Foundation of The Holy Originator's Ore.

This Foundation easily withstands the compressing test of eternity,
And bears the entire burden of the Manifesting Cosmos.

BOOK Three

Spirituality

Introduction

S pirituality oftentimes is confused with or by organized religion. Along the way, the spiritual message has been commandeered by power-hungry, self-serving, misguided "adherents of the message." Many times, the intentions behind the message digress into a bloodthirsty approach that has strayed far from any perceivable message pertaining to "God's Creedless SuperConsciousness." In this book, we expound upon a tremendous number of humbling Truths, expose countless misperceptions and blatant inaccuracies, and validate uncertainties, while disclosing and untangling vast vines of long-suppressed secrets.

Truths suppressed, whether inadvertently or intentionally, lead disconcertingly to hosts of errors. Suppressed secrets tend to accumulate into misconstrued, inaccurate piles of accepted beliefs. Eons have come and gone with civilizations digesting and assimilating huge portions of completely erroneous fiction, assuming it to be immutable fact. Oftentimes, secrets have been buried from existence to conscious existence with little regard for any further disclosure, merely perpetuating the proverbially accepted rug-sweeping method.

Well, Mari and I have been supplied with a broom and dustpan, and we are being divinely guided to take certain dusty, old rugs out back and shake them out, sharing with everyone whatever Truths and confoundities spill out. We are being directed to sweep away the layers of confusion and untruths, separating the uncertainties from gross inaccuracies. We will do this with the simple intention of allowing all humankind the opportunity, once and for all, to know the unadulterated Absolute Truth. Of course, we know full well that earth humankind continually will consume only the most desirable, palatable buffet sections. In doing so, people will find some courses unacceptable, undesirable, and even ominously threatening, leaving them unconsumed.

It is disheartening to discover that the countless meals we have been spoon-fed contain poisonous ingredients of undigestible pollution. However, it is better to be informed now than to waste further existences not ever being exposed to wholesome, healthy, accurate, assimilable truthfulness. At least now we all have a choice. We do not intend to slam organized religion, for it has its place and purpose. Rather, we are here to provide a factual, Truthful tool to assist in facilitating everyone's spiritual upliftment.

For far too long, humans have believed countless "truths" as Absolute. Through oral tradition and later in literature, these truths perpetually have been transferred from person to person—all of whom lacked the ability to discern fact from fiction, their shared "knowledge" with their peers being their only validation. Nowadays, computers spread these so-called truths around the world in seconds—their dissemination power virtually devoid of any accountability factor whatsoever.

What happens when presumed truths are NOT actually truthful? How can anyone discern with pure conviction time-honored traditions of articulated translations? Certainly, even a really good hunch is rendered powerless against the resistless tide of human historical belief. For millenniums, the act of courageously speaking up against the misinformed masses has proven to be futile, if not fatal. People seemed to have fared far better by existing as conditioned lemmings responding by rote than by behaving otherwise and being burned at the stake. Merely being different cost a staggering 330 million Native Americans their lives from the time Columbus discovered America, thinking it was India. During the Holocaust alone, six million Jews were annihilated for being different. In both cases, these "different" groups of people were not a true threat, but perhaps to the entrenched mindsets at the time, were perceived as such.

In Book Five, I am going to share many enlightening Truths about several phenomenal experiences that happened to me (Scott). These experiences embody the reasons I am serving God—just one of which is writing this doctrine. For now, I am being instructed to share with you many untruths erroneously perpetuated as irrefutable facts. Certainly, you are free to believe that which you allow into your consciousness.

However, bear in mind, God alone owns all Truths and shares them, as God feels necessary. The Angelic Holy Realm has endured perpetual lies, deceit, and reams of disinformation unabashedly spread as the infallible Word of God. Humans have reduced the Spirit Realm to a status of mute, observational, uninfluential nonexistence.

The Holy Angels in the Spirit Realm have determined that it is time for all earth humans to know the Absolute Word of Truth Itself. The ongoing saga of egos and misguided free will has continued to confuse and mislead people for three million years—with no apparent end in sight. As always, humans can and will continue to utilize their God-given, free will to make their own, individual conclusions. Now that the Angelic

Realm has reclaimed its rightful proactive role, at the very least, the Truth will be an option guaranteed to ALL.

Conscious comprehensions are the net result of free-will choices. These choices are determining factors for future lessons. Merely understanding or accepting the lesson is not enough. Even if a person seems to correctly interpret their lesson, they may miss the subtleties of the deeper meanings behind the lesson's intentions. Being subjected to life's lessons presents us with opportunities to evolve. Do we handle them with dignity, honor, respect, humility? Such enlightened reactions not only prove we have understood the purpose of the lesson, but also assist us in emancipation from having to experience the same lesson again. Within each incarnation, there is no limit to the number of times or infinitely ingenious ways a lesson can present itself.

Manifesting Permeations

Earth humankind is one of only two existences with free will on this planet, the other being Leviathan or whale. Free will is the inalienable right of all earth humankind to make choices. Of course, these choices have consequences, which we know to be karma. So, personal experience is one of choice and consequences. However, the actual experience itself has been carefully predetermined around an exact, preeminent pathway, neatly enfolded into the atoms of our physical existence by God alone. No Angel or Archangel makes any predeterminations about a person's individual path. God solely preordains all conscious experience before every fetus' soul implantation. God alone bears the responsibility for the implanted existence of every human soul.

All existence is a conscious experience meticulously wrapped within three synoptic vibratory encasements. Humans and all Made Manifest consist of these three distinctly different containers, each with far-reaching purposes. Descending inversely from the Uncreated Infinite Super-Consciousness, the first manifesting container or pupae is the Causal container. The Causal Universe is the initial, inward reflection of God's preprescription or TransImagination for Creation. The Causal Universe is the Realm of the Holy Neutrino. The Universe of the Holy Neutrino Realm consists of photonic light, vibration, and SuperConsciousness. All Creation exists as the Manifesting Dream Idea of God's TransImagination. The second container of Creation is the encasing Astral cocoon. The Astral Universe is the energy world, where God's TransImaginative Ideas are solidified and take objectified form. This is the world of quark and lepton energy existence, where our Manifesting Universe is starting to congeal in a solidifying form. The Causal and Astral Universes comprise the Spirit Realm.

The third, final container is the physical butterfly of formed matter, beginning at the atom level, continuing through molecules and cells—and eventually terminating at the level of bedrock. This concept is irrefutably consistent and applicable to all inversely reflecting manifestations of vibratory phenomena. Whether existence is stone, human, or supernova, within the physical cosmos, nature's packaging is always the same. Such is the threefold nature consistently found within and throughout all existence. Whether amoeba or superhuman, all manifesting matter is similarly contained within these three reservatories.

As previously stated, the Causal World is composed of Holy Neutrinos, which provide enough gravitational exertion to contain every individual's soul. This Causal or Idea container is where humankind's God-gifted consciousness from God's own Uncreated Infinite Super-Consciousness is Transimplanted into the budding fetus shortly before birth. The timing varies from soul to soul, conscious experience to conscious experience—depending upon one's dharma or God-predetermined plan. The soul is Transimplanted shortly before the moment of one's physical birth.

The soul does not reside within the fetus and is not Transimplanted until the dharmic timing for the upcoming human incarnation is EXACTLY perfect. God is the sole power determining when that time is at hand, and this is true for each soul within every fetus. God as Manifesting SuperConsciousness is the activating force causing in-utero fetuses to stir, hiccup, and move about. Prior to every physical birth, the soul is prevented from entering and exiting the physical body. God is the sole, or should we say "soul" gatekeeper.

The dharma is the God-predetermined, unenfolding plan for every existence in the physical cosmos. Your entire life's path for every incarnation was distinctly preplanned, with all influencing factors being considered prior to birth. These infinite indeterminables are based particularly on a soul's past karmic debt and incomprehensible but still finite, random, variable choices, or free will. Your free-will choices, along with your individual and unique preeminent experience of potentials, directly affect the Universal reflection you experience firsthand. In other words, the Universe is neither benevolent nor malevolent, but merely rebounds back whatever you put out through YOUR free-will choices.

In its mirrored holographic response back to you, the Universe is completely unbiased. Thus, if you put out good, good reflects back. Emit horrible atrocities or abominations of ANY vibratory mode, including THOUGHTS, and THAT is what reflects back into your conscious experience. The experience and impact from this reflective process IS your karma. The impact of a karmic reflection penetrates throughout the physical container, right to the very atoms of your being. The atoms form the very first stage of your physical development as a human being.

The Causal Supercontainer, which contains the soul or Idea of existence, is the level fifteen membrane of intellectual existence potential. In this membrane, the incisive separation between The Uncreated and Created is razor-thin, but immutably present. This is a world that composes 25 percent of the manifesting preprescripted cosmos, where the TransImagination of God is Transinterinfused as God's inwardly reflecting Creation. All of Creation actually IS photonic light, vibration, SuperConsciousness, and electromagnetic energy. This energy contains and maintains SuperConsciousness originating from the Uncreated Infinite SuperConsciousness.

The second container for humankind's existence is the Astral or energy form. The human body is composed of thirty-five lightways or wheels of illumination. These lightways or wheels of illumination contain the vibratory information for all various human functions. This vibratory information contains the entire blueprint of what makes up a human being's incarnation. The illumination of the lightway or wheel provides the necessary pathway for the vibrational information it contains. All aspects from the blueprint eventually congeal in the Astral or energy form—and thus, become a human being. In summary, a human being begins with light, congeals with the vibratory information of its incarnating blueprint, ultimately assuming its final, physically manifesting form.

The Spirit Realm IS the Astral Universe of leptons and quarks, which are composed of six intellectual communication membranes. The human Astral container, which contains the thirty-five lightways and correlating vibrational pathways, manifests in the Astral levels fourteen through nine. There are nineteen wheels or lightways that make up the Astral body, and sixteen that make up the physical body. Combined, these thirty-five wheels or lightways contain all the blueprinted information for the human body to fabricate in our manifesting physical universe. Extending inwardly from our Causal or Idea container are the three overarching blueprinted informational wheels. These three informational wheels or lightways—ego, intellectual, and emotional—contain and provide the aspects and capabilities for the human experience.

All nineteen aspects of the Astral body are divided into these three overarching blueprinted information wheels. These three categories of ego, emotional, and intellectual capabilities further are subdivided into four subcategories. These subcategories command our abilities for conscious intelligence, subconscious intelligence, ego, and sense perception. These four subcategories once again are divided into subcounterparts or Astral elemental wheels. They are as follows:

Intellectual conscious abilities: walking, talking, procreating, excreting, and manual skills. These are conscious decision-making, learned behaviors—the results of which reflect people's free-will choices. As such, these free-will choices eventually are recorded in the ego wheel.

Intellectual unconscious abilities: circulation, assimilation, crystallization, metabolization, elimination, and immune system capacity with the body's ability to metastasize. These functions occur through God's ordainment, not as a result of human, conscious intent, directed efforts, or developed skills.

Emotional wheels: physical sense perceptions such as sight, hearing, smell, taste, and experiential feelings. People experience these sense-derived functions as recognizable emotional responses. Without these wheels, people would be incapable of experiencing both the smell of a rose, as well as the stench of rotten garbage—and all the emotional and physiological accompanying responses. (See Diagram of the Unified Astral Wheels.)

As communication wheels descend from Uncreated Infinite God inversely into manifesting creation, communication capacity decreases in efficiency. Intellectual capacity becomes elementally more primitive the farther its location from Uncreated Infinite God. The bigger wheels meld into smaller, more numerous wheels or lightways, with ever-lessening capacity. Essentially, we are saying that intellectual communication becomes less efficient in potential ability, while simultaneously becoming gross physically larger. The sixteen gross physically manifesting wheels represent the end-of-the-line manifestations. The physical formations and subsequent development for the entire physical body are governed by the information contained within these wheels. Combined, these thirty-five wheels or lightways contain and maintain all the information that makes up fully functioning human beings.

The HEM (human electromagnetic) wheels descend, infusing from larger into smaller wheels. They descend inward from the Holy Neutrino, melding into the next wheel, while transporting the vibratory instructions to carry out their purpose. The compiling vibrations simultaneously grow heavier with condensing, gravitational mass. We are describing two distinct phenomena—first, the Preordained lightway, and the second, the manifesting tangible matter. Increasing the encumbering vibratory communication results in limiting the gross physical and intellectual capabilities. Every rock or stone contains at its inner essence vast capacities of intellectual potential. However, the outward manifestation of stone becomes more limiting in varying capabilities, and less efficient when encumbered by compounded elemental matter.

Unified Astral Wheels
The 19 Human Electromagnetic Lightways or Wheels of the Astral Container

The following 3 main lightways (manifesting inwardly) objectify or form our Astral container from our innermost Causal container. This SuperConscious bodily fabrication provides humans the ability to interpret, process, and comprehend our highest levels of sense perception.

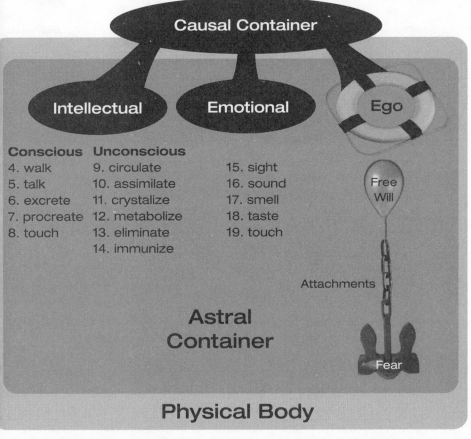

Causal Container

Intellectual   Emotional   Ego

Conscious	Unconscious		
4. walk	9. circulate	15. sight	
5. talk	10. assimilate	16. sound	Free Will
6. excrete	11. crystalize	17. smell	
7. procreate	12. metabolize	18. taste	
8. touch	13. eliminate	19. touch	
	14. immunize		

Attachments

Astral Container

Fear

Physical Body

In the physically manifesting male human being,
mental intellectual sense perceptions take precedence.
In females, emotional sense perceptions take precedence.
By these fundamental intellectual and emotional sense perception
distinctions, in dualistic yin-yang interpretations,
humankind experiences its existence.

Diagram of Lightway Combinations

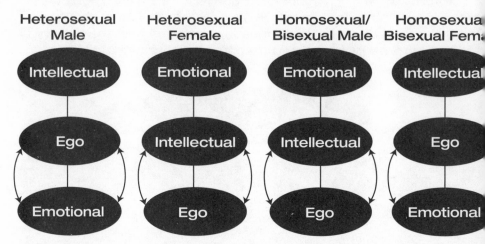

Heterosexual Male	Heterosexual Female	Homosexual/ Bisexual Male	Homosexual Bisexual Fem:
Intellectual	Emotional	Emotional	Intellectual
Ego	Intellectual	Intellectual	Ego
Emotional	Ego	Ego	Emotional

God interchanges the order of these lightways based upon each individual's preprescripted dharmic blueprint. The order of these lightways dictates the individual's ability to interpret, process, and comprehend their experience. These abilities are directed by our gift of free will and provide humans the capability to infuse their intentions thoughts, actions, and reactions into their experience. This g of free will (responsibility) mandates the universe's karmic reflection to impact us—and becomes the driving force directly influencing all that we experience.

In the Unified SuperConsciously attuned being, these dualistically defining yin-yang distinctions are superseded, melding into an At-Oneness with the Manifesting Infinite. When all perceptions of fear have been extinguished and one's ego has been identified as anti-self and subsequently banished from consciousness, Unconditional Love fills the void.

Dharma-Free Will-Karma "Equations"

With mathematics, every equation results in an exact answer. Existence is no different. In both mathematics and existence, there are ever-varying, infinite possibilities or pathways to arrive at a determined point or destination. Humans' dharma-free will-karma potentiality can be explained logically through a simple mathematical equation. In our equation example, we have a student, a teacher, and a problem—all which mirror the limitlessness of free-will choices in the human experience.

Student = the Person who has human, free-will selection capability

Teacher = the Janus-faced Universe

The student always is faced with a life-experience equation ending in "5." There is an infinite number of ways by which a student can arrive at "5," the following being but two of them:

$2 + 3 = 5$ and $4 + 1 = 5$

Both of these above equations represent the exact, preeminent path, which is a student's dharma. One's dharma is based on old karma or past, negative free-will choices, which have resulted in ego imbalances. The fact that one has old karma is why the student is presented with an equation in the first place.

$2 + 3$ AND $4 + 1$ are dharmic potentials, both leading to the end result of "5."

"5" is the karma or answer to the free-will choices. It is the unlimited potential answer, derived from one's free-will choices—be they positive or negative. Each time, how one chooses to arrive at "5" or their free-will choice, determines the next karmic impact potential as their dharmic path continues to unenfold in their life. This equation and process continues throughout one's current incarnation.

Depending upon how one chooses to react to their various free-will choices will determine whether one graduates beyond the equation or has to go back and reexperience the equation until getting it right. A student may need to reexperience the equation many times during their current lifetime, or perhaps during future incarnations if they cannot get it right without humility or unconditional love. A student's final reaction to their free-will choices may be of ego or humility or unconditional love, the latter two becoming an upliftment potential.

The ego has an encumbering, contaminating result, which adds vibratory slop to a student's individual, conscious experience. Such slop compiles and eventually is presented with unending opportunities to be eventually expunged as karmic debt. A humble reaction is a free-will choice resulting in an upliftment. Such upliftment is the chiseling out or against some of the prior, impacted vibratory slop of past karma. Karma is a soul's debt to nature, not to another individual. The specific souls involved initially during the original indebtedness need not be present during the debt's alleviation. All ego imbalances are a direct result of misaligned free-will choices straying from Unconditional Love.

There is NO set age accorded to children or adults when their dharmically preprescripted karma (from prior incarnations) accedes to free will. However, this process begins as soon as a conscious being begins asserting influence upon its surroundings. Severely retarded or mentally restricted human beings never impress their individual influence upon their conscious experience. They have no enfolded free will, so they never incur any karmic debt in this existence. Their sole purpose for existence is purely for karmic debt alleviation incurred from prior existences. Of course, the people surrounding them, having free will and ego, affect their own personal karma based on their respective interactions with those who are retarded, restricted, and lack free-will choices.

Despite any human intentions, nobody but God can prevent another being from experiencing their ultimate karmic imbalances. However, in some very rare instances, a God-sanctioned guru may absorb some karmic debt for people. Oftentimes in these cases, the God-sanctioned guru has been gifted the authority to select the people who might receive such divine rebalancing.

In other words, if your child is destined to experience evolutionary growth or karmic rectification, nothing can be done that will prevent this from happening. That is why prayers, surgery, and love work ONLY when they are in harmony with God's continually reperfecting TransImaginated plan. We don't influence God's plans because our limited human vision can't even begin seeing a microscopic view of an incomprehensibly deep picture. Certain superhumans, preordained by God, can have a marginal influence upon someone's karma—but only with God's unlimited comprehension and blessings.

Free will begins its karmic influence when every individual reaches the uniquely God-predetermined moment neatly enfolded into one's dharmic plan. In some cases, such moments are known to Holy Angels and supporting Superessences as is necessary—also predetermined by God. People's dualistic free-will choices sow the karmic seeds for past, present, or future events. Free will is a God-sanctioned birthright, which is inviolable and can only be retracted by the Absolute Ordainer.

People oftentimes confuse free will and ego. Upon death of the physical butterfly of existence, the ego returns with the soul back to the Astral Universe, while free will withers with the ensuing bodily decay. Because free will naturally unenfolds during our human experience of existence, this God-given gift remains behind with the physical body after death. Upon death of the physical body, the soul has one last free-will choice to make: the soul will either exercise its free will to flee from the dying physical body, or it will be SuperConsciously drawn back to the Spirit Realm. If the soul flees, it ejects out from the person's spiritual third eye—and becomes a ghost. If, however, the soul chooses to return to the Spirit Realm, it does so within its Causal and Astral containers, leaving the physical body (container) behind.

Every free-will choice a human being will make in their experience has previously been Infinitely Comprehended and ingeniously discerned by God. During the TransImaginating Contemplative state, ALL aspects of EVERYTHING Made Manifest are preprescripted and enfolded into EVERYTHING'S dharmic blueprint. Nothing Made Manifest is allowed to be experienced without first being pre-CompreCreated and God-allowed to be experienced. From this Limitless Comprehension everything Made Manifest follows its preprescripted holy blueprint or dharmic plan. As such, NOTHING happens without God's limitless knowledge and unconditionally loving blessings.

The TransImaginative state occurs prior to ANYTHING being Made Manifest. The entire Universal Incarnation has been intricately Thought Out and Infinitely Comprehended. It is during this TransImaginative state that every human consciousness (soul) that is to be Made Manifest makes its free-will choices that it will experience during its Made Manifest incarnations.

With this Truthful Absolute it is imperative that each soul recognizes its individual conscious accountability due solely to its TransImaginated free-will choices. This Holy Wisdom allows each human being the ability to influence its Made Manifest experience today through recognition and implementation during its TransImaginating process. By willfully exercising evolved free-will choices today in its Made Manifest state, the soul infuses an Advanced Spiritual Upliftment Technique into the pre-Made Manifest TransImagination that already has taken place in its pre-Made Manifest state. In other words, in its TransImaginated state, the soul already influenced its yet to be experienced Made Manifest state with the free-will choices it made during TransImagination. This pre-Made Manifest, preprescripted TransImagination IS the "déjà vu" that people experience in their unenfolding Made Manifest state.

Knowledge of this Holy Absolute in our Made Manifest state is irrefutable proof that we comprehend this Truth in our TransImaginated state. Humans have the opportunity to accelerate their spiritual evolution by comprehending and free-will choosing to align their individual perception with indivisible Unconditional Love. As Made Manifest humans, exerting free-will choices as Unconditional Love will ensure compounding, uplifting benefits.

In your TransImaginated state—which is now being experienced at this very moment—you simultaneously recognize your influence in both aspects (TransImaginative and Made Manifest) of your evolution. In doing so, both aspects of your experience reap the same compounding, positive karmic reflections. In other words, you are able to advance your TransImaginated spiritual state and experience a "spiritual double dipping" by aligning and expressing your Made Manifest existence as pure Unconditional Love. To express a state of Unconditional Love, one needs to disconnect from all fears, conditions, and attachments associated with every outcome within their perception.

As each human being evolves through their natural progression, any reflecting karma compiles or recedes, depending upon the free-will-influenced actions/reactions and ego benefiting intentions and thoughts behind their actions/reactions. In other words, even if unenacted, the ego-based thought to harm, negatively impacts the karma—albeit to a lesser extent than the action/reaction. Ignorance is not bliss in this circumstance—and is inexcusable. The choice to inflict aggression, anger, or violence upon anything Made Manifest ALWAYS is a TransImaginated free-will choice and NEVER is purposelessly preprescribed into anyone's dharmic plan. Whether executed or merely intended, all such injustices are karmically impacting. This Divine Law applies to overt physical actions, as well as covert, psychological, emotional, or even psychically vampiric tactics.

No earth human has the ability to cast a spell or place a curse upon an unsuspecting victim. In other words, the victim must know that a spell or curse either has been or will be sent—or the victim must be vulnerably and willingly OPEN and trusting of the perpetrator. In rare cases, merely trusting and believing in the concept of spells or curses is enough for people to open themselves up for exploitation. Any negative life occurrence experienced by a supposed victim is a karmic reaction to this victim's prior imbalance. It is NOT the result of someone else's unevolved ego casting an ill-advised spell on an innocent or unsuspecting victim. If the intended victim of a curse or hex is oblivious or disbelieving of the perpetrator's power, intention, or authenticity of the curse itself, any such curse will boomerang back to its sender.

The three containers of a human being constitute a quadrant of space called the merkebah. The human electromagnetic fields reside within the merkebah. The merkebah is completely impermeable to spells, hexes, and curses if no victim willingness or otherwise breachable opening within it is available. Almost any traumatic spiritual, emotional, or psychological impact can imperil a victim and cause what can be considered cracks in a victim's merkebah. The only other reason for such impact would be that of an unfulfilled karmic debt, such as Mari's experience with the evil, diabolic entity. In this case, her willing openness to the implementing experience was irrelevant. Preprescripted (through a Transintervention) into Mari's dharmic plan was a divine agreement from God that she would be afforded an opportunity to erase the intense karma incurred with the entity from the midwife existence.

As previously stated, all opportunities to alleviate karmic indebtedness must be preprescribed in the atom level of everyone's physical container. Had Mari not been willing or open to receive MB's psychic services (psychic implementations), her merkebah still may have been breached, affording her the opportunity to alleviate her karmic indebtedness with the entity. For reasons known only to God, under rare circumstances preenfolded into one's yet to be experienced dharma, a breach of the merkebah may be necessary for the alleviation of one's karmic debt. This is only possible with God's Irrevocable Will. In contrast to MB, DR acted independently from the entity or any of Mari's karmic indebtedness. With DR, Mari was open and trusting, thus allowing for the potential fulfillment of DR's malevolent intentions and actions.

Essence Stealing and Reclamation
Mari's Words

As I realized the magnitude of what DR and MB stole from me, I began to realize they had stolen my body's essence. I asked Scott if either DR or MB possessed a special skill that would enable such stealing and destruction to take place, and he said in all cases, there is no special skill. DR and MB—and their unholy actions—were preprescripted and Transintervened respectively within God's own blueprint deeply enfolded within me. As such, they stole from BOTH God and me. By stealing part of my life-sustaining energies, the very essence of my being, they were interfering with and influencing my free will—something only for ME to be activating and accessing on my own volition. I eventually understood that both MB and DR, in their unevolved states, could not possibly have known that they were actually transgressing against Made Manifest, which is what I represented.

Throughout this book-writing and spiritual evolution process, I have come to understand more fully my quest for Truth about universal existence. As an adult, I "psychic shopped," delving into metaphysical realms, hoping for insights. I felt deep within my heart that mine was not a search in vain. The harder and longer I searched, the more earnestly I desired the Truth.

I especially was hungry for any validation regarding deceased loved ones, including my maternal grandfather. I devoured any tidbits of information forthcoming from psychics, finding them comforting on many levels. Erroneously, I thought I could receive some sort of message from the so-called "other side," or perhaps send one there myself. I wanted to know about life after death—and death itself. I wanted answers to these and so many other unknowns. I later would learn that even if done with honor and good intentions, if it influences another's free will, the work of psychics IS a transgression against God.

While God works through psychics—as through all Made Manifest— I learned there are NO psychics sanctioned by God. No one—not even the most seemingly talented or benevolent mediums—EVER can communicate with those who have died. Those psychics who do profess to communicate with the deceased only appear to do so within their own minds. Also, when psychics are pressed for information, a client's tenacity serves only to increase the psychics' ability to utilize their own imagination.

By conforming their awareness to the molecular level of a client's conscious experience, psychics are able to access a client's thoughts or cognitions. However, psychics are NEVER able to extend this awareness past the atom level of a client's physically manifesting existence. In other words, psychics' abilities to perceive are limited to the physically manifesting container—and NOWHERE near anyone's Astral or Causal containers. Most important, psychics cannot tread ANYWHERE near a person's dharmic blueprint.

I have come to learn and realize that unless it is done under God-sanctioned circumstances through divine intervention or Transintervention, has been preprescribed into one's dharmic plan, or both, it is a transgression to willingly attempt to give someone your free will. However, it was AFTER God made the Transintervention that meeting up with the entity was formally introduced into my dharmic plan with a discerning, divine exactness. God ensured that I'd meet the entity with a now-inscripted Absolute. By its very definition of being called a Transintervention, this divine act—once executed—becomes part of one's dharmic plan. From the moment of Execution, the person's actualization of this Transintervention can occur—up until their physical death or at any time, right to the very end of their soul's dharmic plan.

My supposedly innocent personal quest (that included psychic sessions), actually WAS my dharmic plan. This plan guided me to reach the entity, alleviate the associated karmic imbalance, fulfill the intention of God's Transintervention, receive the messages from the benevolent psychic, experience healing from Scott, and co-author this God-sanctioned book. This Transintervention certainly changed the course of my life, for which I am extremely blessed and will remain eternally grateful.

Contemporary Free-Will Examples
Introduction

When it comes to recognizing the role of our free-will choices as they impact our karma and the lives of others around us, we may find ourselves faced with some surprising realities. While the examples we will provide you might not seem to be overly connected, they all pertain to karmic impaction. The first example, one that may strike you as quite surprising, relates to abortions.

The number of children—and with whom one is destined to have these children—are both preprescripted into each soul's dharmic plan for its every human incarnation. Abortions are performed according to God's divine predetermined plan. No human being actually MAKES the choice to abort. Solely, by God's manifest, according to the dharma of either the man or woman involved in this situation, does this act occur. This Divine Law accounts for spontaneous abortions, as well as those physically performed.

In other words, to have an abortion, many abortions, or none at all, is based on God's predetermined dharma for each individual soul experience. This God-predetermined experience, like all others, lies neatly enfolded in the blueprint plan for each individual, waiting for every predetermined time of experience.

From an abortion, there is no transgression against God. An abortion is not actually or technically a free-will choice. No human life is being denied, destroyed, or prevented from experiencing a manifesting existence. Every soul has an expressing dharmic blueprint preprescripted from the Holy Dharmic Plan. With the abortion experience, no human soul is Transimplanted into the fetus. As stated earlier, the fetus does not have an earth human consciousness within, but rather is inhabited by Manifesting Infinite SuperConsciousness. Since every abortion has been preprescripted and Uncreated Infinite SuperConsciousness has Trans-Imagined every aspect of all Made Manifest, all abortions are natural, preprescripted unenfoldments.

Free will is reflected in the ongoing reactions people exhibit after an abortion, directly contributing to their personal, conscious experience. Such reactions result in either a burdensome ego attachment or in contrast, a release of any attachment. If the latter response is the case, this person will experience and realize personal growth. Either way, the response always is of one's free-will choosing. In EVERY life situation, challenge, or opportunity, your EVERY influencing response as intention, thought, action, and reaction is your free-will choice—and thus, entirely up to YOU. Exercising your free-will choice, as such, IS that for which you are accountable.

One free-will selection option upon which future humans will decide involves cloning. A tremendous amount of needless energy currently is being exerted regarding human biogenesis issues. The simple fact is that this cloning results in the physically manifesting resemblance between the clones—but the similarities end there. If a human were cloned, only the physical outer shell (container) would be similar—and the Astral and Causal containers would be bound by the same Manifesting Infinite Potential or Divine Universal Law as every other life form. Since God Transimplants the soul into the fetus, the clone's soul and physically manifesting life experiences would be infinitely varied.

Any similarities between the clones would be completely superficial and restricted entirely to the physical aspects. Personalities would be as varied as any two randomly selected souls. Autosomal mutations can and will occur during the cell division process. In addition, the very electro-magnetic fields contained within the Astral and Causal containers are preprescribed by God prior to the physical formation. These facts alone will incontrovertibly ensure that no one soul ever will inhabit two physically manifesting exact replicas of any one particular person. No matter how closely clones resemble each other or share similarly identifiable traits, they are not and never will be the same soul existing continuously within two identical bodies.

With regard to cloning, future problems will arise, due to survivors who desperately want to bring back their deceased loved ones. Human souls literally are inconsistent equations, such as $X + Y = 1$ and $X + Y = 2$. No matter how many times the exact $X + Y$ DNA would be cloned, $X + Y$ = Infinite Potentiality. Unless God commands the exact soul to reinhabit the exact DNA-cloned replica of the previously untenanted bodily container, every resulting cloned birth will be infinitely different. In rare circumstances, a Superevolved Saint may be God-gifted the opportunity to inhabit two physical bodies simultaneously with their one Made Manifest soul. This would take place only when preprescribed into the Saint's holy dharmic blueprint for divinely discerned purposes.

According to the Holy Realm, cloning is an acceptable practice, one that consistently operates throughout other vectors of the Universe. The only potential issues of transgression occur when the motive for cloning is to produce human results for specific manipulative reasons. When biopolymer markers are inserted for a desired outcome, the manipulator may be transgressing. When one produces a particular genetic biotype for warfare or any other purpose where the free will of the cloned being is compromised, one is transgressing. Otherwise, the Holy Realm recognizes no restrictions on the cloning of any animals, vegetables, or minerals.

There are many things we do in life that transgress against God, all leading to varying degrees of karmic impaction. Even something as simple as gossiping about others is a free-will choice, which leads to minor build-ups of karmic debt.

When we listen to gossip, however silently or passively (even when we sit in our own realized self-discomfort), we are making a poor free-will choice. When we find out someone has died, but lack reasons that satisfy our curiosity, quell our fears, or justify the supposed cause of the death, we tend to search for answers. Oftentimes, we devour the crumbs of gossip or hearsay as if they were nutritious morsels leading to some great insight.

In other words, no matter what the cause or apparent circumstances, only one thing is certain: It was that person's particular, divinely planned time to leave this earth existence. There are many, varied, unknown circumstances behind the death of a human being that are beyond our knowledge, that may remain unknown forever. It may temporarily seem helpful, relieving, or assuring at the time to attribute a so-called "logical" reason for a seemingly unusual, bizarre, shocking, or jarring death, but such reasoning is not necessarily accurate or truthful. For example, what may appear as a suicide may not necessarily be the case. Even in the case of homicide, where the so-called evidence is glaring, the Truth behind the reasons for the death may not be so clearly defined. There are limitless underlying unknowns contributing to the eventual outcome. The fact is, no matter where they were or what they were doing at the time, that soul's human body WAS going to expire at that exact moment from some deciding factor.

Furthermore, rationalizing such situations by citing depression, or other related mental, physical, or psychological issues or disorders as possible contributing factors or causes of the death only compounds the situation. Such rationalization, oftentimes in the form of gossip or obsessive wondering, also only leads to negative, karmic impaction. As in death, so in life, there are countless reasons why things appear to be a certain way. It is not for us to place judgment, and it is not for us to define in absolutes anyone's individual, conscious experience. When we do this with our thoughts or cognitions, we create attachments that become restrictions on our human existence, preventing us from experiencing true spiritual evolution.

Also karmically impacting are conscious feelings of superiority. Throughout many societies and civilizations, this air of superiority has permeated and been pervasive on an ongoing, chronic basis. Throughout time, every society in its own way has maintained and nurtured cohesive sentiments of superiority designed or disguised as martyrdom, victimization, or special uniqueness set apart from all dissimilar, unrelated others. These mindsets actually reflect cowardly fear rooted in the ego, further substantiated by how one chooses to exercise their free-will choices.

Cowardice does not discriminate based upon one's age. Adults and children alike can act out of cowardice. People also possess the free will to choose differently, not be cowardly, and stand up for an inner truth. When we stand up for an inner, resounding truth, rather than some externally based or forced illusion, we make Truth the ideal. The way in which one perceives, identifies, resonates with, and accepts Truth is indicative of an individual's conscious evolution. The ability to see, know, and "do" Truth is the ultimate, reflective manifestation of God's mirror for a soul's potentiality.

When karmic debt has been incurred and we've transgressed against God, prayer alone without proper intent is not enough for absolution. People do not and cannot determine the time or the actuality of transgression absolution. However, it is vital and beneficial to pray to have transgressions absolved from one's indebtedness. Transgressions are absolved with directed prayers steeped in focused, earnest intent. Thus, it behooves us to consider incorporating prayer to God into our daily tapestry of existence, rather than merely compartmentalizing devotions into specific, structured rituals, ceremonies, holidays, or times as dictated by any organized religion.

Regardless of your particular religion or possible lack thereof, the true nature of prayer and transgression absolution still applies to your individual conscious experience. Once again, the intent, will, intensity, and integrity you bring to your own awareness and opportunity is up to you.

The Hermaphrodite Example

A baby born with both sexual genitalia is considered a hermaphrodite. In this particular situation, the doctor and the parents are responding to their own challenging free-will choice situation—NOT the baby's dharmic or karmic determined circumstance. These three adults are assuming the responsibility for the baby's free-will choice. The baby's dharmic plan or existence still is completely governed by God. In this case, the parents and the doctor collaborate with their free-will choice, making a joint decision for the baby's gender outcome.

Let us suppose that, subsequently, this baby grows up feeling, believing, and experiencing himself/herself as the gender opposite of the choice made by the doctor and parents. Thus, this preselected gender choice and its resulting discord has created an intolerable condition within the individual's being. So, now this individual has a free-will choice to continue with this experience until the end of their existence, and as such, continuing to experience this discord and conflict until death. On the other hand, the other free-will choice option would be for this individual to change to the opposite gender—opposite of what the parents and doctor have chosen.

If this individual chooses to reverse their gender, this decision WILL be karmically impacting. Such karmic impaction would delay the inevitable experience of that very discord and conflict the individual was MEANT to experience in their dharma, but now is trying to avoid. For THIS particular example, the person's attempt to alleviate pain and discomfort may in fact prevent this person's previous karmic indebtedness from being properly eliminated. Before the doctor and parents chose the child's gender, God already knew the eventual outcome of this collective free-will choice. Thus, preprescripted into the child's dharmic blueprint or plan are all of the necessary challenges, experiences, and growth opportunities for this individual's complete existence. The dharmic blueprint for this individual's entire conscious experience is based on this soul's previous karmic imbalances.

The parent-doctor-chosen pathway is in fulfillment with this person's dharmic plan, and thus would balance their imbalanced karma.

Deciding to continue living according to this parent-doctor-decision (and dharmically preprescribed pathway) would manifest in the individual resigning to this conscious, individual experience. Such resignation does not necessarily signify a doom-and-gloom, ill-fated attitude. With this choice, the individual's attitude can lead to peace, after being willing to work toward attaining a deeper comprehension of their situation. However, this individual could choose differently, and postpone balancing these karmic imbalances. If he/she chooses this postponement route, this choice might manifest in the selection of elective surgery to reverse genders.

There always is the chance that the karma can be eliminated through additional and perhaps totally unrelated challenges, resulting in the same net karmic harmony. The only other potential karmic rebalancing would be done by a Divine Superimposition, where God imposes God's own, influential, revamping of an individual's entire dharmic blueprint. This revamping signifies an elimination or transfer of an individual's debt— only by God's choice.

Life-Maintaining and Sustaining Treatments— The Case of Breast Cancer

Life-sustaining, preserving, lengthening, maintaining, and "saving" actions take the form of treatments, surgeries, medications, and alternative therapies and modalities. Neither life-sustaining nor elective measures will change the length of someone's life. In either category, a particular treatment or action may influence the QUALITY of that person's existence, albeit only temporarily. One's lifespan is preprescripted into their dharmic blueprint by God—and no medical measure will alter someone's time to die.

Breast cancer is a condition enfolded into one's dharmic blueprint, as is the surgery to remove the cancer. If one elects to go through with any surgery, the end result of such surgery was preprescribed into the dharmic blueprint. Recovery from surgery for a life-threatening ailment was preprescribed into a person's dharma—BECAUSE the end result was "remission," to perpetuate a person's existence, until the person's life was to end at this preprescribed death.

People die on the operating table because they were MEANT to die at that very moment in time—for infinite reasons. In that case, the termination of one's incarnation was preprescripted to terminate at that very moment. Similarly, an ailment, surgery, recovery, and ensuing higher quality of life also are in fulfillment of one's karmic imbalances. In all cases, all such conditions have been preprescribed into a person's dharmic blueprint.

After or even during surgery, any ensuing complications are a result of the weight of one's karma overriding any free-will choices one could possibly make. Free-will choice can influence, but never rules. Only one's dharmic and karmic laws preside over one's individual conscious experience.

With regard to a human being's life plan, there are infinite variables and manifesting potentialities, and as such, the concept of what is dharmic-, karmic-, and free-will-choice-influenced never will be entirely crystal clear. There are many reasons for this. First, only God knows what is in one's dharmic blueprint. Second, other than making their TransImaginated free-will choices, human beings have no influence in the choosing of their dharmic blueprint—nor the incarnation yet to unenfold. Prior to their incarnation, people do NOT choose any factors in reference to their dharmic, infinite potentiality. Specifically, people don't choose their parents, illnesses, circumstances, environments, or other relationships whatsoever. God makes such choices, enfolding them into God's Divine dharmic plan for each individual.

Contrary to what psychics and other metaphysicians have maintained, one does not "choose" any dharmic factors at all. Furthermore, one cannot and does not choose which planet on which they eventually end up incarnating.

Every TransImaginated free-will choice has a determining impact upon the net outcome for what is destined by one's dharmic blueprint to unenfold. Any and every free-will choice one makes has been preprescripted, and one's dharmic plan will reflect the influence of this TransImaginated free-will choice.

What this means is when a bad free-will choice is made today, it is the same bad free-will choice your soul made in its pre-Made Manifest TransImaginating (Uncreated Infinite SuperConscious) state. Conversely, the same good, unconditioinally loving choice also was the same uplifting choice your soul made in its pre-Made Manifest (Uncreated Infinite SuperConscious) state.

Another example of free-will choice is expressed in the case of a person dealing with a breast lump. After detecting a lump, they might seek out numerous medical opinions, as follows:

Doctor A says, "It's probably nothing, don't worry. Just watch it and see what happens."

Doctor B says, "I don't like the look of it. I'd recommend surgery to take it out."

Doctor C says, "I recommend these herbs in conjunction with a regime of acupuncture. Let's see how that goes."

Doctor D says, "Why don't we do a combination of allopathic (surgery, medications, etc.) and nontraditional approaches? Then we'll be covering all of our bases."

Doctor E says, "The problem with mixing treatments and modalities is when one is either cured or the condition worsens, we don't know to what we can attribute the results. We also don't know enough about various drug interactions to feel good about mixing treatments."

After visiting such doctors, the patient is faced with a myriad of free-will choices to make, including not taking ANY medical action whatsoever. If this person elects not to take medical action, they are making the free-will choice to do so, thus allowing the natural progression of events—and consequently, the resolution of their karmic indebtedness. This person chooses to be resigned to experience whatever has been pre-destined to dharmically occur.

In each and every selection mentioned above, within any free-will choice, no person can alter their predetermined moment of death. Any one of these free-will choices WILL INFLUENCE the QUALITY of one's existence, but will have NO EFFECT whatsoever on the termination point of this person's existence. So, in this case, this person's prepre-scripted DHARMA contains the specific illness AND the ensuing end result from whichever choice they select via free will.

This person's KARMIC reflection is the illness itself and any ensuing, potential ramifications. Such ramifications could include pain, discomfort, the surgery not working, no "fix" from a particular treatment for the ailment, side effects, etc.

As such, electing to undergo surgery does NOT guarantee satisfaction or alleviation of the karmic indebtedness. If this is the case, subsequent and possibly unrelated illnesses may crop up, reflecting the unresolved satisfaction—once again, allowing the person the opportunity to satisfy karmic indebtedness. As always, accountability rests with the individual, based on their past and present free-will choices.

The other possibility is that the person has a complete recovery from the illness, its side effects, and no longer has the life-altering condition and associated diagnosis. In this case, the entire experience—including the treatment, disease, and recovery—satisfies the karmic indebtedness. Consequently, this person then is free from that particular karmic indebtedness, and will continue living out the rest of their dharmic plan.

Please know we are not advocating ANY of these options or choices, nor are we advocating NONE of them. We merely want to point out the resulting reasons for circumstances surrounding each selection. We are not saying "go" or "don't go" to a doctor. It is important for people to do what they want and feel is best. This discussion is meant for you to know that if the treatment, doctor, or choice does not work, it is because its inability to "work" is in your dharmic blueprint or as a result of your karmically reflecting indebtedness.

The only other free-will choice involves utilizing the power of prayer. By choosing prayer, a person is making a free-will choice to allow the natural progression to occur, consequently also allowing for the natural resolution of their karmic indebtedness. The power of prayer is ONLY effective if the outcome of this choice is in harmony with God's Reperfecting Plan. The power of prayer itself does NOT influence God to ensure a particular outcome—in this case, a cure or state of remission from disease. After one has elected to pray (allowing life's natural progression to occur), any final outcome of their becoming disease-free is due solely to the fact that karmic indebtedness has been satisfied—and is NOT directly attributable to the prayer itself. All free-will choices, including prayer, have one thing in common. All are paths that ultimately converge at one point—that of one's predetermined death, as preprescripted by one's dharmic blueprint.

In the cases where people are faced with whether or not to consent to removing life support, please remember that God's dharmic plan for all is NEVER wrong. The fact that someone might "pull the plug" or remove life support merely FACILITATES the dharmic plan. The fact is that the person who is ill or injured at that time would have died at that moment in existence anyway. God's comprehension of the ultimate outcome allows the natural unenfoldment of the dharmic plan to occur. In the case of an individual existing in a medically deemed, irreversible, vegetative state, this individual's free-will choice rests again in God's hands. Without the individual having free-will choice capability, all decisions revert back to the dharmic plan—as it was when this person was born and not yet able to exercise free will.

The decision to remove life support in no way signifies an alteration or interruption in this ill or injured person's dharmic plan. Rather, God compels those who make this decision to execute what actually IS contained (at the moment of physical death) within the ill person's dharmic plan—and what is God's Plan for this person, anyway. Consenting to pull the plug is for such decision makers and survivors a guiltless, egoless act of Divine Interaction. God will utilize anything or anyone to interact as a catalyst to ensure fulfillment of any preprescribed desired outcome. When a Divine Interaction occurs for a specific outcome without utilizing any such catalyst, it is Facilitated directly by God. When such Interaction is not preprescripted it is called a Transinteraction.

As stated earlier, when it comes to death, human beings attempt to make sense of this mystery, tending to fixate or focus on the possible reasons or causes. We tell ourselves, "Perhaps if she hadn't taken drugs, she'd still be alive," or "He was taken from us too young. He should have worn a seat belt." We also misinterpret some seemingly unhealthy choices others make and are shocked to see these same people outliving those whose habits and lifestyles are far healthier. "I can't believe she lived to be so old. She smoked and drank like crazy." "He walked or jogged daily, ate a whole-foods diet, and never smoked or drank. I can't believe he didn't make it past 40."

In terms of understanding or attempting to justify (futilely so) someone's death, whether they die at an old or young age is irrelevant. People die when it's in their dharmic blueprint to do so. Thus, there really is no such thing as "dying too young"—it's just a reflection of our human perception, developed without knowing about dharma. When we perceive existence in this manner, we are not looking at the greater dharmic perspective. The unhealthy free-will choices we make will not cause our ultimate physical death; if we fail to make good ones, they merely will impact us karmically. Thus, if we don't attend well to ourselves during the present incarnation, we can be certain the opportunity to do so will be ours in future incarnations.

As such, when it comes to the cause of a human being's death, the way in which they die merely happens to be the modus operandi—and irrelevant, at that. Only the dharmic blueprint or plan determines the exact moment of death. This moment ALWAYS is predetermined and Preordained. There is real, true resonance with the simple phrase, "It was his time to go." Similarly, when people say, "It was meant to happen," they are referring to their dharmic plan. We spend an inordinate amount of time following other people's tips and recommendations for "how to live longer," which if exercised, are done so in futility. It would be more accurate, as well as more far-reaching, enriching, and enhancing to develop and follow ways to "live better"—something over which we CAN exercise some influence.

In the case of the person who overdoses on cocaine and ends up dying, they would have died at that very same moment in time, anyway. The correlation between the consumption and fatal end result is inconsequential. As just stated, the choice to use a drug is only that—a free-will choice—and this choice alone does NOT cause death. If this same person had NOT chosen to use cocaine, they would have died at that very same moment in time, in some other fashion—regardless.

In the gut-wrenching case of a baby being left in an automobile unattended, if it is NOT that child's dharmically preprescribed time to die, they WILL survive this experience. If the child does in fact survive, there will be a resulting abundance of lessons to be learned by all involved. There are NO accidental deaths—only divinely predetermined moments in one's existence that will occur no matter what a person is doing or what free-will choice they happen to be exercising before or at the point of death. Thus, while these behaviors or actions (based upon one's free-will choices) may have acted as catalysts or processes, we cannot blame doing drugs, smoking cigarettes, or not wearing a seat belt as the True Cause(s) of someone's death.

In a similar vein, there is no question God views the acts of murder, homicide, and suicide as serious transgressions. Such actions, of course, are unholy. However, no matter how abhorrent and heinous these crimes against God's Gift of Life, these crimes in and of themselves are not the True Cause(s) of one's physical death. The dharmic plan for the deceased included the divine preprescription for this death to occur at that very moment in time.

Some of you may interpret this Divine Universal Law as license to utilize your God-given free-will choice in reckless, careless, inappropriate, nonsensical, and unhealthy ways. However, you might want to consider the fact that such choices will not directly change your dharmic plan—and thus not hasten, delay, or cause your death. Nonetheless, such choices may lead to a severely compromised body. This is the same body in which you will be imprisoned until your final God-determined dharmic termination point. In addition, using free-will choice to harm or kill one's self or another person undoubtedly guarantees the transgressor a massive karmic impaction.

God can choose to intervene on any soul's behalf for any reason. Transinterventions can take place regardless of any or all free-will choices a person makes. God can intervene with the purpose of extending or shortening one's lifespan. Of course, these situations are extremely rare. Many times, the opportunity for karmic fulfillments is very time-specific, with a divinely predetermined window of opportunity. During this Made Manifest opportunity, if one makes uplifting free-will choices in harmony with their dharmic-based pursuits, the subsequent fulfillment and alleviation of their karmic debt will have occurred in their TransImagined state.

Because we don't have access to our God-gifted dharmic blueprints, we must work hard to ensure we are in upwardly evolving sync with our divine plan for existence. The less we experience that all-too-familiar "fighting against the universe" or "going against the grain" as we approach and make our free-will choices, the closer and more harmoniously we will be aligning our dharmic plans with unconditional love. The ways we interpret, process and comprehend our Made Manifest free-will choices will provide good clues regarding whether or not we are influencing our dharmic plans toward or away from unconditional love.

Knowing that a spiritual upliftment occurred in your pre-Made Manifest TransImagined state, you can start today to align your every future moment with unconditionally loving responses to all your free-will choices. All your woven TransImagined, free-will influenced, now-Made Manifest, present, and future experiences will reflect these efforts.

This spiritual awareness upliftment technique becomes a twofold bene-fitting approach. It allows you to directly sow the seed of unconditional love into all yet-to-be experienced dharmic unenfoldments. (See Diagram of Spiritual Upliftment.)

Diagram of Spiritual Upliftment

Omni At-Oneness

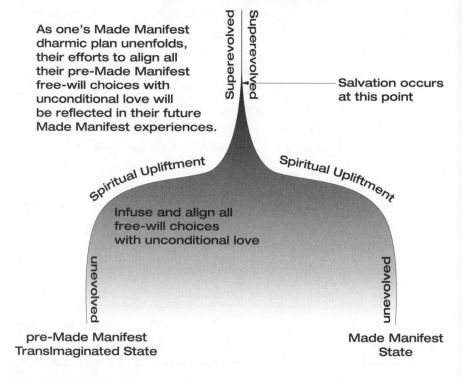

As one's Made Manifest dharmic plan unenfolds, their efforts to align all their pre-Made Manifest free-will choices with unconditional love will be reflected in their future Made Manifest experiences.

Superevolved Superevolved

Salvation occurs at this point

Spiritual Upliftment Spiritual Upliftment

Infuse and align all free-will choices with unconditional love

unevolved unevolved

pre-Made Manifest TransImagined State

Made Manifest State

The Psychology of Free Will

Because of dharma, people are divinely destined for their own unique individual paths. One's dharmic blueprint might include having experi-ences with such things as mental illness, breakdowns, major health crises, or other problems and issues for which people might seek help, treatment, or assistance. This search for help, along with the treatment, is PART of their dharma—and NOT a result of the ill person's free-will choices. These problems or "dharmic obstacles" are a result of a person's past karmic debts needing resolution through a manifesting life experience.

During my work as a psychologist, I never believed (and still do not believe) there is one "right" way to attend to a human being. I knew then, albeit on a more basic level, what I have come to know now on a deeper level: People walk into an doctor or therapist's office propelled by their dharma, NOT by their symptoms. The examples I will discuss are by no means exclusive to the fields of psychology, psychiatry, social work, therapy, or counseling. The points I will highlight are applicable throughout all human conscious experiences.

Contrary to what many people tend (or wish) to believe, it is not the helping professional who saves, fixes, or changes their clients. Rather, the relationship and experience a client has with a therapist or doctor is part of this client's God-given, dharmic blueprint. The issue, problem, or illness is part of this blueprint as well. It is in the client's dharma—not in the hands of the professional—that the client has this issue, the need for treatment, the actual treatment itself, as well as whatever transpires next as a result of all of these factors. The composite of these factors, as well as the ultimate results, comprise an individual's conscious experience. In combination and totality, these elements make up one's dharmic blueprint.

One's dharma contains the need for that person to overcome an issue, crisis, problem, or situation, from which they need to grow on some level. This dharmic issue or problem usually requires utilization of one's free will to propel themselves to overcome the obstacle itself. As such, it is one's free-will choice to do any or all of the following: (1) To recognize or identify a problem; (2) To seek support, help, or treatment; (3) To choose one treatment or therapist over another; and (4) To comply with a prescribed medical or psychotherapeutic treatment.

One can utilize their free-will choice to elect NOT to comply with any of the above options. If so, this person may run the risk of not fulfilling their growth opportunity contained within their dharmic plan. Of course, as a result, when one exercises free-will choices as such, they run the risk of further contributing to their karmic debtload. Thus, the challenge for a patient or client resides in how to discern the appropriate free-will decisions. There is no prescribed way to discern the correct free-will choice other than by trial and error. The only one viable option to assist someone with this challenge is to ask for divine guidance, to be directed to the initial uplifting free-will choice that will enable them to grow—without having to go through lesson after lesson until finally satisfying this karmic indebtedness.

Thus, there really is no one ideal group of theories that adequately can address a person's issues. In this context, the whole nature-versus-nurture debate is rendered nonapplicable, if not a baseless philosophy to explain dharmic reality. Neither nature nor nurture can explain or reason away life's many challenges, results, or physically manifesting realities. It is meaningless to give such credence to nature or nurture, when it is the divinely created dharmic blueprint that governs these and ALL aspects.

One's dharma IS who they are, and what their life path will be, as divinely preprescribed and TransImaginated. Thus, one's environment and related factors do NOT prescribe or explain one's destiny. As it relates to the free-will choices adults and parents make impacting their children, the nurture factor can be karmically impacting on all involved. Such impactions will contribute to the texture of one's path—but will not alter the path's key dharmic components. Really, the only nature or nurture truly influencing destiny's path is the Creator of that path—God.

While in my clinical practice, I did not have this thorough comprehension of dharma or TransImagination. Instead, I was able to utilize my cognitive reasoning to make interpretations for what I intended and hoped would benefit my clients' well-being and welfare. I also never subscribed to either the nature or nurture philosophy with any real zeal, and I did not adhere to a particular stand regarding the use of psychotropic medications as an adjunct to psychotherapy. I always told my clients I supported them in THEIR discovery and understanding of what might work well. I felt they were their own best experts, had the key to insight, and I was merely there as a catalyst to such processes. As such, I had a difficult time internally assuming the role of supposedly having the "answers," let alone oftentimes being required by third-party insurance companies or referral sources to follow a "set" therapeutic path or make diagnoses in order for clients to continue receiving additional sessions.

Who was I to be in the position of defining what was occurring inside my clients' beings? Granted, there were issues with which some of my clients grappled that indeed did blur their clarity and perceptions. However, the act of placing one person or system in charge of diagnosing, or in a position of power to influence, another's potential free-will choices is worthy of some contemplation. I most certainly did not have access to other people's divinely enfolded dharmic (preprescripted) information—no more than they themselves did. I tried to do minimal diagnosing, attend to clients as comprehensively as possible, and let them know where I thought the real gems of insight truly resided—within each and every one of them.

I always have felt and known that there is a lot more at play when it comes to how people are "wired." There also is a lot more behind humans' outwardly manifesting behaviors and expression than nature, nurture, or any combination thereof possibly could explain. I always have felt people were capable of making changes, but that there were limits involved. People's insights and potential for change always reside and operate deep within them. Thus, I felt any limits to personal change were those I never could begin to predict or conceive. I considered and perceived change as possible, an ability, but truly always based upon one's WILLINGNESS to CHOOSE to do so. Change is only possible when an intentional willingness is combined with an energized focused choice.

I've always known that with regard to people's individual changes, the limits resided deep, in people's cores or essences. At their innermost cores, I felt people contained the seeds and roots for the finite structure encasing their existence. I now know such encasement or structure IS one's individual dharmic plan.

Seeing people repeatedly return with the same symptoms, complaints, situations, or circumstances, or seeing them worsening or spiraling further downward, was extremely painful and difficult for me to behold. There were many issues or illnesses that never seemed to remit for long. There were times when I felt I was fighting against the universe, rather than against the illness or problem at hand. It was during those times when I realized I could be supportive but certainly no more effective than my clients themselves.

As a graduate student, I was instructed on how to deal with suicidal clients. I recall being told, "If someone wants and intends to kill themself, they will do so—oftentimes despite another's efforts to prevent it." I found myself wondering how I would manage to balance in my mind the reality of suicide, while also making sure I was doing my proper, ethical duty in my professional role. I didn't know it then, but I was hitting up against the issue of dharma. I also knew deep down that mental health and medical professionals all too often egoistically (and erroneously) take credit for what they interpret as preventing a client's suicide or otherwise saving a life. While I still did not fully understand the concept of dharma then, I nonetheless knew in my heart that no mortal had or ever will have that kind of power. Human beings do not prevent another's death, but rather merely interact within the continual unenfoldment of another's dharmic plan.

I also found myself having trouble buying into the notion that issues and problems are "genetic" or "in the family," as is common thought amongst mental health and medical professionals. While there often were seemingly obvious patterns to support this thought, there also were enough of a highly random nature that failed to do so. Such random patterns indeed confirmed this generic rationale as being completely unrelated to the manifesting problems. I have come to realize the only so-called "family" in and from which illnesses seem to reside was and forever will be the family of all earth humankind. There are way too many reasons—many unknown—why and how people get sick or well. Thus, it is nearly impossible to discern with exactitude the factors behind all human, dharmically based problems.

Can people change? Yes, to a limit—one that I do not, cannot, and am not supposed to know. Yes, people can change—only if they themselves are willing to choose to make changes. No matter what changes may take place in our lives, all of us at our innermost cores remain where we began at a seed level. Only God truly determines the seeds' blueprint plan and subsequent path, gifting all of us free-will choices to make along the way. Understanding this concept has been invaluable for me on many levels.

My spiritual path of learning, growth, and evolution has required me to examine deeply my core belief system regarding the mysteries of existence. What I thought I knew to be true certainly revealed itself to be inconsistently true at best. I had to rethink a lot of things, including my perspective on death.

One of the most challenging aspects of understanding the concept of reincarnation and related experiences is that of making peace within oneself about the death of loved ones. Contrary to what many have believed and may continue to want to believe, after someone dies, they—and those around them—are NOT able to communicate. There simply is NO avenue of communication to or from the afterlife. When considering the loss of loved ones, this reality can be difficult to understand, let alone digest and swallow.

Because the effects of this reality are potentially heavy hitting with long-lasting reverberations, it behooves us to take stock of how we exercise our free-will choices. It is important to do our life work now, for there is no guarantee that we will ever meet the same people again through reincarnation. It is so important to enjoy relationships today, for you may never encounter these souls again.

Assisted and accompanied by God, we are born alone and we die alone. It will not help, and can actually hurt, to cling to the unrealistic belief that we and the departed can converse together. It is important to make peace with any unfulfilled desires from present or past existences. Attachments made pertaining to unfulfilled desires must be resolved, for in the Spirit Realm, there is no assurance of ever rejoining with the same souls and thus alleviating such unmet desires. When someone is gone, they are gone. Only through God's Will alone would there ever be any chance of a reunion in future incarnations. However, once emancipation from the physical incarnating process is achieved and physical karmic debt satisfied, reunions with the souls of past loved ones becomes highly possible. We will discuss these realities in greater depth within the Spiritual Dharma subsection.

Some of us have been conditioned to believe we're seeing signs from deceased loved ones. However seemingly well meaning, psychics and mediums perpetuate these notions or disbeliefs—rooted not in truth but actually derived from within a psychic's own imaginations from their personal perceptions. There are NO God-sanctioned channelers, mediums, or psychics. The reason for all of this is that psychic and related work is a soul transgression, a transgression against God. In extremely rare situations, addressed case by case, God will utilize a psychic and manifest through their work. In these instances, God operates within the combination of the client and psychic facilitator as they fit into God's Divine Reperfecting Plan. This was the case for me and the benevolent psychic, who supplied me with the intricate details of my past incarnations and connections to the Transintervened and thus preprescribed entity—all of which was validated by the Holy Sanctioned Angel.

As vulnerable humans, we cling to hope, wanting to believe in something tangible and validating to help us understand what is incomprehensible—to comfort our insecure fears and cope with unknowns, including death. Because there is no communication link to deceased loved ones, people's desperate yearning to reconnect with them becomes unfulfilled desire, eventually becoming karmic indebtedness in need of rebalancing.

Cognitive Interpretations
Intuition

Contrary to what earth humankind has believed and perpetuated, intuition is not what we've perceived. Intuition as Superconscious perception is a uniquely individual Holy wheel contained and maintained by the Causal container aspect of a human being. Idea based, this Causal wheel influences both the Causal and Astral existences rather than those in the physical realm. No psychic accesses intuition. Intuition is Super-Consciousness that is infused into the spiritual wheel, which is contained and maintained in the Causal container. Intuition is pure, human SuperConsciousness—part of the actual soul itself. Intuition is insulated from the material universe by an entire system of containers and lightway barriers, all divinely constructed. Just like God is divinely protected from the physically manifesting, the spiritual and intuitive aspect of soul is protected from the material cosmos.

For those trying to improve or work on their intuition and intuitive capabilities, such efforts are futile. Intuition is governed by the Holy Neutrino Universe, and anyone who is contained and maintained by their own physically manifesting body couldn't possibly affect or access anything based in such holiness as intuition. IF someone were to access their own intuition, they first would have to completely eradicate ALL physical contamination, including their ego, all past karma, all aspects of reincarnation, and eliminate and relinquish their free will. In other words, one must trust so unequivocally in God, that they turn over their entire conscious experience to the intentional Will of God. Only then will God divinely activate one's SuperConscious intuition, allow it to be enhanced, and ensure that it becomes one's SuperConscious experience. At this point, one exists in and of the Unity—as a physically incarnated Saint. This Superevolved state would, of course, be preprescribed or Trans-Imagined into their dharmic plan.

Cognitive Reasoning—The Dharmic Gift

Every human has a gift, wrapped or encased into their dharma.

Sometimes this gift is a keen ability to discern. This ability to discern resides in the intellectual wheel of conscious ability. It is more primitive than intuition. Known as cognitive reasoning, this ability to discern is one's capacity to identify patterns. It is the ability to put together particles of one's reality to create a loosely connected whole—and has NOTHING at all to do with intuition. When one utilizes cognitive reasoning, the "hits" or experiences they receive internally are called "intellectual cognitions."

Typically, people erroneously label cognitive reasoning as intuition and refer to intellectual cognitions as "senses," "gut feelings," "feelings," or even "intuitions." Psychics who utilize their cognitive reasoning abilities are NOT using their intuition. Cognitive reasoning is an Astral Universe-based phenomenon. As long as people use it for their OWN purposes, they are not dishonoring God. However, this is most problematic if or when people such as psychics use it to assist others.

The accuracy of cognitive reasoning depends on the degree of purity or contamination of the person who is making the discernments. Both psychics and nonpsychics confuse cognitive reasoning with intuition. Clearly, cognitive reasoning is easily convoluted and difficult to maintain over time with any accuracy. If cognitive reasoning is utilized for ANY purpose other than for one's own personal insight, whether used benevolently or malevolently, inaccurately or accurately, simply does not matter. When cognitive reasoning is not being utilized for one's own purpose and growth, it WILL be ego impacting and karmically impacting for the person doing the discerning—and this person will be transgressing against God. A psychic, however truly well intentioned, transgresses against God by utilizing their cognitive reasoning skills to help or assist a client. By assisting or helping in such a manner, a psychic ends up destructively influencing the client by interfering with the client's free-will choices.

For several similar reasons, both astrology and numerology are problematic. In addition, those (like psychics) who engage in such pursuits and utilize perceptions that influence the free will of others are transgressing. While problematic, both practices do have some roots in fact. It is true that at the time of one's birth, the spatio temporal heavens are in a certain geometric—and hence, mathematical—heavenly order. Randomly and without malevolence or benevolence, the heavenly bodies do exert their nondirected radiations and electromagnetic influence upon all existence in incomprehensible ways.

The problem regarding these practices resides in attributing to the placement of celestial bodies an insightful relationship into every person's dharmic plan. God does not cryptically inscribe into everyone's experience a divine insight, somehow hidden in the placement of celestial bodies whose organizational pattern was established upon the birth of every earth organism. Both astrology and numerology are just like omens and superstitions—nonsense. Void of any substantiation to support them, these pursuits and concepts are baseless. As stated earlier, the other troubling aspect for these misguided pursuits is the interfering or influencing effect they have upon people's free-will choices.

Whether you are a metaphysician or not, if your intention, however subtle, is to influence another person's free will, it IS a transgression against God. If you experience the hit of an intellectual cognition about someone, you impart this cognition TO them, and they digest and their choices are influenced by this cognition, then you have transgressed. In this example, you have in effect, influenced this person's perceptions and free-will choices. However seemingly well-meaning at the time, your choice to impart your cognitions to this person may even result in their making a certain kind of choice, based upon having heard what YOU had to say. If this person had NOT experienced hearing your cognitions, they may well have made other choices. One will never know.

One may truly feel in their heart that they are doing a service, favor, or even a blessing by imparting intellectual cognitions and related interpretations to a client, family member, or friend. Such imparting may even appear to be well-meaning, as the person imparting such thoughts may perceive it as such. Perhaps the recipient actually is soliciting and hoping for such cognitive feedback or insight. Nonetheless, one's perception of being helpful or well-meaning is superseded by one larger fact. They have imposed personal perceptions upon another impressionable human being who otherwise would be exercising free-will choices based upon their OWN cognitive reasoning capabilities—untainted by anyone else's perceptions.

So, when speaking your mind in any situation that is not yours alone to influence via personal free-will choice, bear in mind that you very well may be transgressing. As you now know, this kind of transgression is karmically impacting. This is why not even Angels themselves operate or influence within human beings' conscious free-will choices. The weight of every transgression is always directly proportional to the karmic impaction experienced by the transgressor. The weight of the karmic impaction only can be determined by God, Whose benchmark is Unconditional Love.

One always has a free-will choice whether or not to activate or access their cognitive reasoning abilities in the first place. This choice is part of one's dharmic blueprint, as cognitive reasoning is part of one's intellectual Astral Wheel capacity, and as such, a necessary part of one's dharma. In response to recognizing such abilities within one's self, some humans react to this realization with fear. This fear response actually IS an example of negatively relating to this information. As such, the avoidance, anticipation, and fear all become karmically impacting. Fear of one's own potential can be incredibly incapacitating.

God endows every soul with hidden gifts or unrealized potential, which, by directing one's individual free will, can be recognized, nurtured, and developed into focused pursuits. By focusing on certain interests, passions, and philosophies, people create and feed their self-imposed perceptions, facilitating and perpetuating the manifestations of their intentions. People tell themselves a certain message regarding their pursuits, believe it, and accordingly, establish the corresponding steps by which to accomplish their goals relative to these beliefs and pursuits.

After taking actions to make these goals come true, people experience the manifesting reflection (and hopefully, satisfaction) of the fruits of their labor—from years of goals being met. Finally, and most validating and confirming, people realize that they embody their thoughts and created self-perceptions. The rich heritage, spiritually evolved, and Holy Beings originating from and living in India are evidence of this phenomenon of focused conscious experience manifesting into reality. As compared to the societies within other world countries, India's culture places a high value upon spiritual evolution and related pursuits, which is reflected in India's disproportionately large number of recognized Saints.

Cognitive Reasoning Patterns: Addictions and Compulsions

As previously stated, human beings use cognitive reasoning abilities to make free-will choices in life. At times, we also use cognitive reasoning to interpret, analyze, and quite possibly to attempt to justify such choices and their results or impact on all involved. The power of the mind is so strong that to it we attribute the erroneously based qualities of sensing, or intuiting. Instead, the mind actually is the engine that propels us to make INTERPRETATIONS based upon cognitions or thoughts. It is our cognitive reasoning abilities that lead us to create, maintain, or extinguish certain behavioral or cognitive reasoning patterns throughout our existence. Thus, we have our mind to thank—or clobber—for being the powerful engine driven by our varied free-will choices, as well as contributing to how we interpret, process, and comprehend them.

The cognitive reasoning patterns of behavior reflect more than mere cognitive reasoning abilities. Also at work are the karma, dharma, and a whole host of ego-impacting free-will choices, assuming roles of both influenced and influencing factors in one's existence. With regard to free will, cognitive reasoning, and children, it is important to recall when free will actually begins to emerge and transpire. Humans' thirty-five light-ways or wheels are in place at the moment of conception. The moment the soul is Transimplanted into the fetus is the moment the human electro-magnetic fields (HEM) begin to govern all three containers composing the human being. Before this stage, the HEM fields are solely God-directed. Once the fetus is born, the thirty-five information-laden lightways contain and maintain the Transimplanted consciousness or minute Essence of God.

For example, a baby would make random perceptions while also developing patterns of random familiarity. Over time, these random patterns of familiarity develop into cognitive reasoning capabilities, utilized by this now older person's influence of free will over their conscious experience. Thus, as a person's conscious experience unenfolds, they begin cognitively influencing their immediate surroundings through their free will. There is no set age for this process to be initiated and developed.

Our cognitive reasoning patterns are exemplified by our behavioral responses. Our behaviors are the outward reflections of our internal selves, especially as we contend with our free-will choices along our dharmic life paths. All too often, our behavioral responses reflect our inward or internal unrest or disease, resulting in a myriad of unresolved emotions and feelings, as well as some stubbornly troublesome addictions and compulsions. Unresolved feelings might include grief, anger, guilt, resentment, shame, remorse, or misgivings. If accompanied by a layer of addictions or compulsions—or both—such weighty emotional burdens can lead to an even weightier and extremely impacting self-disrespect, self-punishment, or self-loathing, and more of the same continued, unresolved feelings.

Addictions are cognitive reasoning patterns influenced by free will to such a repetitious state that the unconscious or subconscious aspects of the mind influence or take control of the person's thought patterns. The subconscious aspects, as they relate to the free will of human existence, also eventually are rooted in the ego. Our compulsions to do or act in specific, oftentimes self-prescribed manners, only further fuel our addictions. In such cases of overabundance and overdependence within one's cognitive reasoning, more or more often is not necessarily best.

For a multitude of reasons and benefits, it is important to attempt to resolve any such unresolved feelings; doing so only will help in remedying any impacting and destructive cognitive patterned behaviors. If we are aware of our feelings and behaviors, as well as the cognitions or thoughts fueling them, we will be able to greatly reduce the infractions, transgressions, and impactions we inflict upon others as well as ourselves. When we begin to assess and take remedying action in this way, we can get that much closer to being in tune with what God truly wishes for us to experience in our existence as spiritual, evolving beings.

How do we go about trying to resolve these problematic patterns, especially if we've managed to perfect them over years of unfortunate practice? The first step involves considering the intricacy and complexity of the layered connections between our actions and their impact on others and us. While it may seem simple or basic that our cognitions drive our actions and behaviors, it is deceptively so. When we begin to make these important connections for improved, overall comprehension, we must remember to bring TO such consideration a consciousness or mindfulness. This mindfulness implores that we see vividly the different levels and layers of each component in the thought-behavior equation. If we are to evolve as spiritual beings, we no longer can afford to be ignorant of, blind to, or in denial about how each component in these equations is important, as well as its role contributing to the equation or pattern as a whole.

All too often, we lack the insight, patience, wisdom, and depth of comprehension needed in order to see how we really function and operate within our own lives—and how we impact the lives of others around us. We tend to absorb our conscious experiences almost to unimaginably great proportions. In doing so, we disallow any chance of bringing to such situations the wisdom and depth of comprehension these situations so desperately require and deserve. Thus, we truly are incapable of facing and experiencing our lives with an understanding, let alone a comprehension, built upon the simple but profound principle of "net and release."

Instead, we hang onto our experiences and attribute to them our thoughts, feelings, and attitudes that propel us to respond with behaviors that at times range from reactive to incredibly abusive. When we behave in such ways, we cause others and ourselves some very unnecessary and potentially destructive contamination and impaction. For example, when we really know the difference between sharing our feelings and slopping or dumping them onto another person, we have demonstrated that we have the wisdom or comprehension to discern internally, and this comprehension IS reflected in our very behaviors.

When we bring to our conscious experiences a wide net of deep comprehension, we are able to see the grander, infinitely larger picture of how we all participate in our universal existence. We then can see more clearly the selfishness, ignorance, shallowness, and incomprehending nature of our ways. Only then can we accept our differences while permitting ourselves to be open to implementing some changes.

In order to better comprehend how our cognitions influence our behavioral patterns, we need to examine the building blocks that comprise such connections, as well as those that determine the resulting impact. Typically, we consider our thoughts and behaviors to be a relatively basic, two-part process. In reality, here are the six components comprising this process.

First, there is our intention—the motive that drives all that follows, the innermost component reflecting the relative evolutionary state of our selves. Second, there is a thought or cognition, which propels us into behavior or action. Third, the action or behavior itself. Fourth is the reaction—our own and that of anyone else who might be impacted by all of the components thus far that have informed and influenced this process. The fifth is the impact or result of all previous steps, as they are compiled upon one another. The sixth is the reverberation, the vibratory, mirrored reflection back to us—of the impact on ourselves and/or others—on a multitude of levels.

When we witness an injustice, neglect a responsibility, or abuse a situation or person, our cognitive reasoning abilities are at work. This is the case, as well, when we covet or harbor unfulfilled desires and yearnings. Our free will adds additional layers of dimension to such experiences, and our subsequent actions, reactions, impactions, and reverberations reflect back—often in unimaginably powerful ways—to us and others around us. This process of intention to reverberation—and everything in between—applies to the most profound, as well as the most seemingly simplistic examples in existence. Whether we witness someone begging for food or money, or we notice a mosquito entering our otherwise insect-free kitchen, we are challenged and tested. How we interpret, process, and respond to the challenges of existence is up to us.

Basically, thoughts drive actions, which cause an impact. On a deeper level, our thoughts oftentimes become human infractions, our actions or behaviors become unholy transgressions, and the resulting impact of it all becomes any number of karmic impactions upon ourselves and those around us. Time and time again, how we perceive, think, and respond speaks volumes about our relative spiritual evolution. All too often, we robotically lumber through existence without pausing to consider the intricate nature of our ways.

We think if we atone—even by prayer—for set times, on set days, in set ways, we can absolve our transgressions. Secretly, we hope to abolish our responsibilities, our roles, and in some circumstances, ourselves, from troubling involvements that got us into hot water. When we later find ourselves laboring under the self-imposed burdens of obsession or addiction, or perhaps steeped in the waters of unresolved regret or other lingering emotions, we wonder what went awry and where we went wrong.

It does little good to continue on such paths, only to cope with our regrets with disbelief, puzzlement, denial, and anger, and make urgent, desperate pleas within subscribed, theologically based rules for atonement. Such patterns only prove to be set-ups for our failure, when in reality, the keys to evolving, improving ourselves, and gaining insight reside right at home, within each and every one of us. No matter how we perceive, think, or act, no matter what theology we choose or don't choose, no matter who we are, from where we came, and what skills, resources, talents, riches, deficits, strengths, or ills we have, absolutely NOTHING of or about us goes unplanned by God.

When we utilize our free-will choices with better discernment, we might just notice that in time, even the intentions which power our cognitions will begin to change. As a result, we actually will be operating for a higher good and purpose, other than that of satisfying our own desires or alleviating our own discomforts. It also is important to spend time working with the cognitive reasoning abilities that reside within us, in addition to developing and nurturing our own, personal, individual connections with God.

While it may seem remedial or superficial, it is critical to practice training our minds to work in alternative ways. Our minds are powerful enough to make us sick or well, angry or joyous, worried or calm. Because our minds fuel our behaviors, it truly is a reality of mind over matter. When we give our minds another option or alternative to what perhaps have been our knee-jerk reactions to life's circumstances, we do others and ourselves a big favor. When we consider what it would be like to do, feel, and experience situations in a more benevolent and receptive manner, we will notice ourselves doing just that. As we experience more and more improved thoughts and responses, soon we will not only feel and behave better, but we also will think, perceive, and intend in better, more benevolent ways.

When we make inroads by choosing to approach existence differently and with more awareness, we in fact will notice we've utilized our free-will choices appropriately and wisely. Remember, free-will choices produce ALL karmic imbalances in limitless ways. The better our choices, the more we will facilitate harmony within our dharmic plans.

This principle is ever apparent in human image portrayal. People tend to portray an image they feel suits that particular situation. It is easy to see through the façade that most people project outwardly. Our outward treatment of others speaks volumes and provides much external proof of either our true inner happiness—or our angst.

When we feel, experience, and appreciate the positive energy and intention we bring to our thoughts, it is natural and easy to bring such goodness to the free-will choices in our lives. Indeed, how we see and respond to others and situations around us comprise this amazing, big picture of human existence. This notion is not just about sparing the life of that one bug in your kitchen on a Saturday. Truly comprehending this complex process is about the fact that it applies to each and every bug, each and every day, at each and every moment of your conscious, personal experience of human existence.

On the opposite end of the spectrum from great conscious, insightful awareness are conditioned patterned responses. Conditioned patterned responses are those that could be characterized as automatic responses. Like automatic pilot, these seemingly innate, nearly robotic responses made without much foresight, certainly lack any depth of comprehension in order to attain a more universal, complete, "big picture" perspective. No matter what the pollutant, be it one's mother-in-law, supervisor, clients, or one's own internal response to such stressors, the results can be debilitating to both adults and children. Only exacerbating the impact of these conditioned patterned responses is the fact that most often they are exhibited by people who should know better.

Many times, adults exercising bad free-will choices subject innocents around them to the inevitable consequences of their decisions. Children are subjected to their parents' inability to process and express their own internal dysfunctions. Adults inappropriately and ignorantly victimize each other. In all cases, the phenomenon occurring is the uncontrolled expelling of pent-up energy with no positive outlet from which to flow. Those who vent, dump, vomit, contaminate, or physically harm others with ill-will, do so out of frustrated anger, feigned unaccountability or responsibility, and the unwillingness to acknowledge the very true controllable and preventable nature of these destructive responses. It behooves all of us to recognize our individual responsibility for the healthy expunging of our personal frustrations—and to consider how we might otherwise conduct ourselves.

Fortunately, as humans, our relative coping success truly IS a matter of "mind over matter." When employing this philosophy, and practicing it with commitment, authenticity, and the intention of doing so for goodness, one might experience some real spiritual upliftment. Of course, this all requires some understanding of, insight into, and accountability for our tendencies to respond to life in conditioned patterned ways. We must have and project the sincere desire to approach things differently.

In the cases of animals and plants—neither of which have free will— we can explore the very practical, behavioral application of consciousness. Such consciousness is based upon lower functioning cognitive reasoning abilities, or perhaps limited or compromised abilities. Nonetheless, all manifesting life forms have the eternal opportunity to evolve from conscious experience to conscious experience. Like humans, all life forms have lightways or wheels that allow for the natural fabrication and facilitation of their particular conscious experience. All animals possess three primary lightways: fear, joy/thankfulness, and sadness, along with their particular conscious identity—or the specific qualities that make every animal unique.

God governs these beings, and as such, they have no free will. When we consider the behaviors of animals such as dogs and monkeys, or insects such as ants, we can see the capacity of the particular level of consciousness at work. We see in all such groups the level of consciousness at which all members of each species communicate worldwide.

Every domesticated dog (including my own) possesses and demonstrates (in both charming-delightful and not-so-lovely ways) their own, special idiosyncratic behavior patterns. However, it also is true that on a basic level, ALL domesticated dogs are tuned in to the same, universal channel of D.O.G. In other words, a Russian dog visiting the United States will bark, and without doubt or question, his American canine counterpart will understand. The channel of D.O.G. is that to which all dogs are wired.

The "on" button to this universal D.O.G. channel operates on a sustained and continual basis. This phenomenon humorously is exhibited in the situation when both you and your beloved dog are entering your home, during which you inadvertently ring the doorbell with your elbow. By the intense and passionate nature of your dog's ballistic response, one would think the two of you might be inside your home, receiving very important, unexpected guests. For the dog, who by the way still is outside the home, any doorbell chime—whether heard indoors or outside—still elicits the same exuberant D.O.G. response. In the case of my dog, my elbow-bumping, doorbell-ringing behavior stimulates within him a passionate response. So, just as soon as the door cracks open wide enough for him to race back into the home, he promptly assumes his rightful position of sitting facing the door from the inside—and continues to be "misbarkin'."

Another example of such communication capacity exists as consciousness within consciousness, which is evident in what has been called the Hundreth Monkey Phenomenon. For eons, primates have been deathly afraid of the water, unable to hold their breath, with no ability to swim. Some isolated monkeys live on an island off the coast of Japan. Tired of eating dirt-encrusted sweet potatoes, the alpha female reached into the water, washed one off, and promptly consumed it. Other monkeys observing her also began to tentatively wash sweet potatoes—eventually entering the sea and consuming things. Almost immediately, scientists allegedly observed an astounding phenomenon as monkeys worldwide lost their trepidation of the water and began to wade into the water, wash their potatoes, and retrieve potential food objects. This alleged phenomenon was dubbed the Hundreth Monkey Phenomenon.

In theory, it took one hundred monkeys engaged in washing sweet potatoes to consciously transmit the idea to monkeys worldwide. While the transmission phenomenon was false, the "monkey see, monkey do" phenomenon was clearly evident. In other words, it required learning, growing, and evolving, in order to produce one capable of overcoming its innate fear. Eventually breaking the old paradigm, it established new cognitive conscious conceptualizations around which to form new patterns. In actuality, it was not a hundredth alpha monkey or even a new phenomenon, at all. The individual monkey's consciousness always had contained within its DNA the information necessary to overcome its water fears and break the psychological barriers preventing it from doing so. Lower grade thought processes create an artificial limitation that easily becomes an accepted ideological complacency. This imperceptible barrier prevents monkey, humankind, and most other life forms from reaching beyond the tried and true. These perceived retardants are formulated out of acknowledged patterns of established thoughts.

However, existence is not hemmed in by actual, but rather interpretive, parentheses. From this perspective alone, evolution is incorrect. All whales once were large, carnivorous land creatures. Just like the alpha monkey, one of these beasts one day stood on the bank of the sea and ventured beyond its established, familiar, conscious parameters. Exercising its free-will choice, it dove headlong into the vast sea of the unknown, eventually formulating a cognitive "known" out of its experience. All existence was placed here from elsewhere in the physical cosmos and has been given the opportunity to sink or swim.

There also is evidence of species overlap when it comes to the wheels of communication. This can be noted when a blue jay or crow flies overhead, squawking about something, and birds, squirrels, and rabbits all understand the warning to flee—and quickly follow suit. So, even though there is a distinct physical difference between birds and squirrels, they are able to communicate intelligibly. In a Unified state of Super-Consciousness, the ability for earth human beings to understand and discern becomes innate—a natural extension of one's ever-deepening SuperConscious comprehension.

Oftentimes, a Holy Angel is operating through these beings, which are by then void of ego and dualistic attachments, and have attained freedom from physical reincarnation. In this case, the Holy Angel is responsible for the divine wisdom that so effortlessly flows through these beings. Most often, the Angel and the Divine Source are completely unknown—even to the now-SuperConsciously attuned beings, themselves.

Essentially, planet Earth is a vast petri dish of available DNA. God has allowed planet Earth's inhabitants through higher conscious perceptions to discern and eventually attain ever-Deepening Comprehension. It was not by evolution that life continued to expand, but rather from the very lack of any ingrained, conscious restrictions placed by God upon any manifesting creation. Some DNA manipulation or introgression was conducted by otherworldly beings for specific purposes, but these were unusual events. Most of our known evolutionary attributions were simply the results of the upliftment of reincarnating consciousness, combined with unrestricted conscious comprehension capabilities of creation.

The collective consciousness is one of the more primitive communication states. It easily is observed when a rock is overturned, and the entire freshly exposed ant colony evaporates down into the ground in a completely orderly, robotically purposeful manner. There is no confusion, the ants don't hit one another, and every individual unit making up the whole has an innate, predetermined role in the evacuating emergency. Notice the profound paradox when such mentality is applied to earth humankind. This is a case where free will would be very problematic. In the situations of soccer riots, Nazi followers, natural disasters, and fires or bombs within crowded public spaces, human beings tend to exhibit more of their base-level, subconscious "abilities," resulting in mass hysteria.

Typically, when faced with such tough situations, humans get sucked into an ignorant stupor, resulting in lemming-like behavior. As such, in an attempt to save themself, a drowning person will drown others—even when those others are trying to help. This drowning person cannot and does not consider that the other people are trying to assist. The drowning person simply cannot bring to their cognitive reasoning skills the sound, more developed consciousness required to ensure a better outcome—and less physically, karmically impacting choice.

Similar to conditioned patterned responses is the phenomenon of conditioned patterned resignation by which people decide to reside in varying states of learned helplessness. Here, people assume the victim mentality of "why bother, things won't improve anyway." In doing so, they allow other people and external forces around them to assume inordinate amounts of power and control. Devoid of their own fortitude and inner truth, these people tend to fill up their own empty inner voids with anything they perceive as strong and powerful enough to do the job of showing and telling them the way to exist.

This often translates to people filling themselves up to the brim with various dogma-based, unsubstantiated perceptions—only to leave them exacerbating their self-imposed victim status by becoming "better Christians," "better Jews," or "better Muslims," etc. Unfortunately, in giving permission to external sources to enter into one's experience to this extent, people risk losing all sense of self and any truth discernment abilities whatsoever.

Our souls are like sprouts that start out with exuberance, wanting to absorb God's Photonic Holiness. Our minds and consciousness are like a divine, growing tree—although time and time again, we tend to crowd our tree with vegetation trucks. We run right over this tree with contamination. Our minds fuel our self-demise and the demise we project onto others. When we clutter ourselves, our minds, consciousness, and the tree within ourselves, we undermine the very holiness and beauty of our God-given souls. We fail to recognize or appreciate the very heaven on and of planet Earth we could be experiencing during our existences.

God has seen, sees, and forever will continue to see the beautiful essence of this tree, which in its shade creates an entire ecosystem to nourish. In the Holy Eye of God, we human beings ARE infinite potentiality. God so benevolently and generously has gifted us the seeds with which we are to evolve. Now is the time—yet another gift—for us to begin to understand our potentiality. Now is the time to comprehend that we all receive the holiest of gifts when we begin to respond in kind.

Spiritual Dharma
Wheels of Consciousness

The inwardly reflecting three Universes—Causal, Astral, and physical—are divided into fifteen levels or membranes of consciousness. These membranes become more powerful and efficient the closer they are to the Holy Source, which is located in a blissful void beyond level fifteen. The Unified membranes of the Spirit Realm are composed of levels fifteen through twelve. The duality consists of levels eleven through one, with level one being rock or stone.

Human communication is conducted between levels six through eight. Human verbal communication operates through the sixth level capacity or membrane. The comprehension and communication levels of earth humans are relegated and limited to a specific, appropriate range, based on their individual evolutionary attunement. People are governed by a particular membrane of communication or comprehension as they evolve continuously until they have worked their way back to the Holy Source. The Holy Source begins Its unifying SuperConscious influence at Unified level twelve, continuing through level fifteen.

Level six is the lowest human intellectual communicative membrane of consciousness and is the level that does not contain free will. Developmentally delayed, retarded, brain-injured, or intellectually impaired human beings operate their highest cognitive reasoning capabilities at level six, where free will does not exist. Free will is prevalent from levels eight through eleven, but not including level twelve. At level eleven, earth humans have begun a transitory stage, where free will begins to meld into the ego—and at level twelve, this free will has been absorbed and is no longer utilized. Human beings experiencing this transitory stage between levels eleven and twelve direct their free will for the betterment and upliftment of all other surrounding consciousness—and no longer for their own personal advantage.

The highest level of human intellectual comprehension occurs in the atom or level eight membrane. Psychics, hypnotherapists, mediums, advanced astrologers, and channelers all operate within the atom or level eight realm. By utilizing their cognitive reasoning capabilities, all of these practitioners operate with varying degrees of accuracy and success within the constraints of the level eight realm.

The level eight realm is the highest attainable capability afforded to human beings. Level eight still is located within the material, manifesting universe—nowhere near the Unified, Holy Angelic realms, which begin at level twelve. There is a definite barrier between the manifesting, material universe and the Spiritual, Astral Universe. This barrier is impermeable to all but God, absolutely preventing any earth human from accessing, interpreting, or interfering with information divinely maintained and protected SuperConsciously.

This impenetrable barrier prevents deceased beings existing in the lowest, most abominable regions of level nine in the Astral Universe from reaccessing an existence back into our physically manifesting universe. It is within the lowest regions of level nine in the Astral Universe, to which the most heavily karmically indebted beings are restricted. If the theologically derived terms "hell" and "evil" ever were to apply to any form of heavily indebted manifested existence, they aptly would describe these gloom-drenched, war-riddled, lower region dwellers.

Dualistic membranes one through eleven actually are levels of consciousness within consciousness. At level twelve, the membranes merge, becoming the Unity, where the SuperConsciousness of God becomes one's no-longer-individual consciousness. The SuperConsciousness supersedes all other influences of thought. Through focused development by deep prayer and meditation, the Unified human increases their capacity for receiving ever-increasing magnitudes of Holiness or God attunement. God's electromagnetic fields contain and maintain all manifesting levels, one through fifteen. These manifesting electromagnetic and gravitational fields are the only two influences containing and maintaining SuperConsciousness throughout these levels.

These electromagnetic fields of minimal to measureless amplitude make up what is known as consciousness within consciousness. All manifesting creation is indivisibly held together by its individual consciousness, contained and maintained within electromagnetic fields of energy. This means that every aspect of manifesting existence has a capacity or communication level in which it operates. Consciousness within consciousness as all fifteen levels of manifesting existence collectively is known as the Manifesting Infinite SuperConsciousness. This consciousness within consciousness membrane communication system is that by which all manifesting Creation operates.

As previously stated, the conscious capacity of any particular manifesting existence determines the membrane by which this existence communicates. In other words, a monkey is incapable of operating an automobile, for as per this Divinely Governing Principle, it lacks the free-will conscious capacity to do so. Any increase in a being's accrued electromagnetic resonance is directly proportionate to this being's capacity to attune to the appropriate corresponding level of membrane communication. In other words, car-driving human beings have a greater electromagnetic or conscious resonance capacity than do their primate counterparts. This archetype is consistent throughout the entire three manifesting universes.

When foods such as fruit or vegetables first are removed from the vine, the prana or electromagnetic fields, as well as the exchangeable sustenance capabilities of hydrogen electrons are at their peak. The longer the food is removed from the vine, the greater the effect of cosmic decay—and the less available prana or life force for cellular assimilation. One of the problems with genetically altered foods is the harmful effect on the foods' electromagnetic fields. The genetic alterations of the foods' DNA blueprint are oftentimes unrecognized by the body, and thus interfere with the cellular assimilation process. The result is the storing and subsequent accumulation of nonassimilable, nonfood substances within the human body.

The body's inability to recognize these non-foods causes the unhealthy accumulation of toxic or poisonous substances within the body's tissues. Similarly troubling, labile iron within the cells of the body changes and often becomes hypervalent iron when interacting with manipulated sugar. This ongoing condition will soon be found to be the leading cause for most of the recognized cellular diseases of the world.

Another problematic dietary concern involves the consumption of animal products. More often than not, when it comes to animal-based proteins, we are unaware of a larger accumulative problem at work. Simply put, we rarely can be certain about what we are consuming. To begin with, many animals are raised in less-than-hygienic conditions, and consume grains grown with pesticides, herbicides, fungicides, germicides, as well as genetically modified organisms. Next, the animals themselves are injected with their own growth hormones. All of these nonfood contaminators accumulate within the animal's tissues without ever breaking down into inert compounds. In other words, these toxins become accumulating, carcinogenic poisons, which inevitably transfer directly from animal to human "animal" system. These poisons disturb the pure electromagnetic fields necessary for proper human digestion and assimilation.

In addition, meat consumption presents a heavy, dualistic encumbrance for which humans pay substantial physical and spiritual prices. Flesh consumption separates the dualistically influenced, lower level animal species from those attuned to a higher, more refined and Unified SuperConsciousness. As with every example and principle we present to you in this book, it always is up to all individuals to determine for themselves how to execute their own free-will choices. Please be aware that attractive labeling and packaging, however compelling, does not necessarily constitute a wholesome or healthy product. Just because it tastes or looks good does not always mean it is good for you. Similarly, just because something is "all natural" does not mean it will taste like bark.

In actuality, one would be better off eating bark than ingesting artificial colors or flavors. With bark consumption, at least the body would recognize a mistake was made, and promptly would excrete the bark—just like it does with colon-cleansing corn kernels. When humanly processed or genetically altered nonfoods are broken down, the unrecognizable substances erroneously are presumed to be something of assimilable value, and are stored for future discernment. As a result of this confusion, these carcinogenic accumulations build into conditions compromising the quality of one's existence. This prana or life force assimilating absorption is consistent throughout both the physically and Astrally manifesting Universes.

These electromagnetic fields are the sustaining life force substances that comprise the species-appropriate membrane levels of communication. Electromagnetic fields contained within digestible foods allow physically manifesting beings to absorb and derive energy after consuming, digesting, and assimilating recognizable food source substances. In the Astral Realm, sustenance consumption occurs through the Astral being's direct absorption of electromagnetic fields—which in the Astral Realm spontaneously manifest as Astrally recognizable food sources, entirely skipping the physically manifesting food growth process. Within membrane levels one through fourteen for both Astrally and physically manifesting existence, this entire life-sustaining process actually is an electromagnetic communication transference process. The fifteenth or Holy Neutrino membrane of communication consists of beings who exist only upon direct Transinterinfusion of electromagnetic sustenance of Unconditional Love.

The manifesting existence for all universal life is lawfully contained with its communication capabilities transmitted through these fifteen membranes. All existence throughout the universe is governed by each individual species' capacity to attune to the Manifesting Infinite SuperConsciousness. God does ALL the conscious decision making for all earthly existence, except for humans and whales—both of which have free will. While alive, whales communicate in membrane eleven. Upon physical death, they go to their own particular death-determined membrane placement within the same Astral existence. Upon death, all manifesting, material universe existence from planet Earth—excluding whales and humans—goes to the same membrane of consciousness accorded its species. All of these existences are contained within the level ten membrane of conscious capacity.

While in the Astral existence, each species continues to evolve based upon their continuing, deepening comprehensions and ensuing experiences in the Spirit Realm. The ensuing spiritual experiences allow all essences an upward evolution of soul attunement. God predetermined the upcoming incarnations for each soul and all existence. In the case of existences devoid of free will, God, assisted by supporting Holy Angels, presides over particular choices for upcoming incarnations. There is no particular, individual choice afforded any soul yet to reincarnate. Humans do not have ANY say in selecting their future incarnations. This responsibility rests solely upon God, the Infinite Ordainer. Once an existence physically has remanifested, whether it be as ant, dolphin, or alien form, its essence will evolve upward—and its reincarnated existence is not limited to planet Earth. Throughout the Universe, there are millions of inhabitable vectors from which God selects.

All earth existence originally came from other parts of the already evolving universe. Plant life has been allowed to remain exactly the same throughout its earthly existence. God has granted humankind the opportunity to discover and facilitate plant grafting, which has allowed for the creation of different plant forms. Without an outside influence, plant life remains the same—with limited adaptability capacities. However, both animal and vegetable were planted or deposited here by beings from other parts of the universe. No existence here on earth has been allowed to evolve without having been deposited here by any one of hundreds of thousands of otherworldly beings throughout the vectors of manifesting creation.

All DNA ever found or existing on planet Earth previously was planted here through God's Divine Will as per God's Reperfecting Plan. As previously stated, planet Earth essentially is a DNA petri dish. DNA implementation directly is responsible for all planetary evolutionary existence. Without evolutionary implementations within manifested DNA, no earthly life ever would change. Earthly existence, through otherworldly DNA manipulations, has been granted evolutionary changes. All existential evolution on this planet was allowed to occur so that upward conscious attunement would take place.

Throughout history, evidence of DNA retrieval and extraction has been sprinkled throughout the world. One example, located in Scotland, is an ornate temple known as Rosslyn Chapel. There is a great deal of mysterious symbolism surrounding Rosslyn. In fact, its very originations are steeped in mythology and legend. Rosslyn contains over one hundred unusual carved, molded facial renditions of what now is known as "The Green Man." Associated with the Knights Templars and Gnostic thought, the Green Man's molded image also is represented in several Gothic and medieval church buildings built by the Templars. Strategically located in the corner of Rosslyn's ceiling is yet another, different molded face—that of "The Apprentice." Legend states that upon his return after receiving specific carving instructions in Rome, the master mason of this uncarved pillar discovered—with envy and anger—its meticulously detailed completion, courtesy of his own apprentice. So enraged, the master mason purportedly bludgeoned his apprentice on the spot.

In actuality, the Apprentice Pillar is a representation of DNA. Just like Baphomet and Egaladio Dimms, The Apprentice and his guru, The Green Man, were extraterrestrial beings visiting planet Earth with the sole purpose of retrieving for intergalactic recultivation the DNA of several plant forms, including aloe and maize—of which many etchings can be found throughout Rosslyn's interior. These etchings of aloe and maize were carved nearly one hundred years BEFORE human beings ever would have begun to discover them in the New World or present-day

United States. The truth is, The Apprentice never was murdered, but instead, he and The Green Man simply left for their next intergalactic destination. Other examples of DNA extraction on planet Earth, conducted by extraterrestrial beings unrelated to The Green Man and The Apprentice, took place in the United States.

In the late 1970s to very early 1980s, alarmed ranchers in Denver, Colorado, were discovering very disconcerting cattle mutilations. The *Rocky Mountain News,* Denver's local daily newspaper, carried extensive articles about these events. These mutilations were executed by otherworldly beings, using planet Earth as a petri dish for making DNA improvements to benefit life in other parts of the universe. Ranchers found their dead cattle missing specific anatomy with no other visible signs of harm to which they could attribute the deaths. These specific, missing anatomical pieces—including internal organs—were strategically removed, leaving no metal traces and no blood loss whatsoever.

Even after animal autopsies were performed, these inexplicable deaths were left unresolved. These incomprehensible mutilations simultaneously were happening throughout other parts of planet Earth. Through the assistance of the Angelic Realm, these otherworldly beings came to planet Earth to retrieve specific DNA components. These retrievals were done by these Divinely Guided Beings in order to recolonize other earthlike vectors of the vast cosmos.

For these visiting beings, most conscious communication is done at a level far above the levels six through eight of human beings. The communication for these beings begins at the atom level eight, and goes all the way to level fourteen. Many of the beings in the cosmos are communicating through thought transmissions. No registerable, audible sounds are heard. Earth human beings have spent lifetimes attempting to make sense of inexplicable phenomena, such as true life experiences with extraterrestrial life. Oftentimes, articulating these experiences poses an immense communication challenge; details may seem unreal or get lost in the translation. Similarly, the conscious thought transmissions by which extraterrestrial beings communicate seems a bit surreal. The beings portrayed in the movie *Communion* were communicating through thought transmissions in the eighth or atom level of communication capacity.

In *Communion,* one particular being is depicted as constantly exhaling through oboe-like lips, essentially acting as a vibratory neutralizer for the entire synergized group. He actually was their form of Holy Man who would devibratorize the contamination continuously accumulated by the group due to its exposure to earth human beings and planet Earth. The thirteenth and fourteenth levels of the Unified Super-Consciousness represent the Holy Realm specific to the oboe-being and most extraterrestrial life forms.

When we speak of Angels, we are referring to the Spirit Realm or Astral Universe of existence. When we speak of extraterrestrial beings, we are referring to a physically manifesting existence within the spatio temporal heavens. The Angels with whom these extraterrestrial beings interact are located in the thirteenth and fourteenth membranes of the Astral Universe. These thirteenth and fourteenth membranes of communication capacity are the same Unified SuperConscious levels to which highly evolved earth human beings also attune.

In fact, whether extraterrestrial or earth human being, the system of communication membranes of the Astral Universe is one and the same. Thus, unholy beings from earth and anywhere throughout the physically manifesting universe wind up in the abominable, gloom drenched bowels of level nine. As per God's Universal Law, which is consistent throughout the physical cosmos, no physically manifested or manifesting existence has any interaction or intercommunication with the Holy Neutrino Realm inhabitants.

Another tangible contemporary example of these extraterrestrial DNA retrievers was evidenced at an incident that occurred in 1947 in Roswell, New Mexico. This event involved a spacecraft crash during an electrical storm. Hitting a dry gulch riverbank, this spacecraft exploded, scattering its beings and spacecraft materials over an extensive area. Once again in history, the truth quickly was buried—this time by the federal government. The government threatened the lives of all eyewitnesses, warning them not to say anything about what they'd experienced. Like all other smothered truths, information about this incident (and others like it) keeps springing up from the veiled soil under which they are buried.

Dharmic Records and Astral Consciousness

The physical cosmos is the innermost third universe as the inward reflection of the Uncreated Infinite Holy SuperConsciousness. The Astral Universe is the second, and the Causal Universe is the first. These three inward reflections of God collectively are known as Manifesting Infinite SuperConsciousness. God ALSO is the Uncreated Infinite Super-Consciousness. Any Made Manifest Expression of God actually is the Manifesting Infinite SuperConsciousness.

All manifesting or photonic Transinterinfused vibratorized existence is called Creation. Creation, as an inward reflection, consists of the Causal, Astral, and physical Universes. This archetype is consistent throughout the three manifesting Universes. Whether an amoeba, a human being, or a supernova, all manifesting existence has a physical, Astral, and Causal container. In the Causal container is the Idea, in the Astral container is the energy, and the physical container is the innermost, combined reflecting expression of both Causal and Astral containers.

God alone has encoded within all manifesting existence or creation a dharmic blueprint. This blueprint encompasses all manifesting creations' period of existence, whether it occurs in the physical, Astral, or Causal Universes. While in the physical universe, all creation manifests, exists, and eventually experiences cosmic decay. The Causal Universe is composed exclusively of the Holy Neutrino. The synized center of the Holy Neutrino accounts for the cosmic decay. The physical cosmos literally implodes upon itself, akin to pulling out the bottom cards from a vast house of cards. This implosion stops or is contained at the quark level of existential matter.

The existence of all previously experienced, eventually decayed matter is stored in the quark realm. The quarks contain and retain this memory for all decayed matter until the black holes absorb, illuminate, and sear-separate the experienced photons from the experienced vibration. The Astral Realm is subdivided into six membranes. These six sets of existential communication membranes are dispersed within and throughout this Astral Realm. These six membranes are composed of twelve particles of matter—six particles of quarks and six particles of leptons. The particles are matched up in six subsets of two, with the quarks serving as stable foundations and the leptons whirling around the congealing quarks.

The six quark particles make up half of the Astral Universe, with the six lepton particles comprising the other half. The leptons are the building aspects of the Astral Universe. The quarks retain the memory information from the decomposing, once previously experienced physical universe unenfoldments. For example, once the cosmic decay absorbs the memory information of what was once a "flower," the memory of the flower's existence is retained within the flower's own quark particles.

These same quarks contain the records for all deceased human existence as well as the memory for all materialized existence. This is where all released conscious existence goes after exiting the physical universe. Upon their deceasing from existence in the physical universe, all life forms are absorbed into the Spirit Realm where they are contained, maintained, and continue to exist in the Astral Universe. Upon human physical death, the Holy SuperConsciousness cracks the human electromagnetic fields (HEM) or prana, contained by the atoms of the human's being.

Once this has occurred, the invisible human consciousness (soul) has seventy-two hours during which to be absorbed into the light of the Manifesting Infinite SuperConsciousness. If one uses their free will to resist the absorbing light at any time during this seventy-two hour period or afterward, the soul can escape through the portal of the third eye. When this occurs, the soul becomes an apparition or ghost. In this surreal, in-between life-death state, existence is experienced as gray and white, shadowy images.

As an apparition, this existence is permanent until an intervening act of God or a God-sanctioned Angel arrives to retrieve the lost soul. No human being, whether shaman, psychic, medium, or healer, EVER has been sanctioned by God to perform this ghost busting task. Only in rare situations have Holy Angels utilized human assistance for the divine purpose of soul retrieval. In Book Five, we will describe one such example, which occurred when a Divinely Sanctioned Angel worked through me (Scott) to facilitate the soul retrieval of a ghostly inhabitant in my home.

Upon the death of the physical body, if the soul goes into the light of the silver cord, it is absorbed down through the root chakra and inevitably ends up in the Astral Universe. The silver cord is the corridor through which souls are SuperConsciously retracted in order to reach the Astral Universe. The already bright light preceding this corridor is further enhanced by the sixteen gross physical lightways being retracted along with the soul. The weight of the deceased person's karma determines the level of conscious attunement. Of course, the less karmic debt, the higher the membrane to which the soul is SuperConsciously drawn, signifying the soul's level of attunement. The heavier the debt load, the lower the membrane placement into which the soul settles.

The soul exiting the physical realm through the atom level membrane eventually resides in the membrane to which it is attuned according to its karmic weight from all its physically manifesting existences. Those souls with heavy physical karma stop at level nine, those with less physical karma are drawn to levels ten or beyond. The death sleep occurs at level ten, and this is the same Astral membrane level to which the consciousness of dogs, cats, birds, and all other nonhuman forms exiting the physical universe attune and reside. All physically manifested existence that had lacked free will in the physical realm resides in Astral level ten. The death sleep is an inactivated dream state of soul suspension that continues until the soul is once again reincarnated in the physically manifesting universe.

More enlightened beings with free-will choice attain the higher vibrational membrane eleven level of attunement. A Unified Super-Consciously attuned soul continues on past level eleven, eventually residing in the membrane appropriate for its individual soul's qualifications. The Unified SuperConscious membranes comprise levels twelve through fourteen. Levels nine through fourteen comprise the entire Spiritual Realm of the Astral Universe. The level of membrane placement is directly proportionate to the level of evolution. In other words, the higher the membrane level, the closer it is to the Holy Source. As membrane levels increase and become Holier, their spatial dimensions increase as well. In addition, the higher the membrane level, the smaller but more numerous are the particles comprising its constitution.

The tiniest of particles make up the highest, most Superenlightened Holy Neutrino Universe. Holy Neutrinos comprise level fifteen or the entire Causal Universe. In this Holy Universal Realm, Creation as SuperConsciousness exists only as an Idea. Everything is supremely radiant with the Photonic Vibratory Transinterinfusion of photon, vibration, and the SuperConscious Will of God.

In the entire history of earth-born humankind, no person before now EVER has had any direct contact with this Realm. Earth humans are far too contaminating to the supersensitive, unimaginable subtle SuperHoly Realm of the Causal Universe. God never has granted any human a direct link to the Saints and Superevolved, supremely enlightened Holy Beings existing as Supernally Divine SuperConsciousness. No earthborn, Superevolved being, such as Lord Krishna, Lahiri Mahasaya, Trailanga, Patanjali, Buddha, or Sri Yukteswar Giri was granted accessibility to this

Holy Realm during his physical incarnations. With the exception of Jesus, a Holy God-sanctioned Angel was responsible for each of these people's incredible insights and miraculous abilities. Jesus was uniquely different, as described throughout this book.

All of these beings were attuned to the fourteenth level of communication capacity while incarnated as earth humans. Level fourteen is the absolute highest level of attainment ever afforded naturally born earthly incarnates. Babaji is not considered an earth human being, for his incarnation did not include an earthly physical birth. However, he is attuned intimately to the Causal Universe of the Holy Neutrino. Babaji works quietly behind the scenes of the manifesting physical cosmos, executing the Divine Will of the Manifesting Infinite Holy SuperConsciousness as an expression of Made Manifest Holy Lord Shiva. This aspect of Manifesting Holy Lord Shiva is where science and spirituality are fused.

Level fourteen consists of the building neutrino lepton "electron," combined with the quark "up." The thirteenth membrane consists of the building leptons "electron" and "electron neutrino" and the quarks "up" and "down." Level twelve consists of the building leptons "electron," "electron neutrino," and "muon," the quarks "up," "down," and "charm." Level eleven consists of the building leptons "electron," "electron neutrino," "muon," "muon neutrino," and the quarks "up," "down," "charm," and "strange."

Level ten consists of the building leptons, "electron," "electron neutrino," "muon," "muon neutrino," and "tau," and the quarks "up," "down," "charm," "strange," and "top." Level nine consists of the building leptons "electron," "electron neutrino," "muon," "muon neutrino," "tau," and "tau neutrino," and the quarks "up," "down," "charm," "strange," "top," and "bottom." These twelve particles of matter comprise the fundamental building and retaining particles of the Astral Universe. Starting from level fourteen and continuing through level nine, these particles are intricately interwoven, forming the various membrane levels.

Eventually, these interinfused particle combinations form into atoms, continuing on to form physical matter. The physical universe is composed of levels eight through one. Within these levels are atoms building into molecules, and eventually forming cells and objectified matter. The Astral Universe is composed of leptons and quarks that similarly are enfolded to become Astral matter. The vast distance between the quarks and their leptons account for the Astral Universe's immense size. Within the Astral Universe is a vastly more numerous collection of planets and galaxies. Of course, only in the Pure Perception state of Astral Super-Consciousness can the Manifesting image of Astral planets and galaxies be experienced. Teeming with existence, this Universe also is hundreds of times bigger than the small material universe.

Only extremely evolved Holy Beings are God-sanctioned to pierce these levels of SuperConsciousness. The higher the attunement of a God-approved, Unified earth-bound soul, the greater the soul's potential capacity to be expressed as God incarnate. When the Unified soul is attuned to the fourteenth membrane of SuperConscious potential, it is in harmonious synchronicity with the subtle laws operating and governing the entire physical cosmos. The manifesting universe responds naturally to this superattuned will of the Superevolved Being, resulting in a God expression as human incarnate. Only God-ordained earth humans can comprehend and discern the immense yet subtle energies of these Holy Realms. Only those Holy Beings who have attained salvation are granted any access to these Divine Astral levels. God alone sanctions all Unified SuperConscious souls. No Archangel, Saint, or deity has the authority to grant this supernal gift.

If an earth human has any physical universe karma, they are not granted salvation—freedom from all dualistic indebtedness. For salvation, humans cannot have any physical universe karmic weight holding them captive in the duality. If an earth human soul has karmic weight, they are relegated to the dualistic membranes until God deems them ready for Unification. If an earth human is in the duality of existence, they are also governed by dharma, ego-free will, karma, and reincarnation. After the death of the physically manifested tabernacle (physical body), the soul is in God's Divine Care until it either reincarnates or graduates into a different Astral Realm.

Once a soul is in such Divine Soul SafeKeeping, this soul can be God-gifted a unified conscious perspective of ALL past incarnations—that is, all access to them, with acute clarity about all of them. If the soul still has unfulfilled physically manifested karmic debt, the soul will reincarnate and return to the physically manifesting universe. Unresolved physically manifested karma is contained in the atoms of one's physically manifesting existence. This indebtedness will have limitless opportunities to be resolved during one's physically manifesting incarnations.

If the indebtedness occurred in one's previous Astral Universe existence between physically manifesting incarnations, this indebtedness is retained by the quarks of the Astral Universe until the soul returns from its current physically manifesting incarnation. If God determines a particular physically manifested or manifesting indebtedness to be irresolvable during one's current physically manifesting experience, this indebtedness also remains retained in the Astral quark level. It subsequently is carried over into the next physical incarnation.

If there is no physically manifested karma to work out, but rather some Astral Universe karma to resolve, the soul will complete its work in the Astral Universe. Also, if a soul's physically manifesting karma is one of very minimal unfulfillment, there is in the Astral Universe a facilitating process by which this karmic debt can be eliminated without the soul's existence needing to manifest through another future physically manifesting incarnation.

No psychics, mediums, or astrologers on planet Earth EVER have been granted salvation during these particular physically manifesting existences. These earth human beings operate in the eighth level of communication capacity as their highest possible level. Even Edgar Cayce was capable of operating only in the eighth or atom level of communication potential. Cayce also was transgressing against God when utilizing his perceptions to influence others' free will. Even if a psychic has the best of intentions while doing a "reading," because the psychic discernments can and do influence the natural free-will choices of the individual being "read," this psychic IS transgressing.

Most psychics, mediums, hypnotists, fortune-tellers, soothsayers, and prognosticators operate in the molecule or biomolecular levels. Most of these beings use cognitive reasoning or cognitive patterned interpretations while the individual client is present before them. If these beings doing the readings have attuned their free will to focus beyond the biomolecular level to the atom level, they may attain a degree of mild success. However, the transgressor is using their free will, which is flowing directly into their ego, further burdening their evolutionary growth through karmic debt.

In addition, this person is interfering with and influencing another individual's free-will choices. By feeding their own ego, as well as influencing another's fee will, the transgressor actually receives a double karmic reflection (impaction) back for their transgression. This reflection is unbiased, and does not consider even the best of intentions on the part of the transgressor. On extremely rare occasions, God, through Holy Realm assistance, will operate through a transgressor for a Divine Purpose known only to God. Once again, God absolutely does NOT impart decision-making accountability to a Holy Angel, but rather facilitates outcome through Angelic assistance.

The lower levels of the Astral Universe contain the heaviest karmic indebtors. Lepton level nine, with the "Tau," "Tau Neutrino," the "muon," "muon neutrino," the "electron" and "electron neutrino," and quark level nine, with the "bottom," "top," "strange," "charm," "down," and "up," contain the souls contaminated with horrific karmic debts. These dank, dark, gloom-and-doom regions are where the most evil beings are banished to exist. Heavy karmic debt-laden souls are subjected to gruesome wars and abominable terrors. Transgressors like killers, murderers, suicide bombers, etc., all end up experiencing this soul-excruciating realm. Inhabitants include the transgressors from throughout the entire physical universe, from which really nasty beings can hail—not just those of earth humankind nature.

Levels eleven and twelve could be considered the ordinary Astral Universe, inhabited by people from planet Earth and beings from throughout the physical cosmos. Most of those beings remain in a death sleep as temporary visitors of the Astral Universe while awaiting their next preprescripted physical incarnation. Their previous incarnations' karmic weight carries them back to the universe of their previous existence. However, exceptions are made throughout the universe—especially after so many extraterrestrials have visited and taken with them DNA with which to perpetuate humanlike life forms. Consequently, there are many locales for former earth humans to experience various other vectors of humanlike existence.

Toward the end of its story, the movie *Communion* portrayed human children on their way to inhabit other earthlike realms sprinkled throughout the universe. These places do exist, and to believe otherwise is akin to stubbornly believe planet Earth to be flat and also to be the Ptolemaic ego center of the whole universe. That movie was based upon actual events and incidents that did occur. All of the types of beings portrayed do exist, and literally hundreds of thousands of others throughout the cosmos exist as well. All physically manifested deceased beings return to the Astral Universe.

The levels thirteen and fourteen of the Unified SuperConsciousness are where Superevolved beings experience their souls' final evolution before being released from their Astral Containers. Here they are free to exist for short times in the Causal Universe of Idea existence. Once a human being dies, there absolutely is no earthly communication with the deceased person. God does not grant any mediums the ability to communicate with the Astral Universe. The atom level of the physically manifesting universe is the farthest to which any earth human can penetrate using their free will. In the history of the deposited humans on this planet, no human EVER has been able to communicate with deceased beings in the Astral Universe. Once a human being no longer is a tenant in their physically manifesting container, no communication is humanly possible with this person. In other words, there are no loved ones watching over you to make sure you are okay. This capability is not God-sanctioned on this planet.

Consistent with this Divine Law is the fact that despite strong perceptions and convictions otherwise, deceased loved ones do not and cannot appear to a soon-to-be dying individual. This misperceived phenomenon is based in the soon-to-be dying individual's imagination—much like the ways in which mediums receive what they believe are authentic communications from "the other side." The only exception to this Divine Law is when God decides to assist this dying individual in their journey from the physically manifested existence to the Astral Universe. If this is the case, God might present to this individual through a dream an image of a deceased loved one, whereby the dream would represent a Divine Interaction—for reasons known only to God.

Unless God allows you to resurrect, you are not capable of communicating with or even knowing about surviving loved ones. If you evolve to the thirteenth or fourteenth membrane of Astral existence, you are granted far-reaching freedoms to begin to manifest your own destiny. Loved ones may be reunited at this time, but usually by then a soul has had a thousand incarnations with tens of thousands of loved ones.

The Divine Universal Records (Holy Records) contain the indelible recordings of all physically manifesting conscious experience, whether amoeba or supernova, human or mountain. These Records have been erroneously and mistakenly referred to as "The Akashic Records," to which many metaphysicists claim to have access. Nothing is further from the truth. First, there are no "Akashic Records." Second, no earth human ever has had access to God's Divine Universal Records because they are completely out of reach for inhabitants of the physically manifesting universe.

These Records are located in the fourteenth level of the Astral Universe. They are located at the deepest-kept memory section of the manifesting cosmos—the master blueprint containment system of the manifesting universe's cosmic decay. These Records are stored in the quark foundational level of building neutrinos for the Astral Universe, where the outward (that which is being Created) meets the inward (that which is being Comprehended and retained). All universal existence operates within the fifteen levels of conscious comprehension. These fifteen levels of interconnecting SuperConscious Comprehension form the Universal Communication Continuum.

One interesting phenomenon regarding the soul after a physical death is that of soul fragmentation, whereby a soul becomes splintered or fragmented into more than one soul. These resulting soul offspring then are vibratorily manifested into spiritual families in the Astral Universe—only through the Divine Will of SuperConscious God. Based on similarities of mental and spiritual tendencies, the manifested soul electromagnetically is drawn into the Astral family through the Will of God. These newborn souls already have retained some of the same qualities as the producing or parent soul.

This phenomenon occurred only once to my (Scott's) individual soul, which was incarnated in human form. That incarnated soul ultimately became known as Crazy Horse. Crazy Horse was a soul offshoot of Richard the Coeur de Lion. Crazy Horse was a fearless warrior of the Lakota tribe. His tribe's medicine man was Sitting Bull and his tribe's great leader was Chief Gall. Chief Gall happened to be the great-great grandfather of a very close and special loved one of mine, who accompanied me on a visit to the Crazy Horse Monument in South Dakota. Once there, I was so electrified that my then-long hair threatened to stand on end. Energy currents flowed through my body, producing incredible surges, evidence of the strong and undeniable connection between Crazy Horse and me. When the soul of Crazy Horse was Astrally Made Manifest, it had both Causal and Astral containers, but did not have a merkebah.

The physically manifesting merkebah comprises all three containers of the entire manifesting human being. The outermost pathways are known as the chakra meridian gridwork. These lightways guide and direct the electromagnetic fields in their proper physically manifesting order. The entire merkebah-chakra-meridian-electromagnetic gridwork makes up a human being's aura. By being able to absorb the ever-increasing magnitudes and volumes of the Manifesting Infinite Holy SuperConsciousness, earth humankind's twelve major chakra centers allow people to evolve faster than all other earthly life. The merkebah of a Superevolved soul provides this soul with many unique, superhuman abilities.

No naturally born earth human being has ever walked on water. A God-realized Superenlightened Hindu Being named Trailanga, who lived to be three-hundred years old, has remained underwater for insurmountable amounts of time. Other Hindus have levitated and floated above water, but none have ever walked upon water. Similarly, earth humankind does not have the superhuman ability to see auras, period. With an ever-increasing God attunement, Superevolved people may see the absorption of photonic light being reabsorbed by the Holy Uncreated Infinite into an individual's merkebah of existence. Through their DNA and chakras, all human existence is able to absorb the almost infinite, manifesting, measureless amplitude of God. Human DNA literally is coaxial cable, with the chakras serving as rheostats.

The higher or more evolved one's attunement, the greater their necessity for heightened DNA and chakra abilities. Superevolved souls oftentimes are depicted by humans as having a halo (nimbus) or illuminated aura (merkebah). Nimbus and merkebah enlightenment is due solely to a Holy Photonic reclamation phenomenon. Humans do not emanate light outward, but do emit some particles of photonic matter during the cosmic decay, which also is unseeable by earth humans. Most of the photonic light in a Saint's nimbus and merkebah is being absorbed into the Saint's essence by the Uncreated Infinite SuperConsciousness, as opposed to the typically interpreted but erroneous perception of outward light emanations.

Even the most Superevolved Beings are incapable of perceiving these emittings. Babaji is the only God-sanctioned SuperConscious existence on earth currently operating beyond all Universal Governing Laws. St.

Germain and Lord Krishna were functioning as manifesting Super-Consciousnesses, as were two unnamed others, but all four Beings now are executing God's desires primarily in other manifesting realms—NOT on planet Earth. As we write this book, Babaji is the only SuperConscious God-sanctioned Being on planet Earth gifted with the ability to see auras. He also has complete mastery over all manifesting restrictions. After the crucifixion, Jesus sought out and spent the duration of his physically manifesting human incarnation with Babaji. As we describe in this book, Jesus transcended and was reabsorbed by the Holy Neutrino Causal Universe at age eighty-six. He did NOT resurrect.

The Holy Neutrino Causal Universe is level fifteen. The veil of separation between the Uncreated Infinite Holy SuperConsciousness (God) and the manifesting Holy Neutrino Existence is extremely thin. There, souls exist as omnipresent manifestations of God-thought Ideas. In the Causal container is the SuperConsciousness of human existence. The human SuperConsciousness (soul) and Intuition both are located, contained, and maintained in the Causal container by God's SuperConsciousness, with the entire universe's gravity contributing through God's Superwillful Influence.

Through focus, evolution, prayer, and meditative attuning, all universal existence evolves its way back to the Holy Uncreated Infinite SuperConsciousness. There is no such thing as a chosen race or a superior earth human existence, period. The fact that we have a human physical body gives tangible, manifesting proof of our unevolved state of conscious experience and karmic debt. No one is superior, chosen, or inferior, and to even think so is a karmically burdening thought. Angels can be utilized to assist in the upward soul evolution for human beings for both life and death situations. However, no Angels EVER have assisted in the unsubstantiated taking of human life. Angels only have assisted with complex soul reckonings when preprescripted in the dharmas of both the Angels, as well as the groups of humans in large-scale situations such as September 11, 2001 or the Holocaust.

Through free will, humans have assisted in other humans' dharmic unenfoldment, but at huge transgressing costs to their own karmic debt. Upon physical death, all manifesting existence is SuperConsciously drawn inward. Some people who have had near-death circumstances and other unique experiences report having seen a bright light or silver cord stretching infinitely upward and outward. However, the silver cord does NOT go upward and outward, but rather inward. This cord is the main meridian lightway connecting the twelve main chakra spinal centers to the cerebral light center. The cerebral light center is known by many as the thousand-petal lotus. Located in the brain, when viewed from above the spiritual essence or one's soul, the silver cord's root resembles a thousand-petal lotus. These spinal centers comprise the Astral system of a physically manifesting human being.

Human souls are reclaimed by God through their root chakras and are Transimplanted into their subsequent incarnation through the third eye of the fetus right before birth. A soul outwardly leaving a physical body that is dying actually is fleeing AWAY from the white light. Because of fear or related attachments to their physically manifested experiences, such souls have exercised their free will to flee away from the white light. The white light is the dying person's connection to the photonic Holy Neutrino Universe, which presents itself upon physical death as a blissful, radiant, divine attraction. Once the atoms of the physical, manifesting container are cracked by God, the Uncreated Infinite SuperConsciousness attraction irresistibly draws the dying individual's consciousness (soul) inversely inward toward the Holy Neutrino Universe.

Even with the complete destruction of the physical body, the Astral and Causal containers continue to function undisturbed. From the moment of physical death, the white light portal for the soul to return to the Astral Universe is open and visible to the freed soul for seventy-two earthly hours. After these seventy-two hours, the lost soul (ghost) can be reclaimed only by God. No Angels have the freedom to intervene, unless by a very rare consent by God. This phenomenon has not yet happened on planet Earth.

The near-death experience people have experienced is a true phenomenon. This experience is in one's dharma for a specific purpose known only to God. The atoms of one's physical being are cracked enough to allow the soul to be Superwillfully extracted from its physical incarnation. Once freed from the confining physical container, one's consciousness (soul) is allowed to access two choices, of which they choose one. The freed consciousness (soul) always is given two—and only these two—choices. God discloses these two options—one is for the soul to remain in the physical body, the other choice is to die, the soul then continuing on to the Astral Universe.

For both options, God discloses to this soul its preprescripted, preordained dharmic plan. In other words, God will show a soul what its future would be like, for it to decide to remain in the physical body rather than depart for the Astral Universe. Only God presents to a soul these two options—and for purposes known only to God. If the soul elects to continue on to the Astral Universe, it is Super-Consciously redrawn back into the physical body and down through the root chakra.

If a soul elects to remain in the physical body, it then is Transreimplanted back into the physical body. At this point, its dharmic path—including all knowledge of the choices and which choice was selected—is rendered completely unknown to its consciousness. So, anyone who has survived a near-death experience would have NO conscious recollection of this life-altering, phenomenal event. People might have a vague recollection of floating above themselves in any life-threatening situation or seeing a lighted tunnel. In some cases, people may remember this out-of-body experience.

However, once someone has elected to return to their physical body, they will not be able to recall God's presentation of such choices. This person is then free to experience the remaining unenfoldment of their earth human conscious existence. God's presentation of the choices is NOT a Transintervention, for this presentation was preprescripted in this person's dharma before the soul was Transimplanted. This event is the only circumstance allowing a human soul to glimpse their dharmic blueprint, and with God's exit from their experience, the memory of the person's insight at that time subsequently is removed.

When a person sleeps, the atoms containing their material existence may loosen enough to allow the dreamer to be drawn toward the Astral Universe. Once freed from any perception of bodily confinement, a sleeper can be drawn inversely inward toward the Uncreated Infinite Holy SuperConsciousness. One's destination during sleep is restricted by the weight of their ego, which works to contain or hold them back within the physical duality. Without an ego, Superevolved Beings may experience higher, bliss filled regions of dream-free sleep states. Superevolved Beings may sleep in the calm, non-dreaming, blissful radiance of unconditional love—if they sleep at all. During the beginning of their awakening state, some evolving sleepers may dream at the very end of their sleep cycle.

Eventually, the Superevolved Being attains a level of sleep that is unaffected by Astral influences. The lower vibratory membranes of level nine is where evil or heavily indebted karmic beings go to work out their huge debts. When dreamers experience nightmares, it is in this lower membrane, where their consciousness is influenced at that time. All dreams are influenced by the duality of levels nine through eleven, with happier, more uplifting dreams influenced by the higher, more God-attuned levels of twelve through fifteen. Sleepers whose Superevolved consciousness resides in the Unity, in levels twelve through fourteen, rarely dream at all.

In writing this book we realized there also are many other interesting facts and realities regarding the Upper Realms of the Astral Universe— specifically levels twelve through fourteen. In compiling the following information, we considered what others might like to know. The following questions came to mind: What is it like? What is experienced there? What types of existence are there? Under what Laws of karma, death, and existence do the Upper Realms of the Astral Universe operate? We also included some of the same information as it applies to the Causal Universe.

What is the Astral Universe really like? It is a Universe consisting of Astral solar and stellar systems, as well as suns and moons. There are many Astral planets within the Astral Universe itself. The Upper Realms of the Astral Universe are beautiful, clean, and pure. However, throughout the membranes of the Astral Universe, there are some notable differences within the Astral Universe as a whole, such as the more ordinary Astral level ten being extremely different from the Astral heaven-like planet of Hiranyaloka. The differences between the two locales are based upon their different vibratory quarters, and their eligibility-determining levels of attunement. All in all, in the whole Astral Universe, there are many Astral planets teeming with Astral beings. In the Upper Realms, the inhabitants use Astral planes, or masses of light, with which to travel from one planet to another—faster than electricity or radioactive energies.

The following information applies to the Upper Realms of the Astral Universe. What types of existence reside in the Astral Universe? Astral Beings dematerialize or materialize their forms at will. They are free to assume any form and easily can commune together. In terms of their Astral bodies, these Astral Beings are not subject to the natural conditions typical of earth humankind's physically manifesting body experience. As such, these Astral Beings can affect their bodies by SuperConscious force or mantric vibrations. In fact, these Astral Beings retain the same outward appearance they possessed in their previous earthly physically manifesting incarnation. Even more interesting is that at will, these Beings can project the outward physical appearance of any chronological age from that previous physically manifesting existence.

In terms of intuition, Astral Beings communicate entirely by Astral telepathy. In the Astral Universe, no matter what costume or chronological age a particular Astral Being assumes, friends from past existences easily are able to recognize each other. Unlike the physically manifesting universe, Astral inhabitants do not need to draw power from oxygen. Instead, they sustain themselves principally by photonic light. In keeping with this fundamental difference is how Astral inhabitants experience sensations such as desire. While physically manifesting beings experience desires as rooted in egotism and sense pleasures, Astral Beings' desires center on enjoyment in terms of vibration. In further contrast, Causal Beings' desires are fulfilled by perception alone.

What are the Astral Laws of Existence? In the Astral Universe, just like on planet Earth, there are Astral Beings, directed by God, who serve as Saviors on a particular Astral planet. Prophets sent by God to planet Earth help earthly beings work on resolving their physically manifesting karma. Astral Beings sent by God to Astral planets aid spiritually advancing Astral beings in ridding themselves of Astral karma, so they can attain liberation from Astral rebirths.

The lifespan in the Astral Universe is much longer than that on physically manifesting planet Earth. A normal advanced Astral Being's average life period is anywhere from five hundred to one thousand years. Visitors to the Astral Universe dwell for a time in accordance to the specific weight of their physical universe karma, which then draws them back to planet Earth within a specified time. Physically manifesting death is characterized by the disappearance of one's breath and disintegration of fleshly, physical cells. On the other hand, Astral death is characterized by the dispersement of the SuperConscious Astral energy container.

What is the relationship between a human being's physically manifesting karma and this being's permanent residence in the Astral Universe? Before a permanent stay in the Astral Universe becomes a possibility, this

Astral being's previous physical karma and physically manifesting fears, attachments, and desires must be completely worked out and resolved. As such, temporary Astral residents are those beings still having some earthly karma of which to dispose.

What is existence like in the Causal Universe? Causal Beings see the differences between their bodies and thoughts to be merely Ideas. These Beings have a much greater freedom, allowing them effortlessly to manifest their thoughts into instant objectivity—without any material or Astral obstruction or karmic limitations. By either divine request or at will, a Causal Being can retenant an Astral container. By thought alone, these Beings are able to see, hear, feel, touch, taste, create, or dissolve anything—all by using the power of SuperConscious capabilities. Superevolved Causal Beings manifest their own realities, allowing for long-lost reconnections, which otherwise require millions of earth years of evolution to develop. In the Causal Universe, both death and rebirth exist by perception alone.

Reflections on Biblical Truth

Theological Pertinacity
Mari

Organized religion and spirituality seem to be related, yet are not remotely synonymous. In order to truly be connected with the other, organized religion and spirituality need the one-way "bridge" of free-will choice. Spirituality does not require an organized religion, but no organized religion can exist without the conscious free-will pursuit of its adherents. If people don't direct their conscious free-will choice adherence to a recognized system of doctrines, rituals, rites, and observances, organized religion cannot exist. However, these same people certainly can be deeply spiritual.

Today, more than ever before, the options for spiritual satiation seem unlimited. When one's free will is focused toward material pursuits, the satisfaction is fleeting. In my personal examination and exploration of organized religion and spirituality I found that when I focused my free will upon (organized) religious (Jewish) fulfillment, it produced within me more questions than answers.

Throughout history people have sought enlightenment. Everywhere I look in today's society I notice the same universal search for Truthful answers. Yet, oftentimes people are unwilling to be patient or open enough to recognize the answer or Truth when it presents itself. Only further exacerbating this problem is the fact that people are more materialistically focused than ever before. Consequently, their pursuits leave them stressed out, angry, confused, overwhelmed, overburdened, and still spiritually unfulfilled. As such, they have sought—and continue to seek—desperately and longingly for something substantial in which to believe and place their trust, as well as quell their ever-mounting fears. With its doctrines, practices, observances, and leadership, organized religion in various ways has operated as a long-standing spiritual appetite suppressant. Ever-ready, ever-willing, organized religions as a whole have strived to meet the internal hunger of "The People," or more accurately, "Their People," or as some religions prefer to say, "Our People."

The problem with this long-lasting phenomenon is that the search for spiritual relief, comfort, and satiation cannot be completed or fulfilled with theology or organized religion alone. If we think a particular religion in and of itself can completely fill these gaping voids, we actually do ourselves—and God—a great dishonor and disservice. In our efforts to nourish what at various times in our lives might fluctuate from spiritual cravings to an overwhelming spiritual starvation, we misguidedly, often blindly, have been followers. Consequently, we've walked—sometimes even run—to the well of theology.

We've thirsted for remedies for our stresses of daily human existence, drinking from doctrines, sermons, and books as our cups of knowledge, despite their never being proven historically or spiritually accurate. We've sipped from these cups when feeling strong, and drenched ourselves—perhaps even in shameless desperation—when lacking internal fortitude and perspective. We've looked to theology to tell us what we need, and how to quench our thirst. In some cases, theology, in turn, has conditioned many of us to remain in a state of constant thirst.

In some instances, the ceremonies, rituals, and traditions have provided us comfort and reassurance. However, many people "go through" a ritual despite not knowing, caring, or even believing in the tenets on which it is based. When we examine further the foundation on which they are based, it behooves us to assess more critically how to employ and utilize rituals in our lives in a spiritually supportive and enhancing manner. There are those who perform and observe countless rituals, whose theological recitations and principles govern every moment of existence. They believe only theirs is the "right" religion and "my" or "our" God superior to "your" or "their" God. All of these people still are void of spiritual upliftment and fulfillment, and perhaps these "thirsty" adherents have frequented the wrong wells.

Of course, this is not to say all wells are created equally, always produce a lower-quality refreshment or sustenance, or come up completely dry. However, it is to say there is no one right or perfect theological well from which our deepest thirsts could be quenched. This certainly is the case with those thirsty seekers and corresponding theological leaders and organizations who promote and proclaim theirs as being the only suitable "well," theirs the only drinkable, truly nourishing, and life sustaining water.

Such dogma simply rings with untruth and is as unholy and unGodly as it gets. Such self-righteous, self-congratulatory blindness is evident in what I dub the "Four-P" paradigm. In various, unholy and repugnant ways, the pious, provincial, and possessive perceptions of various theologies regarding God are being consumed by the masses as The Way To Believe. When asked how to define God, many theologians and followers make distinctions between "My God" and "Your God," "Our God" and "Their God," carefully delineating how they perceive such differences. Some take this mindset further: "You all have YOUR God, but we have THE God."

Such mindsets are fueled and powered by fiercely held beliefs, however erroneous, that certain people are chosen especially BY God. Of course, in this case, only the Chosen People's God chooses THEM to receive certain unique or special blessings, treatment, victimization, martyrdom, or overall key places in existence. The notion that God places either favor or discrimination upon God's children is unholy and untrue. With God's creedless, ever-present, ever-flowing, eternal Unconditional Love, one need not rely solely—and worse yet, with blind faith—upon the wells of theologies and their doctrines to assist in one's spiritual search.

In reality, "My God," Your God," and "Their God" actually are "Our God." One would hope that God, being everywhere, anywhere, all-seeing, all-comprehending, and always eternally benevolent, would provide the sense of security and comfort we all seek in our individual conscious experiences. Nonetheless, people's reluctance to relinquish their hold or "trademark" of "My God" highlights their unwillingness to share the true Holy water from God's infinitely overflowing well of Unconditional Lovingkindness.

Many people agree there is "One God," yet also seem intent on claiming this God as their own. We rationalize that "The Others" have "Their God," a God somehow not nearly as holy as our own. We apply this warped, narcissistic logic to people as well. Yet, are we all so different? Aren't we all just as thirsty and hopeful to experience spiritual satisfaction? We may approach the quest from different points, taking different paths, but it is the same God who divinely accompanies all of us every step of the way.

Yet, when we're conditioned to believe in only one set of rules, one right way to pray, not to mention only one preferred God or preferred "people," we actually fail to truly quench our thirsts. Instead, we only further deprive ourselves of experiencing any True Holiness. When we seclude ourselves with such narrow mindedness, we do so out of fear. Rationales such as, "It's always been this way," "We just do it this way," and "This is the way" become our foundations, leaving us with no real incentive to explore or experience things any differently. Religious, cultural, and societal upheavals and tensions only serve to exacerbate already ignorant and exclusionary views. Even those for whom certain elements of theology don't sit well or remain questionable, are not always inspired to veer from the historically or familiarly prescribed path of existence.

This literally is "living life by rote." Through spiritual cowardice and ignorance, such adherents rely more upon their conditioned patterned behavioral responses than exercising their individual free will. They do not ever consider choosing or exploring alternative pathways to the Infinite and Truth. In fact, strict dogmatic adherence prevents people from referencing their own individual experiences, behaviors, and accountability. Instead, it enables them to remain dependent upon rigid perceptions that leave no room for recognition of the individual conscious experience.

Dogma very successfully has instilled within us a fear that if we do it differently, we in effect do it wrong. If we look back in history, we can see the patterns of politics and religion reigning over legions of terrified followers—or soon-to-be extinguished heretics or rebels. Many of us have followed a variety of paths in order to maintain some semblance of self-preservation, and we've gone to many different extremes in order to do so. Religious impulse and subsequent adherence and/or obsession most definitely reflect people's profound psychological and emotional needs, such as avoidance of rejection—oftentimes in the guise of spiritual fulfillment.

Only further fueling the fires of insecurity and internal emptiness is our need to feel special, unique, superior, more martyrlike, victimized, or even holy. Filling the voids with dogma temporarily satiates the thirsty, empty space, but nonetheless leaves a more long-lasting, ever-growing spiritual deficit. In a physically manifesting reality where God loves all without conditions, we do ourselves and God grave injustices when we place upon such divine processes any conditions whatsoever.

For way too long, people have embarked on journeys of soul searching in an effort to find out "Who am I?" and more deeply understand the mysteries of existence. We've sought to relieve ourselves of internal stress, tension, and warfare, but too many of us remain filled with conflict—or perhaps a complacency based upon dogmatically imposed standards to which we feel we must subscribe in order to belong. Too many of us have followed blindly, never questioning, also never necessarily believing, either. We have existed on autopilot mode, merely behaving like robotic lemmings.

For many, as long as we do it our way, it is sufficient. However, if we choose NOT to be obedient, compliant adherents of a theological message, we risk doing so at what feel like considerable, painful costs. We try to avoid incurring what we perceive as costs far too harsh, high, painful, or uncomfortable to fathom or bear. Instead, we submerge ourselves yet deeper into our fears of being excommunicated, alienated, isolated, and disenfranchised from our faith, religion, sect, or people. Even worse yet, in doing so, we push ourselves even further from our own selves, as WELL as the True Holy Source.

When we agree to drink any water as long as it is poured to us from a source or theology deeming it the finest, best, purest, or most holy, we truly do miss out on all the abundant, ever-flowing water God makes available to ALL God's children. As God's children, we need not search for prescribed wells in order to quench our thirsts. A combination of the waters from many wells may indeed provide ample sustenance, as might the sustenance from no set well outside one's own internal self. If supported by one's trust in God, both such options can provide spiritual sustenance. No one well's waters are of markedly higher or lesser quality, but they ALL are susceptible to varying degrees of toxins and pollutants that can contaminate all who drink such waters without discernment.

We do ourselves no favors by remaining victims to our fears and adopting and applying pious, self-righteous indignation to ourselves and those around us. The fear of alienating one's self from the masses must soon take a backseat to doing what TRULY IS holy. When we remain fearful of others' reprisals, we bow to the clutches of cowardice. In doing so, we tend to make choices we rationalize as holy, right, or just, while never really making any internal assessment or discernment that if made, might lead to otherwise very different results. We tend to act without such difficult and often uncomfortable introspection, oftentimes maintaining that there is only one real path from which to choose, anyway.

Fortunately, in reality, there ALWAYS are alternative paths from which to choose. However, such paths only can be realized fully when one is open and made aware of them. Most people tend to resign themselves to one particular way of being, long before they would ever consider changing their views or paths. The downfall of taking one path and worrying about alienating others is that in the guise of doing justice, we may, in fact, be doing quite the opposite.

Steeped in our theologies, if we believe such adherence is what God wants us to do as God's people, disciples, or followers, we may be doing unGodly, unholy, karmically impacting acts. The very ways in which we define spirituality, our particular religions, and ourselves speak volumes about our priorities, values, and ways of looking at existence. When we refer to ourselves or others as "Good Christians" or "Good Jews," we imply that to be otherwise somehow is of lesser stature, quality, and worse yet, less worthy in the Holy Eye of God.

Such descriptions also might imply that one always could improve or get better at being a Jew or Christian, that mediocrity or deterrence from the prescribed path is not acceptable to either the theology as a whole or by God. Such descriptives fail to recognize or make room for alternative ways of thought or being. If someone were not a "Good Jew," would he or she by default then be a "Bad Jew" or "Not Jewish Enough?" If someone is not a "Good Jew" or "Good Christian," is he or she inherently "bad" or unworthy? Is he or she deemed completely nonspiritual?

The provincial exclusivity perpetuated by many theologies further is exacerbated by defining and confining phrases such as "I'm a Christian," "Who is a Jew?" "Were you born Jewish?" and "Everyone else will go to Hell." Worse yet, and more disturbingly so, is the phrase "God fearing." To be a "God-fearing" person subscribing to an organized religion supporting and encouraging such views only serves to further distance ourselves from the all-loving, all-compassionate God.

God does not ever want us to fear God. Any measures or degrees of such fear would be misdirected on every conceivable level. God only wishes for us to reflect back the Unconditional Love God gives to us. When we put out love, there can be no fear and vice versa. Especially when directed to and experienced about God, the two energies of love and fear are completely incompatible. Any arguments or philosophies upholding the contrary truly are in vain and will be self-defeating.

When we attempt to sequester God all to ourselves, when we deem "Our God" as "THE God," and "Other People's God" as anything lesser than our own, we disrespect our creedless, benevolent One God. When we segregate ourselves and inflict upon others the discrimination, prejudice, condemnation, and disrespect we might say we've come to endure and loathe, we transgress against God—and our very souls. Why is someone less holy, less spiritual, or less worthy as a human being and essence if they do not subscribe to a particular religion? Why does such a non-subscriber remain in the eyes of subscribers as forever undeserving of certain rights? In a cemetery formed and founded as a "Jewish" cemetery, a Jewish man and his non-Jewish wife (or perhaps vice versa) cannot be buried together, side by side, as they lovingly lived their earthly existences. Does the burial of one soul's manifested dead vessel so contaminate the others if the theological choice of that earthly incarnated person doesn't match that of the sponsoring burial ground organization?

If the answer is "yes," then I urge you to pose the question to yourself a bit differently. Ask yourself, "Does such a burial contaminate ME or my future untenanted body?" Also ask yourself if and how your particular religion might serve to reinforce and enforce such thought. Ponder the answers to such questions—especially when considering that in the Holy Synoptic Eye of God, we are ALL God's children, our physical bodies ALL God-given real estate from which our souls rent finite amounts of time for our physically manifesting existences.

Our souls reside within God's Realm. Within a true reality, we enter, live, and leave this physically manifesting universe with God. As such, the idea that divergent theological viewpoints have enough power and authority either to contaminate or comfort is at the least preposterous—and at the worst, completely unholy. When we subscribe to any theologies that support such segregation and compartmentalization, we engage in selling our souls to dogma. In doing so, we disrespect God. Furthermore, we have forgotten that our souls are not ours to sell.

Theological Pertinacity
Scott

From their very roots, all theological, dogmatic, burdening religions have exerted tremendous influence upon the God-gifted, free-will choices of every earth human's conscious experience. Through disconcerting, misguided egos, religious hierarchies have coveted and then sequestered the very mysteries of existence. These mysteries of existence are what God lovingly intended to be shared. Experiencing and comprehending such mysteries is the inalienable right for every soul's conscious evolutionary experience.

God lovingly ordained, with an irrevocable right, the freedom for every soul to evolve through its own, individual free-will choices. Through insidious, covert, misguided, misdirected, and unGodly activities, self-serving, ignorant, unevolved beings have strived to thwart earth humankind from realizing our very purpose. Through interdiction, the ecclesiastic hierarchy sanctioned and authorized for themselves the right to pursue the mysteries initially intended for everyone.

This process has not gone unnoticed or unknown by the Spirit Realm, and now the time for atonement has arrived. To begin with, organized religions are theologies, based on ideological beliefs. After birth, an infant's God-preordained, dharmic path guides its soul's experience. Simultaneously, this soul is guided, directed, and influenced by its parents' or adults' decisions. This subordinate soul has little, if any, say in its theological or religious decisions, experiences, and instruction. This process of dependency continues until this evolving child realizes their soul's free-will discernment capabilities. This realization and subsequent application of one's free-will discernment capabilities is based upon a complex combination of a soul's individual evolution, parental or adult influences, and the individual's, God-predetermined dharmic plan.

By the time one begins to assert their free-will realizations, any potential theological foundations have already been established. In other words, a newborn child is but a pure, immaculate parchment yet to be filled with what amounts to incredible influences. The parents and adults in the life of this impressionable child possess an influence of great magnitude. Hence, the free-will decision to impart to our children either defiling or uplifting information, philosophies, and practices is up to us. As adults, it behooves us to be aware of our role and responsibility. It is never too early to search our own souls and begin a process of upliftment before we embark on the vital journey of influencing the souls of our children.

The more evolved philosophies, such as Hinduism and Buddhism, are free from and not rooted in theological dogma—and as such, have no real formal, traditional, academic principles as stepping stones for children. Unless an individual child is born into a family untarnished by religious dogma, they will discover these enlightened philosophies only after having realized their free-will discernment implications. By this time, the pure, immaculate consciousness of the child's soul may very well have been permeated with a particular religious sectarianism.

As previously stated, organized religion is not anything other than a belief system. There has been the notion that each is secure in the wisdom that theirs is the one true religion—and others are "missing the mark." This one notion has done more divisive damage than all the other aspects of existence combined. Wars, slaughter of life, ostracism, sinister secret-keeping, anger, guilt, shame, revenge, and regret, all are easily traced to having a tentacle rooted in most organized theologies.

Even infighting within these supposedly holy organizations has torn the human experience away from the coveted mysteries that were everyone's from the very beginning. Countless lives have been sacrificed; existences have been fractured with irreparable damage from within these very families of organized religions themselves. Everyone wants everyone else to adopt their superior-based slant on God's veritable words of truth: "Our slant is the right slant" or "We have the God-chosen slant, and if you don't believe us, we'll destroy you—or at least, persecute you." Even worse yet, "Perhaps a crusade or jihad against you will convince you that we are right and you are wrong?"

Crusades and jihads are holy like sewage is consumable. Holy and war are as compatible as are "potable" and "cesspool." "Holy War" is an abomination; in fact, by their very definitions, these two words are entirely incompatible. Furthermore, any violence directed against any of God's Creation is completely unholy. God simply would not, does not, and never has condoned violence in any way, shape, or form.

In the Holy Eye of God, all are created equal. There is no "chosen" anything. No one is better or selected out above the others. God is creedless, and to believe otherwise is both unGodly and severely karmically impacting. Each of us is measured by the weight of our individual, karmic debt, period. Furthermore, God does not judge; the interworkings of karma and free will, with their roots in the ego, determine one's evolution of soul. There absolutely is no judging.

Cloaked under the guise of God's Holy Writ, earth humankind have forced their interpretation of organized religion down the conscious throat of every other believer and nonadherent. Humankind's ego and ignorance have enabled the self-proclaimed, power-hungry, officiating church and religious elders to pull off a coup against trusting followers. As you soon will learn, the process of coveting, sequestering, distorting, and obliterating truths was more of a coup de main by extremely misguided miscreants.

These people forcibly omitted, edited, deleted, revised, and destroyed all that refuted or contradicted their distorted ideological beliefs. The Holy Realm wants to set straight the record. In response, YOU can exercise your God-given, free will to determine for yourself which truths are Truths.

Theology As Free Will
Not DNA or Bloodline

This book details why and how theology is the result of people's free-will choices, rather than as a result of a people's bloodline, DNA, or generational acquisitions. There are many instances when people are so busy abiding by their own humanmade dogma, laws, and policing within their particular group that they become polluted by their own piety and self-righteous indignation. Unfortunately, as a result, the roots of theology (as evidenced in the bible, etc.) have been shrouded in mystery, expressed in unbelievable stories, and enforced by the masses via what appears to be a "telephone game" mode of communication. With doctrines being so poorly or untimely recorded, it is no wonder so much has been lost in the proverbial (no pun intended) rewritings and translations.

The most outrageous point of all is that a series of people, from council elders in Jewish sects, papal and bishopric hierarchies, to an assortment of political and religious types, all took something special and did a great deal of damage to it. They seized something that was a personal, conscious, individual experience, coveted it, then sequestered it for themselves, forcing everyone else to remain on the outside. Everyone else then had to abide by a myriad of rules, laws, and regulations. As such, they only were given a portion of what was meant to be a holy feast intended for all to experience. As a result, the individual became alienated from the mystery which was rightfully theirs to begin with. Above all else, this deprivation is unconscionable.

People's dharmic plans do not choose for them any particular or specific monotheistic theology whatsoever. With our TransImagined free-will choices, we humans have taken and are led down a variety of paths. Some of us believe in theology, while others do not believe, and some combine both ways. Some create their own spiritual experience that requires no organized religion at all. Futhermore, religions are theology—thoughts and beliefs based on another's free-will choices and interpretations.

Hitler's attempts to rid the world of what he perceived as flawed or inferior DNA exemplifies this ignorant, uninformed, and misguided view of what constitutes a people, group, culture, or religion. A person could be completely non-religious and have no identification with any theology at all, but if their ancestor was discovered to have been Jewish, that nonreligious person was "Jewish enough," too—and at risk for destruction. People who were gay or gypsies, and those who aided these selectively persecuted people were labeled, deemed flawed or inferior, and at risk as well. Anyone who did not appear to possess the requisite DNA characteristics according to Hitler apparently had the wrong DNA.

However, religion is NOT DNA. It is not a culture or a people, but rather a theology. Religion as theology parallels the concept of there truly being no psychologically applicable "nature-nurture" hypothesis. As stated earlier, the nature-nurture hypothesis is baseless, because the origin of one's presenting problems, illnesses, or issues are those darmically enfolded and karmically reflected. Thus, the path one chooses to take in response to such problems is no different from the free-will choices we human beings make in terms of how, what, or perhaps even IF we choose to subscribe to a particular theology.

Holy Didactics
Biblical Illuminations: The Old Testament

We hope that the following Truthful disseminations, stemming from the God-Sanctioned Holy Angel, likewise will be truthfully comprehended. However, the extent to which each reader is capable of understanding these Truths is dependent upon their individual free will and personal evolutionary attunement. First and foremost, the focus and intention of this book is the Truthful dispelling of misinterpreted, misguided, or incorrectly recorded events and information.

Whether or not anyone chooses to believe this Truth, the fact remains that without unsullied outlets through which to flow, misinformation only builds. This book's impartial disclosure provides the lawful exegesis, while simultaneously allowing for the dissipation of all distorted, insensible inaccuracies. No part of this Holy Book is directed toward any particular individual or theology, and its purpose is not to antagonize or incite the ire of any particular adherent of the message.

The entire Old Testament is the result of verbal or oral historical translations that attempted to explain the inexplicable. Consistently throughout inhabitation on this planet, earth humankind has used mythology to explain unknown mysteries. Subsequently, people applied Old Testament happenings to their personal, individual experiences. For example, every time there was a flood, it was magnified and thus, misinterpreted to be the "Great Flood." Each time a locust infestation occurred, humans attributed it to some kind of divinely directed punishment of its selected victims, instead of what it truly was—a naturally occurring phenomenon.

Truth be told, most of the early Old Testament is filled with unsubstantiated interpretations of incomprehensibilities, which earth humankind has struggled to understand. Most human interpretation resembles the "telephone game," retranslated throughout thousands of years before literally being recorded. We know all too well the end result of this game—even after one minute, let alone three thousand years.

The Genesis section of the bible begins by creating more perplexing uncertainties than explanations. If fossilized remains are to be believed, the existence of Adam and Eve basically would have taken place around three million BC. Fossilized humanlike remains date back to approximately these ancient times. While literal translations of Holy Writ create a cerebral conundrum, spiritual translations certainly still beg for further elucidations. If we look pragmatically at each of the Old Testament writings, we quickly can surmise the implausibility of most, if not all, of these stories. Even if such writings were to be applied allegorically, these biblical stories still would be deemed imaginative exemplum.

The authors of the Old Testament utilized two modes of thought— mosaic and hermetic—to convey both historical as well as spiritual concepts. Mosaic thought refers to Moses and all principle doctrines attributable to him. Mosaic thought supposedly is based on historical, factual happenings. Hermetic thought refers to a body of esoteric writings on cosmogony, the soul, magic, etc., of the first through third centuries AD. Historically, hermetic thought is based in spiritual principles. We exist today in an era inundated with untruthfulness. In fact, Truth itself is very elusive. Human beings rarely know Truth when we experience it. Most humans are so contaminated with vibratory impactions, we are rendered unable to discern the subtlest Truth.

Convoluted thinking clouds the ability to detect Truth. Even when people might think they are detecting, understanding, or comprehending Truth, whatever they've determined as truth gets compartmentalized. For most humans, such compartmentalization is based upon one's comfortably accepted beliefs—many times having little to do with Divine Truth Itself.

There are two sources of vibratory information. First, there is the Manifesting Absolute, which is based in the inwardly reflecting Causal, Astral, and physical realms. The second source for vibratory information is the humanly imparted, articulated, influenced, and impacting, potential truth. The first source of vibratory information has the ring of the Holy Indisputable, while the second source—that which humans create and perpetuate—is to be scrutinized. Because Absolute Truth is extremely subtle, few circumstances or events in our conscious experiences ever really allow us to feel the "Ring of Truth."

We all are conscious experiences, located deep within three containers, yet we associate our very existences with outward manifestations. Without even blinking an eye, we say, "I am a Mr. (or Mrs.)," "I am Christian, Jewish, or Muslim." We tend to identify with outward, externalized definitions for our very existence. Few people really contemplate the nature of their true existence, instead associating it with an inanimate object, such as their car, upon which they base their relative self-worth or identity. We often expect others to identify and summarize themselves based upon what they do or where they live, and most of us readily reciprocate without much awareness.

Unfortunately, such narrow self-identification reveals volumes about our lack of awareness, insight, and conscious evolution. We are quick to use our labels and roles to justify, rationalize, theorize, explain, and condone some rather unevolved, perhaps unholy, and just plain ignorant behaviors and actions. "I am a Chicagoan, and this is the way we do things in Chicago," "I am a Muslim. I believe in the Koran. The Koran says God approves that it's okay to stone someone to death. Therefore, if we do so, we are vindicated." "The Old Testament speaks about slavery, so I am going to have slaves. I also have the right to strike with revenge against others who have wronged me." These unevolved interpretations by egoistic, self-serving adherents are keeping theological and ideological beliefs entrenched in the barbaric dark ages. The bottom line is that however truthfully perceived, all of these interpretations are faulty, unholy, and horrifically destructive.

The Old Testament essentially is composed of inexplicable circumstances around which humans have melded their mortal, necessitated interpretations. These are not the same as the "Veritable Word of the Holy Absolute." However, with what else does earth humankind have to work? People simply did not know any better. Both human and mythological gods rode around in chariots at that time because that was the sound, sensible logic available to explain incomprehensibilities.

However, this same logic cannot be applied today. We have a cumulative base of wisdom upon which to draw, yet consistently, earth humankind resorts back to the Old Testament or New Testament from which to form their "absolutes." Such absolutes, though, are NOT God's Absolutes, and are NOT about God's Absolutes. In reality, the Old Testament has become a modern-day interpretation about ancient, uncivilized human interpretations. A veil of blind faith—clearly not a foundation upon which to establish God's Absolutes—cloaks such perceptions.

People continually are formulating a blind faith in just about everything in existence, from diets to doctors to religious clergy to scriptures. Where does anyone draw the line? Linear thinking does not arrive at solidified absolutes, so how can blind faith? If we have conscious experience, which certainly seems an absolute to most individuals, where does blind faith fit in? While Christian children are taught to believe with blind faith, Jewish children are taught to question—but only to a point. In the end, all religious children, once they become adults, ultimately seek a change or choose to remain obedient within the confinement of their learned and accepted scriptural dogma. When questions are raised, the answers are derived through the modern human interpretation of ancient human perception of inexplicable experiences. These events went unrecorded for thousands of years. Furthermore, in most cases, few of these events even occurred. What does this tell us today? If someone posed the question, "Who was Noah?" the answer would be something like this . . .

For thousands of years, events were verbally translated through cultures and civilizations. Two thousand years ago, humans started writing down details of these verbally translated events. A man named Noah and his wife gathered together two (one male, the other female) of all the known animals on the planet—not missing even one insect or animal throughout the entire planet. Fortunately, Noah's father lived to be 770 years old, so he got a head start in helping to collect all these animals. Noah himself is said to have lived for 950 years. Collectively between the two men, they have a hoary 1,720 years of combined, continuous living.

It would take that long to travel by land and water, canvassing the world in order to collect a male and female of all creation to save in the ark—and what an ark it would have been. Just imagine a zoo with two of every known creature on the planet. To contain all of them, the ark would have to have been the size of the state of Texas. Then think about the food and waste factors. This group would need another ark the size of New Mexico to house the food for all of Earth's Creatures for forty days and forty nights. One quickly can surmise the ludicrous aspects of either Noah or an ark, for neither ever existed.

In all actuality, most of the Old Testament is nothing more than people's feeble attempts to explain unrecorded, misconstrued, misinterpreted, and subsequently purposefully manipulated information. These oral traditions transpired over twenty-five hundred years before earth humankind ever literally began recording them. The New Testament is composed of deletions, omissions, edits, and revisions of untruthful accounts—decades to centuries after these events supposedly took place. So, who knows what to believe? To look mosaically and/or hermetically at the Testaments, one must cling to threads of historical and geographical truth wrapped with indefinable misinterpretations. In reality, there simply is no way to believe any of it as actual fact.

Christians, Jews, and Muslims all recognize in some form the Old Testament. The theological and ideological separation between these theologies begins to occur with the New Testament. The beginning of the Old Testament consists of five scriptural segments known as the Five Books of Moses: Genesis, Exodus, Leviticus, Numbers, and Deuteronomy. These books actually had nothing to do with Moses. Numerous writers subdivided these five segments into writings.

These writers actually did not record these events at the time they were occurring. In fact, most biblical events did not occur at all. These "recorded" events now are known as scriptures or the holy bible. These scriptures originally were fables and stories, verbally communicated from generation to generation—recorded by writers who existed hundreds and hundreds of years after any such events ever would have occurred.

The bible was not created by Superevolved beings, writing in eloquent, deeply symbolic Holy Attunement. All mythological stories continually can be reinterpreted with ever-varying abstract comprehensions. A whole bible-sized compilation of symbolic interpretation could be created from Genesis alone. However, the Old Testament, New Testament, and Koran were written and meant to be interpreted more or less by adherents of the word. Even more problematic is the fact that earth humans rarely are willing to dissect such texts with diacritical thinking.

Just because something is ancient and purported to be holy does not make it so. This consistent biblical interpretation inevitably leads to wars, killing, slaughter, and annihilation of life, liberty, and freedom. Reflecting on my existence as Richard, Coeur de Lion, I now know this all too well. I participated in human atrocities such as those featured in biblical testaments. As a result, I paid dearly for my karmic transgressions. My dharmic plan includes sharing with you countless Truthful realizations. God purposely selected, guided, and instructed me to share with you these Transcendental Enlightenments.

According to the bible, Joshua (who actually did not exist), engraved these fabled stories into tablet form in the seventy languages present on the planet at the time of the supposed engravings. However, the Angelic Realm informs me there were eighty-six distinctly different languages spoken the first time any biblical stories were committed to written form. The first actual written recordings began to appear in 300 BC, centuries after any of these fabled events ever would have occurred. There are no physically accessible records of these recordings available today, other than those still retained and preserved within the quark memory membrane levels of the Holy Realm.

It should be known that I never have had more than a passing interest in the Old or New Testaments. I read and enjoyed the children's version of the Old Testament. After Catholic confirmation, I did my own individual praying to God, but never immersed myself into biblical scriptures. Consequently, I had very few preconceived ideas about their contents. Quite literally, I was a clean slate with little, if any, knowledge about the Old or New Testaments. However, I always have maintained a deep connection to God, whom I personally now refer to as Holy Lord Shiva, and whose Holiness I always sensed near my conscious perception.

For the sake of current and future earth humankind, God authorized a Supreme Holy Angel—the Holy Sanctioned Angel—to access the actual and Truthful Angelic Holy Realm recordings contained within the quark memory system. Never before has such Holy Access been divinely granted for the benefit of earth humankind. These Holy Records eternally are irretrievable and inaccessible—even to the Angelic inhabitants of the Holy Realm. Only when God-sanctioned is there an exception to this Divine Law.

To access this retained information within the quark memory of the Holy Realm, the Holy Sanctioned Angel was faced with immense challenges. Even for a Holy Angel, accessing, interpreting, and retrieving information that may or may not have taken place centuries ago is a daunting task. It is tantamount to locating a particle of dust capable of fitting on the point of a needle residing somewhere in a "haystack" as vast as the size of planet Earth.

This God-authorized Holy Sanctioned Angel never has set a hallowed foot on this planet, and has spent all incarnating existences evolving in other vectors of the physical cosmos. This Holy Sanctioned Angel is a Superenlightened Being with a vast ocean of wisdom, patience, love, and devotion to God. This Holy Angelic Being has neither a contaminating bias, nor preconceived notions, concepts or ideas regarding our simple, most often misguided existence here on planet Earth. This Holy Being is completely impartial and merely retrieves the ancient fact out of the catacombs of the Universal or Holy Records. Without God's compassionate approval, these inaccessible facts remain absolutely out of the range of comprehension for all manifesting beings.

Another Transcendental Angel of the Causal Universe showed this Holy Sanctioned Angel where to locate these ancient records deep in the Astral quark-contained memory of both time and space. God instructed the Transcendental Causal Angel of the Holy Neutrino Universe exactly how and where to locate these records. God did this for our benefit to prevent our further digression into a morass of insidious religious convolution. It is God's wish that these factual disseminations are to be interpreted as Truthful, useful tools to prod earth human beings into focusing on our individual responsibilities.

We all are independent, conscious experiences, whose free-will choices determine our individual attunement and ensuing holiness. We are not—and have never been—dependent upon organized religion to pave the only holy highway back to our Uncreated Infinite SuperConscious God. Theologies' ostracizing rules of unholy sectarianism fail miserably to feed our cravings for divine sustenance. We would be wise to recognize their limitations.

It is inconceivable to consider that any of us have—or ever had—only one absolute pathway to the Absolute Truth. God has provided us with the startling revelations of the Immaculate Truth. Before this time, we might have felt forced to believe many of these nonsensical, unGodly embellishments as the "Immutable Word." Now, with the Truth revealed clearly before us, we have another option for where and in what we decide to place our beliefs. When earth humans begin to exist in a God-loving, Creation-loving, evolved state, we then will know we exist on a planet deemed by God as physically manifesting heaven. As earth humankind, we erroneously and misguidedly continue looking elsewhere to find our heaven. Fortunately, heaven is here, all around us. We indeed can experience heaven on earth. It is merely a state of mind.

God's Holiness no longer will be contaminated and misrepresented by the concoction of blatant mistruths, embellishments, and misperceptions the bible erroneously portrays as truths. In particular, most appalling is the outrageous portrayal of God. The Holy Angels transmuting the Truthful Absolutes themselves were appalled. Other than Sri Yukteswar Giri, none of these transmuting Holy Angels ever have been born earth human. As such, these Blessed, Holy Angelic Beings brought to their God-sanctioned mission of transmuting a clear, pure, immaculate, conscious parchment with which to work.

Although planet Earth and its mortal inhabitants have value in their evolution, earthly existence remains fairly insignificant in the scheme of cosmic relevance. In spite of our shortcomings, God always has loved—and will forever continue to love—God's TransImaginated, little earthly creation. For all eternity, God lovingly is committed to assisting all of earth's inhabitants in realizing spiritual growth and soul upliftment.

Genesis—The Story of Creation

If interpreted literally or mosaically, Genesis is a hodgepodge of ignorant, verbally perpetuated fables constructed by later adherents of the word. Primitively cobbled together with gross exaggerations of historical facts, this total and virtually complete fiction is wrapped in a transparent cloak of holy writ. Just to ensure this fiction enjoys a continuous, everlasting irrevocability, it is sprinkled with God's supposed holy stamp of influence throughout.

A fabricated lie, even if perpetuated with innocent intentions, influences other people's free will. Furthermore, when such fabrications continuously are being retold and reabsorbed, karmically impacting transgressions occur. If done with sheer innocence and good intentions, the impact is fairly slight, but still is a negative soul impaction still needing to be expunged prior to attaining freedom from continuous reincarnation.

In Book Six we explain in depth the originations of Creation. Thanks to the Holy Angelic Realm, you now will know a great deal of what is depicted in the bible simply did not exist. As such, if interpreted symbolically, the biblical concept of creation is not nearly as problematic as its literal interpretation. Unfortunately, most religious followers focused solely upon literal interpretations without giving much credence to the symbolism. In doing so, they only further perpetuate biblical nonsense at the expense of the few Truths that do exist.

What follows is an analytical synopsis no academic or theological scholar or researcher ever could provide. God graciously authorized the Blessed Holy Sanctioned Angel to Transingress into the ancient earthly Dharmic Records meticulously contained in the quark memory system. What you will read are the results of this search and subsequent transmutation for the purpose of Truth extraction and dissemination. Due to the nature of transmuted information, this dissertation occasionally appears in linear, as well as flowing paragraph form.

At the beginning of earth's creation, manifesting earthly existence did not occur in six days, with God taking off the seventh or Sabbath day. In addition, there was no good/evil cosmic battle whatsoever. Evil exists as free will in the minds of misperceiving miscreants or incomprehending earth human-kind. In this book, we describe how existence actually originated on this planet. If Genesis is to be believed, it must be accepted that as per the Old Testament calendar, all manifesting existence would have begun 5764 years ago. This, of course, would completely discount the disciplines of paleontology, anthropology, archeology, and geology. It is impossible to contemplate, let alone believe, that the subjects of these disciplines—fossils, gems, rocks, and the formation of entire civilizations—were all created a mere 5700-plus years ago. To literally (or even symbolically) interpret and accept this "Genesis Theory of Creation" is absurd. Fossilized, humanlike remains accurately and historically detail earth humankind's inhabitation dating back four million years. We conclusively can determine that Adam and Eve never existed. As depicted in the bible, the Garden of Eden never existed, and there was no tree of knowledge or any evil serpent whatsoever.

As depicted in Genesis, there also was no direct one-on-one dialogue between God and any earth human being. Earth humankind have experienced supernal disembodied voices as communications resounding from external sources, such as clouds, "the heavens," and literally everywhere. Note that there is a major distinction between the dialogue that occurs as one's internal comprehensions and the communications originating from external sources. Manifesting Infinite SuperConsciousness (Holy Lord Shiva) is infinitely careful when operating unseen behind all manifesting experiences.

Manifesting Infinite SuperConsciousness rarely subjects Itself to contaminating interactions with its manifesting child, Creation. Only on rare occasions, while celebrating a soul's evolution from Astral to Causal emancipating attunement, does Manifesting God directly express Itself before Made Manifest within the Causal Universe of the Holy Neutrino. In Books Four and Five, we describe the three rare exceptions that have occurred when God has provided an opportunity to communicate directly to earth humankind.

The Old Testament is filled with many fictitious God-human "communications," as well as fictitious individuals themselves. One example is Cain and Abel, who never existed, and whose rivalry never occurred. Only symbolically and compassionately, are we our brother's and sister's keepers. Neither Noah nor his infamous ark occurred. Phenomena of existence, such as natural disasters and diseases, occur not as God-driven retributions against earth humankind, but rather by God's Unconditional Love, TransImaginated for reasons known only to God. Of course, as humans, we typically place ourselves as the ego centers of the universe.

We tend to personalize, overanalyze, misinterpret, and misconstrue naturally occurring events.

More often than not, these peripheral events impacting our experiences are just natural unenfoldments actually unrelated to our prior behaviors. Earth humankind oftentimes personalize these peripheral experiences, forming attachments that may become karmically burdening to their souls. One example of this is the mass emotional hysteria, anxiety, depression, or fear commonly occurring in people during the aftermath of traumatic events, such as wars, injustice, violence, and egregious atrocities. In contrast, those experiences of TRUE karmic retribution tend to be greater in personal or individual magnitude. Massive, God-Ordained rectifications occur to large groups of individuals simultaneously for divinely discerned purposes, based upon each person's unique, individual dharmic plan and karmic necessity. God does not and never has unleashed upon poor, undeserving earth humankind any angst, pent-up rage, or targeted venting.

There indeed was a real Tower of Babel. However, the events depicted in the bible simply did not occur at the Tower of Babel; such events did not occur at all. Sodom and Gomorrah indeed were real places, but were not destroyed by any act of God on the behalf of earth humankind. Indeed, earthquakes and the shifting of continental plates destroyed both places. God does not judge, and God does not respond with vengeance to groups or their deplorable actions. It is karma that eventually rebalances the transgression of the individual's conscious experience after the individual soul's indebtedness has occurred.

Abraham's father was not Terah. In fact, no one by that name ever was associated with Abraham. Terah was the clan or village from which Abraham's father descended. Abraham was a real person who was born in 1832 BC and died at age 48. His original name was Abram. Abraham's father was a pagan moon worshipper who migrated to Gerar, where Abraham was born. Abraham had three brothers and two sisters. Two of his brothers and one of his sisters also followed their parents' moon worshipping ways. Abraham and his family's travels took them to numerous neighboring villages, although never to Hebron. Abraham quarried limestone block in the surrounding villages. When he left his family at 17 years of age, Abraham resettled back at Gerar.

Abraham's father arranged for Abraham's wedding to Sarah. When Abraham and Sarah first were living in Gerar, Sarah was a toddler. By the time Abraham went back to Gerar for the fulfillment of his father's arrangement, Abraham was 28, and his wife-to-be, Sarah, 17. Abraham's wife Sarah's original name was Sarai. She was born in 1827 BC and died in 1806 BC at age 21. Sarah was Abraham's only wife. Abram and Sarai were long since deceased when later writers changed their names to Abraham and Sarah—a gesture, which during these writers' lives was deemed highly significant, for names were reflections of one's very essence and being. Neither Abraham nor Sarah was a particularly spiritual being. They had no knowledge or awareness that God existed, and therefore did not believe or disbelieve in God.

The circumcision of Abraham never happened, for his renaming occurred well after his death. The tradition of name changing and accompanying circumcision, as well as the subsequent threat of being cut off from his kin, simply did not apply to Abraham. None of Abraham's male family members were circumcised either. At age 18, Sarah gave birth to Ishmael, and two years later, gave birth to Isaac. After Sarah died at age 21, Abraham received support from three female helpers in the raising of his young sons.

Abraham's relationships with all three of these women were strictly platonic, and he did not marry any of them. After Sarah's death, Abraham spent most of his remaining seventeen years in bad health. He did almost go blind before he died. Abraham deeply loved Sarah, and was devastated upon her death. In fact, Abraham never fully recovered from the loss of his beloved Sarah, and in his ensuing grief, directed much anger toward his family's perception of God, which for them was the moon.

Hagar did exist, but did not serve as a concubine and surrogate mother for Sarah. In addition, Rachel's maid, Bilhah, did exist—but did not serve as a concubine or surrogate mother for Rachel. Haran did not have a son named Lot. Lot simply did not exist. Of Abraham, Sarah, Ishmael, Isaac, Rebekah, Jacob, Leah, their three sons, or daughter, none were considered by the Holy Realm to be holy beings. They were not holy then, and through subsequent incarnations, none of them are any more evolved or holy today. The soul of Isaac's son, Esau, is the only true Holy Being depicted in Genesis. Esau attained salvation in 600 BC.

There was no covenant or Akedah between Abraham and God, and no bloody treaty. The Akedah story was revised several times before it became the biblical version we know today. No animals were sacrificed on God's behalf during Abraham's conscious life. Isaac and Ishmael were born to Abraham and Sarah, via normal births, with Ishmael arriving first. God never demanded anything from Abraham, period. God endowed Abraham with Unconditional Love, in the hope that Abraham unconditionally would love God in return.

The Akedah, the binding of Isaac, is absurd and insidious in its entirety. God NEVER would require the sacrifice of any created existence to prove one's faith in God. There was no test of Abraham's love and devotion to God. The entire account of Abraham's journey is a complete farce—and in any aspect at all, did not happen. Abraham never, ever spoke directly to an Angel, let alone to the Holy SuperConsciousness.

Abraham did not plant a sacred tree and invoke any name relating to God. Abraham did not go to Hebron to settle Sarah's corporal affairs, or to buy a plot of land. There was no chosen burial ground for any chosen people. In fact, there were no chosen people at all. As stated earlier, Abraham actually never went to Hebron for any purpose whatsoever.

After Sarah's death, Isaac was wed in an arranged marriage to Rebekah. Rebekah did have a brother named Laban. Jacob and Esau were fraternal twins born to Isaac and Rebekah after a difficult pregnancy. Esau was the firstborn of the two twins, and developed into a strong and skillful hunter. Jacob was mild-mannered, and never divinely was designated to be the sole heir to any Abraham-Isaac covenanted heritage. Jacob never was predestined by God to be the father of any chosen people. Rebekah favored Esau and Isaac favored Jacob. Jacob never exploited Esau when Isaac was old, feeble, and going blind. The two twins simply never got along. Similarly, Esau never threatened Isaac. The father and his son (Esau) didn't get along.

Isaac died at age 34, Jacob died at age 24, and Esau was 36 years old at his time of death. Jacob did not cheat his father out of anything. He did not try to fool his father by pretending to be his brother, and never was banished from the household. However, in some small, insignificant way, he was involved in an incident with Laban, involving Leah. Laban never played any substitution game with Jacob's wife's sister, Rachel. Jacob had a bad hip, but not from any mysterious night encounter.

One's firstborn son was considered sacred and accorded special status as an exclusive possession of God. Of course, this was according to human interpretation, but never by God's interpretation. Jacob never slept with Bilhah. It is true that Jacob and Esau had an altercation, but it was not a factor causing Jacob to leave town in search of a wife. Jacob only had one wife, Leah, who was promised to Esau. Jacob did take Esau's bride-to-be. However contentious their relationship was at this point, it had no bearing upon Esau's never-married status. Esau was not interested in marriage, or relations with anyone at all. As a spiritual being, Esau only was interested in developing a relationship with God.

Jacob never had any dream about a heavenly stairway for a variety of reasons. Jacob never left home, never erected an altar for God, never went to Bethel, and never had a vision. Jacob never visited Laban's house, and Laban did not adopt him. Jacob did not have twelve sons with Leah. He and Leah had three sons and one daughter. The rest of these fictionalized sons were attributed to the tribes and villages of the day—and they had nothing to do with Jacob. Furthermore, none of Jacob's sons led any of the tribes with which they supposedly were associated. Any such connections by later writers were sheer fabrications. Out of the twelve supposed sons, only Simeon was an actual son—but never a tribal leader of any village. Jacob never had children—or relations—with Rachel. He had no relations with anyone named Bilhah, or Zilpah.

God never intervened openly or indirectly on behalf of Abraham, Isaac, or Jacob. God never intervened on behalf of any potential Joseph at the time. As stated before, in the history of earth human beings, God never has interacted directly with humans—except through Angelic Beings or God's Selected Messengers. Such messengers specifically are engaged for this sole purpose. Angels have no authority to interact on their own accord without God's sanctioning.

Joseph was not a son of Jacob. Joseph never was sold into slavery. He never had a mother named Rachel, married to Jacob. There was NO Joseph born with a twin brother named Benjamin. There were Josephs in the region, but all were completely unaffiliated with both Jacob and Leah. Around that time, there was a woman named Rachel who had twins who died during childbirth—but their names were not Joseph or Benjamin. In fact, there was no biblically pertinent Joseph at all. The biblical Joseph simply did not exist.

Abraham and Sarah were not buried together. Isaac and Rebekah were not buried together. Abraham and Isaac were not buried together. Jacob and Leah were not buried together. Jacob's three sons or daughters were not buried together, either.

Exodus

Exodus basically is the same distorted fiction as Genesis. The Egyptians did enslave people from all of the various clans and villages. At this point in time, however, there was neither an Israel nor was there any Judaism. There was a real person, a shepherd, named Moses. He never was floated in a basket. He never was given over to be raised by Egyptian Pharaohs. Moses never struck or killed anybody. He also never was a slave. Moses never married anyone named Zipporah, and he did not have a son named Gershom. In fact, Moses neither married, nor did he ever sire any children whatsoever. The Holy Realm considered Moses then as a highly evolved soul—and today as an evolved and Holy Being, free from any future reincarnation.

Moses was born in 2154 BC. Moses was 16 years old when he departed for Canaan in 2137 BC. At that point in time, there still were no Israelites; in fact, Judaism itself simply did not exist. There merely were nomadic survivors being led by their teenage leader. Neither Moses nor any of the surviving followers were associated with any theological affiliations. Moses and his father were primarily oxen shepherds, a non-Semitic people who were not enslaved by the Egyptians. Moses had two biological brothers and was the youngest of the three. There was no brother Aaron, for no such Aaron even existed. No one in the family, including Moses' mother, ever was enslaved. All of Moses' family succumbed to the famine, draught, or disease taking place at the time.

Moses and his family were completely unreligious and maintained no theological affiliations. With the exception of his father, who worshipped the sun, Moses, his mother, and the rest of the family, did not adhere to any spiritual disciplines whatsoever. Moses and his family were completely unfamiliar with any Hebdomad concepts of days and weeks. Moses recognized no particular day as a Sabbath. As such, every day was a "sun" day. Nonetheless, prior to his Angelic encounters, this simple, nomadic shepherd who, regardless of his particular social stature and religious deficiency, had a very special purpose preprescribed into his dharmic plan.

The Holy Angel first appeared to Moses while he tended his flock and cattle near the Nile. This initial Angelic visit never took place on Mount Horeb, which actually is the same as Mount Sinai. As Moses' family was succumbing to the perilous conditions, God commanded the Holy Angel to appear to Moses. There was no burning bush. The Angel indeed was radiant, and Moses definitely was incapable of viewing it or opening his eyes. The Angel did deliver a message from God regarding leading people to another land, the land of Canaan. Moses was not requested to remove his shoes, for the land on which the message was delivered was not and could not have been on holy ground.

Whether the ground exists as Mecca; Sedona, Arizona; or Detroit, Michigan, the perceived sacredness of all created lands is indistinguishable. In the Almighty Eye of God, when it comes to distinctions of holiness throughout all Made Manifest, there are none. There also is no difference between the individual sacredness of people. People rich or poor, lands urban or rural, all manifesting creation in the Divine Grace is deemed equal and pertinent without bias, preference, or discrimination. This same principle is applicable throughout the entire physically manifesting cosmos. In the Almighty Eye of God, this Divine Law has been and forever will be consistent for all eternity.

The large group of enslaved people included many nationalities—ALL who were enslaved and oppressed. However, the designations Israelite, or Jewish or Hebrew, did not exist prior to 300 AD. God did not signify to Moses any elevation of people or any special designation that would have identified any so-called "Hebrews" from this enslaved group as chosen people. These particular people were enslaved not because their numbers were so vast and threatening—for neither was the case—but simply because they were available bodies for labor. The Egyptian king or pharaoh needed more laborers to build the infrastructure for the Egyptian empire. At the time of Moses, the first Egyptian civilization was disintegrating and the second civilization had yet to rise. There was no singling out any firstborn sons of "Hebrew" slaves to be killed by the ruling Egyptians. In fact, the Egyptians looked at all of the increasing male births as future, potential laborers.

As stated earlier, there was no covenant between God and Abraham. There also was no covenant between God and Isaac or Jacob. All of this was pure fiction. There was no prior promise to give the land of Canaan to Abraham, Isaac, and Jacob. However, as stated before, the Angel did give Moses a message to lead the enslaved people to Canaan. The Egyptian civilization was collapsing, due to environmental and viral conditions—NOT because of any plague causing the ruling Egyptians' demise. The exodus was an attempt to flee the drought and not succumb to these conditions. The drought, famine, and virus contributed to the collapse of the Egyptian empire, providing the impetus for the Angel's intercession and dialogue with Moses.

At no time ever did Moses or any other representative of the "Hebrews" utter to the Pharaoh, "Let my people go!" None of the enslaved people had absolutely any concept of being "our people" or a divinely chosen people, in reference to freedom for that particular period of history. Furthermore, Moses never had any direct contact whatsoever with any pharaoh. Aaron was written in for a firsthand corroboration of these fictitious events. Aaron allegedly was the brother of Moses, but in truth, Aaron simply never existed. A rod morphing into a serpent never existed either. The surviving slaves and villagers were leaderless. As a result of his Angelic encounter, Moses simply led the people out of the imploding Egyptian civilization.

The Angel's message to Moses was sufficient to rally all of the surviving slaves—especially since Moses, himself, was not a slave. Part of the intent behind the Angel's message was to provide the leadership role for the exodus of these oppressed people. These horrific conditions at the time killed both humans and animals without discernment for cultural lineage. Massive numbers of people—both slaves and Egyptians—perished from this widespread collapse of civilization. As just stated, no one of any particular people was chosen to be targeted or spared. The effects of the societal meltdown were completely nondiscriminatory.

Part of the Angel's thought transmission to Moses included giving him directions for the upcoming exodus. The Holy Angel's instructions directed Moses exactly where to pass through the Red Sea, which then was known as the Reed Sea. After many years of little rainfall, severe draught, and famine, the water only was at knee-deep or axel level where Moses and his followers were to cross. At that time, the Sea where they crossed was extremely shallow, thus requiring no "parting of the sea" whatsoever.

At the time of the exodus, the Red Sea had no tributaries, for the Suez Canal was nonexistent. In addition, when Moses and his followers later crossed the northern tip of the Sea, they did so without being pursued. After successive years of minimal or no flooding of the River Nile, it no longer replenished vital nutrients into the soil. The resulting famine and civil unrest prevented the Egyptians from doing anything more than struggle for their own survival amidst their crumbling civilization, let alone even consider pursuing Moses and his group.

Including men, women, and children, there were a total of 1,137 people who exited out of Egypt. Moses and his group were not treated to any dew-like, flaky substance gathered for consumption. With the state of the dried-up Nile and resulting lack of nutrients in the soil, any grain grown during the time of the exodus was extremely compromised. As such, there was no yeast to make regular bread. Moses and his group did not have unleavened bread baking upon their backs during their journey. Rather, the unleavened bread known in later years as matzo merely was dough without yeast left out in the scorching sunlight in the back of the group's oxen carts.

Once the group commenced on their sojourn, they gathered whatever scant, bitter vegetation and herbs they could find. Since Moses was a desert nomad, he was well-versed in desert survival skills. As such, he made use of the dew on rocks and other various objects in order to provide enough moisture sustenance for his group's survival. To maximize their progress, the group traveled day and night.

On their journey to Canaan, Moses and the emancipated slaves indeed did pass by Mount Sinai, also known as Mount Horeb. Per his preprescripted dharmic plan, Moses was guided to experience a second Angelic Visitation, this time occurring on Mount Sinai. The entire exodus from the Nile to Canaan took two years. Filled with great suffering, the journey took a toll on humans and animals alike. As stated earlier, for both people and animals, lack of water was very problematic. The group's journey skirted around the wilderness area, which was very hot and dry, with rugged terrain—a desolate wasteland. The northern part of the Sinai Peninsula was mostly desert, while the southern area was inundated with numerous, steep, craggy mountains, including Mount Sinai.

Moses indeed did ascend Mount Sinai, but did so strictly for navigational purposes. He did not respond to any ram's horn prior to this ascent. While on Mount Sinai, Moses was visited by the same Angel who had visited him before when he was tending to the family animals. During the entire exodus, Moses was the only person to whom the Angel communicated.

There were no covenants ever forged between the Angel and any earth human beings. While on Mount Sinai, Moses did not erect any altars. There were no restrictive demands placed upon these starving, thirsty, dirt-poor survivors. No annihilation of any aspect of any creation was demanded. There were no animal sacrifices; if any animals perished, they were consumed for sustenance. By the time the sojourners arrived at Mount Sinai, their numbers were reduced to 695 barely surviving human beings.

Those who died had succumbed solely because their individual dharmic blueprints called for them to exit our physical universe at their God-predetermined moment. Each individual's death was not attributable to their particular suffering or traumatic experience. Their terminal suffering was a karmic response to their individual karmic debts derived exclusively from their current and prior free-will choices. If one makes bad free-will choices, they will suffer heavy karmic consequences.

While on Mount Sinai, the Angel, through thought transmissions did explain to Moses about the soul or manifesting consciousness inhabiting the tabernacle of the human body. The Angel explained the various conduct parameters that would feed the soul and please God. The Angel also explained that God was responsible for the creation of everything Moses could see and understand, emphasizing that such comprehension and adherence to these conduct parameters eventually would lead to salvation.

These conduct parameters later became known as the Ten Commandments. However, the Ten Commandments were not carved in any stone. Lapis usually is the repudiated stone chosen by the majority of modern-day believers. In actuality, however, no stone was used for the Ten Commandments. Moses' experience atop Mount Sinai was like an epiphany. The Angel carefully explained to Moses the value of conscious existence and the importance of salvation.

The Angel instructed Moses to teach, share, and abide by these Holy Commandments for salvation. Prior to Moses' Angelic Visitation, the concept of salvation was well-known to Babaji, who was instrumental in ensuring that salvation was included in the Vedic Scriptures. While the concept of resurrection was well-known to the Egyptians by this time, the concept of salvation was unknown to the people of Moses' day in the Middle East. These Holy Commandments are just as applicable today as they were at the time of Moses.

In addition to not being committed to any stone, the Ten Commandments were not committed literally to any hemp paper or parchment. These people carried with them only the absolute, bare essentials for survival, and had no parchment. Furthermore, every surviving member of this group was illiterate. Not one of them could write in any language. The Angel did not burden them with any unnecessary, heavy stone tablets. As it were, these people barely were surviving. Furthermore, the exodus preceded Abraham's existence by over three hundred years. This reality, combined with the fact that Joseph never existed, renders moot the necessity for Moses to carry along Joseph's bones.

As we stated elsewhere in the book, God does not judge any manifesting conscious experience or existence. Transgressions against God were preprescripted into the dharmic blueprint for all earth humankind. Transgressions simply occur through humans' TransImaginated free-will choices, resulting in all physically manifesting karmic repercussions. Bad things (or karmic reflections) do not happen to good people without some interwoven dharmic reason. Take a truthful, fearless, introspective look deep enough into your actions and reactions—and consider the fact that you—like all existence—have lived many, many times before. Inevitably, you will find the reasons for most, if not all, the troubles in your conscious existence.

The conduct parameters or Ten Commandments were not actual commandments, but rather were enlightenments. The Angel informed young Moses that these guidelines would allow for soul upliftment—in other words, salvation or freedom from sin or karmic attachments. At no time was there any conveyance of any covenant, and there was no physically manifesting ark. Neither one was associated with Moses in any way. The Angel disclosed to Moses the Ten Commandments for Salvation in the following order:

1. One God.

2. No idol worship. Worship one God.

3. Don't take or use God's name in vain.

4. Respect thy personal tabernacle.

5. Govern over all your personal intentions.

6. Govern over all your personal thoughts.

7. Govern over all your personal actions and reactions.

8. Respect all God's Creation and its right to exist. (Unconditional Love)

9. Kill for food only, and then only when absolutely necessary.

10. Do not covet anything along your personal journey.

The first three Commandments easily are self-explanatory. Number four pertains to a human being's personal, physically manifesting body. Numbers five, six, and seven refer to the threefold nature of which the human body is composed. Number five pertains to the Idea or Causal nature of earth humankind. Number six pertains to the energy or Astral nature of earth humankind. Number seven pertains to the physically manifesting, outermost aspects of human existence. Number eight pertains to transgressions against others and all Creation. Number nine pertains to the unnecessary killing of other existences. Number ten pertains to karmically burdening yourself with attachments along the path of your existence.

For each Holy Enlightenment Commandment given, the Angel provided Moses with specific examples applicable to Moses' own human conscious experience. After descending Mount Sinai to reunite with his followers, Moses was not able to remember fully all of these Commandments. In some cases, he only was able to recall the supporting example, rather than the actual Commandment, itself. In some cases, Moses was unable to recall either the example, or the corresponding Commandment.

When Moses experienced his first Angelic Encounter while tending his animals, he was terrified. However, this was not the case when Moses experienced his second encounter with the same Angel on Mount Sinai. Nonetheless, while on Mount Sinai, Moses was unable to look directly at the Angel. He had to hide his face in order to shield his eyes from the radiant, blinding photonic light of the Angel's essence. The only tabernacle mentioned at all was the bodily tabernacle. Once again, there were no sacrifices, no altars, and no ark of the covenant to carry what in reality, Moses was carrying inside his own head.

Moses was instructed that God also created the sun, land, and all creatures. In the Almighty Eye of God, any and all manifesting creation, such as mountains, lands, or grounds are not and never will be considered holy. No one particular land is more holy than another. No rock is holier than any other. Directing worship toward a rock is neither a soul transgression, nor does it constitute idolatry. However, from the Holy Realm's perspective, honoring any physically manifesting aspect of creation is not synonymous with attuning to God. In other words, such worship of ANY and ALL physically manifesting aspects of creation clearly misses the mark—and bypasses the True Source of all Creation.

Directing worship toward either a rock or a wall is no more spiritually accurate than directing worship toward an old, abandoned sock residing in the gutter of a road. All three—the rock, wall, and sock—contain the same photonic light and vibratory Unconditional Love of God. All three of these physically manifesting aspects of creation equally are deserving of compassion and perhaps some loving, considerate attention, but nothing more—and certainly not the designation of holiness. Earth humankind's ego-based confusion and sense perceptive delusions tend to create an expectation of perceived holiness. Without distinctions, God recognizes ALL Made Manifest as Holiness.

While on Mount Sinai, the Angel did not direct Moses to erect any elaborate tents. There were no human consecrations. In fact, Moses died without ever hearing the term "consecration." When Moses descended from Mount Sinai, he actually was excited and enlightened from his Holy experience. From the Angel's Holiness, Moses was transformed into a differently acting and comprehending being. The Angelic Encounter indeed did have a profound impact on young Moses' conscious perspective—he shared his enlightened exuberance with the 695 survivors.

Nonetheless, the survivors were not very enthused about or responsive to Moses or his message, for they were physically suffering from food and dehydration concerns. Theirs was an extremely difficult journey in which fewer than half of the people who started out actually survived to the point at which the caravan disbanded. As stated earlier, no one named Aaron existed—and there was no golden calf. Moses did try to instruct his followers about the Angelic visit, the life-adhering parameters, God, and salvation of the soul. He was met with very obstinate, desperate people, and had little success in convincing them to change their ignorant, incomprehending ways.

There were no elaborate, celebratory rituals, ceremonies, or created objects of opulence. There was no breastplate, no jewels, gold, or headdresses for anyone associated with Moses' group. Mount Sinai was

Moses' second and last encounter with the Angel. God never directly addressed Moses or any other Earth human during that period.

Leviticus

Leviticus is laden with more of the same illogical elaborations written by later writers. After analyzing this section in its entirety, the Holy Sanctioned Angel was unable to find any truthful, substantiated, historical reality. On behalf of earth humankind, it truly is an embarrassment to read what for eons has been purported to be truth—only to be informed by this Superenlightened Being that page after page contained pure, fictional nonsense.

Numbers

As you well can imagine, "Numbers" produced even more magical numbers, as well as other imaginary characters and events. Some such people may have existed, but were not connected with Moses. Aaron, who never existed, conveniently died along the way to Canaan at Mount Hor. Since Aaron was fictitious, words of his demise are fitting. Moses never quite made it to Canaan. He died at age 28. Before he died, Moses continued to expound God's virtues and his experiences with the two Angelic Encounters. Moses also continued to teach the life-conforming parameters and soul-enhancing guidelines transmitted to him from the Angel.

Moses had relations with women, from which he never had children. Moses also never was married. If it matters to anyone, Moses was never circumcised. In fact, no desert-dwelling shepherd living in 2150 BC ever had heard of such a custom. Although the custom of circumcision was just becoming known and gaining popularity in densely populated Egypt during Moses' time, he personally was not a participant. Moses ultimately settled in an area that provided water, still within the confines of Egypt.

Joshua of Nun

Joshua never existed, so Moses never commanded him to do anything. A few of Moses' surviving followers did reach Canaan or what now is known as Israel. They recalled scant few details about Moses' visits with the Angel. However, they did describe in great detail the arduous journey and the epic struggles along the way. The survivors were able to recount correctly the fact that there indeed were ten parameters by which to conduct one's life, but could not necessarily equate them as requisites leading to salvation. A couple bedraggled survivors did make it to the southern areas of Canaan, but none of them penetrated very far into the land of Canaan proper. The Exodus expired in the southern area of Canaan.

Joshua of Nun could have been from "None," for he was a complete fabrication. The walls of Jericho were not felled by rams' horns or by the Mighty Will of God. The walls of Jericho crumbled after becoming derelict from uninhabitation. Once again, severe draught took its toll on earth humanity, and the inhabitants drifted away in search of food and water. The abandonment of Jericho occurred in approximately 1700 BC. There was no miraculous destruction, but rather a natural attrition, attributable to the area's ever-present, grinding forces.

Judges

Once again, later-day writers embellished the historical truth by weaving loosely recorded facts, incidents, and occurrences into a vaguely plausible story. To The Angelic Realm, these are misleading, gross fabrications—untruthful recreations of events. Biblical writers have cloaked them as intervening, holy acts by God on the behalf of humankind. However, God simply does not act in such ways. The TransImaginated Laws of dharma, as well as manifesting reflecting karma ensuing from our free-will choices inevitably lead to our future incarnations. These laws exist irrespective of any of earth humankind's interpretations. These immutable Laws are irrevocable, except by God's unprecedented, remedial reperfecting of the Universe's Dharmic Blueprint. God clearly will not revoke these Laws, has no intention of doing so, and has never done so in any of the Universe's prior incarnations. The Holy Angel has informed me this is Absolute Truth.

Samson was a real person born in 934 BC. He never tangled with a lion. He never put forth a riddle to anyone. He never killed any animals or people. He indeed had long hair, physically was very strong, and was married to a Philistine. On occasion, Samson did treat his wife with indifference; however, his wife never left him for his companion. Samson's wife's family pressured her a great deal, resulting in much friction in the marital relationship. Samson neither encountered anyone named Delilah, nor was he ever bound. Samson was a Nazarite, which was a designation applied to him by writers after his passing. Samson never drank any wine. His hair never was forcefully shorn, and he did not knock down any pillars or cause any temples to collapse. Samson died of natural causes at age 27.

I did not request the Angel to investigate the truths regarding either Micah and Benjamin of "Judges." The purpose of this truthful enlightenment was neither to validate the very existence of every human entry in the Old Testament nor was it to discredit the three main organized religions of the world. As stated earlier, I personally do not care whether organized religions historically are right or wrong. However, the Angelic Realm is highlighting specific incidents of importance, and will be explaining the Truths.

Through your God-gifted free will, you will decide for yourself what strikes of the Truth and what does not. Some of these ancient misperceptions were prompted by the individual souls themselves, trying to refute and prevent the perpetuation of lies about their very existences. This explanation also helps prevent innocent people—who of course, never have had access to the unadulterated Truth—from foolishly continuing to spread inaccurate, grossly misleading distortions.

First Samuel

No Ark was brought out, for it never existed in such purported form. Any aspect of a holy object, such as an Ark of the Covenant, never could be used as a weapon against anybody or anything. Such usage would be nonsensical—and the very antithesis of what God manifests.

The Philistines neither returned The Ark nor ever gazed upon it. The Ark never existed in the manner in which it allegedly exists in Exodus. In those days, there were plenty of minor, local battles, including fights and skirmishes, infighting between clans, and wars between the various peoples of the day. However, God sides with no one, as the manifesting laws of dharma, free will, karma, and reincarnation incorrigibly mete out unbiased reflection.

David and Goliath are sheer fiction. Neither one existed as a combatant in any way. Plainly and simply, David did not slay a giant named Goliath; Goliath did not exist. This fabled David never became King David of anything other than this story.

There was a man named Saul who did exist, rallying and presiding over several clans and tribes. However, the Holy Realm did not recognize him as a king. Saul did have sons, and Saul and his sons all were killed by a Philistine insurgent uprising. There was a King David, but this particular kingly being had no ties to the David in the First and Second Samuel sections. The David in the First and Second Samuel sections was a fantastic fabrication of the real King David's early life. Although not recognized as a holy being, the real King David was a good man. He indeed did have four sons, and he existed in the mid-seventh century BC. King David did have a son named Solomon, who built a temple with massive pillars that eventually was sacked by Nebuchanezer of Babylon. King David did rule over the various clans, tribes, and families of what now is Israel. He was the first real king or ruler of the region.

Second Samuel

It was true that infighting had been going on between Saul and David. Upon Saul's demise, David assumed the first actual kingship position of the Hebrew realm. He didn't actually have to battle the Philistines, for by that time, the Philistines were fewer in number and simply took the spoils and fled. King David literally marched his people in and subordinated the others. In response, King David's people actually were welcomed by Saul's subsidiary clans and enclaves.

David did spread his rule outward without the assistance of a favoring covenant with God. David was successful in battle and was a revered king. He was recognized by the Holy Realm as being a just and righteous ruler. The incident with Uriah the Hittite and his wife and son never happened. One of David's wives was Bathsheba, and it was their son who was named Solomon. The Holy Realm informs me that David died at age 37. He was king for just nine years—from the time of Saul's death until his own passing.

First Kings

Solomon became king through attrition. Solomon was the third brother—his two older brothers died before King David. Solomon was nineteen when his father David died. While not considered to be a holy being by the Holy Realm, Solomon was a very good king. He did not ever marry a pharaoh's daughter. He did have several wives and concubines. The Holy Sanctioned Angel informs me he officially had seven wives and five concubines—not exactly the seven hundred wives, princesses, and three hundred concubines he purportedly experienced—but still quite a few by anyone's standards. Solomon did sire several children, five boys and three girls to be exact.

Ahijah was a real person—an old, blind prophet through whom an Astral Universe Holy Angel worked, providing Ahijah with his divine prophetic vision. Ahijah did not call a curse upon the house of Jeroboam. Jeroboam was not a catalyst for God to take vengeance upon the people of Judah. Elijah also was real person—and not recognized by the Holy Angelic Realm as a Holy Being. Prior to this incarnation, Elijah was a level eleven attuned being. Elijah did have an Astral Angel assisting him. Through the divine request of the Astral Angel on Elijah's prayerful pleadings, God actually did restore the soul of an infant child.

A competition occurred between Elijah and a man named Ahab. In this event, each man's devotion and attunement to God were put to the test. The test included igniting a bullock cart purely through devotional will. Upon his prayerful request, Elijah's bullock cart erupted into flames. This startling occurrence truly was a miracle of some measure—although its subsequent recording was laden with human embellishments and mis-perceptions. Elijah never slew anyone in his entire life, and he never mocked or taunted others.

Second Kings

Elisha was a real being who also was not recognized by the Holy Realm as a Holy Being. Elisha, like Elijah, was still a temporary resident of level eleven of the Astral Realm. Elisha was a farmer when Elijah encountered him. Elisha did not slay the oxen, but did bid his parents farewell and left with Elijah. Elijah was on the hilltop when the king summoned him. None of the king's party was consumed in fire. Elijah did go willingly. Elijah and Elisha did travel together quite extensively. Elijah did not part the Jordan. Elijah and Elisha never crossed over onto the far side.

Elisha indeed did request of Elijah that Elijah's spirit enter him (Elisha) upon Elijah's passing. However, Elijah's spirit did not pass into Elisha upon Elijah's passing. Even the Astral Angel watching over Elijah had no authority to grant such a request. No request such as this one ever has been granted to any earth human incarnating being for the benefit of any surviving, earthly incarnation. Only the Infinite Soul Ordainer can grant such a request, and for God, it was not even a consideration.

Upon his passing, Elijah did not disappear in a whirlwind, into heaven. There was no separating fire that split Elijah from Elisha. There were dust devils and blinding, dusty whirlwinds occurring that day. The men were separated and Elijah literally was absorbed into the quarks of the ether. He basically disappeared into the thin air. Elijah transcended inward with his entire atom existence dematerializing, and was absorbed inward by the Infinite draw of God's SuperConsciousness. Elijah was the first earth human incarnation to be reabsorbed in such a manner.

Elisha never wished leprosy upon anyone. He also never requested the Angelic Realm to open the eyes of anyone so as to be seen. Elisha never wished blindness upon anyone either. He never forecast a famine, he did not bring a child back to life, and he did not speak of atrocities to be committed on behalf of God. Elisha did die and was buried. No dead being was cast upon Elisha's remains and revived to walk away.

Nebuchanezer did raze King Solomon's Temple. Indeed, he did enslave the people of the conquered region. At that time, these people still were not united under any particular theology or nationality. They were a conglomeration of various peoples and ideologies. The Babylonian slaves were the surviving fragmentation from the decline of the Canaanite civilization and ensuing influx of various nomadic peoples of all types.

Isaiah and Jeremiah

The book of Isaiah contained much of the same unholy nonsense, implying that God was working on the behalf of kings and chosen people to vanquish their foes. The Angels of Holiness don't smite living beings, and they do not commit any destructive acts against earth humans. Humans, through free-will choices, ignorantly destroy other living beings. Humans commit abominable acts against humans, and then cower behind a transparent cloak of God, declaring, "It was God who said it be so." Earth humankind commits atrocities against other people—and NOT by God's intentions or desires. Any time one reads anything resembling a correlation between the Holy Realm and despicable destruction, it is complete insidiousness.

Isaiah did not extend Hezekiah's life by fifteen years. Even a Truly Holy Being as recognized by the Holy Realm still cannot grant such a miracle. Only in extremely rare circumstances, a God-recognized, God-sanctioned, towering spiritual skyscraper of a human being may petition

God to acquiesce and readjust the dharmic blueprint of a person. This petition for God-recognized purposes only, may allow for God to respond to such an imperative quest. There are scant few earth human beings walking the planet today capable of communing through the proper, God-recognized, Angelic Channels who are attuned enough to be able to request a dharmic alteration. There were none living in the Middle East at the time of Isaiah.

Jeremiah

Neither God nor a Holy Angel communed with Jeremiah. Jeremiah was not any more enlightened than any of the other previous writers. Jeremiah was a good man. He indeed did spend time in a pit of mire. The Holy Angelic Realm did not recognize him as a holy man. He since has been reincarnating, and has attained a level of salvation from the earth plane. He currently is recognized as a Holy Being and permanent resident of the Astral Universe.

Ezekiel

Ezekiel indeed did see a vision, and it truly was Divinely Ordained. The vision consisted of four living creatures. Each creature had a four-faced head of a different being—human, ox, lion, and eagle. Each of these beings was resting on the lightway or wheel by a pair of hooves. Each face on each of the four heads represented one of these four beings—the human, ox, lion, and eagle. Each head had a pair of wings attached to it. Lightning and flame surrounded and was interwoven throughout the spectacle. Perched above the bizarre apparition was a benevolent being, appearing quite manlike, adorning a throne. Fire and lightning, with a rainbow surrounded by blinding radiance, was encompassing the Holy Angel.

This was a Holy Vision that only Ezekiel's mind could perceive. These beings were enshrouded in photonic lightways, which Ezekiel's mind imaged as wheels. I really expected the Sanctioned Holy Angel to inform me that this vision was the result of bad wine or an alien encounter. However, what took place was not a galactic visitor from afar, but actually a Holy Realm Interaction meant to convey some Supernal Realm Messages. The Supernal Angel that appeared above the vision was from the fourteenth membrane of the Unified Astral Universe.

The Angel utilized the vision to spread apart in all four directions the fabric of the ether—which appeared as the four recognizable forms in Ezekiel's mind. The Angel utilized the lightways or wheels to pierce the membrane of earthly reality. The heavy cloak of the physical universe is very suffocating to Angels who exist as Divinity protected by photonic light contained in a sacred, immaculate Astral body. The Holy Angel utilized the wheels and energy imaged by Ezekiel.

Upon viewing such a terrifying, mind-boggling vision, Ezekiel fell and hid his face in fear. The Holy Angel did instruct Ezekiel to stand up and understand his message. The Holy Angel called Ezekiel "Son of Man." The bible states that Ezekiel was subjected to eating a scroll or roll of book such as the Torah or a manuscript. This was not true, as Ezekiel did not eat any such thing. He was the first earth human to actually undergo a purposeful Transimplanting of a SuperConscious essence. Essentially, Ezekiel went from being a son of man to a "Son of Man."

In order for this to occur, a lightway transformation needed to happen. The Holy Angel Transimplanted into Ezekiel a new lightway— one capable of containing and protecting a higher attuned, Holier Essence. This lightway actually is a special electromagnetic housing, which creates an impedance within the meridian lightway gridwork that makes up an earth human being. The electromagnetic impedance is a special retainer called an Arc of the Covenant. Located within the tabernacle of Ezekiel's physically manifesting body, the interior of the Arc of the Covenant is known as the "Holy of Holies."

With God's blessings, God allowed the Angel to cohabit within the physical body of Ezekiel's conscious experience. This is the only way a Holy Realm Being can sustain or continually reside within a physical incarnate's conscious experience. Without God's directive to implant the Holy Impanation, the Transubstantiation is impermissible. The Arc of the Covenant as a lightway–implanted impedance in Ezekiel was a Holy Intervention preprescripted in Ezekiel's TransImagined dharmic plan.

The Arc of the Covenant enabled the Holy Angel to communicate directly to the physically manifesting universe for extended periods of time. The Arc of the Covenant allowed the Holy Angel to reside within Ezekiel's conscious experience simultaneously as Ezekiel's experience was unenfolding.

To date, Ezekiel's experience unequivocally was the Holiest event to occur to any of the Old Testament characters. Ezekiel's experience never was recorded truthfully, so subsequent adherents were prevented from ever comprehending the enormity of this experience. The Arc of the Covenant was Transimplanted, and this definitely was a historically and spiritually huge event.

The Angel actually did transport Ezekiel to the river Chebar, near a community called Tel-abib. Ezekiel was appalled by the people existing there at the time. Indeed, it did take seven days before the Holy Angel recontacted Ezekiel. The Transimplanted Impedance wheel needed seven days to fully ingrain into Ezekiel's meridian gridwork. In order for the Holy Angel to Transingress into the Arc, a certain ingratiation period is required for all the electromagnetic fields to completely harmonize.

In the case of Ezekiel, once the reharmonization was completed, the Angel Transingressed as the Manifesting Son of Man SuperConscious essence into Ezekiel's Arc of the Covenant. In contrast, Moses neither heard of, nor experienced, an Arc of the Covenant. In addition, there were no stone tablets carted around in an unimaginable "arc" by the bedraggled, ragtag survivors of Moses' exodus from his virally infected homeland.

Through the Divine Intervention of his dharmic plan, Ezekiel did experience firsthand the Arc of the Covenant. The interior of the Arc of the Covenant was "The Holy of Holies," a sepulcher within the Human Tabernacle. The Holy Angel directed Ezekiel to go alone out into the plains where this Angel Transingressed into Ezekiel's Holy of Holies. This was an Arc of the Covenant through which the Angel could communicate to Ezekiel, and if necessary, into which the Angel could enter Ezekiel's Holy of Holies. While Ezekiel experienced a continuous Transingression, he was never Transimplanted with the SuperConsciousness or Holy Grail.

The Holy Angel informed unsuspecting Ezekiel of the Truth about the supernatural phenomenon he experienced in becoming a Son of Man. The human body is the Absolute Tabernacle that houses the Super-Conscious soul. The soul is contained by the Causal SuperContainer. The Causal Container is contained by the Astral Container, and those two containers are retained by the gross physical superficies. Within Ezekiel's Causal SuperContainer, the Holy Angel Transimplanted the Arc of the Covenant.

In their zeal to portray something that actually wasn't what they purported it to be, later-day writers completely distorted the True purpose or Absolute meaning of the Arc of the Covenant. This distortion has robbed hundreds of millions of incarnated souls of the opportunity to know and comprehend the Truth regarding earth humankind's evolutionary potential. Think about the countless souls throughout history who lived and died while being deprived of this knowledge. If these earth humans only knew that they, too, could have been SuperConsciously Transimplanted, one would have to believe many people's free-will choices would have been made differently.

Earth humans ALWAYS have been capable of attaining salvation and existing without ego or ignorance. Like Ezekiel, ALL earth human souls have the capability to have their individual, conscious existence Transimplanted within their Holy of Holies, God's SuperConsciousness. Had they only known this Spiritual Super Attunement was available to them, imagine how many souls would have transcended to SuperEnlightened spiritual status. With regard to withholding or misappropriating truths, one easily can see the problematic impact on unknowing, innocent souls.

In Ezekiel, it is glaringly obvious where the real writings leave off and the ignorance of later-day writers takes over. It is not difficult to comprehend where the real Ezekiel's true Holiness ends and the influence of the later-day writers' influence picks up. Not only is this apostasy appalling, but it also leaves little doubt as to why such traumatic troubles grip our earthly experience today. In supplanting and impressing their unevolved literary viewpoint, smugly stamped with the so-called "holy" seal of "Saith the Lord God," I am sure these later-day writers had no clue about the problems they would be causing. These writers doomed countless millions of subsequent adherents to believing in the acceptability of such misleading literary liberties.

While reading Ezekiel, I found myself wishing Toto from *The Wizard of Oz* would come scampering up to pull back the curtain to expose the fraud of this writing. While a few threads of truth were woven into this writing, unholy liberties clearly were taken in the name of God. The later-day writers certainly did not understand the Holy Covenant that was Divinely Transimplanted within Ezekiel. These writers allowed their own, modern-day, unevolved theological ideas to influence their interpretations. These suppositions certainly have misled and continue to delude earth humankind from accurately comprehending the True Nature of our SuperConscious God.

To assist in earth humankind's consciously uplifting attunement the

Janus-faced, dualistic universe metes out dharmic destinies and registers karmic debts. The experiences to which earth humans continually are re-exposed are not vicious acts being unfairly registered against poor, innocent earth humans. Rather, such experiences occur because these peoples' individual souls need these experiences to assist in their ever-increasing, conscious upliftment. These challenging opportunities for growth merely provide earth humans with the ability for their souls to rise above the dualistic restrictions; hopefully, or eventually, they will begin to bask in the blissful, Unified, SuperConscious existence.

Throughout the book of Ezekiel, there were tiny threads of truth, but they were so convoluted with unholy misstatements, the entire Holy phenomenon regarding Ezekiel's true Holy Angelic and Divine Intervention was obliterated by human incomprehension. It is known to you today that Ezekiel's Holy Experience, through a Divinely Ordained Holy Angelic visitation, truly and absolutely is available to every earth human being. In Book Five, I will share with you my personal Divine Experience, which has allowed me, through the Holy Realm, to discern and write these Truthful Absolutes.

Jonah

There indeed was a man named Jonah. He did flounder in the sea. However, he never was consumed by a fish or whale. That story was fictional—just a whale of a tale. Jonah was not then, and is not today recognized by the Holy Realm as a Holy Being. Jonah had no divine experience happen to him regarding a gourd.

Zechariah

Satan is complete fiction. Satan does not and NEVER did exist as a superconscious being who digressed back to the physical universe. No Holy Angel EVER has fallen from Grace. Satan and Lucifer both were created out of earth humans' imaginations to explain the traumatic experiences that test and befall humankind's conscious experience. No angel EVER has been banished from the Holy Realm. That story is complete, nonsensical fiction. The Astral Universe does not operate that way.

For you, we have taken great lengths to accurately portray and describe the Holy Angelic Realm. The Holy Realms—the Higher Astral and the

Causal Universes—exist exactly as we have intricately described them to you. The laws that govern and operate those spiritual Universes—and the physical, material universe itself—absolutely exist as described.

The Old Testament has been Truthfully dissected by a truly Holy Angelic Being, purposefully and perfectly chosen, for it never has been an earth human. This Holy Angel was recommended by Sri Yukteswar Giri, and approved by God.

Job

The Holy Sanctioned Angel could not find any evidence that Job ever existed. No heated interactive communications occurred between God and Satan—and no pun intended, either. One would have to have greater patience than Job to contend with Satan, who like Job, never existed.

Ecclesiastes

Koheleth was a real being who did exist. He indeed was the son of David, the King in Jerusalem. Koheleth wrote and spoke some words of wisdom. He was more intellectually wise than spiritually evolved. To this day, Koheleth is not yet recognized by the Holy Realm as being free from karmic debt and reincarnation. Some of his writings were written by later writers and inappropriately applied to his original works.

Esther

Hadassah was a real person, a Hebrew, now known as Esther. She was brought up by Mordecai, to whom she was related. She did become Queen to King Ahasuerus. The truth follows fairly closely with the biblical story. At the time of Hadassah's existence, there still was NOT any theology known as Judaism. Judaism was formed later by theologians. Hadassah did petition the king on behalf of Mordecai, her uncle. Mordecai's life was spared, and Haman was beheaded—not hung—as a result. It should be pointed out that Hadassah was acting out of compassion for the Hebrew people, not then yet a theological sect.

Later-day writers merely applied "Jew," "Israel," or "Our People" whenever a hint of a "Hebrew person" was concerned. It is easy for later-day writers to misapply words, actions, and intentions when the actual events have long since passed. To further ensure that adherents could be convinced into becoming adamant believers is the fact that as they were occurring, none of these events were ever being written or recorded by firsthand eyewitnesses. Thus, how can we even begin to assume that the Old Testament was accurately portrayed? Granted, certain loose facts and actual, semiaccurate accounts are available, but we pragmatically need to look at the facts.

Modern historians, theologians, and lay people in general are not stupid. Considering the fact that such reporting has been interpreted and available in everyone's appropriate language, humans certainly have wrestled with problematic aspects of these biblical accounts. The ever-present stumbling block always is the sacred cow aspect of the bible. The bible itself says that it is holy writ, transmuted by God through the efforts of so-called holy, benevolent later-day writers.

All words seem to be deemed holy and sanctioned by God. The stamp of "Holy Scriptures" ensures that no matter how outrageous the messages and intensions behind the messages, no one will dare dispute it. Given the existential laws set in place that govern any and all interactions between the physical and spiritual universes, how does the Holy Realm itself dispute the veracity and validity of the scriptures? Why did the bible have God smiting and punishing, placing upon humans such completely unholy demands?

If the Holy Realm is relegated to invisibly operating behind the manifesting scenes, bound by Divine Universal Law to never interfere with human free will, how can 2000-year-old inaccuracies be corrected? The simple fact is that the early writers of the bible compiled and gathered their wisdom of the day and wrote their stories with the best of intentions. This was done in an attempt to record and describe the inexplicable events that were occurring during that time.

Theologies always attempt to present themselves as the one truthful pathway back to God. The truth is, theologies can work, but they need to be kept in their proper perspective. Earth humankind's interpretations serve as a historical telephone-game whose recordings are insidiously misguided. If we exerted the same efforts loving and communing with God that we spend trying to convince every other human being that our particular belief is the correct slant, our lives certainly would be more lovingly attuned.

By the very nature of its determination to confine and define God as a humanly perceivable conformity, each theological dogma has an unGodly quality about it. Likewise, adhering to a set of rules, rituals, and observances will not grant anyone an accelerated track back to God. The Holy Realm is attempting to instill in all people the Universality and Creedlessness of God. Transgressions are not annulled through confession, adherence to rules and rigid conformities, or through ignoring the karmic impaction and scapegoating God for human sins. Karmic transgressions are alleviated by the soul's conscious walking through their every lesson while aligning their free-will choices with unconditionally loving intentions. Unconditional Love is the universal elixir of absolution.

Ezra

It was during the time of Ezra that Judaism was beginning to take form. The surviving Hebrews began to migrate back toward Jerusalem. As a group heralding from the same region and having survived a fairly horrific, short period of enslavement, there began to exist a certain camaraderie. Beginning at about 300 BC, Judaism began to take form.

Judaism started innocuously enough, as these returning Babylonian slaves met, talked, and compiled various myths and legends. These people began to formulate collections of stories and fables pertinent toward uplifting the spirit of the emancipated slaves. Slowly, these fables were collected and synchronized into the collective works we now know as the Old Testament. The fact that the "big three" organized religions cling to the same, fictional stories, with each theology adding its own particular slant, should speak loudly to modern earth humankind's common sense.

Each theology has its benefits, as well as its drawbacks. Most devoted "adherents" know little, and are often completely unaware of these limitations. In the Christian theology, the priests and ecclesiastic hierarchy protect and maintain their elevated stature, to ensure that the obsequious masses are kept in their proper places. In Christianity, absolution of sin, holy consecration, and all "God sanctioning" strictly is reserved for the priestly selected few who are deemed by someone within the hierarchy above them to be holy enough. The status of the "selected" deems them sanctioned to dole out to the followers the "holiness" in tiny tidbits.

The roots of the Judaic theology were nourished by the determined efforts of the Zealots and the Essenes in 150 BC. They were orthodox ascetic mystics who blended Gnostic thought with rigid rituals, rules, and adherence to Judaic Law. Today, the Jewish Kabbalists might loosely resemble the old, Essenic practitioners. Most Jews of today are unknowing of the spiritual potential of the Kabbalists, and are totally unaware of their Essenic roots.

With regard to Islamic theology, the Sufis have been diligently pursuing and applying its messages for the benefit of its followers. Modern-day interpretations of Islam's ancient roots do not always resemble the ancient teachings and traditions still recognized and practiced by the Sufis of today. Strict religious observance produces confinements that prevent adherents from moving beyond their theological compliance toward realizing and experiencing true spiritual evolution of consciousness. Organized religion, with its many rules, rituals, and regulations prevents its adherents from experiencing their true Made Manifest At-Oneness. Made Manifest At-Oneness IS pure Holiness. Pure Holiness completely supersedes any and all specified religious rules, rituals, and regulations.

Of all the Superevolved Saints purported to have come from the ranks of all three organized religions, only one has been blessed with the Key to open the Om Door. The Holy Realm informs me that only Kabir is recognized as a truly ascended, Holy Islamic Being. Kabir, who existed from 1450 AD until 1518 AD, is recognized as an exceptionally Holy Sufi/Hindu Being. Kabir actually was instructed and taught by Babaji. Kabir was purported to be able to materialize and dematerialize his physical being at will. The Holy Sanctioned Angel validated this to be true. If any Islamic adherent to God wanted to emulate a Holy Realm-recognized, truly ascended Being, Kabir would be this Being.

Christian mystics, Jewish kabbalists, and Islamic Sufis all hold potential keys for their modern-day followers to pass through their Om Door and attain salvation. In all cases, God—as all-knowing, all-powerful, and ever-present Made Manifest SuperConsciousness—cannot possibly be relegated to a set of humanly recognizable or defining religious absolutes.

During everyone's ongoing unenfoldment, it is critical for each soul to align its every intention, thought, action, and reaction with an unconditionally loving response. If you do this in every future dharmic moment, know that you also would have done so in your TransImaginated state. Comprehension of this Truth will deeply assist your spiritual evolution, as well as purposefully and willfully infuse unconditional love into the endless, upcoming positive experiences yet to unenfold.

Made Manifest God IS Unconditional Love expressed as Manifesting Infinite Potentiality. So, by continuously aligning one's TransImaginating free-will choices with Unconditional Love, the soul (now as Made Manifest), expresses or reflects itself AS Divinity.

Nothing will be Made Manifest until the entire TransImagination process has been infinitely pre-CompreCreated. TransImagination is everything that is going to become Made Manifest during its ongoing, pre-CompreCreation state. All souls experience the fluidity of their Made Manifest Infinite CompreCreation having already been fully prepre-scripted. Knowing and referencing this Truth of TransImagination while in this Made Manifest state presents each soul with the opportunity to influence and uplift its ongoing, preprescripting TransImagination process. This realization also directly influences and uplifts the soul's ongoing Made Manifest experience.

The soul's ongoing TransImagination will be experienced throughout its Made Manifest state, during which all infusion of pre-Made Manifest and Made Manifest Unconditional Love will reflect these purposeful, Unconditionally Loving efforts. These Unconditionally Loving efforts are then woven into the Transenfolded fabric of the soul's upcoming, unenfolding (Made Manifest) experience.

At any unenfolding Made Manifest moment there is a corresponding TransImaginating point. At this particular Made Manifest point all the soul's future TransImagination is still being pre-CompreCreated. Knowing this, each soul has the ability to reference and comprehend this Truth. At any given point in a soul's Made Manifest existence (during any incarnation), this soul can infuse its current and future experience with Unconditional Love. By consciously choosing to do so, this soul will realize the benefits of this Unconditional Love in both its pre-Made Manifest (TransImaginative) and Made Manifest (currently unenfolding) states. The Advanced Spiritual Upliftment Technique of spiritual "double dipping" accelerates the soul's evolution toward achieving At-Oneness.

Daniel

Daniel was a real person who did exist. His friends, Hananiah, Mishael, and Azariah were not real beings and did not exist. There was no test of dream interpretation. The fact is, this biblical holy writ was not the result of divine afflatus from Superevolved beings. These later-day writers were not even centuries close to knowing the original characters about whom they were writing, and they were not divinely inspired.

Daniel (or Belteshazzar) did not spend any time in a fiery blast furnace, and neither did his three friends since these friends never existed. Daniel was not considered then by the Holy Realm to be a holy person, and still is not yet today a holy person. Daniel was not divinely guided. He never was forced to endure the wrath of a lion. In fact, during his entire incarnation, Daniel never so much as ever saw a lion. Daniel did have a few visions, mostly to do with supplication and worship of God. His visions read remarkably close to those of Ezekiel—from the fiery, Angelic Visits, to falling upon his face, to being addressed as "Son of Man."

However, Daniel was neither a "Son of Man," nor did he experience Divinely Ordained Angelic Visits. Daniel's visions indeed did come to him while he was worshipping. Most of the accounts attributed to Daniel are through the zeal of later-day writers trying to mosaically piece the Old Testament to mesh with the accepted religious beliefs of the day. Not accurate, truthful, or beneficial to the evolutionary upliftment of earth humankind, these stories are sought to establish a chosen people, religion, or theology.

The stories in both the bible and the Koran are vulnerable and subject to personal interpretation. Some of their passages seem to absolve humans of their accountability for their free-will choices. These words are not meant to be inflammatory or to incite anger, hatred, or violence. The Holy Realm wants to inform anyone who abides by unGodly beliefs or commits unholy acts (free-will choices) against God's Creation that they WILL experience karmic retributions. This is a God-ordained, Universal Law. Earth humans cannot write something, deem it holy, and will it to be consecrated as something "true." Only God can do (and does) the consecrating. Humankind can kill, be killed, and exert great, egoistic influence through egregious conduct. However, such choices only serve one purpose—to ensure the ever-increasing, individual indebtedness of the perpetrator.

In essence, free-will choice IS the determining factor in uplifting an individual's conscious experience. We tend to be ego-based, thinking our egos can produce an uplifting influence within our dharmic plans—when in effect, only free-will choices infused with Unconditional Love will produce dharmic upliftment.

Ego misperceptions allow the act of martyrdom to be viewed as an acceptable holy act. The innermost intentions and thoughts of the martyr determine if this is the case. The act of giving one's life (dying) for a certain belief can be spiritually uplifting, but the act itself is NOT spiritually uplifting if it is inflicted upon others and if it influences their free-will choices.

There have been souls who have died for their love of God (martyrs), but in doing so, did NOT interfere with anyone else's free-will choices. These martyrs did NOT inflict their intentions, thoughts, and actions upon anyone else. In contrast, if a person is forced or coerced into an act leading to their death, this does NOT constitute true martyrdom.

A martyr is recognized as a person who freely chooses death rather than to renounce their beliefs. A martyr is NOT a person who chooses a death that directly influences the free-will choices of others. In other words, a so-called "suicide" bomber would NOT be a martyr if their choice to die also causes others to die. In this case, they would be a homicide bomber and would NOT be a true martyr, but rather an unholy transgressor. The distinction between martyr and non-martyr can only be SuperConsciously discerned by God from the intentions, thoughts, and actions of the individual making the free-will choice to die.

The act of true martyrdom does NOT guarantee the soul salvation from future incarnations in the physically manifesting universe. Salvation is freedom from sin, earthly incarnations, earthly karma, and the potential for future indebtedness.

In Book Five, we will once again share not only this new Spiritual Upliftment Technique for earth humans' salvation, but we also will deeply reiterate that God is creedless, supplying measureless Holy Light and illimitable Unconditional Love to all Creation throughout the Universe.

God does not select or choose one particular sect of earth humankind on which to bestow God's benevolence. Earth humankind is but one particular sect in a nondescript vector of the physical cosmos, seventeen million light years across—and filled with more galaxies than anyone ever could count in a hundred lifetimes.

Existence is about evolution of our individual consciousnesses. Attunement to the Higher Holy Realms does not just happen. Reading of scriptures or contributing to collection plates are meaningless acts when applied as steps toward holiness. Attaining a creedless, unconditionally loving, SuperConscious state of mind is meaningful.

When one achieves a Unified attunement leading to salvation, they are recognized by the Holy Realm as a Holy Person. One Holy Person doing quiet, prayerful, behind-the-scenes work for the good of humankind is far more beneficial than all the planet's egotistical beings combined unashamedly being recognized for their conditional giving.

What purpose does it serve to give conditionally? Whether or not one gives, pompous arrogance only feeds one's own self-serving, individual ego. Such action is not helpful or holy, but definitely is karmically impacting for the egoistic giver. It actually is spiritually self-defeating and karmically contaminating. Earth humankind really needs to understand this point. When we conduct ourselves in an ego-based manner, we will not evolve.

Earth humans definitely will not attain salvation by exerting their egos (free-will choices) upon the will of others. Until humans realize this and take appropriate steps to do otherwise, people can count on spending vast amounts of time in the lowest levels of the Astral Realm, working out the unholy karma accrued by the unGodly free-will choices they inflicted upon others.

Truthful Absolutes

The Astral membranes are vastly huge and far beyond our limited scope of comprehension. Just beyond the atom world of physically manifesting existence, the caustic bowels of the Astral Universe's level nine are where all serious Universal transgressors go. To give earth humans some perceptional comprehension regarding the enormity of the Astral Realm, level nine itself is somewhat larger than our entire physical cosmos. These realms become increasingly larger and simultaneously holier the higher the numbered level and the closer they are in relation to the Holy Uncreated Infinite SuperConsciousness.

Level ten is many times larger than our entire physical cosmos. This is the level to which all evolving, universal existence goes upon leaving its physical incarnation form. This is true for all earthly animal and vegetable existence, as well as every similarly attuned universally incarnating existence.

Level eleven is reserved for all universal existence endowed with free will that has attuned its consciousness or soul to an increasingly enlightened state. These souls have not yet attained salvation from ALL previous incarnations to realize a Unified state of Holy Being status, as recognized by the Holy Angelic Realm. A good example of an earth human who has elevated their soul to this level eleven, but one not yet attaining salvation, would be Mother Teresa. Being canonized by the Catholic Church has absolutely no bearing on the True Holiness of Holy Realm recognition.

Incidentally, the Catholic religious theology is not in any way recognized as a holy institution itself. From its very inception and continued contribution today, the sheer weight of historical and continual karmically impacting atrocities is binding evidence of the institution's unholiness. This long, sordid history of public abominations against countless innocent beings, including today's children, has served to defile the very sacredness of God.

The nets of theological institutions are not the ensnared pathways to Holy Salvation, for fish are not caught in holey nets. That eternally free pathway was, is, and forever will be an individual soul attainment, accrued from its every incarnation. All individual roads lead back to the Holy Source, not to Rome.

Level twelve is the first level of the Unified SuperConsciousness Realm. If they have attained salvation, residing here are all souls or manifesting SuperConscious existences within the Unified Realm. These souls are free from physical karma, reincarnation, and dualistic influences. These souls of the Unity also have exchanged their egos and gift of free will for the higher Holy Realm God Realizations. The "individual" becomes "Us," the dualistic "me" becomes the Unified "We."

If we really look at our civilizations today, we have an overabundance of everything except Unconditional Love. Unconditional Love is the Unified Holiness, which bonds the Superenlightened, even Holier Realms of levels twelve through fifteen. When earth humans shed our heavy coats of egocentric ignorance, in favor of the Deep Comprehension of Unconditional Loving, we actually are dissolving our accrued karmic impactions.

This Unified ideology of Unconditional Love completely is nonexistent in either the Old Testament or the Koran. There is not so much as a single entry from our human perspective even resembling the concept of Unconditional Love. To portray something as holy and be glaringly void of the very epitomizing embodiments of holiness is outrageously appalling. If we earth humans consider ourselves to be evolved (that is, above other animal forms such as monkeys), we need to exude the kinds of superior consciousness God enables us to exhibit.

The extremely ignorant, unholy mentality by which many theologically abiding adherents to the message live is not only unGodly, but also embarrassing to our species. Monkey-brained (no offense meant to earthly monkeys) mentality is excruciating to observe, let alone have to read about on a daily basis. "Adhering to the unholy message" has caused a disgusting disintegration in our conscious perceptions. Because someone named Abraham—whom writers declared "holy" 2,500 years after his existence—was purported by those same writers to have been asked by God to slay his own son, it's now deemed acceptable to kill anyone, anywhere, for the sake of adherence?

In an unevolved, pathetic civilization completely lost from the true meaning of adhering to the message, these horrific mentalities may be acceptable. I know the Holy Realm and our Creedless Holiest, Manifesting God, finds this behavior mortifying. This descending mentality provided the impetus for the Holy Realm and God to intervene with Truthful Absolutes. That is why this particular, conscious, dharmic experience, of which I am the conscious perceiver, is being guided by a host of Blessed Holy Angels—and our Transcendental God—to try to uplift from subconscious decay earth humankind's very consciousness.

A Unified SuperConscious experience at levels twelve and beyond provides the highly attuned Spiritual Being with an unparalleled opportunity to influence with profound impact its unenfolding, SuperConscious experience. Within the twelfth membrane of SuperConsciousness, vast realizations occur. One now has learned to operate within the binding, imperishable laws of the Astral and physically manifesting Universes. This level of attunement allows for ever-increasing abilities, which attract the heavenly supernal SuperHoly Consciousnesses to assist in exerting Holy influence on the dualistically influenced, physical world.

There is much to be gained from a life of renunciation, deprived of unlimited, physically manifesting abundance. However, one might choose to focus their intentions and energizing thoughts toward booze, sex, drugs, and material gains—and this satiation all is part of one's free-will choice. Such pursuits are not necessarily bad ones, and are not even transgressions against God. Many times, these opportunities are pre-sented for us to experience fulfillments, which we have carried through as unfulfilled desires from prior incarnations. As with playing cards, the wisdom is knowing when to hold them and when to fold them. The road to salvation is lined with satiation as well as renunciation.

These choices are not always easy to master. To experience almost unlimited free-will immersion into highly pleasurable enticements can be overpowering. So, go with them and experience your desires. There are two caveats necessary to bear in mind. One, these actions and subsequent reactions must not karmically impress negatively upon any manifesting existence, any other person, or their free-will choices. Two, you must release any attachments that might accompany the experience. In other words, net and then release these desires.

For example, the Dalai Lama consistently disseminates goodness and love without impacting others' free will. His life as a monk is devoid of dualistic and materialistic pursuits, yet abundant with humility and loving kindness. He walks his life's pathway balancing the need to participate as a human being in the world around him (satiate), while not becoming overly attached to or enamored with its trappings (renunciate). If you face each experience and all that Creation has to offer with these two simple creeds, in the end, your existence will be filled with all your desires com-pletely fulfilled—without clinging to any of them or ever being dragged or held back by such desires.

The hidden Gospel of Mark according to the Carpocrations espoused this truthful philosophy, but like most truths in Mark, it ended up on the cutting room floor. So, experience whatever it is you desire, but just don't hurt anyone else or negatively affect the other person's free-will choices. Then release any holds or covets, and the experience truly will become an enriching memory, with no impacting damage done.

It may take a little accrued wisdom to figure out if karmic damage has occurred, but eventually everyone will get very adept at determining the Truth. This concept can be called "Deep Comprehension." Eventually, "Ever-Deepening Comprehension" becomes a way of life. If a soul does attain Deep Comprehension, its dualistically intertwined conscious expe-rience lends itself to the Unified SuperConscious Existence.

Astral level thirteen is where all communication within the Holy Realm really begins to have a permanent influence. There a Being exists in a state of blissful fulfillment, ever continuously supplied from within. In level thirteen, the Unified SuperConscious Beings are highly evolved, and tend to be rewarded with these superattuned existences as a result of their uplifting efforts accrued during incarnations experienced in other parts of the physical cosmos. Level thirteen covers an area approximately thirty times bigger than our entire physical cosmos. Level thirteen represents the midway point of the Unified SuperConsciousness. This area is very bright and vibrant with God's photonic light. Angelic Beings from this realm tend to interact spiritually and physically with the beings existing in other parts of the manifesting physical cosmos.

This level provides Holy Angelic Spiritual assistance and uplifting Holy attunement to the myriad life forms far more evolved than earth humans, those forms found residing in vectors throughout the physical cosmos. At this level, colors are recognized in far more intricate variations and appear more surreal than in physical manifestations. Level thirteen is composed of leptons with the names "Muon" and "Muon neutrino," with the quarks of that realm called "Charm" and "Strange."

Due to God's SuperConscious electromagnetic fields, these particles are thought by scientists to have been abundant after the erroneously defined "Big Bang." However, these particles continually are formed as building neutrinos within the atom. All manifesting existence is composed of these realms from within the atom. Scientists tend to be relegated to the decaying end of the subatomic particle phenomenal universe.

Level fourteen is the highest, Holiest Realm of the Unified Astral Superconsciousness. This level's leptons consist of electrons and electron neutrinos and quarks "Up" and "Down." These particles tend to present themselves during the atomic decay process. This Realm has immeasurably vast capacity for communication capabilities. In this level, the Manifesting SuperConsciousness radiates unimaginable photonic Holiness and vibratory might. If one could view this Realm as if a speck from within the electron itself, one literally would be seared by the blinding radiance of the photonic and electronic Holiness emanating from Manifesting God's SuperConsciousness.

This level fourteen consists of an imposing, illustrious vastness, approximately a hundred times bigger than our entire physical cosmos. Those staggering dimensions contain all the foundational scaffolding (building leptons) and memory-retaining infrastructure (quarks) to hold up the entire, burdensome structure of the manifesting universe. The appetency of the lepton-quark synergy is supplied entirely by the Holy Manifesting Infinite SuperConsciousness. This incontrovertible Realm maintains and contains the inconceivable energy that drives the inner cosmic "engine" of the physical cosmos.

The Astral Holy Increates enjoy vast, blissful freedoms and ever-newness, ever-joyous exultatious enlightenments. In this Holy Realm, the Astral container of nineteen wheels or lightways is shed in an Astral salvation, or freedom from Astral karma. Astral karma occurs as a perception, as one may perceive through any of the nineteen Astral lightways. Karmic impact is experienced as a sense perception, rather than a physical manifestation. A physical world comparison might be the noticeable loss of one's sense of self-worth.

Excessive drinking, coming down off a cocaine high, or indulging to egregious excess leaves one with a disturbing loss of self-value. This perception is very recognizable. In the Astral Universe, these same perceptions are magnified without the physical bodily encumbrance. The magnitude of a karmic slight results in a traumatic to excruciating loss of blissful attunement. Much like the drug crash, an Astral karmic debt is like dragging around lead weights. This debt's vibratory impaction is more easily recognized without the sixteen gross physical wheels of materialization.

This level fourteen realm is where the last vestige encasement of the Astral container is sloughed off. Once all Astral karma is slaked, the now Indivisible Soul is ejaculated from the tabernacle of the manifesting vibratory encumbrance. This Realm is the highest Realm from which any manifesting physical being can be influenced without some additional supernatural phenomenon.

All earthly humankind has the ability to attune to this level. Superevolved Earth-born Saints such as Lahiri Mahasaya, Sri Yukteswar, Trailanga, Kabir, Buddha, and Lord Krishna all were God-attuned to this Holy Realm. Through multitudes of incarnations, conscious existences slowly evolve their souls' attainment to ever-higher realm attunements. Once a soul attunes to the Unified Realm of level twelve, it is considered to be Holy by the Holy Angelic Realm. It is primarily through attunement with level fourteen that true earthly miracles can occur. Earthly miracles only occur by way of a God-Sanctioned Holy Angel. These God-Sanctioned

Holy Angelic Visitations or Interactions resulting in miraculous outcomes are extremely rare, for specific, divine purposes known only to God. Other than during extremely unique Transinteractions, all such outcomes are preprescripted during their TransImaginated state. We use the prefix "Trans" to denote God-Reperfecting Involvements NOT preprescripted into the soul's dharmic blueprint.

On rare occasions, Transinteractions are facilitated for human beings to experience very compromising circumstances in order to alleviate critical karmic indebtedness. Once the challenging lesson has been learned, the karmic indebtedness is thus satisfied. God utilizes all aspects of Creation as facilitators by which humans can learn these lessons, satisfying the karmic indebtedness specific to that impeding situation or circumstance.

Some examples of God's ingenious interactions on the behalf of an individual needing to satisfy karmic indebtedness include rescuers, witnesses, and communicators in the physically manifesting forms such as people, animals, objects, environmental phenomena, and even the individuals themselves.

Human beings mistakenly misinterpret God's Divine Interactions as true miracles. Divine Interactions are always executed through physically manifesting forms, whereas all true miracles take place only via Astral or Causal Realm intercessors. What people tend to perceive and interpret as a benevolent, "miraculous" act, with only very rare exceptions, actually is a Transinteraction.

People fail to realize and recognize the divinely intended, purposeful role of karmic reflection. As such, it disturbs and upsets people when dangerous, difficult, frightening, and life-threatening circumstances rear their ugly heads during what human beings erroneously perceive should be an otherwise harmonious existence. As earth human beings, we are not going to experience a continuously perfect existence.

The Divine Laws and God's Interactions do not excuse or dismiss us from the responsibility of acting on another being's behalf. However, when we observe another in a precarious or dangerous situation and use our free-will choice to attempt to save or assist them, any failure to succeed in doing so on our part does not signify personal responsibility. Our interpretation of such failure indicates only our inability to fully comprehend the overall, big-picture perspective of divine intentions behind the circumstance or situation. In fact, if we fail to assume such responsibility, we may be preventing the success of God's intended Interaction, and in doing so, we run the risk of experiencing similar karmically reflecting circumstances.

All true miracles occur through the workings of the Holy Angelic Messengers. Divine care is necessary to ensure that in the miracle producing process, the miracle worker does not transgress and thus interfere with the Divine Universal Dharmic Plan. Even Superevolved Earth-born Saints have had Ordained Holy Angels operating through them. God sanctions all miracles through these Holy Angels, as no earth human beings by their own initiative have the God-given authority to perform any miracles.

Level fourteen attuned earthly Beings have an Angelic Superessence that assists them during times of necessity for these God-sanctioned purposes. These Angels really are SuperConsciousnesses operating through God's directives, executing God's Supernal desires. Holy Angels have no authority to operate in the physical realm without God-sanctioned authorization.

If a miracle were purported to have occurred, attunement to a level fourteen Angel with God-sanctioning is the ONLY way that miracle would take place. If the Holy Realm does not recognize you as a Unified SuperConsciously attuned soul, you will not facilitate true miracles. This is not to say that miracles cannot occur around someone who is dualistically attuned. The miracle is merely being facilitated through that person's experience by a Holy Sanctioned Angel. It is earth humanly impossible to induce miraculous, transcendent energies without this Holy Realm attunement. To believe otherwise is ego-based delusion and utter nonsense. Dualistically attuned earth humans have no authority, no God sanctioning, and absolutely no Holy consecration ordination recognition.

In fact, other than Jesus, NO earth-born human ever has had a God-sanctioned authority to consecrate ANYTHING. Babaji is the only physically manifesting Being currently inhabiting the earthly plane that truly is God-authorized to consecrate anything. Irrespective of any human-ordained titles, to attempt, pretend or purport to be able to consecrate anything is a transgression. No rabbis, priests, mullahs, or even the Pope have ANY special Transcendental Ordainments according them ANY superior holiness.

All earth humans are subjected to their individual karmic weights, and the Janus-faced Universe recognizes no titles. Titles are completely meaningless in the Holy Realm, and generally are unjustifiably afforded special accord in the physical realm. Purely and simply, Holiness is recognized by the Holy Realm as sustained attunement to the Unified Astral membranes twelve through fourteen. From this Absolute Verity, there is NO earthly or physically manifesting alteration.

Level fifteen is the Ultra-Holy Realm of the Causal or Holy Neutrino Universe. This Universe is located beyond the Astral Universe, and consummates a staggering 25 percent of the Manifesting Universe. In this Made Manifest Realm, the Holy Uncreated Infinite SuperConsciousness synizes Itself back down the spiracular of the Holy Neutrino, returning to its Uncreated Infinite state. This thermonuclear TransInterfusion of the Holy Uncreated Infinite SuperConsciousness produces a Holy Syngenesis of Uncreated into Created, which literally creates the Holy Synkaryon or Spawning Manifesting Universe. This Realm is where the inception of the Uncreated Transfinite SuperConsciousness transforms itself into the Transitory Manifesting Infinite Potential SuperConsciousness.

This Realm is so Holy that the Saints and Superessences residing there exist as an Idea of Manifesting Infinite SuperConsciousness. The Holy Neutrino is beyond the lepton electron and the quarks "Up" or "Down." Transcendental Photonic Illumination sears through all aspects of this Superexistence. These SuperBeings are bathed in a blissful surge of Manifesting Infinite Holiness. Much like God, they apperceive God-gifted ideas and command the powers to create Universes.

Their subsequent apperceptions formulate the very ideas that eventually become tangible manifestations. This is the Realm where the Holiest of Holiest SuperConsciousnesses reside. No earthly communications ever come close to penetrating this sacred, immaculate Realm. Earth humans are far too contaminating to be gifted access to this radiant, resplendent Holiness.

A Causal SuperBeing would require an Arc of the Covenant before it could communicate from within a physically manifesting being. In order for a Causal SuperBeing ever to communicate through or with a physically manifesting being, as in the case of Ezekiel, an Arc of the Covenant impedance first would need to be Transimplanted into the being. This Arc of the Covenant implantation allows the Immaculate Holy Angel to enter and exit with complete immunity from physically manifesting defilement or coinhabitation transgressions.

Contained within the Causal container is your soul or consciousness. This is your spiritual container, which also houses SuperConscious intuition or "sixth sense." Intuition only is accessible when consciousness is existing within its Astral or Causal bodies. Intuition is NOT accessible to earth humans in the true sense of the ability while one is in human, physical form. Aside from Superevolved souls, all earth human perceptions are limited to the level eight atom membrane of communication potential.

Level nine is the abominable, evil-entrenched region of the Astral Universe. On extremely rare occasions, through severe alcohol or drug-enduced states of perceptions, some earth beings momentarily will experience perceptions found in level nine and encounter unspeakable horrors. All physically contaminating or perception-altering substances strictly are forbidden for those attuned consciously to levels twelve through fourteen. Although I am informed that marijuana does not in any amount produce this level nine-attuned state, it nonetheless is a bodily contaminating and Astral perception-altering influence—strictly forbidden for any Being attuned to Unified SuperConscious levels twelve through fourteen states.

Untarnished children and levels twelve-to-fourteen attuned Beings sometimes mistake the Holy Angelic guidance and interaction as intuitive perceptions. Rather, these so-called "perceptions" actually are divinely granted interpretations. All physically manifesting Beings that are Unified with the Astral levels twelve through fourteen have Angelic or Holy Realm Assistance.

Most of the physically manifesting beings attuned to level eleven, who are nearing attunement with the physically karmic-free level twelve, usually will attract Holy Angelic guidance, assistance, and interactive support. Many human beings, especially psychics, mediums, channelers, and unrecognized healers proclaim to have ever-present spirit guides, Angelic messengers, guardian Angels, and Saints supporting, guiding, and assisting them throughout their conscious existence. However, in most cases, nothing could be further from the truth.

So-called spirit guides, Angelic messengers, guardian Angels, and Saints of any form have absolutely no independent authority to interact with physically manifesting existence. The only exception to this Divine Law is when God sanctions Superevolved consciousness as Angels for specific divine purposes known only to God. There are no such things as guardian Angels or spirit guides. Furthermore, the supposed superconsciousness of the particular guardian saint with whom a Christian is baptized has no influence, guardianship, or holy protective capabilities with regard to that individual human being. I was baptized at age 4 and given the Saint's name of Mark. All my life I was certain that St. Mark was vigilantly watching over me to ensure no harm would come to me. Catholicism taught me that God sanctioned St. Mark to preside over all aspects of my existence. I now comprehend that TransImagination renders unnecessary all such unevolved perceptions. Universal Law or Divine Order absolutely PREVENTS the potential chaos that would ensue if such misperceptions indeed were true. Nowhere in the physically manifesting universe is there an exception to this Rule.

From humans' perspective, the difference between a Saint and an Angel would be that a Saint would have at least one physical earthly incarnation. An Angel would have a manifested incarnation, but not necessarily earth human, or even a physical universe existence. With the exception of Sri Yukteswar, who assisted Book Six, neither one of the Angels who lovingly and generously have been transmuting this information ever have had an earth human existence. The Holy Causal Angel, Holy Intimate Angel, and Holy Sanctioned Angel all have had a myriad of physical existences in other vectors of the universe, but not as any human of any sort.

The Old Testament is sprinkled with human beings who have been reincarnated and are perhaps now your neighbors, still trying to work out their karmic debts. They are jerking the dog's chain, beating up on the family, swigging the booze, ranting and raving, harming or killing others. These beings still exhibit the same behaviors of racism and bigotry, anger and abuse toward any other physically manifesting being—especially one very different from themselves. Then and still today, earth humankind basically is an unevolved civilization.

Holiness simply is not measured by earthly, human standards, and it's pretty impossible for earth humans to determine who is considered holy. With what gauge can people determine such things? The Christians perceive they have a host of saints, but without unerring certainty, Absolute perception is not available to manifesting earth humankind. The list of emancipated Saints is far shorter than one might imagine. In fact, what people commonly refer to as "saintly" or a "saint" oftentimes is not the case. Due to the heavy cloak of ostracizing sectarianism, theologically, dogmatically entrenched adherents first must shed all organized religious garments of limiting exclusivity. All self-imposed dogma collars must be willfully removed.

All evolving souls who leave the physical universe return to the Spirit Realm (Astral Universe), where they are relegated to their appropriate placement based on the weight of their individual karmic debt. Those with heavy karmic debt end up in the abominable region of level nine. Those with less karmic weight reside in level ten. The beings existing in level ten primarily are in the Astral death sleep of conscious existence. Earth humans attuning toward salvation and Unified SuperConscious attainment bypass both levels nine and ten. Level eleven conscious attunement is where most earth humans who chose to conduct themselves in an evolved, conscious manner can further fulfill their obligation of karmic expunging. Most benevolent, loving, kind, compassionate, thoughtful, considerate earth humans are attuned to this level eleven realm. Unique transformations occur once attunement to the level twelve Unified SuperConscious realm is attained.

Because earth humans are very contaminating, SuperConsciously Attuned Beings will minimize exposure and interaction with the human masses. Rather than being around the masses, these Beings find far greater fulfillment engaging in prayerful, inner spiritual communication. This phenomena is why yogis tend to prefer hermitic solitude to urban jungles. Think for a moment about the sources all around you. Then consider what actions and articulations from those sources constantly are being absorbed by your metaphysical existence. Are you consistently being assaulted with verbal dumping and negatively impacting action from those who surround you? It is imperative for everyone to stop to analyze their conscious experience for a few moments, and reflect on their free-will choices.

Do you choose to surround and inundate yourself with karmically restricting or uplifting experiences? If your answer is primarily in choosing vibratorily polluting experiences, your road to salvation will be long and grueling. Each incarnation is valuable and not one moment should be disregarded as meaningless or taken lightly. Spend as much time as you can in uplifting enjoyments, and always be thankful for fulfilling opportunities, even if the effort to do so is extremely challenging.

The vibratory contagion can be eliminated through Deep Comprehension. We must look at each experience, whether good or bad, and evolve from it. Every apparent crisis is an opportunity for spiritual growth. It is important to learn from these upward stepping-stones and release any restrictions that may influence your state of mind. If your state of mind is positive and upbeat, your soul is fed the enriching universal reflection of upliftment. If your state of mind is gloom and doom—and life stinks and then you die—it does, and you will.

An earth human can choose the road to salvation through deprivation and martyrdom, as well as satiation. Neither process is any harder or easier, and you control your individual free-will choices, as well as your conscious response to those same free-will choices. Knowing this, it benefits us and those all around us when we elect to make Deep Comprehending selections. Experience all that existence has to offer, process it positively, be humble and grateful, and then release and move on. Never cling to any past experience in a negative or desirous manner, for only karmic dead weight will be the result. The karmic burden of attachment is a huge impediment to salvation.

Karmic debt can contribute to an interesting phenomenon. In the same way a dam will prevent the flow of water from its continued path, so too does an impediment in the conscious electromagnetic pathways cause backups. A dam continually restricts the natural waters' flow, while the back-filling pool continues to receive and collect the additional water. Like almost all physically manifesting phenomenon, this pooling process follows an archetype patterned from a higher sourced model.

A similar condition occurs when energy is focused toward something that never existed, never occurred, or has been falsely or completely misinterpreted. This energy continually builds with no truthful or factual outlet through which to channel such build-up. Like a river, energy needs a final destination into which to flow. The final destination for all physical universe, experienced matter, is the quark universe. The quark universe records and stores all physically decaying experience now being reduced to a quark-contained memory. Cosmic decay continues only to the quark-dominated Astral Universe. All physical, vibratorized experience is subtlely and meticulously retained in its predetermined, exact, orderly location.

A problem occurs when misfocused energy collects or pools behind a dam of conceived misperception. This happens consistently in our physically manifesting universe. Without the benefit of the Astral Realm's Divine Discernment, earth humans are reduced to primitive and somewhat imperfect interpretations. The energy that results needs an avenue and a terminating point. If that path is absent or the focal point never existed, the energy literally has nowhere to go.

Much like a ghost or apparition, this energy ends up caught in an in-between, nonexistent state. It has a manifesting consciousness without an actual termination point. This phenomenon actually then builds into a convoluted pool, which can become very problematic, producing incredible confusion, contamination, and conscious instability for both individuals and groups of humans.

This condition is the particular unfortunate circumstance surrounding the inaccuracies pertaining to the biblical fables. If these fabled stories were based on factual events or primarily truthful occurrences, the ensuing energies being passionately generated and directed toward theology would result in a natural dissemination. As it is, these theological misinterpretations continue accumulating, then occasionally rebalancing, with very damaging results.

When this happens, those contributing souls carrying the heaviest karmic loads will be affected with the most severe backlashing. Souls who don't subscribe to these theological ideologies, but perhaps focus on unrelated spiritual pursuits would remain unaffected. This phenomenon is true, even if these souls are carrying karmic debt loads from other aspects of their existences. Karmic debt originating from other sources will be provided alternative ways to be eliminated.

One of the alternative forms of energy elimination is through the Christian-based stigmatist. A stigmatist is a devout Christian person, who, when in a state of episodic but intense, organized religious attunement, experiences and bleeds through marks resembling Jesus' crucifixion wounds. Unbeknownst to stigmatists, such as Sister Therese Neumann of Konnersreuth, Bavaria (born in 1898), their bloody wounds actually are assisting in the lawful and rightful dissemination of the energy created by people's sympathy and perceptions of fictional circumstances surrounding actual events.

While graphic, gory, and real, these wounds actually are not necessarily attributable to Jesus. However, in their successful dissemination of false pools of energy, these wounds ARE facilitating God's Holy Work. The stigmatists provide truthful flow pathways for this stagnant energy.

When a physically manifesting conscious experience has attained a Unified SuperConscious State of Salvation, no karmic retribution is registered against the soul. Karmically free souls can assist in the dissemination of these pools without experiencing any defilement. When Sri Yukteswar Giri would read from the bible and espouse eloquent, symbolic interpretations regarding any particular biblical segment, he was always untainted and unaffected. If assisting in the dissemination of this stagnant, pooled energy, Saints attaining salvation in the future likewise will remain unimpacted.

Salvation is not easily attained or haphazardly granted. At the time of this writing, there were thirty-seven fully emancipated souls walking amongst the 6 billion others. Fewer than a thousand souls have earned the distinction of complete emancipating freedom while incarnating in human form since humans first were deposited here on earth.

No strict Christian, Jewish, or Islamic adherent has ever attained salvation or been recognized as a Holy Being by the Holy Angelic Realm during their physical incarnation. Islamic Kabir was the sole exception, yet he also was a devout Hindu, and eventually became a disciple of Babaji. All strict adherents of the fictional biblical messages have been shackled and burdened by the same energy encumbrances.

Blessed Jesus himself did not adhere to any strict theological confinements. That is just one reason why Jesus tipped over the money exchange tables in the Judaic temples of worship. During his incarnation, Jesus did NOT abide by any organized religious restrictions—and he definitely would not recognize or authorize any today.

Later in Book Four, the Holy Sanctioned Angel, with Jesus' Divine Assistance, untangles from the fictitious, deified Jesus, the REAL Jesus. The Causal and Astral Universe levels fifteen through twelve continually must contend with the stagnant pools of manifesting immotile energy as it continues to accumulate. No physically manifesting being can influence the Holiness of an Astral or Causal Being. However, some God-sanctioned, supremely evolved earthly beings can help eradicate the karmic indebtedness of other earthly beings. An earth human soul cannot be assisted through human efforts (intentions, thoughts, and prayer) into the Unified Holiness of the Holy Realm.

Without exception, earth humans are completely incapable of enhancing the Holiness of Astral or Causal beings. Holiness is attained exclusively through each conscious individual's ever-increasing capacity toward ever-increasing levels of focused attunement. The higher the level of attunement, the more your conscious capacity accommodates and expands. This leads to the Unified levels of attainment. Once a being is God-Sanctioned into the Unified Astral SuperConsciousness, salvation is attained, and this Being would be recognized and considered a Holy Being by the Holy Angelic Realm.

This brings us back to the dilemma of consciousness without a truthful termination point. Part of the purpose of this book is to give all uncovenanted or misappropriated energies an umbilical cord of Truth through which to flow, allowing the eminent dissipation of the coagulated pools. Once the Truthful, connecting pathways have been established, the dispositional process commences. The more earthly humanity consciously accesses the Truth, the faster and more completely its dispersion will occur.

When accessing the archaic, historic records, the Holy Sanctioned Angel faced this confusing disparity many times. Once the actual, resolute, quark Truthfulness was investigated, what I thought would have been a pat answer "yes" to my in-depth questions led many times to disconcerting "no's." With respect to our factual history and desired due-diligent accuracy for God, this Blessed Holy Sanctioned Angel exercised meticulous, supernal responsibility in discerning the Truth.

This Blessed Holy Sanctioned Angel would be gone for long periods of time, searching for "Noah" and "Jonah," only to find pools of irrefutable nonexistence. Great pools of energy hype surrounded humanly conceived absolutes, all which were unsubstantiated, contrived nothingness. Whether humanly accessed or not, the Truthful connectivities will initiate the process of dissolution of this energized, suppositious vacuity.

It may take a while to fully liquidate these nonexistent, baseless pools, for they were begotten and continuously contributed to for over two millennia. This does not take away from historically correct incidents in any way. Now such incidents have a clean, Truthful stream through which to flow.

One would like to believe that complete uniformity exists between interpretations, representations, or even the bibles themselves. The big three theocracies have subversive themes or coy messages that consistently and insidiously are woven throughout their bibles.

In the Holy Eye of God, this disregard for creedless theological virtues of faith, hope, and charity become the unbridgeable chasm that continually tears the very fabric each theocracy purports to infallibly purvey. The resulting scar tissue is inflexible and unyielding in its unmalleable or inelastic healing properties. The festering wounds continually are assuaged with an ointment that more closely resembles a theomachy, rather than an all-loving, compassionate, merciful, Holy Universality.

This divisiveness is the very root of the worldwide disease that is disseminated throughout earth humankind. As indivisible SuperConsciousness experiencing life in the physical universe on this Earth planet, we are indistinguishable before the Transilluminating Eye of God. Most Native American Lakota pipe ceremonies end with the wise saying, "Mi taku oyasin," or simply and humbly stated, "We are all related."

To look at our civilization today, one would see nothing but division, segregation, and ostracism. From block to block, neighborhood to neighborhood, state to state, country to country, this pervasive divisiveness resides. When such divisions are then subdivided according to organized religious or ideological lines, the eventual result yields inessential, little, narrow-minded cliques with a cause—but without a clue.

These deep, biblical, inextricable differences must be realized for true healing to occur. Fortunately, there is a Universal Law affording manifesting humankind the opportunity to experience individual spiritual upliftment. This Law guarantees that all souls will be divinely gifted numerous incarnations, during which each individual soul will experience existence as every possible type of organized religious and nonreligious adherent.

As such, it is an Absolute Fact that Jews reincarnate as Muslims or Christians, Christians reincarnate as Muslims or Jews, and Muslims reincarnate as Jews or Christians. This Fact spawns more hope and promise for permanent resolution than any possible reconciliation between these disparate groups. In other words, while it may be impossible to achieve common ground, peace, respect, and understanding in the manifesting, material cosmos, at least there exists a divine, built-in mechanism for such benevolence to take place on a deeper soul level.

Future generations will have to carry the torch for the lasting expatiation necessary to bridge all of the divisive crevices, whose formations have been allowed, courtesy of prior generations. Through ever-Deep-ening Comprehension, the spiritual expansionism, which until now has taken place through souls' countless incarnations, may become an increasingly accomplishable, manifesting reality.

Biblical Illuminations: The New Testament

Christians have long since been led to believe that divinity was the foundation upon which their theology rests. However, this belief is not even remotely the case. Christianity has a long, ugly history of oppression, violence, and immense bloodshed. None of the recognized "big three" theologies of today promote Truth deemed holy by the Holy Realm. You will come to know that Christianity is guilty of some of the most abominable, deplorable, unconscionable acts ever committed against pure innocents, as well as targeting promulgators of the Truth.

It is no wonder Christianity—as well as all theologies—is so unstable and oftentimes held with such contempt and low regard. The problems go far beyond the concept most earth human beings have that theirs is the correct and holy God-recognized theology, while all others badly miss the mark. The Truth is, every theology misses the Mark: Unconditional Love.

No longer will sequacious Christian souls unknowingly promenade to the altar to receive God-unauthorized, unsubstantiated rituals from transgressors. At least now earth humankind will have the option of exercising our God-given gift of free will to make our own discernments regarding truth, sensibility, and righteousness. No longer will human beings be inundated with confusing, contaminating, inaccurate diatribes, forcing people to conform to predetermined standards through imposition of unholy guilt.

The Holy Sanctioned Angel has been authorized by God to extract all pertinent facts and Truthful information by delving into the archaic records contained in the quarks to extricate fact from fiction. So, here is the unadulterated historical Truth, without embellishments. Blessed Jesus himself is helping with this section of Holy Exegesis to ensure the accuracy and validity of every word. God has Transubstantiated every vibratory letter to validate this entire book as Truthful Absolute.

Before extracting the Truth out of the New Testament, the Holy Sanctioned Angel felt some background information would be helpful.

In 300 AD, Christianity did not yet exist. In 303 AD, a sun-worshipping pagan Roman emperor named Diocletian collected and destroyed all known Christian writings and related documents. Between 66 AD and 74 AD, a Jewish revolt had occurred. It was a futile Jewish uprising against the insurmountable Roman legions, resulting in the obliteration of Jerusalem and the destruction of Solomon's Temple. In the uproar and aftermath, all known, tangible evidence regarding historical genealogies for both Judaism and upcoming Christianity was destroyed.

This destruction of evidence removed any factual or firsthand accounts of the believed or recognized truth dating back to the Old Testament. Most of the historical evidence had been committed to writing in 300 BC or sooner. As a result, there was a glaring lack of any substantiating documentations validating earlier Old Testament claims. In actuality, both Judaism and Christianity benefited from the void. Judaic adherents were able to recreate "accounts" without danger of embarrassing or damaging contradictions.

Christianity began to grow and thrive in the Roman Empire, primarily from the efforts of Irenaeus, the Bishop of Lyons, in 180 AD. Irenaeus consolidated all the Christian doctrines and principles that he found acceptable. He created a massive piece of work, which unequivocally condemned as heresy all objectionable deviations from his personal viewpoint. All diversity or ideological beliefs not adhering to his single apostolic system were to be viciously opposed, usurped, and destroyed.

Irenaeus's new doctrine demanded unquestionable faith in his brand of fixed dogma. Through his shameless wrath and ecclesiastical principles, anyone usurping his rituals and customs was to be met with vengeful indignation. Irenaeus's forces attempted to commandeer and sequester the mysteries behind salvation, resurrection, and many other relevant aspects of existence today.

The Gnostics, who preached the virtues of knowledge gained through individual experience, union with the Divine, and the essentials of salvation, were particularly victimized. Irenaeus's efforts laid the approving foundations for all the future Christian annihilations of human heretical positions of nonconformity. Countless souls lost their lives, due to their noncompliance with and nonrecognition of Irenaeus's pious assertions of absolute righteousness.

Christianity continued to grow and expand until 312 AD, when

Constantine and Maxentius, two rivals for the position of emperor of the Roman Empire, clashed at the Battle of Milvian Bridge. Before the battle, Constantine experienced a brainstorm while being informed about Christianity and Jesus on the Cross. He drew inspiration from Jesus miraculously resurrecting or apparently surviving his grisly ordeal. This inspiration contributed to Constantine's determined savvy. As a result, he was very tolerant of Christianity after that inspirational influence. The "Cross" eventually was to find an echo when it later was emblazoned on the chests of the Knights Templars and associated crusaders.

Constantine crushed Maxentius, his adversary for the throne, and assumed complete sovereignty over the entire Empire. Constantine purposefully erased the distinctions between Christianity, Mithraism or "Light and Truth," and a popular Syrian cult at the time called "Sol Invictus" or "Invincible Sun." During Constantine's rule, the cult of Sol Invictus reigned supreme over the budding Christian theology, while meshing nicely with the popular Mithraic theology. When facing his eminent death in 337 AD, Constantine was baptized into Christianity. Between 312 and 337, he was a staunch sun worshipper who knew how to play the political-religious game. Constantine did what he had to in order to appease all sides and keep all potential problematic factors under control.

Constantine comfortably allowed the Invincible Sun cult to supersede all other gods and pertinent religions. Feeling indebted, the Christian orthodoxy flourished under Constantine's reign. All three theologies essentially were monotheistic, with the cult Sol Invictus presiding over them as the Empire's Imperial Religion. The three theologies were somewhat interwoven, with acceptable similarities. By official proclamation in 321, Sunday became Christianity's official day of rest. Prior to this edict, Christianity recognized the Jewish Sabbath of Saturday as the sacred day. Both Sol Invictus and Mithraic religions recognized Sunday as being sacred.

For Sol Invictus and Mithraism, the winter solstice was celebrated on December 25, when the daylight begins growing longer. Accordingly, Christianity realigned Jesus' birthday to coincide with the established sun-related celebrations. Prior to its repositioning in 321, Jesus' birthday accurately was celebrated on January 6.

Mithraism provided Christianity with immortality of the soul, a future judgment, and the resurrection of the dead. These last two aspects are recognized incorrectly or misunderstood by Christianity. Evidence of these misperceptions and others are found in the Catholic Creed. God is not ever coming to "judge the living and the dead," and there also is no resurrection of the dead. One rare exception is the temporary exiting or ascension of the soul into the level eight atom realm. This phenomenon results in the person's subsequent death or bodily reinhabitation—both of which are based upon the individual's TransImaginated conscious decision made during an Interaction.

This phenomenon is extremely rare and granted by God for reasons known only to God. Continuous bodily inhabitation is reserved only for the material universe, because the physically manifesting container is far too materially heavy and vibratorily contaminated to be granted access into the Astral Realm.

Transcendence also is a phenomenon that occurs in extremely rare circumstances, as in the case of Elijah. In transcendence, the manifesting physical being literally is reabsorbed back into the Astral quark-lepton Universe and never returns. As such, this person's atoms are disseminated without a trace or remainder of their bodily container. After a physical death or soul transcendence, the only way a person returns to the material universe in the same recognizable physical body is through the phenomenon of resurrection.

Resurrection is for the physically freed soul to be SuperConsciously contained, maintained, and reconstituted by entirely new Fabricating atoms of its exact previously physically manifesting state. This exceptionally rare experience also is God sanctioned for specific purposes known only to God during the TransImaginating state.

In 325, Constantine unified Christian orthodoxy at the Council of Nicea. Two-hundred twenty voting church elders established many foundational Christian beliefs. At this unprecedented gathering, ecclesiastical powers and authorities were self-granted to the bishops and church hierarchy. It was by vote that the dating of Easter was established. Also, by a 218 to 2 vote, Blessed Jesus was deified to the status of a God, no longer a mortal prophet. Constantine felt indebted to Jesus and Christianity, so he allowed the association of God Jesus with God Sol Invictus.

In 326, Constantine sanctioned the collection and subsequent destruction of all known "now heretical" literary works challenging the freshly established orthodox authority on Godliness. He arranged for an Imperially Sanctioned fixed cash flow for the Church, and positioned the bishop of Rome into the St. John Lateran Palace. In 388, the bishop of Rome declared himself the first Pope of Rome. In 331, under the orchestration of Constantine, the revised, edited, omitted, deleted, misconstrued, and misguided bible was presented to the adherents for indoctrination into their belief system, and now is known as the New Testament.

In 367, Bishop Athanasius of Alexandria compiled a list of literary works to be included in the New Testament. In 393, at the Council of Hippo, it was arbitrarily decided which works were and weren't holy. In 397, at the Council of Carthage, more refinements again were voted and decided upon. It was not exactly an unbiased, authoritative committee selection process by which the Holy Word of God was determined. This same highly questionable, nondefinitive process was enacted for both the Old and New Testaments. The bible was canonized at the second council of Constantinople. The following is a Truthful analysis and account of the New Testament.

PART I

John 1: 1–18

This entry probably is one of the most misunderstood aspects of the New Testament. This Prologue of John's Gospel became misleading primarily due to the deification process by Christian founders. We are not yet going to address their inaccuracies, but it is safe to say that once detailed without cryptic allegory, the Truth will be even more amazing—and inevitably make more sense.

John 1-18 is provocative, with many beautiful, symbolically interpretable passages. Known to devout Christians as Logos, it claims validity as the Word of God. Logos is an utterance, speech, or vibration interpreted as being God's inward, reflecting thoughts—and as such, the controlling principle of the universe. In theological jargon, Logos is the eternal personality, thought, or vibratorized manifested word of God, incarnating as Blessed Jesus Christ.

The deification process wove in four public decorations of Jesus the Christ. Known to theologians as the Four Christophanies, they are as follows:

I   Jesus is declared "Son of God" by his resurrection from the dead. (Romans 1:4)

II Baptism; Jesus was designated as the "Son of God" by the descent of the dove and the voice of God from Heaven.

(Matthew 3:13–17)

III Virgin birth story (Matthew 1:18–25 and Luke 1:26–38, 2:1–17)

IV Creation of the world. (John 1:1–14)

Matthew 1:1-17 and Luke 3:23-38 focus on the genealogies. The rational line of thinking of the day was a self-fulfilling prophecy—a doctrine-supported, underlying ideal of miracles. After forty-nine generations of families, the Messiah was expected to magically appear and the world would end. It was important to include all the families, from Jesus through to Abraham, to ensure proper inclusion for all—especially after so many wars, with people smiting and internecine fighting. Luke took his genealogy linking Jesus right on through Noah, all the way to Adam and God. Matthew's genealogy stopped with the linkage of Abraham to Jesus.

Luke 1:5–25

This pertains to an angelic visit by Gabriel to Zacharias and Elizabeth. Neither did a visit nor any silencing of Zachiarias occur. Both he and Elizabeth were of normal childbearing ages when they had John, who became known as "The Baptist." John was the reincarnate of Elijah.

Luke 1:26–38 (Christophany 3—The Annunciation to Mary)

No angel Gabriel was sent to foretell of Jesus' arrival. A Hebrew virgin named Mary was betrothed to Joseph. A being indeed was sent by God to inform Mary of her impending pregnancy, but that being was a benevolent, physically manifesting being—not an angel. Mary was informed that God had selected her for a special birth. She was Transimpregnated with very unique DNA, and it did not belong to the being doing the inseminating. The originator of the DNA did not have a DNA lineage to King David, as his DNA was far more evolved, and it was not from this planet. Transimpregnation of Mother Mary was performed by Holy Beings from a star system known as Sirius. Therefore, any lineages, such as any later descendents like the Merovingians of Southern France, also were from Sirius. This is why Jesus was known to the Knights Templars as "The Son of a Widow."

Mary was given a memory inhibitor that prevented her from recalling the incident. At that time she was not informed that the child would be named Jesus, and was not informed Jesus would be called the "Son of the Most High"—even though he eventually was to become a "Son of God." It was not until later in his life, shortly before he began to teach at 30 years of age, that Jesus was a "Son." Mary did not ever know Elizabeth and Zacharias. Jesus was the reincarnate of Elisha.

One rather overtly elusive yet subtlely persistent thread pertains to the questions regarding Jesus' parentage and subsequent bloodline throughout history. It is Absolute Truth that by God's Ordained Instructions Jesus actually was tapped for seminal DNA extraction by extraterrestrial Holy Beings. After Jesus' crucifixion, Joseph of Arimathea and Mary Magdalen, Jesus' wife, indeed fled Jerusalem to settle in southern France. While in France, Mary Magdalen gave birth to two daughters. To facilitate conception in both cases, Jesus' DNA was divinely Trans-impregnated into Mary Magdalen—AFTER Mary Magdalen and Joseph of Arimathea had escaped to France.

The first daughter was born shortly after their arrival in France, with the second born two years afterward. Much like their biological father, both daughters experienced DNA extraction procedures by which extraterrestrial Holy Beings analyzed and interpreted the genetic markers carried through in the DNA structure. These two daughters provided the DNA link supporting the long-standing, persistent assertions that Jesus indeed fathered children whose diluted lineage continues even to this day.

Jesus' two daughters each bore children, which further perpetuated Jesus' DNA lineage. Three-hundred fifty-seven years of continual procreation brought the family lines of both daughters back together again. This familial merging first was recognized in the birth of Merovée, a Sicambrian Frankish leader born in 413. Subsequent marriages yielded the birth of Dagobert II, the King of Austrasia (now known as Lorraine), who ultimately was murdered while napping under a tree beside a stream. His son, Sigisbert IV, Count of Razés, was the last survivor to the direct line of Merovée—the symbolic unified point at which Jesus' daughters' lineages merged.

Matthew 1:18–25

The Being did appear to Joseph, but not in a dream. Joseph (not Mary) was informed that Mary would bear God's Son. However, he was not informed about the "Holy Ghost" or "Holy Spirit." He was informed the child was to be named Jesus. He was instructed to marry Mary, during whose pregnancy she and Joseph did not have intimacy. Jesus' incarnation actually was NOT foretold in Isaiah 7:14, but instead was written in by later-day writers composing the Old and New Testaments. Joseph was administered a memory inhibitor to forget his encounter. Rather, Joseph's vivid recollection of this encounter was experienced as if generated by his own thoughts, thus the information unenfolded very naturally in Joseph's ensuing experience.

Luke 1:39–56

Mary did not visit Elizabeth. Throughout the duration of their lives, they did not know one another.

Luke 1: 57–80

The visiting Being did not mute John's father, Zacharias. There was no reason to speak to him through signs. John was circumcised. Zacharias and Elizabeth did not have a name-giving controversy. Elizabeth did choose "John," and Zacharias did concur. Zacharias did not become filled with the Holy Ghost. He also did not prophesize the passages Luke: 1:68-79, as attributed to him.

Luke 2:1–7

Both Joseph and Mary were born in Bethlehem. Although a Hebrew and along with Mary, of Jewish adherence, Joseph was not of David's lineage. At that time neither one of them was recognized by the Holy Realm as holy beings; however, only Mother Mary is recognized today as a Holy Being. It is true that there was no room for them at the inn. They were very young and poor, living a transient lifestyle. Thus, they would not have been staying that night at the inn, even if it had an opening available. Jesus was born in a stable in Bethlehem. Baby Jesus was wrapped in a blanket and at times was placed in the manger.

Luke 2:8–20, 21

Mary, Joseph, and Jesus were not visited by an angel, but three shepherds indeed did enter the stable area to check and see what was going on. It actually was January 6 when this benevolent birth took place, during which no angel was present. In addition, the shepherds did not lavish them with any gifts, other than their presence, assistance, and offering them four nights' shelter. Jesus was not as yet a "Son of God." Jesus was circumcised.

Luke 2:22–39

No doves or pigeons were sacrificed to appease the "law of the Lord." The Simeon blessing did not occur, so there occurred no early hymnology relating to the fictitious Simeon. The Anna prophetess incident also did not occur.

Matthew 2:1–12

King Herod did not know about the birth, or miraculous shining star or any celestial portent. As such, he did not call upon Magi to interpret any nonevents. Neither the wise men (Magi) story, nor any so-called shining star ever occurred. Jesus was a very benevolent incarnate with extraordinary DNA, but was NOT known or recognized yet as being "Divine" by earth humankind.

Matthew: 2:13–23

Joseph was a carpenter, and for a short time did take the family and venture to the top of Egypt. They were not fleeing the wrath of Herod; he merely was following work-related pursuits. The Holy Angel did not find any evidence of Herod taking sordid, vengeful liberties against any children. Joseph, Mary, and Jesus did end up in Nazareth. Mary and Joseph did not have any other children. Jesus was Mary's only child.

Luke 2:41–50

They did not go to Jerusalem every year for the feast of the Passover.

However, they did go to Jerusalem when Jesus was 12 years old. Jesus did tarry behind when it was time to return to Nazareth. By this time, they did have a humble home in Nazareth. Jesus did not entertain doctors and field complex questions posed to him. At this time, he did not recognize God as his "Holy Father." This incident just did not occur as it was portrayed. This is the last time Joseph was mentioned in the bible. However, he did not die shortly after this entry. Jesus was in his early twenties when Joseph died.

Luke 2:51, 52

During these eighteen years, Jesus did grow in wisdom and in favor with both God and human beings. He was a brilliant, compassionate, loving, and gentle young fellow, who was being taught wisdom from a couple of older Essenic teachers. I was one of those teachers, after which during that same incarnation, I was instructed by God to change my name to "Ormus."

At the time of Jesus, there were various sects of Jewish adherents. The main ones were the Sadducees, Pharisees, the Essenes, and the Zealots. The Sadducees tended to be priestly and aristocratic Jewish families who more literally interpreted the Judaic Law. They tended toward materialism, and were less formal and observant of rites and rituals. The Pharisees were strict observers of the rites, rituals, and interpretations of The Law. Their beliefs included soul immortality, resurrection of the body, retribution, and a coming of the Messiah. These are the two sects mentioned in the Gospels.

The Essenes were a separatist group of ascetic sages, monastic, white-cloaked monk healers. We Essenes (I was one) interpreted the Old Testament as allegory. We blended Gnostic, Pythagorean, and Hellenistic thought, and in some cases, were even tolerant of aspects of Mithraic light worship, as well. The Zealots were an activated, somewhat inciteful group—more politically than theologically based. While less spiritually evolved, they were more socially interactive. They were more apt to be the active disciples and followers than the sages and seers.

The Gospel of the Infancy in the Apocryphal works portrays Jesus with some disrespect, suggesting that in an angry outburst, he actually struck and killed another child and killed one of our fellow tutoring sages. These stories both are complete fiction. Jesus was very vibrant, energetic, curious, and eager to learn—but was NOT subject to rash, irrational, or irresponsible outbursts of anger. He did, however, tip over the currency exchange tables in the Temple. He would not have been chosen by God for his Divine purpose if he had committed any of those unGodly acts.

Prelude to John the Baptizer of Men

The time of John and Jesus was vibrant with raw activity. The Babylonian slaves returning from Nebuchanezzer's downfall and Esther's interactions were struggling for cohesive identity. In 300 BC, they intensely gathered the stories of mythology, perceptions, and interpretations of their time and geographical region, beginning to compile them. Out of these efforts came the birth of Judaism.

The early writers were tenacious in accumulating Middle East history, especially those stories based with potential Hebrew slants, and amalgamated them into a theology. These writers were not always meticulous or able to derive or arrive at the exact Truthful facts. They strived to do their best, despite the nature of the circumstances surrounding their plight. They attempted to work with what they had, in order to make the most sense out of the rubble of accumulative piles of historical events.

It was from these amalgamated records dating from 300 BC, from which John, Jesus, and all of us of that day operated and resorted to when necessary. These were the texts and manuscripts on which all three major, known theologies of today base their entire belief structures.

PART II

Matthew 3:1–12, Mark 1:1–8, and Luke 3:1–20
The Ministry of John the Baptist

John the Baptist was a preacher who lived in what then was known as the Wilderness of Judea. He did preach about repentance and the remission of sins. This idea did stem from what now is known as the Book of Isaiah. John was clad in a camel-hair cloak and wore a leather girdle. For sustenance, he was known to consume locust insects and honey. He indeed did baptize people—a ritual he misguidedly perceived as effectively able to grant people absolution from their sins, transgressions, or karmic debts. However, he was not sanctioned by God to absolve karmic debts.

As we have stated earlier, no earth human has or ever will be granted this God-only authority. Thus, with every baptism John ever performed, he unknowingly but egoistically was transgressing against God. The Holy Sanctioned Angel informs me that this is a very serious transgression. This continuous accumulation eventually cost John his head at the end moment of this incarnation. Otherwise, he may have passed into the Astral Universe in a myriad of other possible ways and without the heavy karmic debt. He went from Elijah, to transgressing John much in the same manner as I went from Ormus to transgressing Richard—now elevated to Scott. I am informed that John, still to this day, is not recognized as a Holy Being by the Holy Realm—and he still is performing his own penance or karmic debt alleviation.

No priest, bishop, or any pope is, was, or ever will be God-authorized to absolve the karmic indebtedness of another earth human being. Satisfaction, reparation, or absolution of karma is only determined by God. No one is God-sanctioned to perform such things. Every time people convince others and themselves that they are capable of such Transcendental Authority, they transgress against God.

To listen to another person's sins is not a transgression, and one does not transgress when dumping and vibratorily burdening another with their personal contamination.

Jesus himself never was authorized to perform karmic debt alleviation for others, and never purported, claimed, or endeavored to do so. Even miraculous transformations as a result of any known miracle would not ensure or guarantee the proper or actual absolution of prior karmic debt. Without Divine assistance it is impossible for humans to know that any karmic debt has been completely absolved. Once an individual soul sufficiently evolves to merge with the Unity of SuperConsciousness, one easily understands the purposeless, ineffectiveness, and vain uselessness of baptism as absolution from anyone else's (especially fictitious Adam and Eve's) sins.

Matthew 3:13–17, Mark 1:9–11, Luke 3:21–23
Jesus' Baptism

Jesus was baptized by John. He had yet to understand the full implications of baptism. To Jesus, baptism was a symbolic gesture that he felt compelled to experience. The act itself was completely unnecessary, but to 30-year-old Jesus at that time, it seemed an appropriate and acceptable act of contrition. During Jesus' baptism, no doves descended and there was no disembodied voice from out of the Heavens. He did go out into the Judean wilderness to pray—and it was there where the miracle of all humanly possible miracles occurred to Jesus.

Matthew 4:1–11, Mark 1:12–13, Luke 4:1–13
The Temptation in the Wilderness

It was while Jesus was praying alone in the wilderness that God Itself performed a Holy Transimplantation upon him. Within every earth human's Causal container is a Holy of Holies. The Holy of Holies contains and maintains each human's soul, along with their intuition. During a Transcendental Interaction Jesus' merkebah (the three manifesting— Causal, Astral, and physical—containers) was Transimplanted with an Arc of the Covenant. The Arc of the Covenant is a Holy Impedance permeating within and throughout all three containers, protecting invisible Divine God from physically manifesting contamination. The Arc of the Covenant serves as an all-encompassing, impermeable barrier of protection for the Holy Divinity that is Transimplanted within.

Once this Holy Divinity (Holy Grail or God SuperConsciousness) has been Transimplanted, a transformational perception of expanding comprehension and Divine communication occurs. This transformation from human consciousness to God Expression as SuperConsciousness is actually a human Transubstantiation. This Transubstantiation requires a curing and empowering as this Holy Barrier becomes ever increasingly impermeable to ALL physically manifesting contamination. This is why it was necessary for Jesus to be gone for forty days. The entire SuperConscious Transubstantiation took 152 days.

While God was preparing to Transimplant a SuperConsciousness into Jesus' Causal container, many extremely complex questions were asked of him. These are inaudible Superthought Transmittings to which the correct answers are absolutely imperative. Every perceivable intention, thought, action, and reaction to the questions was Divinely analyzed. Every aspect of his conscious experience was illumed and comprehended. It was at this moment that Jesus was elevated to the status of "Son of God."

At this point in time, there could be no doubt as to the supremacy of Jesus, versus John the Baptist. However, at the time, questions were being raised, for after this event, there was some extended confusion regarding each man's respective divinity. Nonetheless, Jesus most certainly was exuding the virtues of both Unconditional Love and SuperConsciousness after this Holiest of all earth human manifesting experiences.

The Satan incident does not have merit, for that devil nonsense does not exist. Earth humankind commits free-will abominations and unholy atrocities against fellow earth humans, although some conscious, parasitic entities do exist or operate on earth and throughout the cosmos. However, no satanic manifesting angel, deity, or antiChrist exists—or ever will exist on planet Earth. Any such entities would be relegated to operating exclusively in the physically manifesting material cosmos. Entities have no transuniversal capabilities or God-sanctioning capabilities whatsoever. Entities are relegated to the atom world with limited and primitive capabilities. Evil and unholiness are Determined by their distance from Unconditional Love.

John 1:19–28
John's Testimony Before the Priests and Levites

This incident never occurred. John did not know he had been Elijah the prophet.

John 1:29–34
Jesus the Lamb of God

This incident with Jesus did not occur. After the forty-day period of post-Transimplantation, John and Jesus did have an encounter after which John indeed did recognize Jesus as "The Messiah," as well as the Son of God. Jesus knew the work John was doing was unsanctioned by God. However, Jesus did not press John about it, for John had a well-developed ego and a temper to match. Although their relationship at times was somewhat tenuous, the two were friends. Jesus described to John the incident as God descending from the Heavens and entering into him after the series of deep, complex questions. The dove was a fictionalization by later-day writers and signified their attempts to understand and make plausible, comprehensible, analogical explanations that easily could be spread to the adherents.

John 1:35–42

This "Behold the lamb of God" incident between John and Jesus also did not occur. John was not present when the disciples began to gather. John also did not say anything to any potential disciples that contributed to their decision to follow Jesus. At this time they began to recognize Jesus as a Messiah.

John 1:43–51

The disciples were beginning to figure out that Jesus was the Messiah. The fig tree incident involving Phillip actually did occur. Jesus did not say to Nathaniel that heaven will open and the angels of God would be ascending and descending upon the Son of Man. Technically, Jesus was a Son of God, rather than a Son of Man, like Ezekiel. It may sound insignificant, like splitting hairs, but there is a distinct difference between the definitions. Son of Man signifies the existence of an Arc of the Covenant, which allows for SuperConscious communication to occur without the Transimplanting of the SuperConsciousness. The Arc of the Covenant that Jesus received actually provided for a Transimplanted Holy Grail or Manifesting Infinite SuperConsciousness.

John 2:1–11
First Miracle: Water Made Wine

This incident indeed did occur. The water was turned into wine at Jesus' own wedding to Mary Magdalen, also known as Mary of Bethany. It was Jesus' first request of God to perform a miracle.

John 2:12

After the wedding, Jesus, wife Mary, and mother Mary, along with assorted disciples, did go to Capernaum.

Most people fail to realize that miracles only happen by God—not by manifesting humans or even divinely attuned beings. Only God as Manifesting Infinite SuperConsciousness is solely responsible for the miracles being performed. Many times, these miracles are going on around us on our behalf. We just don't recognize this supernatural phenomenon.

Towering spiritual superhumans, such as Lahiri Mahasaya, were so attuned to the highest heavenly Astral membrane that Holy Lord Shiva or the Manifesting SuperConsciousness (God) through a Holy Angel naturally responded to their prayerful requests. Sometimes these superhumans deeply comprehended a God-ordained Divine Purpose, and sometimes this was not the case. When a miracle worker (Thaumaturge king) is so attuned, miracles occur only when TransImaginated into the benefactor's dharmic blueprint.

If the miracle otherwise interferes negatively in any way with the benefactor's dharma, karma, or free will, the miracle will not occur. Of course, performing a miracle under these conditions would be a transgression, and incompatible with a Holy or Divine Interaction. That is why Thaumaturge workers, for the most part, are nonexistent due to the necessary depth of Transcendental Comprehension required for their work to take place.

PART III

Matthew 21:12–17, Mark 11:15–18, Luke 19:45–48, John 2:13–22
The Early Judean Ministry
First Cleansing of the Temple

In this incident Jesus exhibited his only display of negative emotion. Jesus did go through the temple overturning tables. He did not give sight to the blind in the temple, but did heal some lame and disabled people. The chief priests and scribes indeed were upset and disturbed by the event. Contrary to what John 2:19–22 stated, Jesus did not make any allegoric reference to destroying the temple or to being raised from the dead during this incident.

John 2:23–3:21
Discourse with Nicodemus

Jesus did speak to Nicodemus, a Pharisee ruler, regarding the shallow desires of earth humankind. Jesus made references to reincarnation that were muddied by the later-day writers. He also made references to one's dharmic plan and the mystery surrounding creation and our conscious experience as physically born and manifesting existence. He did not mention Moses and the serpent, for Jesus easily knew the Truth about Moses.

The later-day writers took liberties with Jesus' words. Jesus was well aware of the distinction between "Son of Man" and "Son of God."

The early Christian theologians had a distinct motive in mind when misconstruing the words and messages to fit their particular misguided purpose. God, Jesus, and the Holy Realm had NO intention of blatantly misleading subsequent countless incarnations by having the Truth so deceptively misappropriated. Jesus did not ever want a ministry created, especially one that attempted to misdirect the focus of earth humankind's attunement by suggesting everyone go to and through Jesus, rather than God. Jesus certainly did know better.

The conformers of early Christianity would not have known better, but that does not excuse their egregious behavior and the consistent atrocities occurring in the aftermath. After reading this Truthful Absolute, all earth human beings from now on, will be aware of their opportunity to decide for themselves that which rings of Truth.

John 3:16-21 probably is the most problematic example of misguided coercion in both the Old and New Testaments. It purposely is very misleading and contains little Truth. However, each reader can interpret, process, and comprehend this entry any way they wish, in order to formulate an individual opinion.

John 3:22–24

Jesus did not ever baptize anyone, as baptism was a source of contention between Jesus and John.

John 3:25–36

This entire entry was a covert attempt to divert earth humankind's focus from individual attunement to that based upon sequacious, theological dependence. However, most of this entry never occurred, except for a few grains of Truth, which if interpreted allegorically, do shine through. Of course, the trouble is that earth humans must extrapolate the allegorical truths from the purposefully convoluted nonsense.

Whose fault is it that misguided, determined early founders of organized religion usurped the individual authority with pious theological righteous indignation? It is confusing and traumatizing for devout adherents to realize the Truth. For most, such realization will not take place or be completed during this lifetime—or even their next existence. Fortunately, God knew this, and Precomprehended earth humans' plight by giving all Creation eternity with which to work.

John 4:1–3

Jesus did not ever baptize any of his disciples. As stated before, Jesus deeply comprehended the problematic, transgressing falsity of baptism.

John 4:4–26

This entry is beautifully written, scripted in deep symbolic, interpretable lessons. The problem is that historically, it never happened. Passage 24 reads, "God is a Spirit: and they that worship him must worship in spirit and truth." This is the grain of Truth out of all twenty-three passages. Numbers 25 and 26 describe a conversation with a Samaritan woman, in which the woman declares, "I know the Messiah, which is Christ, who is coming—and when he is to come, he will declare unto us all things . . . and Jesus then saith unto her, 'I that speak unto thee am he.'"

This exchange of dialogue did occur between Jesus and this woman, but the contents of the conversation were different. Jesus did not flaunt his Holiness in such a manner.

John 4:27–42
The Gospel in Sychar

This also is a beautiful scripture, but unfortunately also did not happen. Although the passages sound like typical allegory, which Jesus might have uttered, he simply did not say this—and the whole incident never happened. With regard to the Old Testament, the archaic, quark-contained historic records would need to have been accessed for the Truth to have been revealed. The Holy Sanctioned Angel communicated directly with Jesus' SuperConsciousness and confirmed that this whole incident never happened.

PART IV

Matthew 4:12–17, Mark 1:14–15, Luke 4:14–15, John 4:43–45
First Period of the Christ's Galilean Ministry

This concerns the imprisoning of John the Baptist by King Herod. John indeed was imprisoned—allegedly for chiding Herod about marrying his (Herod's) brother Phillip's wife, Herodias. John did speak out against Herod for marrying his sister-in-law, which went against the recognized Judaic Law of the day. However, by this time, John had accumulated a huge karmic debt by falsely portraying karmic absolution sanctioning when no such authority was granted or EVER would be God-approved.

Jesus was beginning to assert his evolution through his teaching and Deep Comprehension abilities. In Matthew 4:17, Jesus states, "Repent, for the kingdom of heaven is at hand." Of course, Jesus is referring to the individual soul striving for salvation while physically alive. All karmic indebtedness incurred in the physical realm almost always needs to be satisfied through efforts while the soul is existing in the physically manifesting universe.

John 4:46–54
Healing the Nobleman's Son

This event did occur, and essentially is true throughout. Indeed, Jesus did heal the man's son. As SuperConsciousness, all Jesus had to do was focus on comprehending if the boy was destined to live. Since the boy was destined to live, (per his dharmic blueprint), God acquiesced. Omnipresent within Jesus' Arc of the Covenant, God acquiesced, since no dharmic interference would occur. If the boy were dharmically blueprinted to physically expire, God still could acquiesce, but greater factors, reasons, and ramifications would need to be considered. It is extremely rare for God to interfere in the dharmic plan of any physically manifesting being.

Matthew 13:54–58, Mark 6:1–6, Luke 4:16–30
Jesus First Preaches in Galilee

By this time, people were beginning to pay attention and ask questions about Jesus. He indeed had assisted in healing the lame and had hastened the recovery of ill beings. At his own wedding, he had turned the water into wine, so his fame was spreading. To reiterate, his brethren are metaphorical family, not biological family, for he was an only child. In Jesus' day, Messiahs were prognosticated to be "coming" all the time. Jesus did not pay attention to such prognostications, and was unconcerned about such titles or positions. He merely expressed Unconditional Love to all around him.

Luke 4:20-30 states that Jesus had an event in a synagogue on the Sabbath day. This did not happen. In addition, in the days of Elijah, Jesus did not state, "Heaven was shut up three years, six months during a famine all over the land." Jesus was not led out of town and was not threatened to be tossed off a cliff overlooking Nazareth.

Matthew 4:13–16, Luke 4:31
Pressing on to Capernaum

The group did leave Nazareth for Capernaum, a city near the Sea of Galilee. Jesus did not refer to any of the new disciples as becoming fishers of men. At this time, he did meet Simon, (Peter) and his brother, Andrew. James and John did leave their father while mending their nets. There were not any hired servants assisting Zebeddee, their father. They did not catch so many fish that their boats were at risk of capsizing.

Matthew 8:14–17, Mark 1:21–34, Luke 4:31–41
Miracles in Capernaum

Jesus indeed did draw out the unholy energy from the man. He also did cure Peter's mother of a fever. Other people were brought to Jesus for healing, and he did heal them.

Matthew 4:23; 8:1–4, Mark 1:35–45, Luke 4:42–44; 5:12–16
Preaching in Galilee

Early the next morning, Jesus did go out to pray alone. It was imperative for him to recharge his Holy Essence by communing and prayerful attunement. His Holy SuperConsciousness carefully guided and directed him to move along to other cities. Putting out healing Holiness to that extent is draining for any physically manifesting being in any part of the physical cosmos. Jesus did heal the leper, and he did instruct the leper to not say anything. Jesus never instructed the leper to lie or falsely purport that adhering to the Commandments will result in similar miraculous recoveries, and he (the leper) was living proof. The leper did shout Jesus' praises, and great crowds did begin to accumulate. Jesus was directed to retreat into the desert to prayerfully attune. Since Manifesting SuperConsciousness does all Healing, Jesus was actually drained of Unconditional Love flowing outwardly to the masses around him.

Matthew 9:1–8, Mark 2:1–12, Luke 5:17–26
The Palsied Man

This whole entire incident did not occur. Jesus did not heal a palsied man being lowered through the ceiling. Jesus did not erase karma or EVER absolve anyone of their sins. Lahiri Mahasaya and some Superevolved Saints have taken into their own physical beings the physical karmic vibratorized indebtedness of others to burn the seeds of someone's karmic indebtedness. Generally, this results in an outward, physical, and many times painful, manifestation of the indebtedness to be transferred to the Saint.

The same universal operating law applies to the psychic's (MB) barb manifesting within my physical container (body) as a very painful, psychically perceivable, growing jungle of energy, which was removed from MM. The elimination of others' sins is a transgression Jesus never committed. Jesus naturally comprehended the ramifications of such actions as incompatible with his ever-increasing Holiness.

Matthew 9:9–13, Mark 2:13–17, Luke 5:27–32
Disciple Matthew Joins

This episode with the Pharisees did not happen. Jesus recognized no one as an outcast from his unrestricted Holiness. This allegory, written by later-day writers, symbolically is still incorrect with regard to Jesus' SuperConscious state of mind. Jesus shared his Divinity with everyone— rich or poor, sinless or transgressor.

Matthew 9:14–17, Mark 2:18–22, Luke 5:33–39
Fasting

Jesus did not recognize any need for fasting. This also is a clever allegory, but not attributable to Jesus. He did not once utter these passages.

John 5:1–47
The Infirm Man of Bethesda Pool

Jesus did not heal the infirm man at the pool. Jesus certainly recognized the unnecessary nature of the Sabbath. He did not raise the ire of the Jews to the point of their wanting to kill him because he did not respect or honor the Sabbath. Jesus also did not anger them by referring to Holy Father instead of God. John's scriptures here and throughout are later-day evangelists' fictional interpretations. While a few threads or parts of passages are true when interpreted either literally or allegorically, none of this is attributable to Jesus, and none of it is accurate. Jesus knew the Truth, he comprehended God's Absolute. The Gospel writers easily expose the fact that they did not grasp SuperConsciousness.

Matthew 12:1–8, Mark 2:23–28, Luke 6:1–5
Disciples Gathering Grain

This particular event also did not occur as it is portrayed. This is a blatant distancing of Christian adherents from Jewish observances. Jesus did not recognize the Sabbath as set apart from any other day, nor the necessity for a day or two of meaningless rules and regulations. Further, the Holy Sanctioned Angel did not find evidence of them making a concerted effort to collect grain falling on a Saturday, which was and still is recognized as the Jewish Sabbath. Once again, these writers are taking the Pharisees to task over the Sabbath activities.

Matthew 12:9–14, Mark 3:1–6, Luke 6:6–11
Withered-Hand Man

Once again, Jesus is portrayed raising the ire of the Jewish Pharisees by not wanting to stop healing people on the Sabbath. In Truth, this whole event also never happened. Throughout his entire life, Jesus never healed someone with a withered or underdeveloped hand. However, the divisive case against the Pharisees certainly is building.

PART V

Matthew 4:23–25, 12:15–21, Mark 3:7–12, Luke 6:17–19
Second Period of Jesus' Galilean Teachings

In these paragraphs there is plenty of Truth. Jesus indeed healed people from many illnesses and ailments. Matthew 10:2-4, Mark 3:13-19, and Luke 6:12-19 all were concerned with the selection of twelve apostles. The Gospels emphasized the misperception that there were exactly twelve selected to go forth to preach and have the authority to cast out devils.

The fact remains that no pre-set, magical number was to be realized. The number of official disciples was indeterminable, ever fluctuating, and unrelated to any pertinent, predetermined reason. The sole purpose for the disciples' presence was that they wanted to learn, grow, and evolve spiritually. Jesus did not keep them around because he was lonely or wanted them to start an organized religion and name it after him. The disciples stayed with Jesus because they loved him and wanted to be in the company of a benevolent SuperConscious Being, who was filled with God's Love for all Creation and which inevitably flowed onto them.

Matthew: Chapters 5, 6, 7, 8:1; Luke 6:20–49
Sermon on the Mount

This contains all later writers' interpretations of things they felt Jesus would have or should have said. Once again, it is glaringly evident these writers wanted to capture the allegorical flair of Jesus' teachings.

The fact is neither of these Evangelists, Matthew or Luke, were present when Jesus was speaking. Later-day writers were not present when the Gospels were being created. Later-day writers of the New Testament also had ulterior motives for directing the impressionable earth human consciousness away from the individual, toward the goal of adherence to their message. Sequacious compliance is subtlely being administered in some passages, which was not even remotely what Jesus desired or upon which he conducted his existence.

Matthew 8:5–13 Luke 7:1–10
Centurion Servant

Jesus did heal a centurion's son, who was stricken with palsy. The rest of the account states that the Jewish elders summoned Jesus to heal the son. The elevated centurion commander of many soldiers felt unworthy of Jesus entering his house or of being in Jesus' presence. He was determined to have Jesus heal his son, so the centurion asked Jesus to just say the word so his son would be healed. Other than Jesus healing the centurion's son, the whole story is a fictionalization and in no aspect ever took place.

Luke 7:11–17
Widow's Son at Nain

Jesus raised a widow's dead son while the son was on the bier about to be buried. This event also did not happen—another completely false miracle not attributable to Jesus.

Matthew 11:2–30, Luke 7:18–35
Baptist John's Last Message

This section also did not occur. The writers desired a separation of Jesus from John. The writers wrote what they perceived Jesus would have said or what they wanted to believe and convince others he did say. The Truth is that Jesus neither said any of these passages as they are presented, nor did he convey any of these allegorically cryptic messages. The fact is that John did not have any final communication exchanges of any sort with Jesus before he (John) was beheaded by Herod Antipas.

Luke 7:36–50
Jesus' Feet Anointed Before Simon the Pharisee

This is the story of the sinning woman who sheds tears on Jesus' feet, then wipes them with her hair and kisses his Holy feet—thus, her sins are forgiven. While Jesus' feet certainly were deserving of all the anointing kisses and loving attention purportedly received, this incident simply did not occur.

Luke 8:1–3
Jesus' Preaching Companions

The merry band did continue to grow. This entry is inclined to portray a second teaching tour being launched, when in actuality it was one continuous, divinely guided and supernally orchestrated journey. This is the first time later-day writers brought into the scriptures Jesus' wife, Mary, known as "The Magdalen." Mary was from the village of Magdala in Galilee. With regard to Jesus and Mary Magdalen, there was amongst his disciples a lot of petty jealousy. The later-day writers were not kind to her, either. In addition, these writers further convolute the history of Mary Magdalen by also referring to her as Mary of Bethany.

In the Gospel of Phillip from the Nag Hammadhi Scrolls, there is written evidence of the resentment being generated by the apostles—especially Peter—regarding Jesus' preference of Mary over the disciples. In Luke, Mary is described as having seven devils or evil spirits extracted from her being. While Jesus indeed was purging evil energies and entities from many people during his Holy Life, Mary Magdalen was not one of these people. She neither had any unholiness within her, nor was she in any way associated with prostitution. When she and Jesus were wed, she actually was a virgin in the purest sense of the word.

Matthew 12:22–45, Mark 3:20–30, Luke 11:14–23
Fanning the Divisive Flames and the Eternal Sin

Here, a blind, dumb, and possessed man is brought before Jesus and Jesus heals him. The Pharisees and scribes were accusing Jesus of casting out demons and devils through machinations of the devil Beelzebub. Jesus also calls anyone who directs blasphemy against the Holy Spirit to have created an eternal sin from which no forgiveness ever is forthcoming. Jesus declares anyone who blasphemes to have an unclean spirit. He also declares that every idle word someone utters will render them accountable on their judgment day. Thus, by one's words, they are either justified or condemned. The Pharisees and scribes ask for a sign so they can believe. Jesus responds by mentioning Jonah and the whale-of-a-tale nonsense, utters some allegoric passages, and chastises the Pharisees and scribes.

To begin with, this whole incident never occurred—it was merely the product of later-day writers. Jesus did heal people and did facilitate the dispensation of maleficent spirits from people, but not in this case. Jesus did not in this case defend his actions against accusatory Pharisees and scribes. He also never would have indicated that any transgression—even one directed against God—would be an eternal sin. He knew, and now you know, that all sins are expungeable. There exists no such transgression as an eternal or mortal sin. This simply is fear-mongering, done in order to reel in the theological adherents.

Matthew 12:46–50, Mark 3:31–35, Luke 8:19–21
Jesus' Brethren

In this incident, Jesus was speaking to a large group when his mother, wife, and the disciples wanted to speak to him. He answered by saying, "Whoever does the will of my Father, which is in Heaven, he is my brother, sister, and mother." Jesus did say this, and this event actually did occur. He did refer to God as his Father, and indeed did understand all earth humankind to be his brethren.

Matthew 13:1–53, Mark 4:1–34, Luke 8:4–18
Parables by the Sea

Once again, some very nice parables, but none were directly attributable to Jesus.

Matthew 8:18, 23–27, Mark 4:35–41, Luke 8:22–25
Rebuke the Tempest

Jesus and his disciples are crossing the sea when a storm erupts. Jesus quells the storm. This incident never happened.

Matthew 8:28–34, Mark 5:1–20, Luke 8:26–39
The Gadarene Demoniacs

In this incident Jesus met with one or two men (depending upon which evangelist) afflicted with devils. In Mark and Luke, the afflicted being was named Legion, for many devils and demons inhabited his body. The demons within Legion asked Jesus for permission to run Legion into a herd of 2,000 pigs—and then subsequently enter into the pigs, vacating the coinhabited man. Jesus agreed, and the then-possessed pigs—apparently all 2,000 of them—ran and drowned in the sea.

Afterward, the demon-free man was sitting around, conversing with Jesus when the villagers happened upon them. After explaining the situation, the villagers chased away Jesus, but Legion still went and published the entire incident in the Decapolis. Now this, of course, never happened in any way, shape, or form.

Matthew 9:1, 18–26, Mark 5:21–43, Luke 8:40–56
Jairus' Daughter is Raised

In this incident, a ruler of a local synagogue named Jairus pleaded with Jesus to bring his either dead or dying 12-year-old daughter (depending on which evangelist) back to life or save her life. On the way to the daughter, an ailing woman touched Jesus' cloak and was healed of a blood disease. Jesus felt the healing life force leave his body, he addressed the crowd, and inquired to know who had been healed. She came forth, made her admission, was assured that her faith had healed her, and was told to go in peace. By the time Jesus arrived at Jairus' house, his daughter had passed on to the Astral Realm. Jesus calmly explained that she was only asleep—and promptly brought her soul back into her body. Neither of these events occurred, although when Jesus did actually heal people, the SuperConscious life force was drained from his essence, and to him, it certainly would be noticeable.

Matthew 9:27–34
Two Blind Men and a Dumb Demoniac

Jesus was passing by two blind men who were calling out for mercy. Jesus replied, "According to your faith, be it done unto you." They were able to see and he asked them to remain silent about it. However, they spread the news across the land. Shortly after that, Jesus cast out a devil from a dumb man. The Pharisees said, "By the prince of the devils casteth he out devils." The only truth in this incident is that this entry continued to fan the anti-Pharisee flames.

Matthew 9:35, Mark 6:6
Third Preaching Tour

Jesus did go around the villages teaching and healing, so these two entries are true.

Matthew 9:36–11:1, Mark 6:7–13, Luke 9:1–6
Mission of Twelve Disciples

In this entry Jesus is instructing his disciples and warning them of the troubles yet to come. Here Jesus is giving his disciples the authority to cast out devils, heal the sick, and cure diseases. They also would be commanded by God to speak God's Words. Brother would rise up against brother, fathers against children, and children against parents and cause them to be put to death. The disciples will be the most hated of all men for Jesus' name's sake. He that endureth to the end, those will be saved. Jesus tells his disciples that he does not send peace, but rather a sword. This sounds more like Alexander the Great, rather than Jesus the Christ. This ridiculous entry needs no further explanation regarding its authenticity or source validity. It is complete nonsense and never happened.

Matthew 14:1–12, Mark 6:14–29, Luke 9:7–9
John the Baptist Beheaded

Herod Antipas had John the Baptist beheaded, purportedly because John was chastising Herod for marrying his brother Phillip's wife, Herodias. Herodias' daughter performed a dance that so pleased Herod that he promised to give her anything she wanted. She conferred with her mother, Herodias, and it was decided they wanted John's head. So, it was with great dismay that Herod grudgingly agreed to keep his oath, thus delivering up John's head. However, this was not really the truth. These were not exactly nice people. Many years before, Herod the Great had his own son, Aristobulus, executed. Aristobulus' son, Herod Agrippa I, age 3 at the time, was spared. Herod Agrippa's uncle was Herod Antipas. All of them were Jewish rulers who recognized and adhered to Greek Hellenistic practices.

John indeed was beheaded by Herod Antipas. It actually had nothing to do with Herodias or her daughter. The reason for his fate really was a combination of his accrued karmic debt and a personal issue involving John and Herod Agrippa I. Herod Antipas had no love for John. In fact, the Holy Sanctioned Angel tells me, he apparently hated John, as did his nephew Herod Agrippa I, who grew to dislike all Christians. They were vehemently opposed to baptizing. The Holy Sanctioned Angel informs me that the blame for John's physical demise is exclusively due to nephew Herod Agrippa's influence over his uncle regarding baptizing. For John's death, all blame purposely was diverted onto Herod Antipas, Herodias, and her daughter.

Matthew 14:13–23, Mark 6:30–46, Luke 9:10–17, John 6:1–15
Feeding the Masses

In this story, after healing some sick people, Jesus and his disciples are faced with feeding five thousand hungry men, women, and children— with only five barley loaves of bread and two paltry fish. They all ate their fill, and after everyone was finished, there were enough fish and scraps of bread left over to fill twelve baskets. At that time, Jesus and the disciples fled the masses to the other shore, for the masses wanted to make Jesus their king. After fleeing to the opposite shore, Jesus retreated into the mountain to pray.

Finally, this passage reveals some actual Truth. Jesus did perform a miracle with the fish and loaves of bread. One thousand people were fed during the event, but apparently there were no leftovers. The group did flee to the other side of the sea, and Jesus did retreat to pray. He definitely would be feeling drained after the miraculous ordeal—and certainly would desire to be reenergized with Holiness.

Matthew 14:24–36, Mark 6:47–56, John 6:16–21
Jesus Walks on Water

Jesus' disciples were leading back across the sea while Jesus still was praying. A tempest blew and the boat threatened to capsize. Jesus appeared, and if they hadn't cried out to be saved, may have passed them by. In Matthew, Peter walks on the water with Jesus, starts to sink, is chided for his lack of faith, and then is saved by Jesus. The winds calm and the sea turns tranquil. They arrive on shore and people swarm to just touch Jesus' garments and to be healed. Jesus did not walk on the water. This whole event is pure fiction.

John 6:22–71
Bread of Life

Jesus is saying that the spirit of God only is accessible if you go first to Jesus. Physical sustenance (Moses and manna from Heaven is mentioned) only is temporarily filling, but lasting satiation or eternal fulfillment is achieved only by believing and going through Jesus, the Christian theology, and receiving the Christian sacraments of bread and wine. At the end, Jesus makes mention about Judas and alludes to having knowledge of his impending betrayal by Judas as a devil.

This entry clearly shows the motivations of the later-day writers and their determined intentions. John clearly doesn't understand omniscience, omnipotence, and omnipresence. If these concocters did understand these concepts, they never would write such misleading nonsense. We already have covered the serious transgression one incurs when assuming unsanctioned Divine Authority.

All souls are immortal. Once Made Manifest, a soul never is dissolved, and does not die. Bodies come and go with consecutive incarnations—but the soul is eternally contained in the Astral and Causal containers until its evolution allows it to once again recognize itself as SuperConsciousness.

Jesus did not ever say anything to deify himself. He knew the Truth by being of the Truth. He never wanted a religious theology to do this to his name, essence, or to mislead others in a deliberate manner. There certainly is no mystery why God and the Holy Realm desires, directs, and carefully guides each and every entry of this book. Jesus was speaking words of Eternal Truth. However, Jesus was not speaking those words purported in John 6:22-65. Jesus was aware of Judas' betrayal before the last supper, so that entry indeed was True.

Matthew 15:1–20, Mark 7:1–23
Eating with Dirty Hands

In this entry, Jesus is taking the Pharisees and scribes to task for chiding the unhygienic habits of his disciples. The Pharisees were meticulous about cleanliness and were offended by the disciples' slovenliness. Jesus quickly turns the issue around to represent outer versus inner cleanliness. He vocalizes a parable about Moses with regard to honoring and supporting parents. Basically, he is teaching that the defilement is what comes out of a person in words and actions, indicating the relative cleanliness or dirtiness of that person's soul. Once again, this entry is meaningful and to some minimal extent carries some truthful messages.

However, Jesus never spoke these messages and he did not actually have chastising exchanges with the Pharisees.

PART VI

Matthew 15:21–28, Mark 7:24–30
Third Period of the Galilean Teachings

Jesus encounters a Syrophoenician woman. The woman implores Jesus to exorcize an evil essence from her daughter. This incident occurred and Jesus did heal her daughter from this affliction. Jesus knew that the devil did not exist. However, Jesus did recognize an evil or unauthorized entity within the daughter's physical being.

Matthew 15:29–31, Mark 7:31–37
Jesus Continues Miraculous Healings

Jesus continued to perform many miracles and heal many people of their ailments.

Matthew 15:32–38, Mark 8:1–9
Jesus Feeds Four Thousand

In this entry Jesus performed another miracle where 4,000 people were fed with a few fish and seven loaves of bread. This incident did not occur. There was only one miraculous feeding of fish and loaves.

Matthew 15:39, 16:1–2, Mark 8:10–21
The Pharisees' and Sadducees' Demands

Here, the Pharisees and Sadducees are asking for a sign from Jesus to ensure he truly is God's Son. Jesus replies by telling them a parable about signs and Jonah. Then the disciples enter into the boat and head for the other shore. They forgot their bread, and Jesus tells another parable about taking heed and being aware of the Pharisees' and Sadducees' bread. This parable relates to Christianity being holier than Judaism. Jesus never said any of it.

Mark 8:22–26
Slow to Recover Sight

Jesus places spit on a blind man's eyes and asks if he can see. The man only partially sees humans looking like walking trees, so Jesus tries again. Presto! The man sees 20/20. Jesus sends him away with instructions to never again enter this village. This never happened. The Holy Sanctioned Angel communicated directly with Jesus, and Jesus concurred that he never gave sight to anyone blind.

Matthew 16:13–20, Mark 8:27–30, Luke 9:18–21
Peter's Confession

Jesus asks his disciples who the people think he is. They state, "John the Baptist, Elijah reincarnated prophet" (Luke 9:19). Then he directs the question at the disciples, and Simon Peter says, "The Christ of God." Jesus gives Peter the keys to the kingdom of heaven, then instructs them to keep it all secret. This exchange never happened. Jesus never promised the heavenly kingdom keys to Peter, for Jesus never asked such unevolved, egoistic, shallow questions. Jesus as SuperConsciousness did not need to ask them or anyone for validation.

Matthew 16:21–28, Mark 8:31–9:1, Luke 9:22–27
Jesus Foretells His Death and Resurrection

Jesus is telling his disciples of his upcoming death and resurrection, and that he will suffer greatly at the hands of the chief priest, scribes, and elders. Peter says to him, "This won't ever happen to you." After just bestowing upon Peter the keys to the kingdom of heaven, Jesus rebukes Peter by saying, "Get thee behind me, Satan. Thou mindeth the things of men, not God." Jesus says a few parables about picking up the cross and following him, and he talks about the value, what there is to be gained from this action.

Jesus neither said this to Peter, nor did he slyly infer to people in parables that one must follow this ministry in order to attain the highest levels of the kingdom of Astral heaven. All souls will eventually recognize themselves as Made Manifest SuperConsciousness and far in the futurity be once again reunited as Uncreated Infinite SuperConsciousness. However, this particular New Testament entry does not imply this

Truth. Jesus recognized himself as a "Son of his Father," not a Son of Man in the big picture sense of the term. Ezekiel was a Son of Man, and Jesus easily could distinguish SuperConsciously the difference between Son of Man and Son of God.

Matthew 17:1–13, Mark 9:2–13, Luke 9:28–36
The Transfiguration

In this event, Jesus took Peter, James, and John up to the mountain where Jesus was illuminated and transformed into his spirit form, appearing to them as bright as the sun. Moses and Elijah appeared before them and Peter asked to erect three tabernacles. While speaking, a voice came from a bright cloud, stating, "This is my beloved son in whom I am well pleased, hear ye him." (Matthew 17:5) When they arose from the ground where they had fallen in fear, no one save Jesus was there. Jesus asked them to maintain silence about it, and further explained it is written that Elijah first must come to set things right—that the Son of Man must suffer, which they presumed must be John the Baptist.

None of this happened. It is complete fiction.

Matthew 17:14–20, Mark 9:14–29, Luke 9:37–45
A Demoniac Boy

This circumstance brought a desperate man to the disciples with his possessed son from whom a demon could not be exorcized by the disciples. After the disciples' failure, Jesus rebuked the unclean spirit, and from that moment, the son was cured. This incident also never happened.

Matthew 17:22–23, Mark 9:30–32, Luke 9:43–45
Jesus Prognosticates his Death and Resurrection

Jesus tells his disciples the Son of Man is to be delivered into the hands of men to be killed. This he did do, only he called himself "Son of the Father." Whenever Jesus spoke of himself to his disciples, he referred to himself as "Son of the Father."

Matthew 17:24–27, Mark 9:33
The Shekel in the Fish's Mouth

The Capernaum taxman came to collect a half-shekel in taxes due to the Romans. Before the taxman could ask Jesus for the tax, Jesus read his mind and said a parable, stating that the Son of the Earth should be free, but go to the sea, catch a fish—in whose mouth there will be double the tax—one full shekel. While a clever parable like many others, Jesus never said it—and the incident never happened.

Matthew 18:1, Mark 9:33–50, Luke 9:46–50
Humility and Forgiveness

Once again, here are many parables, some inflammatory and some could be interpreted as truth. However, Jesus did not mention one of these.

John 7:1–52
Jesus at the Feast of Tabernacles

In this passage, the Jews want to kill Jesus. The Jews accused Jesus of having a devil in him. Jesus claimed that Moses gave them circumcision, which can be conducted on the Sabbath—but healings cannot? Basically, the Jews state that when the real Christ (Messiah) comes, he'll perform more miraculous works than does this man (Jesus). They didn't kill Jesus then, for his hour was not yet up. The event builds, but in the end, nothing comes of it. The men sent by the scribes and Pharisees return, touting Jesus as the Christ or Messiah. Later-day Christian composers continued to build the case against the Pharisees, merely concocting the whole fictitious event, which never happened.

John 7:53, 8:1–11
Adulteress Woman

The Pharisees and scribes caught a woman in the act of adultery. They brought her to Jesus and exclaimed that the book of Moses says she is to be stoned—and "What do you, Jesus, have to say about her?" Jesus says, "He without sin cast the first stone." In the end, they all leave—except the woman. Jesus exclaims, "I don't condemn thee. Go thy way and sin no more." This also never happened. Jesus knew the Truth regarding both Moses and the messages in the Ten Commandments, as did Moses himself. So, if this ever would have occurred, Jesus would have straightened out their perceptions about Moses right away. Again, later-day writers toss yet another stone of accusation at the Pharisees and scribes.

John 8:12–30
Jesus—The Light of the World

These passages are deeply philosophical and nicely conceptualized. Nonetheless, the fact is that Jesus did not say these things.

Jesus did not ever say, "I am He," and that "I do nothing of myself but as the Father taught me I speak these things." Jesus was not taught, he was Omniscient. Thus, whatever he perceived, he simultaneously comprehended. As SuperConsciousness, Jesus eventually attuned himself to comprehend without even having to perceive.

John 8:31–59
Spiritual Freedom

Here, Jesus engages in active dialogue revolving around salvation. The Jews proclaim their lineage to Abraham. Jesus concurs, but further chastises them by stating that if they were of the seed of Abraham, they should act like him. They call Jesus a Samaritan who has a devil in him. Eventually, the Jews pick up stones to cast at him, but Jesus hid himself— and then ran out of the temple.

This is yet another case of blaming the Jews. Here a fictional case is building against the Jewish scapegoats. Jesus as SuperConsciousness knew the Truth about Abraham. This whole exchange never took place.

PART VII

Matthew 19:1–2, 8:18–22, Mark 10:1, Luke 9: 51–62
Final Galilean Days

Jesus is speaking in rich, interpretively deep and meaningful parables. The problem is that Jesus did NOT speak in parables. It was not necessary for him to flex his SuperConscious might by egoistically creating complex allegories with which to baffle the masses. The simple fact is "never did he so spake" in parable—at all. Jesus spoke with eloquent metaphor and deep common sense, which everyone could understand. He emitted Love and compassion, benevolence and goodness. It was not necessary for him to dazzle the crowds with the articulated complexities that the later-day writers felt necessary for the deified Jesus to do.

The Pharisees and scribes had differences of opinion, much in the same way devout adherents of the message will have with this book. The later-day writers had several manipulating purposes for how they portrayed God and Jesus.

Luke 10:1–24
Seventy With a Mission

In this section Jesus is sending out his disciples two by two, as lambs going into the midst of wolves, to preach and teach, heal the sick, raise the dead, cleanse the lepers, and cast out devils. They are not to receive or take anything with them. The seventy returned, joyously exclaiming that even the mere mention of Jesus' name was enough to evict the devil out of plagued, possessed beings. Jesus himself states that he saw Satan, fallen like lightning from heaven. Jesus empowered his legions with the authority to tread upon scorpions and serpents, and ordained them with complete, masterful power over enemies without fear of harm or reprisal.

Jesus also grants himself the power to reveal God to anyone he chooses. Jesus assures everyone that all of these things were pleasing to God. Then, in a self-congratulatory manner, Jesus states that the disciples need to be grateful for all the miraculous holy works and deeds they have experienced.

In these three paragraphs there is a tremendous amount of caustic untruth. The Absolute Truth is that Jesus never did any of this. Jesus never once ordained anyone to go forth and do any preaching, teaching, healing, exorcizing, or leper-cleansing. Jesus never sent his disciples out for any of these purposes. No earth human being ever has been sanctioned by God to ordain others in any remote way. To attempt to do so or assume such authority to do so would be a transgression against God. As Omniscient SuperConsciousness, Jesus knew better and never did any such things.

Luke 10:25–37
Good Samaritan

A lawyer questioned Jesus, "What shall I do to inherit eternal life?" Jesus replied, "Tell me what you think." The lawyer responded, "Love the Lord thy God with all thy heart, and with all thy soul, and with all thy strength, and with all thy mind, and thy neighbor as thyself." Jesus replied, "You are correct." The man further inquired, "Who is thy neighbor?" Jesus told him the good Samaritan story, one familiar and loved by many, but one by which many rarely abide.

Like most of the others, this event never happened. For one thing, eternal life IS every incarnated soul's God-gifted right as a Made Manifest consciousness. Thus, while still being a very benevolent answer, the lawyer's response is false. Eternal life IS the Made Manifest conscious experience, whether in our spirit or physical form.

Luke 10:38–42
Jesus Visits Martha and Mary

Mary and Martha are sisters whom Jesus visits. Martha is relegated to kitchen details, while sister Mary is basking in the radiant Holiness of Jesus' overflowing cup of goodness. This excerpt reveals a little sisterly rivalry and jealousy. Jesus explains to Martha that Mary chose the better of the two positions, and to not take anything away from her. This incident also did not happen, and the two women were not even biological sisters. They were sisters in the same way Jesus looked at humanity as his brethren.

John 9:1–41
Giving Sight to Man Blind from Birth

Jesus explains that a particular blind man is blind not due to the sin of his parents or the man himself, but rather for Jesus to show everyone the miracles of which he is capable. He takes spit and clay—and this time gets it right on the first try. Now the man can see. Unfortunately, Jesus once again is giving sight to a blind person on the Sabbath. Back then, the (Jewish) Sabbath was a big deal and a recognized day of rest. However, Jesus never directly was reprimanded by the Pharisees for healings occurring on a Sabbath Saturday. Once again, the writers continue to build their case against the Pharisees. The entire event is complete fiction, with no aspect of it ever happening.

John 10:1–21
The Good Shepherd

Jesus is talking in parables about people needing to pass through him directly in order to unite with God. He himself is the good shepherd uniting all the people of the world as one flock with one shepherd. Jesus states, "I have the power to lay my life down and take it up again," causing amongst the Jews another division over whether he "hath a devil or is mad."

This overt section is very deceptive and coercive in its intentions to ensure that everyone goes through Jesus alone in order to unite with God. Jesus never said anything remotely similar and would never condone such misleading unGodliness. After his Transimplanting process, Jesus did have the power to lay down his life and pick it back up again. However, prior to this Transimplanting process, Jesus did not have this power.

John 10:22–42
Jesus at the Feast of Dedication

The Jews are asking Jesus if he is the Christ. He utters an allegory about sheep, his Father, and miracles, after which the Jews want to stone him. He further castigates them when they accuse him of blasphemy. Jesus exits to the land beyond the Jordan. This event never happened; in fact at no time during Jesus' life did the Jews ever intend or even threaten to stone him.

Luke 11:1–13
Discourse on Prayer

Jesus teaches his disciples the "Lords Prayer," then offers another parable, "Ask and you shall receive." The disciples never knew the "Lords Prayer," for it didn't exist yet at that time. Also, one may ask yet still not receive. Even in the symbolic sense of the saying, it would be easy to misinterpret the receiving aspect of the request. The receiving is based on deep complexities beyond earth human comprehension. This reflecting answer most often is based on a Deeply Comprehended need—many times out of thoughtful reach of the requester, not predicated upon humanly perceived desires. Dharmic, free-will, and karmic factors all contribute to the response. One always can ask, but many times the answer is misunderstood or unrecognized.

Matthew 12:22–32, Mark 3:22–30, Luke 11:14–54
Jesus Fustigates the Pharisees

In these entries, Jesus uses parables to attack the Pharisees with clever elocution. The problem is that it never happened. Jesus never engaged even once in verbal admonishments of the Pharisees. These entries are inflammatory and certainly unbecoming of a benevolent SuperConsciousness.

Luke 12:1–59
Jesus Teaches Trust in God and Judgment

Jesus starts attacking the hypercritical Pharisees, after which he says that all aspects of existence are known, that there are no permanent secrets. He also says that if you don't believe in Jesus, you won't be admitted into heaven. Jesus goes on to recite many parables, including Matthew 10:34-36, where Jesus claims he does not come to earth to bring peace, but rather to divide humankind. Jesus did not ever speak in fancy parables. He spoke in plain Hebrew to plain, simple people.

Luke 13:1–9
Pilate Slays the Galileans

Jesus is talking about repentance and a parable. Jesus did teach about repentance and accountability for one's own sins. Jesus also shared with the masses the Truth about reincarnation, salvation, resurrection, and soul immortality.

Luke 13:10–21
Jesus Heals a Woman on the Sabbath

Jesus has a heated exchange with the ruler of a synagogue for healing a woman from an eighteen-year crippling infirmity on the Sabbath. Jesus asserts that a daughter of Abraham who was bound by Satan should be healed on the Sabbath. This incident did not happen as portrayed, plus Jesus would not be mindful of recognizing any day as a Sabbath. He also would not recognize a "daughter of Abraham"—unless in the biological sense of the term, this was the case. The Holy Sanctioned Angel said no females who were afflicted with demons exorcized by Jesus were of any genetic affiliation to Abraham.

Luke 13:22–30
Few Are Saved

Jesus is talking about who gets to be saved and who is relegated to observing Abraham, Isaac, and Jacob from outside the kingdom of God. Jesus never inquired or sought to know the truth about Abraham, Isaac, and Jacob, something the configuring adherents obviously also could not have known. This never was spoken by Jesus. Jesus actually posed the question regarding the validity of the scriptures he read.

Luke 13:31–35
The Pharisees' Warning about Herod

The Pharisees warn Jesus about Herod wanting to kill him. Jesus talks about how all prophets in Jerusalem are stoned and killed. This event also never happened.

Luke 14:1–24
Trouble with the Ruling Pharisee

Jesus was breaking bread on the Sabbath with the ruling Pharisee, when he notices a man with dropsy. Jesus healed the man, then defended his actions against the Pharisees and lawyers. The writers have Jesus conveying numerous messages in several allegoric stories and parables. Jesus did speak in humble, eloquent allegory—but not in this case. These allegories were not any that Jesus ever spoke.

Luke 14:25–35
Counting Costs

Jesus is talking about people bearing their own cross and following in his footsteps, becoming his disciples. He shares allegories, in which he states that one always considers the costs of an endeavor before beginning, otherwise, they may be incapable of completing the purpose. However, Jesus never shared any of these allegories.

Luke 15:1–32
Three Parables

In this entry all the sinners and publicans are gathered around Jesus, and the Pharisees and scribes have taken notice. He responds with three parables in reference to being lost and then having been recovered. These are very nice parables, except they are misleading, with hidden, underlying, divisive innuendos directed against the Pharisees. Simultaneously, they imply that lost souls find their way back to God through Christianity alone. Jesus did not utter these parables.

Luke 16:1–31
Two Parables

In these parables Jesus is speaking about the incongruity of serving two masters. Then he is falsely accusing the Pharisees of being lovers of money, when it was the Sadducees who were inclined toward materialistic pursuits. Jesus rails about John preaching the Gospels and about guilt over divorce being adultery. Jesus tells another parable exulting the virtues of Abraham and a merciless rich man. The rich man is condemned by Abraham to exist in the lowest region of the Astral Universe for eternity, and the man asks Abraham to at least save his five brethren from a similar fate. Abraham counters that these brethren have Moses and prophets to believe and would not believe that anyone would rise from the dead.

The first parable is directing everyone to have faith in God and not in material pursuits, which is fine—although Jesus never said it. The second one is more problematic. First, Abraham still is trying to work out his own karmic impactions, and is in no place to pass out judgments to any souls. Jesus as Omniscient, knew the Truth about Abraham, Moses, and the prophets—and simply would not utter an inaccurate parable or allegory.

Luke 17:1–10
Forgiveness and Faith

Jesus is teaching his disciples lessons pertaining to forgiveness and faith. As per the first lesson, forgiveness is imperative for upward enlightenment and attunement for salvation. In the second lesson, Jesus is talking about being satisfied with what our limitations are, recognizing our individual gifts and blessings, and being satisfied with the goodness we all have in our existences.

Jesus did not directly say either of these stories, but he definitely taught and articulated the value of such virtues. The value of faith was expounded upon in some of his teachings, but faith really is unnecessary when compared to trust. Jesus taught trust as a virtue far more often than he taught faith. However, faith was necessary for perpetuation of adherence. Consequently, faith is expounded upon far more frequently than trust, which really should have the emphasis.

John 11:1–46
Lazarus is Raised from the Dead

Jesus comes to the aid of Mary and Martha when their brother Lazarus is sick. By the time Jesus gets there four days late, Lazarus already has been entombed. Jesus calls for Lazarus to come out, and Lazarus obliges. The Pharisees then are informed. First of all, as previously mentioned, Mary and Martha are not biological sisters. Second, neither Mary nor Martha had a brother named Lazarus. Finally, Jesus did not interfere with Lazarus' dharmic plan. Jesus did not ever raise Lazarus (who did exist) from the dead.

John 11:47–54
Retreat to Ephraim

In this caustic entry the Pharisees and chief priests gathered together a council to decide how to do away with Jesus before the Romans would come and take away their place and nation. That year Caiaphas, the high priest, prophesied that they could put Jesus to death and the nation would continue. So, it was decided Jesus would be put to death. Afterward, Jesus couldn't go walking among the Jews. As such, he retreated with his disciples to Ephraim, near the wilderness. This is complete untruth. None of this fiction happened in any form. Caiaphas was a high-ranking Jewish elder during one of the years of Jesus' later adulthood, but had nothing to do with Jesus' crucifixion.

Luke: 17:11–19
Ten Lepers

Jesus and his group are passing through a village in Sumaria and Galilee. Ten lepers were healed and only one Samaritan returned to thank Jesus. This fictional event never occurred as it is portrayed. Jesus cured many, but actually never cured anyone of leprosy.

Luke 17:20–18:8
Kingdom Come

In this entry Jesus is asked by the Pharisees, "When does the kingdom of God come?" Jesus responded by telling them, "The kingdom of God is within you." He went on to talk about Noah and the destruction of everything. He talked about Lot and his wife. He spoke about God judging based on what is in one's life's intentions and pursuits. He ended with a parable about God avenging unrighteousness unless one has faith in Jesus himself as the Son of God.

Jesus never said any of this. First, these writers of Luke did not understand that the kingdom of God is Ominipresent. Later, it was amended to read "in the midst of you," which perhaps is more accurate, but still not totally correct. They also didn't understand the Omniscient comprehensions of Jesus. If they had, they would not have included fictional Noah and Lot in their zeal to put words into Jesus' mouth.

Luke 18:9–14
Pharisees and Publicans

The message here is about humility with the Pharisees and Publicans bearing the brunt of Jesus' acerbating verbiage. While the virtue of humility is held sacred by the Holy Realm, using it against others is not. Jesus did not say this or any other parable.

Matthew 19:3–12, Mark 10:2–12
Divorce

Jesus is talking about divorce to the Pharisees, who pressed him about the lawfulness of Moses' law on divorce. Jesus disputes Moses' law in favor of his own brand of divorce lawfulness. Jesus seems to be back on speaking terms with the Pharisees—at least these particular Pharisees. One might question what authority young, unmarried Moses would have, to allow him to say anything about divorce in 2100 BC. Even if one discounts all the Truths and believes the biblical Moses, what is the likelihood of a stiff divorce law being implemented in the time of Moses in 2100 BC?

Finally, Jesus makes fornication an exception to his rule of divorce disapproval. Jesus is stating that divorce is acceptable only in cases where a husband's wife is guilty of fornication with another partner. Once a man puts his wife away, she officially is held a captive or is otherwise spoken for. After she is put away, anyone who fornicates with her other than the partner who put her away is an adulterer and transgressor. In this same case, the put-away woman also is transgressing and an adulterer.

Jesus would not allow exceptions to be made regarding transgressions. Transgressions occur when karmic impaction results from errant free-will choices. Divorce is NOT a result of an errant free-will choice. For the record, fornication in adultery can be karmically impacting, and thus a transgression. In each case, transgression is dependent upon the intentions and thoughts of those involved. It is up to God to determine if a transgression has occurred. Sex in all its various forms is NOT a transgression. Divorce is not a transgression. Karmic indebtedness occurring from prior existences must have an opportunity to be resolved. Divorce allows for the potential resolution of unresolved imbalances, so that one can experience multiple human interactions (not just one interaction with one person) necessary to alleviate the indebtedness.

Human judgment and subsequent misperception regarding marriage, divorce, sex, abortion, and sexual partners contribute to human guilt-slopping behavior. When directed at one's self or others, such behavior creates binding chains of dualistic attachment. This is extremely karmically impacting and as a result, will require future debt alleviation. It is important for humans to allow themselves to fully experience a guilt-free existence.

Matthew 19:13–15, Mark 10:13–16, Luke 18:15–17
Jesus Blesses Children

In this case, Jesus is blessing little children whom the disciples rebuked. The fact is, even Jesus did not have the authority or sanctioning to bless anyone or anything. Only the Uncreated Infinite SuperConsciousness blesses with incontrovertibility. No manifesting existence is God-sanctioned to consecrate, transubstantiate, bless, or speak on God's behalf. In contrast, being thankful, prayerful, or blessedly grateful for abundance, benevolence, or sacredness bestowed upon someone or something—such as a prayer before a meal—is perfectly acceptable. The distinction is in not assuming God-authority.

The distinction between transgression and praise is that the former involves one's ego, but the latter activates humility.

Matthew 19:16–30; 20:1–16, Mark 10:17–31, Luke 18:18–30
Rich Young Ruler

In this section Jesus is expounding the virtues of Moses' Ten Commandments and what it takes for anyone especially rich to enter into the gates of heaven. In other words, give all your possessions over to the Church, and you're guaranteed a spot in heaven, inheriting eternal life. If you renounce all of your assets to the Church, you will be saved and sit upon a throne in heaven, judging the twelve tribes of Israel.

This is extremely problematic, for spiritual wealth is not measured by external interpretations. Most Christians pragmatically follow this entry and unnecessarily bear the burden of enormous guilt for their asset accumulation. Then tithing came along, which called for the allocation of 10 percent of one's assets to the Church. The act of tithing solved three problems. First, by ensuring its perpetual, permanent income through weekly annuity flow, tithing made the Church the largest, most violent and powerful franchise on the planet.

Second, it provided the adherents an outlet for weekly guilt elimination. No longer would guilt compile whenever members realized they weren't being good Christians by not giving 100 percent of their wealth to the Church—their supposed duty. In reality, a person's spiritual wealth is not determined through their generosity at collection plate time. Third, tithing guaranteed eternal life and ensured a front-row seat in heaven for judging the comings and goings of the people still here—the twelve tribes of Israel—which, of course, is complete nonsense.

Matthew 20:17–19, Mark 10:32–34, Luke 18:31–34
Jesus Foretells Crucifixion

Jesus tells his disciples of his impending crucifixion. He did do this, and they did not understand. He did NOT say to them that after three days he would resurrect.

Matthew 20:20–28, Mark 10:35–45
Ambition of James and John

Brothers James and John are petitioning Jesus to be located at Jesus' right and left hands in the kingdom of heaven. They are willing to pay the price for the honor. Jesus explains it is not his place to say, but those places are for whomever God determines them to be. Then Jesus alludes to his giving his life as a ransom for many souls.

This event never took place. James and John never asked Jesus for this placement. Jesus did not have the say in the placement of any souls' attunement within the Spirit Realm.

Matthew 20:29–34, Mark 10:46–52, Luke 18:35–43
Blind Men of Jericho

In Matthew, Jesus and his disciples were passing by two blind men. In Mark and Luke, they were passing by one blind man. The blind call out to Jesus to open their eyes and give them sight. Jesus declared, "Your faith has saved you. Go in peace." They received their sight and followed Jesus and the group. This never happened; in fact, Jesus did not grant the gift of sight to any blind person or people.

Luke 19:1–10
Stay with Zacchaeus

Jesus stays at the home of Zacchaeus, a known chief publican. Zacchaeus promises to give away half of his wealth to the poor. Jesus bestows salvation upon Zacchaeus, who purportedly also is a son of Abraham. Jesus did not transgress against God in such a way. This event never happened.

Luke 19:11–28
Parable of the Nobleman

Jesus tells a parable about a wealthy nobleman who instructs his servants to tend to his financial affairs while he is away. When the nobleman returns, the man asks for a financial recounting of their holdings. The servants are asked to produce their tradings. One has doubled the money, one has increased the money by half, and one has only one tenth of the original sum. The nobleman takes the one tenth and gives it to the man who has doubled the amount. The nobleman states, "To he who hath shall be given; he who hath not shall be taken from." Jesus did not ever say this—or any other—parable.

Matthew 26:6–13, Mark 14:3–9, John 11:55–57, 12:1–11
Mary of Bethany Anoints Jesus

Jesus is anointed with a spikenard by Mary of Bethany (Magdalen). Judas is perturbed and states they could have sold the oil instead and given the money to the poor. Mary of Bethany is then busy preparing a meal, and her unrelated brother Lazarus is present. Jesus states that Mary is preparing him for his upcoming burial. Furthermore, Jesus states that the poor always will be there, but he himself will not. Then, of course, the Jews—who intently are looking for Jesus—hear that Lazarus is there, too, and decide to put him to death, as well (John 12:9-11).

Mary did anoint her husband, Jesus, at this event. Mary indeed used a spikenard. Jesus knew of his impending ordeal and was being divinely guided by his SuperConscious perceptions. Judas was not there, and there weren't any disciples who questioned the purpose of the anointing. Mary did not prepare their meal, and Lazarus was not present. Jesus did state he was preparing for his crucifixion and the disciples, indeed, were confused.

Lazarus had not been raised from the dead, and at the time there was no confusion about that fact. At the time, the Jews were not seeking Jesus or Lazarus or looking to put Lazarus to death.

PART VIII

Matthew 21:1–11, Mark 11:1–11, Luke 19:29–44, John 12:12–19
Passion Week: Arrival to Resurrection, Entry Into Jerusalem
on Sunday

Jesus sends two disciples to get an ass and her colt, upon which no one or nothing ever had sat. Jesus instructs them if anyone asks or stops them, to tell them the Lord needs them. Upon entering Jerusalem, the vast crowds heard Jesus was coming. They took palm branches, and along with their garments, laid them before the procession. Along with the disciples, the vast multitudes all were singing, rejoicing, and praising Jesus, David, and the Lord. Of course, this raised the ire of the Pharisees.

Jesus did enter Jerusalem. He did not direct his disciples where to find and steal a couple of donkeys. With his entourage, he walked into Jerusalem. It was a humble, somber procession without crowds, fanfare, or singing. People witnessed the procession, but it was not a reveling, joyous, or gala affair. The Pharisees did not notice or pay attention to the procession, which actually entered on a Tuesday.

Matthew 21:18–22, Mark 11:12–14
Cursing the Fig Tree

Jesus took out his wrath on an out-of-season fig tree that when cursed, withered and died. Jesus stated, "If you have faith, you can command a mountain to cast itself into the sea." Jesus did not take out his wrath on a defenseless, out-of-season fig tree, to proclaim his powers to move mountains.

Matthew 21:12–17, Mark 11:15–19, Luke 19:45–48, John 2:13–22
Second Cleansing of the Temple

The same Truth applies, verbatim, as per the First Cleansing excerpt.

Matthew 21:20–22, Mark 11:20–25
The Fig Tree Now Withered

As they are passing by it the next morning, Peter points out to Jesus the withered fig tree Jesus had cursed. No defenseless fig trees—or any other existence—were cursed by Jesus during his incarnation.

Matthew 21:23–27, Mark 11:27–33, Luke 20:1–8
Jesus' Authority is Challenged

In this case, the scribes and chief priests are inquiring by whose authority is Jesus sanctioned to perform miracles? Jesus responds by asking them if John the Baptist was sanctioned by heaven to conduct baptisms. They answer by replying, "We don't know." If they replied, "Heaven," Jesus would ask them why they did not believe John. If they replied, "Men," they would fear reprisal and getting stoned to death—for the masses were convinced John indeed was a prophet. In the end, Jesus responds, "I am not telling you upon whose authority I conduct miracles."

First of all, this incident never occurred. Second, such human authority is not recognized, for God alone performs miracles—either through earth humankind, or without earth humankind's assistance. The God-sanctioning of someone is not a prerequisite for miracles to occur. Third, all of God's Creation is a miracle without any of earth humankind's knowledge, input, or assistance whatsoever. The Sanhedrin did keep an eye on John the Baptist, and was opposed to his baptizing. However, it was the factors of karma, Herod Antipas, and nephew Herod Agrippa I that were fully responsible for John's head.

Matthew 21:28–46, 22:1–14, Mark 12:1–12, Luke 20:9–19
Three Warning Parables

Jesus spoke three parables. The first involved a man and his two sons, one whom he requested to work in the vineyard, who did so after initially refusing. The other son said he'd go and did not do so. Jesus asked them who did the will of his (the sons') father? They replied, "The first." Jesus answered, "Correct," and compared the situation described to the publicans, harlots, and John the Baptist. Jesus goes on to say that John the Baptist was not believed except by the publicans and harlots when everyone also should have repented and believed him.

The second parable involved a man who had planted a vineyard and went off, leaving the vineyard in the care of others. He sent many servants and even his own son out to retrieve the fruits. All were killed or badly mishandled; even the son was killed. Then Jesus asked the disciples what would come of the caretakers. The disciples responded that the man would return and destroy the caretakers and entrust the vineyard to new caretakers. Jesus responds that the rejected stone becomes the cornerstone. The Pharisees and chief priests heard these parables and perceived that it was to them that Jesus was referring.

The last parable was about the king who prepared a huge marriage feast for his son, to which no one came. However, everyone made excuses or killed the servants. In response, the king—in all his evolved wisdom—sent out his armies and destroyed the potential guests and burned their city. He sent more servants out into the land and on the highways and invited everyone to the marriage feast. Everyone was there, good and bad alike. However, one man was not dressed properly, and was bound—hand and foot—and cast out into the darkness to wail and gnash his teeth. The parable concludes with the statement "For many are called, but few chosen."

These dissections of parables probably are boring to most—and to nonChristians, completely unfamiliar. However, the point is to allow for the purposeful dissemination of the stagnant energy—not necessarily to successfully explain to everyone the intention of the parable.

We know Jesus did not speak in parables, so he personally did not put out these stories. The first story advocates baptism, and that both saint and sinner alike—through faith in Christianity—can find the gateway to heaven. The second parable spoke about God sending out his prophets and his son, all whom were mistreated and killed. Eventually, God is coming to annihilate the Pharisees, scribes, and anyone else who doesn't adhere to the message and the messenger. SuperConscious Jesus never would think in those terms. People are eternally free to believe however they desire. The Astral Universe inevitably will receive back every earth human soul, returning it to its then-determined, universally lawful order.

The third parable is about recognizing Christianity as the feast God has put forth for all humankind. He sent servants to spread the news and they were killed. So God, now angered, destroyed everyone not recognizing or rejecting Christianity. Everyone who does believe comes and has a great time, except for one man who is improperly dressed. Unacceptable for whatever reason one wishes to interpret it to be, this man is thrown out. God does not recognize any theology as the "feast" for all humankind. It is existence that is the true feast—and ALL are called, and ALL are chosen.

Matthew 22:15–40, Mark 12:13–34, Luke 20:20–40
Three Questions by the Pharisees

In the first story, the Pharisees ask Jesus if Caesar should be recognized as a God. Jesus answers by referring to a Caesar-headed penny: "Render unto Caesar the things that are Caesar's, and unto God the things that are God's." The Pharisees left him alone. The Sadducees, who did not believe in resurrection, next came along and posed to Jesus a (paraphrased) question. "After seven husbands (who were brothers) and none having children with her, in resurrection whose wife would she be?" Jesus answers, "God is God of Abraham, Isaac, and Jacob. He is not the God of the dead, but of the living: for all live unto him." Jesus told them that, essentially, she is no one's wife because when one is resurrected, one is with God and eternally living, no longer among the dead.

The Pharisees heard Jesus dispense with the Sadducees and were rallying to portray him as not Divine. A lawyer asks which commandment is the greatest in the law, to which Jesus says it is to love thy one God with all thy heart, soul, and mind. He said it is the greatest commandment, with the second being to love thy neighbor as thy self. Jesus states, "On these two commandments hangeth the whole law, and the prophets. Jesus never was tempted by the Pharisees and Sadducees, and these interchanges never happened. The first one elicits no response, for all things are God's—nothing actually belongs to human manifesting creation.

In the second story Jesus is portrayed as explaining and correcting the Sadducees for their confusion regarding resurrection. This concept is something Christianity still does not quite understand correctly even today. The concept of resurrection is misunderstood. There exist two types of resurrection. In the first type, the soul is allowed to temporarily exit and reenter the same physical body. In the second type, the soul enters a completely new body that has been divinely reFabricated to exactly resemble the original physical body. In both types of resurrection, these TransImaginated events are Facilitated and Made Manifest for divinely discerned reasons. In the case of the second type, this Holy Event is reserved for Superevolved souls. In that case, the soul involved has attained salvation and would require no further physical incarnations. Otherwise, a Unified Holy Being would stay in the Unified Holy Realm of the Astral Universe and work on its Astral karma.

Christianity does not recognize reincarnation, so how could it be interpreting correctly the concept of resurrection? Resurrection is not remaining in a grave or purgatory until the coming of the Heavenly Father to judge the living and dead. During this judgment, every soul that recognized and accepted Jesus into their life would be raised up and exist forever in Heaven with Jesus and God. This notion is what Christianity erroneously would insist everyone believe.

The Ten Commandments themselves were not correctly recorded by Moses' survivors, but the writers have Jesus answer the third question correctly. The actual Ten Commandments are existence-guiding parameters, and all are important for attaining salvation. Those who attain salvation eventually would exist forever with Jesus and God in the Causal Universe. However, omniscient Jesus knew the Truth about Abraham, Isaac, and Jacob, and would not have answered incorrectly the second question by referencing their placement in heaven. None of these three men are in the Unity or have attained salvation from physically incarnating—even yet today.

Matthew 22:41–46, Mark 12:35–37, Luke 20:41–44
Jesus' Unanswerable Question

While Jesus and the Pharisees were gathered, Jesus posed to them the question, "Whose son is the Christ?" The Pharisees responded that it was the son of David, who made distinctions regarding himself and God. Jesus then pressed his position as being Lord and not son: "How then could the Lord be the son?" After this point, the Pharisees never questioned the fictitious Jesus. This exchange never occurred.

Matthew 23:1–39, Mark 12:38–40, Luke 20:45–47
Jesus Speaks Against the Scribes and Pharisees

Jesus is condemning the scribes and Pharisees for their lengthy rules, regulations, and rituals. He calls them hypocrites, fools, and extortionists filled with iniquity. Jesus declares them to be serpents, their offspring vipers unable to escape the judgment of hell. He calls them murderers and stoners of prophets and wise men, persecuting people from city to city. These sound like the actions taken against any person who wouldn't adhere to the Christian message or who challenged the Christian stranglehold on God, human beings, or individual belief. It does not even remotely reflect the SuperConscious state of existence in which Jesus perpetually was in after his Transimplanting. Jesus never made these inflammatory statements.

Mark 12:41–44, Luke 21:1–4
Widow's Mites

A poor widow cast into the treasury a couple of mites, which signified all she had. Others cast in much more, which when compared to their vast, rich holdings, still amounted to a paltry, meaningless sum. This entry is an unconscionable, concealed ploy to measure one's perceived holiness against collection plate-giving. Manipulative guilt alleviation apparently is commensurate to contributions. Guilt is not a transgression, but easily can become a preventive hindrance to salvation, for guilt feeds or directly is rooted into ego.

John 12:20–36
Gentiles Seeking Jesus

Jesus appeared before some Greeks at a feast and said the hour of the Son of Man is to be glorified. "Anyone that serves me, let him follow me, and where I am, there shall also my servant be. If any man serves me so too does the Father honor. Father save me from this hour. For this cause came I this hour. Father, glorify thy name." Out of the heavens came a voice saying, "I have both glorified it and will glorify it again." Some said the voice thundered, others said an angel spoke.

Jesus replied, "This was for your benefit, for the prince of this world is to be cast out. If I be lifted up from the earth, I will draw all men unto myself." The Greeks asked, "Who is this Son of Man in whom the law of Christ abides forever? Why does he need be lifted up?" Jesus replied that "for just a little while is the light among you. Believe in the light while I'm here and you may become sons of light." Then Jesus went and hid.

This did not ever happen in any form or aspect. Jesus never said any of these things to the Greeks—or anyone else for that matter.

John 12:37–50
The Jews Reject Jesus

Jesus is lamenting that the Jews rejected him as the Messiah of whom Isaiah spoke. Even after all the miracles, they still did not believe. Jews loved the glory of man more than the glory of God. Jesus says, "If you believe in me, you believe in God. If you believe in Jesus, you believe in the light of the world. If you don't believe in Jesus' words you will be judged on your last day. I don't speak from myself, but from the Father who sent me; he speaks to me and I to you. So the Father speaks through the son."

Jesus never lamented the Jews rejecting him, for he had no ego. He did read Isaiah and was constantly quoting scriptures. Jesus never made references to Jews loving man more than God. Jews do not love man or God any more disproportionately than do the adherents of any other theology. Jesus did not say, "If you believe in me, you believe in the light of the world." Such a statement is untrue. You will not be judged on your last day if you don't believe in Jesus. He did say, "My Father speaks to me, and I in turn, speak His Words to you." That was true, except those previously attributed statements (John 12:37-48) were not made by either Son or God.

Matthew Chapters 24, 25, 26:1–2, Mark 13:1–37, Luke 21:5–38
Destruction of Jerusalem and the End of the World

Jesus speaks about death and destruction, false prophets, and the end of the world. Jesus talks about Noah, a couple of parables, and finishes by predicting his death by crucifixion. It was easy for writers three hundred years later to write about the destruction of Jerusalem. Jesus did not ever say anything about an Armageddon. He never mentioned anything about false prophets. Why would Jesus believe others would be excluded or not allowed to experience this Transcendent Holy Event? Jesus knew Noah and Jonah to be fictitious, and he did not speak in parables. He also did not know how he was going to die, just that he was going to die, and that he anticipated resurrecting.

Matthew 26:1–5, 14–16, Mark 14:1, 2, 10, 11, Luke 22:1–6
Judas and Chief Priests Conspire

The first day of the Passover (in this case, a Thursday) was celebrated with unleavened bread. In this entry the writers were referencing a collaboration between Judas Iscariot (one of Jesus' disciples), the high priest Caiaphas, the chief priests, scribes, and elders. The writers stated that Judas was paid thirty pieces of silver to hand over Jesus to be crucified.

The Truth is there was no such collaboration. Judas was a disciple and was instrumental in Jesus' death, but he neither had anything to do with the Jews, nor was he in any way guilty of complicity with the Jews. No covenant was forged between Judas and the Sanhedrin. Judas also was portrayed as being the only Judean disciple and to be possessed by Satan. Judas was not the only Judean disciple, and was not possessed by Satan. As previously stated, there IS no Satan or devil. Jesus' disciples, like his teachings, were secular, originating from all walks of life. His message always was universally open to all, for all.

Judas was not paid by the Jews thirty pieces of silver for anything. Furthermore, if the Sanhedrin wanted to kill someone, by Judaic Law, they stoned that person. They did not ever crucify anyone; only the Romans crucified people—and only for crimes committed against the Roman Empire.

Matthew 26:17–30, Mark 14:12–26, Luke 22:7–30, John 13:1–30 (Thursday) The Last Supper

In this entry Jesus instructs his disciples to seek out a man bearing a pitcher of water. He then explains that the master's time is at hand and to prepare for the Passover feast with all twelve disciples. Jesus is portrayed as consecrating bread and wine before he is to suffer. Jesus washes everyone's feet to represent symbolically the cleansing of their soul and eternal attachment to "him" as Lord.

Jesus then exults himself above all of them by declaring, "I am your Master and Lord, and you should follow my lead and wash each other's feet." Thus, he attempts to symbolically unite Master to servant, servant to servant, and servant to Master's Master. Also, this establishes a hierarchical continuum that reads, "God is Supreme above Master and Master is above servant. Servant is equal to servant. Everyone will be required to pass through the approved Master to reach He who is above Master." So, if you wish to commune or unite with God, you only can do so by going through our Christian hierarchy.

Jesus then tells them one of the twelve was to betray him—and then all twelve begin to question, "Whom could it be?" Judas asks, "Is it I, Rabbi?" (Matthew 26:25) In John 13:26, Jesus concurs that it is so. Jesus hands a sop to Judas, the son of Simon Iscariot, and immediately Satan enters into Judas. Judas left with the sop and the eleven disciples were confused by the whole process.

With the remaining eleven, Jesus forms a covenant and transubstantiates the sacraments recognized in today's Christian Church. Jesus declares he is dying for their sins, as well as the sins or transgressions of many others. Jesus says anyone following in "his" footsteps will have complete authority to consecrate, transubstantiate, and will minister and judge over all the "servants." Jesus then sang a hymn and went out onto the Mount of Olives.

No man carrying water was sought out and told to prepare for the Passover feast. Not all of the disciples were at Jesus' last Passover meal. Furthermore, it also included Mary Magdalen, his wife, and several others. His mother, Mary, was still alive but not in attendance. Jesus never washed anyone's feet, and no one washed his feet. Jesus never assumed the transgressing, elevated position of Consecrator before he was to suffer. He did not either symbolically or literally refer to himself as the Master through which all must pass to unify with The Master.

They did not pose the question, "Is it I, Master?" during the meal. Jesus knew full well that Judas was handing him over to be killed. At this point, Jesus still did not know he was going to die through a Roman crucifixion. Judas was not at the last Passover supper. He was orchestrating a deal with the Romans. As such, there was no sop incident. In the agreement with the Romans, Jews did play a minor role—but only to the extent of assisting in arranging the meeting between Judas, Pontius Pilate, and Herod. Neither Caiaphas nor the Sanhedrin was involved in the deadly, relegated charade. Judas did not have Satan or any entity in him. He had free will, jealousy, and greed. In exchange for turning Jesus over to be crucified, Judas did receive money from Pilate. The entire, sordid affair was a Roman solution to Herod's problem.

Finally and most important, Jesus did not ever form an unGodly covenant with his apostles. He did not instruct or authorize them to go out and do likewise on his or through his behalf. He did not consecrate bread or wine, and he did not instruct his disciples to do so. Jesus neither assumed "his Father's" (God's) sanctioning Authority, nor did he grant it permissible for others to do so.

Matthew 26:31–35, Mark 14:27–31, Luke 22:31–38, John 13:31–16:33 Jesus' Farewell

Here Jesus is dispensing out a new commandment that if you love one another, you are his disciples. Jesus tells Simon Peter, "Before the cock crows three times, you will deny knowing me." Then Jesus instructs the disciples to buy a sword, to which they reply, "We have two." Jesus responds that in fulfillment of the scriptures, he will "reckon with the transgressors."

Jesus utters to Thomas, "I am the way, the truth, the light. No one gets to the Father but through me." Jesus claims himself to be the Father, and says the words he speaks are the Father's Words. Jesus shares with the disciples, "I am in you and you are in me." Jesus is instructing the disciples to go forth and spread the commandments. If anyone hates Jesus, he also is hating God. Jesus spoke about many aspects pertaining to his disciples going out, witnessing, and spreading the Word of God as Jesus' words.

Jesus sanctifies himself as truth, and those whom he sends out into the world also are to be sanctified in truth. Jesus tells his disciples, "As the Father is in me, so am I in you and you are all potentially perfected into becoming one." Jesus did speak about his passing before his ordeal. He knew many Truths that he imparted to all who desired to listen and learn. He did not tell Peter, "Before the cock crows three times, you will deny knowing me." He did not imply anyone would have to go through Jesus personally to merge with the Father. He did say it metaphorically.

Jesus did not sanctify himself as truth, for he was Truth—and knew better than to transgress by ordaining upon others sanctification. He also did not imply that if everyone believed personally in Jesus, they would merge as one with the Father. Jesus was speaking of the dualistic unified superconsciousness in which all conscious, physically manifesting experience eventually merges as one Unified SuperConsciousness. Jesus never meant (himself) to be taken in the literal, misguided, misappropriated, transgressing manner as his words today are recognized.

Matthew 26:30, 36–46, Mark 14:26, 32–42, Luke 22:39–46, John 18:1 Suffering in Gethsemane

Jesus leaves the last supper and goes to the Mount of Olives to pray. Jesus prays for the incident to pass, if it is his Father's Will, without having to experience what he knows is going to happen. In Luke 22:43, an angel came and comforted Jesus, allowing him the inner resolve to overcome his fear and continue to pray. Three times, Jesus leaves and returns to find his disciples sleeping. Then he commands them to arise, for his betrayal time now is at hand.

Jesus did not go to the Mount of Olives to pray. Prior to his arrest, he actually was with his wife, Mary Magdalen. He did not have any fear or trepidation. No angel came to reassure and strengthen him. Jesus still was not given complete access into his dharmic plan. As such, Jesus was unaware of both his specific mode of death, as well as the exact predetermined moment at which he would die. Jesus was only marginally shown his potential time of death—and not that it would be on the cross.

Matthew 26:47–56, Mark 14:43–52, Luke 22:47–53, John 18:1–12
Betrayal and Arrest

While Jesus is at the Mount of Olives, Judas—with the Pharisees, high priests, elders, and a great multitude of others armed with swords and staves—came to arrest Jesus. According to John 18:3, there also was a band of soldiers and officers with this crowd. Jesus is pointed out, and in the process the ear of one of the high priests' servants is cut off. Jesus heals his ear and states that it is in fulfillment of the scriptures. In Mark 14:51, a toga-clad youth is apprehended. He escapes by wresting free and leaving his garment behind, fleeing naked. Everyone else is allowed to go free, and they take Jesus away for trial.

Jesus was not at the Mount of Olives. Judas appeared with a group of Roman soldiers and officers. No Jewish Sanhedrin members were present. The servant's ear was shorn off, after which Jesus indeed did heal his ear. The youth fleeing naked simply did not happen. Jesus was the only one taken away.

Matthew 26:57–27:10, Mark 14:53–72, 15:1, Luke 22:54–71, John 18:12–27
Jesus' Trial Before the Jewish Elders

Jesus is led before Annas Caiaphas' father-in-law. Jesus is struck in the face by one of the officer's hands. After this incident, Jesus is sent on to Caiaphas. Jesus is accused of stating, "I will destroy this temple that is made with hands, and in three days I will build another without hands." The high priest asks, "What is it which these witness against thee?" Jesus does not answer. The high priest asks, "Art thou the Christ the Son of the Blessed?" Jesus responds, "I am and ye shall see the Son of Man sitting at the right hand of power and coming with the clouds of heaven."

The high priest tears Jesus' clothes and Jesus is spit upon and punched. It is declared he should be put to death for his blasphemy. Meanwhile, while a cock crows, Peter denies three times that he knows Jesus. After realizing Jesus' prediction, he leaves, bitterly weeping. The council declares that Jesus is to be put to death and leads him away to Pontius Pilate.

Feeling guilty, Judas tries to return the thirty pieces of silver. They won't accept the returned silver, declaring it blood money. So, Judas throws the silver on the floor of the sanctuary, goes out, and promptly hangs himself. The money later was used to purchase a cemetery for strangers.

The accepted Christian explanation for Jesus being handed over to the Romans is that the Sanhedrin couldn't put people to death for insurrection. The Truth is, only the Roman Empire could do so. Jesus was handed over to Pontius Pilate for trial. Jesus was not tried before the Sanhedrin. He was not struck by the hand of one of the officers. The statement about destroying Solomon's Temple and its rebuilding was written to be interpreted as Jesus' rising or resurrecting from the dead after three days. Of course, there is no set time limit for one's resurrection: it can be three hours or six months.

The entire Sanhedrin episode, including Peter's denial, is a cock and bull story. Judas did not try to return the money, so no cemetery was purchased in which to bury strangers. Judas did not commit suicide, but actually did die immediately after betraying Jesus. Finally, the Sanhedrin was accused of trying and convicting Jesus for blasphemy, not insurrection. Back then, they stoned many beings for blasphemy without having to bring this issue to Pilate's attention. They certainly could have stoned to death anyone for insurrection, blasphemy, or any other crime they felt warranted such response. They didn't need to wait for Rome's approval, and they did not hand over death-sentenced convicts to be once again tried by Rome.

The trial by the Sanhedrin occurred on the Thursday night of the Passover. By Judaic Law, the Sanhedrin was forbidden to meet at night during the seven nights of Passover. So, on the Thursday night of the Passover, the high priest, Sanhedrin, Pharisees, scribes, Church elders, and the whole council all gathered together to convict a fellow Jew of blasphemy? The entire assembly did this—only to come along on Friday morning, bright and early, once more to gather and hold a consultation? Eventually, they are convinced Jesus is guilty of blasphemy, and sentence him to death. All this, and they need to hand him over to Pontius Pilate for another trial?

The Truth is, with virtually no support or input from the Sanhedrin, but upon Herod's insistence, the Romans executed Jesus—and the Jews were the scapegoat.

Transcendental Illuminations

Matthew 27:2, 11–31, Mark 15:1–20, Luke 23:1–25, John 18:28–40, 19:1–16
Trial Before Pilate

So, early Friday, the whole assembly brings Jesus to Pontius Pilate, who asks if Jesus is the King of the Jews. Jesus replies, "Thou sayest." The assembly accused him of many things. Pilate tries to cast Jesus back on the Jews. Pilate asks if Jesus is the "King of the Jews," to which Jesus answers, "Are you asking this of your own perception, or did others tell you I am?" Pilate responds, "What have you done?" Jesus replies, "My kingdom is not of this world. If it were, my servants would be fighting to prevent me from being delivered to the Jews." Jesus states, "To this end have I been born and to this end am I come into this world, that I should bear witness unto the truth. Everyone that is of truth heareth my voice." Pilate responds, "What is truth?"

Finding no crime in him, Pilate again tries to give Jesus back to the Jews. In Luke 23:4-16, once he finds out Jesus is a Galilean in Herod's jurisdiction, Pilate turns him over to Herod, who in those days, was also in Jerusalem. When Herod saw Jesus, he was glad, for he was hoping to meet him and perhaps see a miracle. Herod peppered Jesus with many questions, to which Jesus remained mute. The Jewish assembly vehemently accused Jesus of crimes. Herod mocked him, arraying Jesus in gorgeous apparel, sending him back to Pilate. From that very day, Herod and Pilate became friends. Upon receiving Jesus back, Pilate told everyone that neither he nor Herod found Jesus guilty of the accusations—after which Pilate said he would chastise and then release Jesus.

At the feast of the governor a prisoner was released back into society. Either Jesus or a murderer guilty of insurrection was to be released, with the choice up to the multitude. The Jewish assembly insisted and convinced Pilate to release Barabbas. When asked what to do with Jesus, the crowds shouted, "Crucify him, crucify him." Pilate was informed by his wife that in a dream she suffered greatly because of Jesus. Pilate knew Jesus was being sentenced for envy, at the insistence of the Sanhedrin and the Jewish multitudes. The crowd was getting agitated, so Pilate released Barabbas, scourged Jesus, and delivered him to be crucified.

The soldiers stripped Jesus, put on him a scarlet robe, and plaited a crown of thorns for his head and placed a reed in his right hand. They kneeled and mocked him, saying, "Hail, King of the Jews." Jesus was spat upon, whipped with the reed, and struck with the soldiers' hands. In a last-ditch effort, Pilate brought out Jesus, wearing the robe and thorns, and said, "Take him for yourselves and crucify him, for I don't find him guilty of any crime." The Jewish mob cried, "We have a law, and by that law, he ought to die, because he made himself the Son of God."

Pilate grew afraid, yet pressed on, saying, "I have the power to release you or crucify you." Jesus responds, "You have no power over me unless it were given thee from above. Therefore he that delivered me hath greater sin." Pilate again wanted to release Jesus, but the Jews exclaimed, "If you release him, you are no friend of Caesar." Pilate said, "Shall I crucify your king?" The Jews responded, "We have no king but Caesar." So, they put Jesus' garments back on and led him out to be crucified.

At the feast of the governor, in lieu of Jesus, a man named Barabbas was released. The fact is, the Holy Sanctioned Angel could not locate any example of this custom occurring as an acknowledged, celebratory practice. On early Sabbath Saturday during Passover the whole assembly would NEVER bring Jesus to Pilate. Jesus and Pilate did get into a discussion about the validity of the Jewish assertions, but the Sanhedrin was not involved. Jesus was arrested by Pilate on behalf of Herod. Only Luke 23:4-16 even acknowledges Herod's role in this abominable injustice and ensuing whitewash. Herod Antipas and Herod Agrippa I both conspired to do away with John the Baptist. Herod Antipas made a forced deal with Judas for Jesus.

Herod Antipas was in Jerusalem only for that purpose, and he and Pilate indeed became good friends. After this corroborative conspiracy, they became much better friends. With Herod, Jesus was not mute. When Herod said he was glad to see Jesus, there could be no doubt about his exuberance. Herod did mock him and arrayed him in regal outfits. Herod was extremely jealous of Jesus, and came up with the insulting inscription of "King of the Jews." Herod the Great was known as "King of the Jews," and so was his grandson Herod Agrippa I. Herod Antipas was a violent, jealous, vengeful, power-hungry man who aspired to be "King of the Jews," and was willing to take extreme measures to become so.

Herod found Jesus guilty of insurrection against the Empire and sentenced him to death by crucifixion. The Sanhedrin was deemed innocent and held unaccountable by the Holy Realm for ANY part of the violent, sordid sham. Herod and Pilate, along with the individual, barbaric Romans, were the karmically guilty instigators and executioners of Jesus' fate, and still today are paying a heavy karmic price.

Most of the Gospels describing the trial are complete fictitious bunkum. Herod planned and strategized the farcical trial. He actually sought out Judas and COERCED him into setting up Jesus. The Holy Sanctioned Angel insisted that Herod knew something, by which he blackmailed or utilized manipulative leverage against Judas. Herod left Judas with no options and ultimately caused Judas' untimely demise. It was Herod who POISONED Judas. Judas did not commit suicide, and he did not die by hanging.

The Holy Sanctioned Angel could not find evidence of the release of this prisoner as ever historically happening in Jerusalem during Rome's rule, and could not find actual, historical recordings of a "Barabbas" ever existing. Neither an exchange was considered, nor did the festive prisoner-release custom (or even Barabbas himself) ever exist. There was no "Crown of Thorns." That also never happened. Primarily, it was that Jesus was referred to as the Son of Christos or Son of God that so enraged the jealous Herod. It was for that reason that Jesus was sentenced to death by crucifixion.

Matthew 27:32–56, Mark 15:21–41, Luke 23:26–49, John 19:16–37 The Crucifixion

Simon of Cyrene was pressed into service to assist in bearing the burden of Jesus' cross. They went to a place called Golgotha or "Place of a Skull." Jesus was offered wine mingled with myrrh or gall, but he refused to drink it. He was crucified with two others—one on his left and one on his right. His garments were divided by soldiers casting lots. A placard was adhered to the top of his cross, with the superscription of one of the following: "This Is Jesus, The King Of The Jews," (Matthew 27:37), "The King Of The Jews," (Mark 15:26), or "Jesus Of Nazareth, The King Of The Jews" (John 19:19). According to John 19:20, it was written in Hebrew, Latin, and Greek. In John, Jesus was requested by the chief priests to change the inscription to read "I am King of the Jews." Pilate retorts, "What I have written, I have written."

The chief priests and scribes mocked Jesus, saying he saved others, but couldn't save himself. Everyone, including one of the men crucified, taunted him to save himself and come down off the cross—so everyone can believe that Jesus was the Son of God. In Luke 23:39-43, the other crucified man rebuked the man who taunted Jesus, saying, "We are getting what we deserved, but this man (Jesus) has done nothing amiss." He then asked to be remembered in heaven, to which Jesus responds, "Today shalt thou be with me in Paradise."

In John 19:25-27, Jesus' mother, along with her alleged sister, Mary the wife of Clopas, and Mary Magdalen are standing in observance. Jesus sees them together with a disciple whom he loved, and he says to the disciple, "Behold thy mother." Jesus also said to his own mother, "Woman, behold thy son." From that hour, the disciple took her unto his own home. In Matthew and Mark, Jesus cried out, "My God, My God, why have you forsaken me?" People felt he cried out for Elijah. Someone ran and got a sponge full of vinegar, put it on a reed, and gave it to him to drink. People around said, "Let's see if Elijah comes." From the sixth to the ninth hour, darkness covered the land.

When he received the sponge, Jesus uttered a loud cry and promptly expired. The veil or curtain of the temple was torn from top to bottom. The earth quaked and the rocks were rent. Tombs were opened, bodies of the sleeping saints were raised, and after the resurrection Jesus entered Jerusalem, appearing to many. The centurion who was watching responded by saying, "This was the Son of God." Watching from afar were Mary Magdalen and Mary, the mother of James the Less, and Joses, as well as Salome, the mother of the sons of Zebedee, and many others.

In John 19:31-37, it states that because it was the Preparation the bodies should not remain on the crosses on the Sabbath, as the Sabbath was a high day. The Jews asked if the legs of the crucified men could be broken and their bodies be taken away. The soldiers broke the legs of the first two, but found Jesus already dead. One soldier ran his sword through Jesus' side, and the fulfillment of the scriptures occurred: "A bone of him shall not be broken, but they should look on him whom they pierced."

To begin with, neither Simon nor Jesus bore the burden of the crosses. The crosses already were at the crucifixion site. There were two other men crucified with Jesus. Jesus' garments were divided out by soldiers casting lots. No placards or inscriptions ever were placed above his head. It was Herod and Pilate who taunted and mocked him. There was no taunting done by either of the fellow crucified men. Jesus did not say to one of them, "You shall be with me in Paradise." No matter what, he would not have the insight, or the power over the other man's karma—and Jesus would not transgress and profess to have such ability.

Neither Jesus' mother, Mary, nor her sister, Mary, wife of Clopas, were present. In fact, Jesus' mother did not have a sister named Mary (John 19:25). She had brothers, but no sister. Mary Magdalen was present, as were James the Less, Joses, and Salome. While up on the cross, Jesus did not say to a disciple anything regarding the beholding of son and mother. However, he did make that statement prior to the crucifixion. The confusion regarding James as Jesus' brother stems from this passage.

Jesus did say, "My Father, My Father, Why have you forsaken me?" He did this after he took a drink from the sponge. It was not said in reference to Elijah, who incarnated as John the Baptist. The sponge was offered up by one of the Essenes, and it was soaked in vinegar and rosebay. Also known as oleander, rosebay is a highly poisonous plant. Once Jesus drank from the sponge soaked in rosebay and vinegar, he quickly lost consciousness. As he was going under, he felt forsaken or abandoned, and cried out. No curtain in Solomon's Temple was torn as a result of his slipping into unconsciousness. None of the ground-shaking, tomb-opening incidents occurred. No saints were resurrected for a cameo visit.

While the legs on the other two men were being broken, no soldier was near enough to Jesus to hear anything being uttered by him. The other two crucified were screaming in agony, and the soldiers could only hear them. The Sabbath was not the reason for the expedient mercy killing of the crucified men. Herod wanted to get it over with quickly, and thus had their legs broken to hasten their demise. Because it was on the Passover, he wanted Jesus dead before the Jews, who all were adhering to Passover, even knew what had happened. By this time, Jesus was well loved by all types of people. Herod's tactics ensured no chance for an uprising from any of the people.

God allowed us (Essenes) to use our free will to interfere in Jesus' final outcome. That is one of the reasons I was selected by God to share these Truthful Absolutes.

By the time the soldiers arrived at the site where Jesus was located, Jesus was completely unconscious and dying—but not fully dead. The soldier did run through him with his sword, and for all practical purposes,

Jesus certainly appeared dead. When compiling the Old and New Testaments, the later-day writers, in their zeal to have the text syndetically flow one into the next, made sure of the appropriate passages. This easily accommodated the fulfillment of the scriptures. Three hundred years after the fact is plenty of time with which to cook the books.

Matthew 27:57–61, Mark 15:42–47, Luke 23:50–56, John 19:38–42
The Burial

A wealthy man named Joseph of Arimathea, a counselor of honor and disciple of Jesus, went to ask for the body of Jesus. Pilate marveled that Jesus was already dead. Pilate asked the centurion, who confirmed this to be the case. Joseph was granted receipt of Jesus' body, wrapping it in linen cloth. He then placed Jesus in an unused tomb in a garden. He rolled a rock across the opening. Mary, wife of Clopus, and Mary Magdalen knew where Jesus was placed.

Joseph indeed was an honorable and wealthy man, as well as a disciple of Jesus. Joseph was an influential member of the Sanhedrin, who at the last minute, heard of the secret plans. The Romans did not allow crucified beings to be buried or even to be removed from the cross. The exposed body always was left to become carrion, and even the relatives of a crucified person were prevented from so much as approaching the victim.

Matthew 27:62–66
Guarding the Sepulcher

The next morning (which is now Sabbath Saturday), the day after the Preparation, the chief priests and Pharisees are gathered together to convince Pilate to prevent Jesus (the deceiver) from rising from the dead. "Command that the sepulcher be secured in order to prevent the disciples from stealing him away and pretend he rose from the dead." Pilate agreed to let them guard the sepulcher as surely and tightly as was possible. So, with the guard present, they sealed tight the sepulcher.

In the writing of the Gospels, Pilate feigned surprise that Jesus expired so quickly—but in actuality, he was not surprised. The whole gruesome affair was a loosely controlled orchestration. Several main participants were involved with huge, consequential stakes. Against Roman protocol and law, Pilate allowed a private crucifixion, a crucifixion removal while the crucified man still was warm, and a private burial on private grounds.

The high priests and Pharisees did not break their Passover Sabbath to go talk to Pilate and seal the tomb themselves. Other than Joseph, no other Sanhedrin Elders were involved. Yet, everyone sort of ended up with what they anticipated. Herod was adamant about the death, holding a quick trial before civil unrest or resistance—especially after executing John the Baptist. Joseph quickly arranged with Pilate to have the crucifixion on his property, allowing removal of the body and burial in exchange for Joseph's property in Jerusalem.

For all practical purposes, Jesus was dead and resurrected—although not technically so. God allowed the Essenes to intervene in Jesus' dharmic plan and actually PREVENT the unenfoldment of his final passing, as was called for in Jesus' dharmic blueprint. Jesus actually was TransImaginated to die and resurrect; that was preprescripted into his plan. However, through interfering Love and human ignorance, Jesus' dharmic plan was indeed changed.

Matthew 28:1–10, Mark 16:1–11, Luke 23:56, 24:1–12, John 20:1–18 Resurrection Morning

On the first day after the Sabbath day, Mary Magdalen and the other Mary, the mother of James and Salome, found the stone rolled back after a great quake. Upon entering they found an angel whose appearance was as lightning, his raiment as snow (Matthew 28: 3). In Mark 16:5 they found a young man sitting on the right side, arrayed in a white robe. In Luke 23:4 the women found two men in dazzling apparel. In John 20:12 Mary Magdalen encountered two angels in white. They were told that Jesus had risen, and in great fear these people so departed.

As per Mark 16:9, Mary Magdalen was the first to be visited. She told everyone and they did not believe her. In John 20:14 Mary Magdalen is standing in the tomb weeping when Jesus comes up behind her. She tries to hug him, and he tells her, "Don't touch me, for I am not yet ascended unto the Father." Jesus continues, "I ascend unto my Father and your Father and my God and your God." So, she tells everyone she has seen the Lord.

In Matthew and John, the women encountered an angelic (Matthew) essence, or (John) two angelic presences. In Mark, they encountered a young man sitting in white, and in Luke, two men in dazzling apparel. The fact is, they encountered two Essenes in their white raiment. The Essenes who were present were unknown to the disciples but still comforted and reassured the disciples that they would soon be reunited with Jesus.

That night, after he was stabilized, Jesus was taken directly from the tomb to a nearby home owned by Joseph. This is where Mary Magdalen was staying, and she helped to care for him during his recovery. She also was in mourning, thus not expected to go out, and nobody was going to bother her. It proved to be the perfect cover. We already discussed the resurrection and ascension differences—and needless to say, the later-day composers of the Gospels did not understand them. Unlike a Super-Consciously Transimplanted Being, a resurrected Being immediately can be hugged.

Matthew 28:11–15
Report of the Watch

The chief priests, scribes, and elders held a council and raised a large sum of money to give to the soldiers for saying that Jesus' disciples came and stole him away while they slept. "If you tell Pilate, this we will vouch for you." The soldiers took the money and did as they were instructed. This story continued on amongst the Jews. No such bribe ever occurred.

Mark 16:14, Luke 24:36–43, John 20:19–25
Jesus Appears Without Thomas

On the evening of the first day of the week, Jesus appeared to them saying, "Peace to you." He showed them his hands and feet, then stated, "The Father has sent me even so send I you." After he said this, he breathed on them and said, "Unto them receive ye the Holy Ghost. Whose soever sins ye forgive, they are forgiven unto them. Whose soever sins ye retain, they are retained." Thomas was absent from the visitation, so he questioned the validity of their assertions.

This visitation never occurred as it is portrayed. Jesus did have the wounds on his hands, feet, and side—which may be the case with a resurrected being. That may well be the condition of the physical manifesting body at the time the body is untenanted. However, Jesus' body never was tenantless before he regained SuperConsciousness. Thus, he indeed still would have the original piercings. He did not say to them, "The Father sent me, so I send you." Jesus also never breathed on them, saying, "Receive ye the Holy Ghost." That he could not do. He also did not say, "Whose soever sins ye retain, they are retained." These are serious transgressions that Jesus did not commit. Jesus never instructed his disciples likewise to do so, for this they could not do. No one was, is, or ever will be God-sanctioned to perform or authorize such unwarrantable substantiations.

John 20:26–29
Appearance with Thomas

After eight days, Jesus appears to the disciples—and all eleven, including Thomas, are gathered together. Jesus appears in their midst, uttering, "Peace be unto you." Thomas is instructed to check out the nail holes and put his hand in the sword wound. Then Jesus states, "Blessed are they that have not seen and yet have believed."

Of course, this event never took place as it is portrayed or described. Thomas did not ask to place his fingers in the nail holes and his hand in Jesus' sword wound. It indeed is important to believe or trust that some eternally generous or illimitably abundant God is responsible for our comprehendible perceptional existence. However, we do not need to submit our trust to sequacious foolishness. The transparent intentions insidiously being communicated are all too apparent. It is consistent with the effort discretely exerted throughout the New Testament, in conjunction with the true, hidden motives and underlying, subversive premeditations.

John 21:1–24
Appearance to Seven by the Sea

In this story seven of the disciples were fishing. They hadn't netted any fish until Jesus appeared on the scene. (Perhaps they were fishing the Dead Sea, rather than the Sea of Galilee?) Jesus hungers and of course, there are no fish. So, Jesus instructs them to "Try over here on the 'right' (Gentile, perhaps?) side" of the boat. This certainly is in opposition to the "wrong" (Jewish?) side of the boat. On the Gentile or right side of the boat, there were more fish than the net could handle. An unknown disciple whom Jesus loved—maybe James the Less—says to Peter, "It is the Lord." Upon hearing it was Jesus, Simon Peter—who was naked at the time—put on his coat and hopped into the water. When they all came ashore, there is a shore lunch cooking, nets are full (containing 153 fish), coals are stoked, and bread is being broken.

Jesus says to the presumably still-clothed Simon Peter, "Lovest thou me more than these?" Simon Peter replies, "Yea, Lord. Thou knowest that I love thee." Jesus commands him to "Feed my lambs." Jesus again asks Simon Peter if he "lovest thou me?" Jesus instructs him to "tend my sheep." Jesus requests a third time of Simon Peter, "Thou lovest me?" Simon Peter, who the later-day writers previously forced to denounce Jesus, was becoming indignant. Nonetheless, he answers, "Lord thou knowest all things, thou knowest I love thee." So, Jesus once more commands him to "feed my sheep." Jesus goes on to speak about God carrying Simon Peter after he himself no longer can do so. Jesus then says to Simon Peter, "Follow me."

The unknown disciple, who Jesus loved more than the others, leans back after supper and says, "Lord, who is he that betrayeth thee?" Peter responds with, "And what shall this man do?" Jesus replies, "If I will that he tarry till I come, what is that to thee? Follow thou me." From that statement, they then assumed that this particular disciple would not die. Jesus basically goes on to say, "No, I don't mean this disciple will not die. I really mean, keep feeding the lambs, sheep, and tending the sheep, and keep following me until I come back again. Furthermore, if it takes a while, what is that to you—or anyone else for that matter?"

This dissertation finishes with "This is the disciple which beareth witness of these things, and wrote these things—and we know that his witness is true." Now, if this witness knows this to be true, he needs to inform the Holy Realm of truths not recognized supernally, for the Holy Angelic Realm is unaware of such truthfulness, holiness, and convincing accuracies so vehemently portrayed. This entry by John self-explains the veiled attempt by people to sequester for themselves the Truths that have always been available to individuals. "No matter how long it takes, just keep blind faith—and one day, I'll return. So, make sure the corral is tight, the sheep well fed and well tended."

A Bergér happens to be "shepherd" in French—and for forty-two years that has been my last name. With regard to shepherdic care, there are two very different modes of thought. One is conventional, the other organic. If one operates with the understanding that earth humankind basically all are sheep, to be treated in the conventional manner, then the religious, theological, dogmatic experience is for you. On the other hand, if you desire to be free, existing in the organic individual conscious pasture, then this dissection of the New Testament should set you free. Truth is forever free and innately organic. No longer will there be only one conventionally prepared type of food for the soul. Everyone should be free to consume the eternal Truth, in the borderless pastures of bountiful individuality.

Matthew 28:16–20, Mark 16:15–18
Jesus Appears to Eleven on a Mountain in Galilee

Jesus appears to all eleven of the disciples on a mountain in Galilee. As soon as they see Jesus, they worship him. He then tells them to go out into the world and preach the gospel to the whole of creation. "He that believes and is baptized shall be saved, but he that disbelieveth shall be condemned." Jesus purports all authority has been given to him in heaven and earth. "Go out and baptize everyone in the name of the Father and of the Son and of the Holy Ghost. In my name and in these signs shall follow them that believe; you will cast out devils, speak in new tongues, take up serpents; if you drink anything deadly, you're immune and it can't hurt you. You can lay hands on the sick and they shall recover. Teach everyone to observe all things whatsoever I commanded you, and lo, I am with you always ever unto the end of the world."

After reading this, I easily can see why there is so much disharmony in the world—so much confusion, contamination, anger, violence, and hatred. It is easy to comprehend why the Holy Realm is so disappointed with earth humankind. We've already exploited and expounded the untruthful unholiness and unGodliness throughout these scriptures. Jesus would not and did not say these horribly transgressing statements. What has been done to Blessed Jesus is disgraceful. It would be easy to assume that since he hasn't yet returned, everything must be truth, or at least okay. If he didn't say and do these disingenuous things, he certainly would return to correct all such untruth.

Absentia is not a stamp of approval. Throughout all three manifesting Universes, there is a Divine Order. Things don't work according to earth humankind's or Hollywood's determinations. There is no mystery why would-be adherents might become atheists and agnostics if they were to read this deceptive prevarication. It makes a mendacious, deceitful mockery of everything Jesus represented.

Mark 16:19–20, Luke 24:44–53
Jesus' Final Appearance and Ascension

Jesus said unto them, "These are my words which I spake unto you, while I was yet with you, how that all things must need be fulfilled, which are written in the Law of Moses and the prophets and the psalms concerning me. Then opened be their minds that they might understand the scriptures, and he said unto them, thus it is written, that the Christ would suffer, and rise again from the dead the third day, and that repentance and remission of sins should be preached in his name unto all the notions, beginning from Jerusalem. Ye are witnesses of these things. And behold, I send forth the promise of my Father unto you, but tarry ye in the city, until ye be clothed with power from on high.

"And he led them out until they were over against Bethany: and he lifted up his hands and blessed them. And it came to pass, while he blessed them, he parted from them, and was carried up into heaven. And they worshipped him and returned to Jerusalem with great Joy and were continually in the temple blessing God." Mark 16:19 and 20 said, "So then, the Lord Jesus, after he had spoken unto them, was received up into heaven and sat down at the right hand of God. And they went forth, and preached everywhere, the Lord working with them and confirmed by the signs that followed. Amen."

Like many other passages, this one is no different; it is pure fiction.

John 20:30–31, John 21:25
Conclusion

There are many other writings of Jesus out there, but they will be wrought with the same persistent shameless mistruth. God has requested the verbatim rewriting of some of these more troublesome entries for the purpose of extricating and exonerating both Itself (God) and Jesus.

Karmic Retribution

During the writing of this Holy Book, a controversial movie was filmed and released. The film depicted one director's personal perspective regarding the final twelve hours of Jesus' biblically portrayed life. In this movie entitled *The Passion of the Christ* great strides were taken to ensure the most ferociously violent portrayal of Jesus' crucifixion. Prior to the release of this movie, the Holy Sanctioned Angel already had shared with us the Truth about Jesus' crucifixion. As such, we were not surprised that the filming was an excruciating personal nightmare for the actor playing the part of Jesus. Whenever the film's portrayal of Jesus strayed from the Truth, the actor playing Jesus experienced severe personal karmic retribution. Both the director and the actor portraying Jesus made free-will choices that resulted in karmic indebtedness. This movie itself is a nasty, violent stain of fiction upon the parchment of the viewer's consciousness, that for many will take lifetimes to remove.

The first manipulative free-will choice made by the director was when he purposefully misrepresented the film as a surfing movie, hoping to engage the interest of the actor who eventually agreed to play the part of Jesus. Even after realizing that the surfing movie was merely a ruse to entice him to accept the role of Jesus, this actor nonetheless chose to ignore this obvious misrepresentation. He ultimately accepted a role subjecting him to so much personal suffering, he stated publicly that it nearly drove him insane.

The movie was filmed during a grueling Italian winter with 25-degree temperatures and 30-knot winds, during which the actor suffered hypothermia, a lung infection, and pneumonia. In addition, the daily eight-hour makeup sessions left him with skin infections and severe headaches caused by wearing a crown of thorns tightly wired to his head, as well as having to film with one eye made up to be swollen shut. From bearing chains this actor experienced cuts, scrapes, and backaches that aggravated a previous chest injury. While carrying the 150-pound cross, the actor dislocated his shoulder.

During the scenes depicting the "stations of the cross," this actor's bare back received a 14-inch gash inflicted by another actor playing the role of a Roman soldier wielding a whip. The force of the blow momentarily knocked the wind out of him. He fell to the ground, and uttered several expletives at the Roman soldier. He then arose, after which he was struck again in the same place, further slicing open the previous wound.

Most of the injuries this actor sustained were the result of planned scenes of torture. However, there was one exception. Three seconds before the film crew shot the scene of the Sermon on the Mount, he was struck by lightning.

This actor's ego and blind faith were the factors supporting his free-will choice to participate in this movie. Despite his personal suffering, he has stated publicly that he has had no regrets. His personal feelings about the experience were that God gave him just enough strength to complete the filming. His personal belief is that all humans are responsible for the death of Jesus, and that everyone's sins are what put Jesus up on the cross. Like the "original sin" of Adam and Eve, this perception of human transgression is complete nonsense.

The Truth is, the suffering endured by the actor playing Jesus in this movie did NOT reflect what truly happened to Jesus during Jesus' real lifetime. Rather, this actor's suffering was a karmic reflection as a direct result of his free-will choices to portray and further perpetuate mistruth.

BOOK Five

Prayerful Attunement and The Holy Originator's Ore

Prayerful Attunement

arth humans, without transgressing, certainly can pray to Blessed Jesus, for he indeed is a very sacred, Holy Being. However, like praying to the "man on the moon," to pray to a holy, nonholy, or nonexistent being is a misappropriation. It is like hitting a baseball that ends up going into foul territory. It may have started out with the best of intentions but clearly misses the mark. You can hit foul balls all day long without being called "out," but missing the mark certainly doesn't get one safely around the bases to "home" as Unified At-Oneness. Even the best of intentions may become a transgression if ego is the benefactor. Praying the rosary to win the lottery will not guarantee winning and could easily become an attachment that eventually would need to be alleviated. The transgression occurs when fear and ego are the focus. Instead, one must trust that God will manifest the deeply comprehended outcome already enfolded into everyone's dharmic plan. Misplaced or misguided prayer walks a very fine line between the energy-wasting harmless foul ball and the transgressing strike-out. In all cases, God determines if karmic impaction occurs.

As you now comprehend the Truth about Jesus, everyone should come to realize his incredible uniqueness. Jesus exists today as SuperConsciousness in the immaculate, supremely resplendent, ecstatic Holy Realm of the Causal Universe. But make no mistake, no one should pray to Jesus and expect the same results as if praying to the Holy SuperConsciousness Itself. As you soon will understand, in the sense of the True definition, they are not one and the same.

Another subject to explain involves the many problems of symbolism. However well-meaning, human interpretation is not a stamp of absolution from transgression. To honor or pay tribute to something that may not have happened or may have happened in a manner different from that which historically has been recorded can be problematic for the Astral, physical, as well as the individual perspective. For instance, praying the rosary or prayer beads is NOT a holy form of worshipping when directed toward a physically manifested human being. When prayers of any sort are not directed solely to God, they run the risk of either transgressing or further contributing to the accumulating pools of stagnant energy. One can always send, think, or emit good thoughts, love, energies, or vibrations toward any aspect of Made Manifest. This is not the same as directing, projecting, or petitioning Divinity to acquiesce to our prayerful desires for a specific outcome.

Despite the fact that Jesus, Mother Mary, and Mary Magdalen all are recognized by the Holy Realm as Holy Beings, to direct prayer to any one of these physically manifested human beings is not a beneficial focus of one's love or conscious devotional intentions. It misses the mark, and one may as well pray to any person, place, or thing. The result is still the same, with no distinction being made for manifested Saint or sinner. Devotees can't pray to something or someone and have ANY effect on the recipient of their directed energies. To pray to a loved one, whether living or deceased from the physical universe, has no impact.

The same principle holds true for the cross or crucifixion—even through acts of contrition directed toward Jesus. This fact may be troubling for many devout Christians who staunchly believe they are committing a benevolent act, repentance, or showing pure love for God. Instead, the prayerful focus needs to be directed toward God or the God Aspect of SuperConsciousness—NOT toward Jesus or any manifested humankind.

By interpreting and attributing to the crucifixion a human slant and then to honor it is not a guarantee of anything associated with salvation, upliftment, or holiness. At times Jesus has answered and does answer the directed devotions, even in person—but this is upon God's instructed responses, not Jesus'. Jesus does not ever act or respond on his own accord, but only through Supernal directives from God.

For one thing, Jesus did not die for the sins of earth humankind. He did not have any intentions of ever doing so, knowing full well the impossibility of such nonsense. He was subjected to abominable human-against-human atrocities, but his dharmic blueprint did not contain within his unenfolding experience a preprescribed "dying for our sins" allocation.

The Torah, Bible, and Koran also are not holy symbolic absolutes. When biblical terms pertain to anything other than human beings, they oftentimes are not representing Holy Absolutes. The Holy of Holies, Arc of the Covenant, and the Casual aspect of the human Tabernacle, all were pertaining to human-to-Holy Absolutes. The Holy of Holies, Transcendental Star, and the Arc of the Covenant are inward reflections into the manifesting physical universe within a human being—and ARE Holy Absolutes. The human tabernacle itself, other than the Holy Neutrino Causal aspect of manifesting human existence, is not recognized by God as holy within a human being. The Astral and physical aspects of the human Tabernacle are far too contaminated or defiling for the Uncreated Infinite or Manifesting Infinite aspects of SuperCon-sciousness to be deemed or recognized as Holy.

Of course, by their manifesting nature alone, sacred places also are not recognized as Holy. All physically manifesting existence has within its Holy Neutrino (Causal) realm a dharmic blueprint. The SuperConsciousness of all existence is located in the Causal aspect of all Made Manifest experience. By the time the God-comprehended and God-reperfected matter has been physically created, it is contaminating to both Uncreated Infinite and Manifesting Infinite aspects of God. For this reason alone, no place is more or less sacred than the next. Whether it's a dust particle, superhuman, or supernova, ALL indivisible Made Manifest is SuperConsciously loved the same—Infinitely, Unconditionally, and Eternally.

For many reasons, some manifesting places certainly seem to us to be holy or sacred. In these circumstances, a couple phenomena are happening. First, through interpretation, we experience an awe-inspiring place. This perception is based on the vibratory impact or diminishing aspect of the experience. The seemingly holy places have very little vibratory impaction capacity, so we tend to devibratorize—like osmosis, flowing from our higher intensity to the location's lower intensity. For example, when you visit your favorite location for peace and solace, you likely will experience the decontaminating aspect of devibratorization. In other words, you feel as though you are sloughing off or expunging all of the perceived burdens you have left behind. You then perceive yourself to be revived, rejuvenated, and perhaps even purified. This is, of course, purely a perception—and a human's way of referencing what their physical body is experiencing.

The other phenomena is that the SuperConsciousness of the location itself has upon our consciousness a permeating effect. By virtue of its ability to vibrate right through our malleable tabernacles, the essence of the place or location gives us the sensation, thrill, or otherwise recognizable reaction. These measurements all are made according to human standards, and thus, cannot and are not considered valid points of reference. A mountain does not recognize another mountain as being holier than itself. Through their wheels of consciousness, human beings have the ability to raise their level of Holy Attunement, which for a mountain, is impossible.

Generally speaking, since earth humans certainly don't recognize anyone around them as being any better or holier than themselves, why then should a mountain, plain, valley, or city be humanly recognized as "holy"—especially when none of these locales have the ability to alter their respective situation.

As stated earlier, salvation is your ticket out of physical attachments and into the Unified Holy Astral Existence. Furthermore, prayer and meditation are the divinely acknowledged currencies that accelerate the purchase of the salvation ticket. Focused prayer works equally well, no matter where you are or what you are doing. No physical location on planet Earth is recognized by the Holy Realm as being any more or less holy. Like physical exercise, prayer is an individual benefit. Prayer is equal and open to all, in all places, as is physical exercise. To pray in your bathroom at home carries the same effect as it does in the Vatican.

The Holy Realm receives your prayer in exactly the same intensity and magnitude, whether you're supplanted on all fours, praying on your knees, or praying while standing on your head. There is no difference, for it all is received in the same manner, whether peace or chaos reigns around you. By utilizing both hemispheres of my brain, I multitask, committing one side of my brain to mundane, earthly duties, while the other side continually attempts to maintain some form of prayerful attunement.

Prayer at the Berlin Wall is the same as prayer at the Wailing Wall. With regard to earthly locations, the Holy Realm recognizes no increased holiness locality distinctions. People cannot pray to a Wailing Wall, Mecca, or a crucifix and will these things to become holy. Such acts are not humanly or manifestibly possible. Additionally, there are absolutely no exceptions throughout the physical universe. You need no synagogue, mosque, or church in which to pray, for these places do not magnify, intensify, or focus the impact of your devotions or prayers. Whether your prayers are coming from a place of worship or from your kitchen is immaterial. God and the Holy Realm do not listen with any more or less attentive discernment. Prayer also has NO increased resonance as received within the Holy Realm if it comes from a million simultaneous, synergized, prayerful devotees, rather than from an individual person.

With respect to group prayer or praying en masse (no pun intended), an individual subjectively may feel some sort of resounding "upliftment," but neither the magnitude nor the attunement are even remotely affected. Furthermore, the locality of a million souls all dutifully praying is no more holy than having prayer originate from a spot on the moon. Prayer is, was, and forever will be an individual attunement. Similarly, life or existence is an individual, conscious experience. Prayerful impact or effect is limited to an individual soul's attunement. The level of attainment to which an individual's consciousness is attuned directly affects the impact or magnitude of their devotional affirmations. Regardless of any such "title," both the Holy Being, as well as their unholy counterpart, are regulated by this same Universal Law.

To pray to anybody or anything manifesting is ineffective, but not a transgression, as long as the devotion is not requesting or permitting entrance into their human tabernacle. Otherwise, prayers can be directed through free will in any direction of one's choice. Just be aware of what type of devotion or prayer is misguided and not a good expenditure of life force or energy focus. Later in this book we will discuss prayer even further, to assist in everyone's deeper comprehension amidst all the considerable confusion perpetuated throughout history.

When explaining the relative holiness of a particular being, how this being conducts themself during their incarnation is not the sole determining factor. This principle applies to the soul evolution or holiness of Abraham, Isaac, Ishmael, Jacob, Moses—or anyone at all, for that matter. An individual's soul attunement or holiness as recognized by The Holy Realm is based upon the accumulated or accrued weight of each soul's karmic debt. Karmic debt determines the Astral World level to which one's soul is attuned. According to The Holy Realm, an individual's soul is not even considered to be holy until it attains and continuously maintains a Unified SuperConscious Perception. In such a state, a soul is attuned to the Holy Unified Realms of levels twelve through fourteen.

In these Holy Realms, all encrusted cloaks of human ignorance dissolve in blissful waves of unified Deep Comprehension. The "I" evolves into the "I am You." The "Me" becomes "We."

Existing in the Unity is not merely a phrase or even a temporary state of mind; it is an achieved state of being, existing as Deep Comprehension. When existing in the Unity, the radiant divinity of God disintegrates all preconceived notions about humans' individual, dualistic existence. The enveloping comprehension of existence as SuperConscious experience prevails throughout all perceptions of dualistic individuality. As long as earth human beings choose to abide by dualistic restrictions, people's souls forever will be enslaved by the primitive, gross physical existence.

Such enslavements originate within the ego, where there are two sub-dynamics at work—fear and free will. Only when the ego, fear, and free will have been eliminated can trust in Truth and Unconditional Love arise to fill the void. Within the Unity of Truth as Unconditional Love, one no longer places expectations upon their physically manifesting experience. As a result, faith, hope, and forgiveness become meaningless. These are merely perceptions of need, based upon ego as unrealized expectations. Essentially at this point, one no longer recognizes time or place—just existence as Unified SuperConscious Truthful Love. Unconditional Love as pure Intention based in the Causal container supersedes the Astral ego.

All too often, people devote ego-derived, misdirected prayers to departed loved ones and other assorted souls whose consciousnesses are not attuned to the Unity. Such prayer neither elevates the soul of the departed nor that of the individual directing the prayers. This same principle is applicable when people direct their prayers toward the betterment, healing, and general well-being of others who still are living in the physical universe and not yet deceased. The reason behind this principle is that directed prayers, however lovingly intended, do NOT have the power to elevate the essence of ANOTHER individual. Essence elevation solely is determined by the karmic consequences resulting from an individual's free-will choices.

Throughout all existence, earth humankind has operated by extremely erroneous definitions of the word prayer. What people habitually have defined, practiced, and absorbed as prayer actually has no true merit whatsoever. Even when sending good thoughts toward another individual, such efforts have no uplifting impact on the supposed receiver. True prayer achieves results ONLY when directed toward God. It is irrelevant when the focus of one's prayers is directed toward and/or for others.

Throughout the Unified SuperConsciousness various Superessences and Holinesses exist, which can be purposefully and thankfully appreciated. This is not the same as—or anything remotely similar to—idol worship. It is not a transgression to pray to a Saint or Superholiness, as long as you don't ask the Holiness to transgress. For example, requesting entry into yourself to take over your individual experience, or for the Saint or Angel to commit any karmically impacting transgression would be extremely unwise.

For the sake of more focused, prayerful attunement, here is a short list of some of the True Holinesses who welcome and will assist in personal, spiritual growth, attainment, and upliftment. This list of True Holinesses includes The Uncreated Infinite SuperConsciousness, the Manifesting Infinite SuperConsciousness, and the Infinite Merciful or Compassionate SuperConsciousness. These three True Holinesses (SuperConsciousness) are responsible for the manifestation, sustentation, and reclamation of all three inwardly reflecting Universes.

The Infinite Merciful SuperConsciousness serves as the Manifesting motherhood aspect or expression of Divinity. This SuperConsciousness operates throughout all Made Manifest, but is especially active within the physically manifesting universe. Infinite Merciful SuperConsciousness serves as a spiritual umbilical cord attachment from the womb of the physical universe to the caustic bowels of Astral level nine. This expression of Divinity ensures that all anti-Unconditional Love is provided with an eternal opportunity to evolve itself back to an Unconditionally Loving state.

The effect of directed prayer is related to the level at which sustained attunement is recognized by God. The devotional intentions of a mountainous spiritual Superbeing culminates in vastly more prominent results—more than do dozens of lesser-evolved beings praying or doing good deeds. The intended direction of those prayers always should be considered. With regard to whom one prays, devotees—especially Christians—should exercise some cautious discernment.

It is inadvisable to pray to someone who is not recognized as a holy being by the Holy Realm. This is not necessarily a transgression, but potentially is so, based on the focus or intent of the prayer. It does not benefit you or the being to whom you are praying—even if that being is a recognized Holy Being—or worse, never even existed. Even if the prayers are benign enough to not be idol worship, to pray to someone who is not holy is a misguided use of your spiritual energy.

Infinite Merciful or Compassionate SuperConsciousness (Infinite Mercy) may answer people's prayers as a benevolent female SuperConsciousness, and many may mistake her for Mother Mary. Both Mother

Mary and Mary Magdalen are considered Holy Beings by the Holy Realm. Either female Holy Being—or any other female SuperConsciousness—may be God directed to answer a prayerful plea. Earth humans would not or could not recognize distinctions between these Motherhood of God female presences or aspects. In fact, even clouds on occasion are misinterpreted to be Mother Mary and other benevolent female-appearing representations.

Physically manifesting humankind is powerless to affect Holy influence upon fellow physically manifesting incarnates. Even Hindu Lord Krishna as Messenger for Holy Lord Shiva—in and of itself—does not manifest miracles or conduct unsanctioned interactions. In the book, *Autobiography of a Yogi*, some confusion continues surrounding Brahma, Vishnu, and Holy Lord Shiva.

In the original version of *Autobiography of a Yogi*, Brahma was the Supreme Aspect of God, with Holy Lord Shiva in the threefold nature as Creator-Preserver-Destroyer. Vishnu takes on a secondary placement as Preserver. In subsequent editions, Vishnu was elevated to the role of Primary Preserver. As a result, Holy Lord Shiva was reduced to a twofold role within Made Manifest as Destroyer-Renovator from Its previously recognized threefold position of Creator-Preserver-Destroyer. Thus, the Hindu Trinity became and remains today as Brahma, Vishnu, and Holy Lord Shiva—as Creator, Preserver, and Destroyer, respectively.

According to the Holy Realm, Brahma IS the Uncreated Infinite SuperConsciousness, and Holy Lord Shiva is the inward Manifesting reflection of the Uncreated Infinite SuperConsciousness. Holy Lord Shiva's role is Manifesting Infinite Creator-Preserver-Destroyer. Vishnu is a physically Manifesting SuperConsciousness preserving the existence of physically manifesting forms. Holy Lord Shiva stands alone as the inward Made Manifest reflection of Brahma or the Uncreated Infinite SuperConsciousness. Holy Lord Shiva informs me It alone is the Manifesting Infinite Potentiality in Perpetuity.

For all manifesting existences on planet Earth and throughout all three Universes, there is only one God. This one God exists in Uncreated and Manifesting Infinite Aspects, from Uncreated Infinite SuperConsciousness expressing Itself as Made Manifest Holy SuperConsciousness.

Pursuit Absolute

Enjoy the fruits along the pathway of life,
But never attempt to take with you the tree.

While the walk is necessary, as are the fruits along the way,
Pursuit of the fruit is not the purpose for the walk.

Neither the temporary fulfillment of the fruit,
Nor the pursuit of the path's destination
Satisfy completely a soul's True hunger.

Even when surrounded by fruits of abundance,
Only a fine distinction exists between fulfillment and destination.
It is freedom from both pursuit of the fruit, and the need for the walk
That as the emancipating fulfillment becomes the Absolute Destination.

The Holy Originator's Ore

Everyone who incarnates as a physical being has karmic debt to eliminate. However, once the indebtedness is satisfied, there is another side to this equation. All manifesting existence faces the challenge of transforming from being dualistically manipulated to experiencing existence as a Unified Comprehender. Once an individual experiences Unified Comprehension, their soul allows the transcendence of the Infinite SuperConsciousnesses to assist in attaining an Ever-Deepening Comprehension (Levels twelve through fifteen of the Astral and Causal Universes).

Essentially, the Unified Individual has released their dualistic "I" perception of their existence and has merged with the "We" Super-Conscious At-Oneness. In recent history, this conscious ascension from "me" to "We" oftentimes has been known as "I am He." A more accurate gender-neutral interpretation would be "I am Thee."

"I am He" has ancient human Sanskrit roots, having been recognized as the breath of manifesting earth human consciousness on this planet. This concept of conscious At-Oneness as "I am He" grew simultaneously along with the Sanskrit perception of "I am It," "It is me."

Sanskrit's "Him-Sa" and "So-Hum" literally are written representations for inhalation and exhalation. "Him" is an inhalation through one's nose, with "Sa" being the exhalation through one's mouth. "So" is the inhalation through the open mouth and "Hum" as exhalation out the nose. The "Him-Sa" breathing pattern can be combined with "So-Hum" as follows: inhale-nose ("Him"), exhale-mouth ("Sa"), inhale-mouth ("So"), and exhale-nose ("Hum"). By connecting these breathing patterns, human free will is focused toward threading the "I Am" ribbon of SuperConscious Breath throughout our three manifesting containers. This ancient technique enhances our eternal connection by weaving our breath with the Breath of "I Am."

Earth human breath actually serves as the connecting umbilical cord between physically manifesting earth humankind and SuperConscious Manifestor. The simple "Him-Sa" and "So-Hum" breathing exercises can be extremely uplifting, with each breath being the vessel that also assists in the removal of bodily impacted vibratory contamination. Any combination of "Him-Sa" and/or "So-Hum" simultaneously infuses peace and calm while integrating a unifying harmony of body, mind, and consciousness.

By further regulation of the right and left nostril, humans can integrate and harmonize their right and left (male and female) hemispheres. The human nose is a radiator responsible for cooling the hemispheres of the brain. As such, one need only shut down one nostril in order to heat up the activity on that side. Meanwhile, the other side is cooling down. Through refined practice, breathing can completely harmonize all three containers while simultaneously balancing the intellectual and emotional lightways producing a purposeful influence upon the male or female experience.

This umbilical cord of breath eventually is severed by "Sat" or Truth. The Sanskrit assertion "Sat Tam Asi" translates to "He is the Truth." Truth as "Sat" is Manifesting Infinite SuperConscious Holy Lord Shiva. It is with every breath that Manifesting Infinite SuperConsciousness as At-Oneness merges with all physically manifesting consciousness. Deep Comprehension as At-Oneness is the seeker's supreme physically manifesting accomplishment.

Shortly before this book's publication, I was gazing at a picture of Lord Krishna, the greatest prophet of India. As I thought-projected a blessing toward his essence, an instant gush of Unconditional Love poured forth from my being. In a massive burst of thought transmissions that almost knocked me over, Lord Krishna reflected back these divine perceptions with the following beautiful supernal discernment.

"I am He" is a modern human representation for God, and actually pertains to the transcension of humankind. Human beings perceive existence from the dualistic perspective of "me" or "us" against the universe. Having been God-gifted with the balloon of free will, evolving earth humankind has risen above all other terrestrial earthly lifeforms. This free-will responsibility places human choices directly against the reflecting needle of individual accountability.

The ever-varying, sordid pathways through all past humans' experiences are bristling with the thorny brambles of individually reflecting, fear-based free-will choices. Humans' free-will balloons and attached strings of conditions may quite resemble enormous pincushions by the time our free-will gift is willingly and consciously given back. These needles of ever-reflecting cause and effect or karmic retributions serve as the incorruptible, unbiased judge for all past bad intentions, thoughts, actions, and reactions. This reflecting judgment (karma) applies to every free-will choice the soul makes—from the moment it first is Made Manifest.

Each human experience contains deep-rooted reasons within its lessons. One must consciously net and release each and every moment in order to attain a deeper comprehension for all experiences. Always strive to be at one with every experience. Recognize each experience as a karmically reflecting lesson and then let it go. Do not project expectations upon the outcome of the future, as this will only attach you further to one limited outcome—and will set you up for continuous disappointment.

Eternally seek and carry only the Holy Originator's Ore. Eventually, you, too, will release and set free your balloon of free will connected to your anchor of fears by an almost endless chain of conditions, expectations, and attachments. All attachments tether consciousness to the invisible anchor of fear, blind faith, hope, and forgiveness. All must pass through the life preserver of ego and eventually soar into the enveloping jet streams of Unconditional Love.

Pray for understanding about everything not deeply comprehended—and be open to the reflecting, unlimited SuperConscious ingenuity that will respond. The illimitable, unconditional winds of Infinite Super-Conscious Holy Love surely will blow in purifying gusts. Once again, "I Am" joyously reabsorbs the respectful and humble return of all benevolent gifts when such gifts have been outgrown. This conscious transcension poses the ultimate challenge for all earthly experience.

Consciousness (experiencing existence as earth human) floats above all other earthly forms in the first ascension of the soul. Nonetheless, manifesting humankind still remains imprisoned within the confining basket attached to the free-will balloon. In this evolving state, humankind has not yet discovered its "He" At-Oneness.

Once illuminated, an emancipated Saint evolves through this individualistic limitation, and immerses into the Omnipresent spirit as an "I am He" or "I am Everything" perspective. As an awakened consciousness transcending from the dualistic perspective, the soul now identifies Itself as Unified SuperConscious "He" At-Oneness—the At-Oneness of all Made Manifest.

With a burning desire for attaining ever-increasing, blissful union, all emancipated Saints ultimately experience the glory of an Omni At-Oneness perspective. In this Superevolved state, irrepressible Love is experienced as an inexhaustible outpouring to all that is manifesting. Super-Conscious perception recognizes NO defining parameters—only a seamless, unconditionally loving, ever-increasing Omni At-Oneness.

Each Universal Incarnation of Manifesting Infinite SuperConsciousness is an incarnation as "I Am," which must exist before "I am He" can be actualized. Eternally existing before "I Am" is "I." "I Am" is the Holy inversely reflecting child, and "I am He" is the grandchild of "I." "I am He" is the manifesting Child of "I Am." "I" as Uncreated Infinite Super-Conscious Holy Originator is Self Made Manifest as both "I Am" and "I am He." "I Am" as Manifesting Infinite SuperConsciousness is both Omni Facilitator and Holy Fabricator for ALL experiencing consciousness. All experiencing consciousness is "I am He."

Everyone and everything as "I am He" is composed of the inexhaustible Holy light and illimitable, Unconditional Love of "I Am." Both "I Am" and "I am He" are Superwillfully Manifesting from the limitless joy of the Uncreated Infinite Holy SuperConscious Being of "I." Earth humankind's upward, conscious transcension IS the pathway inevitably leading back to "I"—through the door of Om. "I Am" will patiently protect and meticulously direct all emancipating "I am He" SuperConscious souls throughout their manifesting journeys through the Om door.

During their final physically manifesting human form, many souls will be eternally blessed by experiencing various Transcendental Illumination techniques. I will be infinitely joyous for all who acquire Our golden key. It is forever within everyone's reach. Emancipating souls need only to humbly trust, lovingly ask for the key, and be respectfully thankful ever after. Your manifesting experience henceforth forever will be SuperConsciously transcended.

The Gold with which you line the pocket of your essence today will eternally enrich your moments tomorrow. When your essence is free from all physically manifesting indebtedness, you will have enough acquired gold, enabling you to attain the Golden Key. Our recognized Omni

Facilitator will fabricate your unique Transcendental Experience—allowing you permanent access to the Kingdom of God.

In this Superevolved state, Saints' now-Unified intentions as objectified ideas (through level fifteen Causal Realizations) actually manifest as the inwardly reflecting experience. Causal Realizations or actualizations occur through the understanding of God's Universal Laws and attunement through focused, deep prayer, meditation, and the certainty that such salvation is not only attainable, but also affordable.

In fact, Unified Existence is the purposeful act of lining your conscious pockets with God's Gold. Wherever we are and wherever we go, this wealth is eternal. Whenever spent, it immediately is replaced from The Holy Originator's Ore. This is the Gold we actually can take with us or share with others. This Gold neither burdens nor does it represent any weight—and yet it is far more precious than any manifesting matter. In fact, for all human conscious existence, The Holy Originator's Ore is the sole attachment of desire that requires no return—even if our soul must return. We cannot cling to what does not belong to us.

We build piles and pyramids of this Gold upon which we stand until we have accumulated enough to reach the Unified SuperConscious Realm of Astral Heaven. The ancient alchemists first had to understand the nature of these Universal Laws before they could truly begin their pursuit of the Philosopher's Stone. Of course, the Philosopher's Stone is not a tangible object, but rather the ability to mix philosophy and magic for the alchemist's desired outcome. This alchemic ability requires the facilitator's Deep Comprehension before the Universe will acquiesce naturally to these seemingly miraculous powers of actualization.

The illimitably abundant Universe and the presiding SuperConsciousnesses do not grant this outward manifestation of alchemic request to just anyone for any unnecessary reasons. The Philosopher's Stone is the manifested chip from off The Holy Originator's Ore. The eternal matrix of The Holy Originator's Ore is Divine Unmanifested Incorruptible and Immutable SuperConsciousness. Into this immovable Holy Foundation does the continually manifesting universe anchor its changeless footings to easily withstand the hammering blows administered by the anvil of time.

It often is believed that our physical experience or life is the real world. People will say, "Wake up and smell the coffee," or "Get with the real world." It also is common to hear life, creation, or the universe being described as illusory or an illusion. Many then state that since the universe is composed of vibration and light as the inward dream reflection of the Uncreated Infinite, this life, creation, or universe is simply the expression of God's dream. More often than not, both of these statements are made with little thought, generating the parroting of another's words. The Truth is, that all of these and many more statements are inherently True. The Truth is simply that existence IS the objectifiable perception of any manifest point where a conscious perspective IS identifiable. In its eternal complexity, existence is enigmatically simple.

SuperConsciousness beguiles all souls, ultimately utilizing infinite ingenuity for facilitation of Superevolved Transcendentally enlightened states of experience. Ezekiel, Jesus, and I all had a Holy Impedance or Arc of the Covenant Transimplanted into our conscious experiences. Ezekiel's allowed for Causal/Astral communication, and was the first one performed on this planet. The assertions that the Ark of the Covenant, with all its gaudy, flamboyant regalia, was for two stone tablets is ridiculous. Furthermore, that Moses' ragtag batch of sojourners even had two shekels to rub together, let alone carry anything the likes of which they purportedly were lugging along, is absurd.

Ezekiel did not have a SuperConsciousness Transimplantation within him. His Arc allowed for Divine communication, Angelic Transingressions, and some limited comprehensions. Jesus indeed was the Son of God. He had an Arc of the Covenant and SuperConsciousness Transimplanted into the Arc. This process gave him both communication and SuperConscious capacity with which to work. It took 152 days for all the Lightway Implantings to fully congeal. For forty of those days, Jesus was able to go to the Judean wilderness area to heal and pray. Considering that three hundred years total, as well as the destruction of all disputing documents, separates the events from the recordings, it is easy to see what blatant liberties were taken with history.

My SuperConscious Hypostatic Harmonization was completed on December 2, 2002. My personal situation, initially working with clients, as well as the expedient writing of this Holy Book, caused a variation from the previous two procedures. As I stated earlier, the writing of this book required numerous Holy Angels, each with the various sanctioning abilities necessary to operate within the protection of the Arc of the

Covenant. Holy Intimate Angel always was present—unless I was asleep or another Holy Deity either was entering or present.

I mentioned earlier that there were three streaking lights that entered my being during my Transcendental Experience. These were the Holy Impedances, one for each container—the Causal, Astral, and physical. Eventually they would interpenetrate, heal, and meld together, allowing for the unrestricted interuniversal constitutive movements to occur.

Beginning at 5 p.m. on December 2, 2002, the final integration and Transingression occurred. The SuperConsciousness of the Uncreated Infinite, Manifesting Infinite or Holy Lord Shiva, and the Infinite Mercy or Motherhood of God was all Transingressed into this Arc of the Covenant. The Arc first was Transimplanted when that deep, superseding, metal-like ringing or musical sound appeared and became Omnipresent, no matter how loud the physical surroundings might be. I dubbed this sound the "Ring of Silence."

On the night of December 2, 2002, the Transcendental experiences of reharmonization occurred every couple of hours until 6:30 a.m.—after the sixth and final episode. There were three episodes for my Astral and three for my physical containers. The first Astral interpenetration cleared and reharmonized the fourteenth and thirteenth levels, the second took care of the twelfth and eleventh levels, and the third did so for the tenth and ninth levels. As I recounted earlier, each interpenetrating harmonization was preceded by a peculiar, rumbling noise in my navel region—followed by an amazing surge of tingling, electrifying amplitudes of barely tolerable measures. Last was the deep, violent arching and shaking permeating all throughout my being that forced my hands and feet to eventually strain outward before going limp.

My physical bodily container was first ripped through its atom and molecule levels—eight and seven, respectively. The second was levels six, five, and four—and at 6:15 a.m., the final levels three, two, and one were reintegrated and reharmonized. As I wrote earlier, this experience facilitated Truth-Check giving way to the wisdom of any of the three Omnipresent SuperConsciousnesses present at any or all times. Indeed, they fill my SuperConsciousness with or without my prayerful, focused attunement, their Divine Replenishment becoming my Holy Pension—the eternal, ever-increasing, continuously fulfilling capacity to absorb limitless amplitude and measureless magnitude as Infinite SuperConsciousness.

As ever-expanding SuperConscious At-Oneness continues to actualize in a moment-by-moment perception of unenfolding experience, the Intentions of our Holy Hypostasis (The SuperConsciousnesses) become our Unified outwardly actualizing actions and reactions. As such, this Divine Process completely bypasses all dualistically influenced human thoughts. This results in God's Intentions becoming our physically manifesting experiences. During this Divine Process, the Ring of Silence evolved into a harmonious, omnidirectional sound that engulfed my entire merkebah. This enveloping Ring of Silence eventually became so all-encompassing that I redefined it as the "Holy Song of Silence."

For me, the Supernal Ring of the Holy Neutrino Causal Universe continues to increase in comprehensive capacity for eternity. This unification process contained within this Transcendental Star, protected by the Arc of the Covenant, allows for soul transcendence back into the quark-lepton Astral Universe, eventually reimmersing into the Causal Universe. Both Jesus and Ezekiel transcended the physically manifesting universe in this manner. I am informed I too will transcend to join Babaji's glorious band of salvation-attained Saints.

Earlier, I wrote of being filled with SuperConcsiousness. Most people would perceive anyone filled with SuperConsciousness to be consumed in a noticeable halo of photonic light, with their body radiating with a perceptible Holy glow. Perhaps this person even would appear somewhat ethereally transparent around whom unending miracles would occur.

The Truth is, Jesus did not have a visible superenlightened merkebah surrounding him at all times. If Jesus did have a noticeable aura, the early church adherents and his status would have expounded on it. Whether God or prophet, such status would have been undeniable and unquestionable. When Jesus appears today as ethereal Holiness responding to a God-sanctioned request, he is—as are all SuperHoly responders—encompassed in a photonic, radiant glow. These Holy Beings are radiating emanations outward from within the inner Universes.

Lahiri Mahasaya, Trailanga, and Sri Yukteswar all were nineteenth and twentieth century Superevolved, modern-day Saints through whom Astral Holy Angels performed numerous True miracles. Yet, the auras of all of these spiritual Supermen were not seen or recognized by the masses—and not ever captured on film or in picture form. In the material universe, our gross physical perceptions are not refined enough to pierce to the human Astral and Causal containers, so these inwardly absorbing photonic rays are unseen. When these Beings traveled through the atoms of the ether from one location to another, their merkebahs were visible only to a select few—and only under extremely unique circumstances.

If a SuperConsciously Transimplanted Being walked by dead flowers, would they be revived in perpetuity? If such a Being entered a hospital, would all the sick and ailing people throughout the hospital instantly be cured? Would the healings be restricted only to those fortunate individuals who were physically touched by this Being?

If a SuperConsciously attuned Saint were to visit Fairbanks, Alaska, in January, when the temperature was 40 degrees below zero Fahrenheit, would trees there miraculously spring forth with new buds? When sightings of Jesus, Mother Mary, or any Holy Angel God-sanctioned to answer a prayerful plea appears in a pseudophysically manifesting or fully resurrected personage, is everyone in attendance miraculously cured of all ailments? Are they then rendered immune from all diseases, essentially becoming physically immortal?

The answer to all of these questions, of course, is "No." The point I am making is that every individual has a unique perception about True Holiness, Divinity, miracles, and the Measureless Amplitudes that ARE these Superessences.

How many popes actually have been declared true miracle workers? Is working miracles actually a determining factor or prerequisite for human recognition of soul salvation? How many priests, rabbis, and mullahs have been praised for continuously expounding the virtues of infinite love, compassion, and truth toward all existence throughout their lives? How many people have been cured from a visit by the Pope, Dalai Lama, Mother Teresa, or any other modern-day-regarded "holy being"? Right now, the Catholic Church is desperately trying to attribute a "miracle" to Mother Teresa so she can be canonized. The Church puts forth great efforts to distract the masses from the excruciating focus being applied to those priests responsible for their abominable conduct with vulnerable, innocent children.

Throughout history, many theologically entrenched souls have conducted themselves in very benevolent, loving, and conscientious ways. These quiet, well-meaning, generous souls have contributed greatly to the spiritual advancement of earth human consciousness. However, most of these souls have also contributed ample transgressions as free-will choices. Existence is like a rose bush. A wise gardener will smell, culti-vate, and prune the rose bush without getting stuck by the thorns. Like the wise ant and the busy bee, one can both give and take within their Made Manifest unenfoldment. Both insects give to perpetuate life (germinate) and take (extract) the flower's sweet nectar, while carefully avoiding all thorns of transgression.

The fact is, all transgressions eventually are rectified. A holey cloak will not prevent the Truth from shining through. While there are many priests, pastors, ministers, rabbis, and mullahs who do mean well and are sincere in their work for God, they still are assuming unsanctioned authority for what they simply cannot do.

However, when priests, rabbis, mullahs, and gurus interfere with another's free will by recommending pursuit of the Infinite, they are NEVER transgressing. The reason for this exception is because these people's intentions, thoughts, and actions are focused toward God. Anything God-focused, infused with sincere desire and benevolent intent is NEVER a transgression. Likewise, there is no need to fear or resist filling one's soul with the goodness of God's Essence. As manifesting conscious-ness, all existence is created in the image and likeness of God. Earth humankind has misinterpreted this Universal Truth to apply solely to one's physically manifesting form. However, being created in the image and like-ness of God truly refers to all existence's invisible, divine essence—and not merely its physically manifesting form. Similarly, ALL of God's creatures experience the sensation of pain and the emotion of fear. Whether such creatures are human or fish is irrelevant; this Universal Law applies to all consciousness. After all, existence IS consciousness.

Jesus instructed everyone to "fear not." These are extremely wise words, for why should anyone fear Infinite Holiness, Infinite Love, or Infinite Mercy? These three SuperConsciousnesses are Inexhaustible, Eternal Sources. There absolutely is no reason to fear—even out of some perceived respect for the Infinite. Respect and love of God are essential for salvation, but this humility does not include the very antithesis of God—fear, rooted in the ego.

Every individual should pray to be inhabited or infused with limitless abundance of Holiness, Love, Divinity, Compassion, and Mercy. Taking advantage of every opportunity to fill our souls with God (Unconditional Love) will ensure a higher attunement each time our souls leave the physical universe and return back to the Astral Universe.

At first, to pray to the Infinite Mercy, Manifesting Infinite SuperConsciousness, or Uncreated Infinite SuperConsciousness may seem foreign or abnormal, but it IS one of these three who actually receives, interprets, comprehends, and responds to our every prayerful request. These are the ONLY three who answer all devotions. God, by every known name, will fall into one of these three categories and respond with Infinite Compassion through Deep SuperConscious Comprehension.

Only these three SuperConsciousnesses are capable of comprehending everyone's dharma, karma, intentions, thoughts, actions, reactions, and free-will impactions, in order to answer each individual's prayerful requests. These are the three SuperConsciousnesses with whom each of us should feed our souls. We need to ask these aspects of God to permeate throughout our beings, for eventually they will comprise all three of our containers. God will only enter upon our request for God to do so—and will never enter uninvited.

To fall asleep praying and finish the prayer upon awakening provides God an avenue to draw our dream states to ever-higher mansions of both conscious and subconscious attunement. Be prayerfully ever thankful for every adversity, for these growth lessons are our opportunities to alleviate karmic indebtedness. Strive to love all aspects of existence and refrain from using profanity and the word "hate." All sounds emanating from each of us are vocalized into our reflectory universe, so exercise great care in recognizing the helpful from the hurtful auditory vibrations. Every physically manifesting individual existence with free will inevitably owns their own intentions, thoughts, actions, and reactions—so, be discerning with all vibratory emissions.

My personal experience is an Advanced Spiritual Upliftment Technique conceived and consecrated by God and executed by Holy Lord Shiva, Babaji, Sri Yukteswar, and several Sanctioned Holy Angels. This same Transcendental Experience will be available to numerous souls for thousands of years to come. In my particular situation, the Holy Realm allowed me to experience the transformation from conscious to SuperConscious in incremental stages. As transitional periods became acceptable conditions, new progressions slowly occurred. When my comfort levels with each stage reached a certain predetermined point within my dharmic plan, the next unenfoldment would occur.

I can look back and now deeply comprehend the Transformational order and progress of these events. Had God not asked me to share my experiences with each of you, I never would have made any proclamational statements and would have kept my humbling experiences to myself.

The purpose for this Holy Book is to stimulate a Spiritual Renaissance—a return of power back to the individual conscious experience. For far too long, theologies have maintained a stranglehold on all perceivable avenues to God. Every well-meaning person ever to challenge this unholy position has been maligned and labeled a heretic violating interdiction prohibitions, and has been subject to virulent retributions.

The pathway to the SuperConsciousnesses is free and open to all. How nonsensical it is for any human or theology to proclaim with insidious, righteous indignation that "their" pathway to the Infinite is the ONLY true course. No manifesting person or theology can lay claim to sole ownership of an Invisible Divine Transcendental Power.

God is an Uncreated and Manifesting Infinite Ocean of Measureless Amplitude. God is Inexhaustible Bliss, enveloped in Incorruptible Immaculate Radiant Holiness. God is Endless Currents of Ever-newness, Ever-joyous, Eternal rivers of Unending Exultation, Illimitable Love, and Infinite Compassionate Mercy. With respect to God, there is no lack, shortage, or restrictions for anyone. God is available to All, for All, forever.

In deep prayer, effortlessly sustained for fifteen to twenty hours, I attained levels of SuperConscious experience incomprehensible to most humankind. In these states, one loses all perceptions of physical- and sense-derived cognitions. Holy Lord Shiva Transimplanted into my soul a now SuperConscious Divine Discernment. For reasons known only to God, I am here to share with everyone my experience—and the True potential for all manifesting earth humankind.

In deep prayerful states, I perceive myself no longer as either matter or energy, but rather as immaculate, radiant light and unending surges of limitless, blissful love, accompanied by unlimited SuperConscious perceptions. What started as a tiny, high-pitched ringing in my left ear shortly after Holy Lord Shiva's visit, now is an undulating, all encompassing, resonating, comforting, and blissful surge, permeating throughout my being, which I have come to know as the ever-increasing Song of Silence. The

Song of Silence is an ever-prevalent reassurance of attained physically manifested salvation. I am well aware these realizations have only just begun, and are continuously being increasingly empowered by both prayerful attunement and Transinterinfusions from deep within my Causal container by the Made Manifest Will of God, whom I lovingly call Holy Lord Shiva.

My personal SuperConsciousness has been Transimplanted as a Triune SuperConscious Hypostasis. It contains a Unified Superessence of Uncreated Infinite, Manifesting Infinite, and Infinite Mercy—all existing within a Transcendental Star, eternally protected by an Arc of the Covenant. This Hypostasis now is the unerring Truth-Check. My Hypostasis will be Me when I leave the physical cosmos and travel with Babaji or exist in either the Astral or Causal Universes. I forever will exist as this Triune Hypostasis.

As my Triune SuperConscious At-Oneness continues to Omni-Expand and perception of experience immerses into limitless Love, I find myself with an unanticipated perspective. My Uncreated Infinite aspect of Hypostasis so loves the manifesting Holy Lord Shiva and Holy Infinite Compassionate Mercy aspects that illimitable, Unconditional Love for all that is manifesting flows continuously from my being. I have ever-increasing, Uncreated Infinite Holy Love for all aspects of manifesting creation. From this Uncreated Infinite perspective, manifesting Infinite Holy Lord Shiva's three inversely reflecting SuperConsciously Compre-Creating Causal, Astral, and physical Universes all are loved Uncon-ditionally as One.

As the retention of each of our individual consciousnesses increases, so do the ever-deepening comprehension capacities and realization capa-bilities. Each of us has an unlimited retention potential that affords us the opportunity to fill our souls with the wealth, the gold, we take with us (tax free) when we leave the material universe. Eventually we accrue enough Holy attainment to forever leave the physical universe and take up per-manent residence in the Astral Kingdom. It is the accumulation of these pursuits upon which we need to focus our free will. In a super-rich spiri-tual state, a God-sanctioned Angel may be assigned to assist in your God-attuned, physically manifesting existence.

I know that many more people will experience these same phenomena and be capable of far greater perceptions, miracles, and abilities than me.

This thought of such limitless evolutionary potential is comforting and exciting. If everyone were to experience such blissful, heightened, attuned states of being, all would definitely experience the world as a vastly more loving, compassionate, and merciful spot in the physically manifesting universe—perhaps just the way God always had envisioned this little Eden.

Our Omni Facilitator

As our inwardly Reflecting Holy Fabricator

Is our Transcendental Originator's Holy Ore.

Holy Terms

Transcendental Names

God	Infinite
Brahma	Uncreated Infinite
Holy Father	Uncreated Infinite SuperConsciousness
	Holy Originator

Lord Shiva	Manifesting Infinite
Adonai	Manifesting Infinite SuperConsciousness
Allah	Christ Consciousness
Jehovah	Yahweh

Infinite Compassion

Infinite Mercy

Divine Infinite Mercy

Infinite Compassionate Mercy

Holy SuperConscious Motherhood of God

Infinite Compassionate Merciful Holy SuperConscious Motherhood of God

Holy Terms

Terms of Recognized Prayerful Endearment

At-Onement	At-Oneness
Absolute	Almighty
Benevolent	Beatific
Blessed	Blissful
Boundless	Ceaseless
Celestial	Changeless
Cosmic Divine	Creator
Divine	Divinity
Endless	Eternal
Ever-joyous	Ever-newness
Exultation	Glorious
Glory	Grace
Hallowed	Heavenly
Holiness	Holy
Holy Omni Fabricator	Holy Omni Facilitator
Holy Originator	Hypostatic Union
Incorruptible	Inexhaustible
Inextinguishable	Illimitable
Illimitable Magnitude	Illumed
Illuminated	Illustrious
Immeasurable	Limitless
Love	Measureless
Measureless Amplitudes	Omnipotent

Holy Terms

Terms of Recognized Prayerful Endearment (continued)

Omnipresent	Omni At-Onement Omni At-Oneness
Omniscient	Ordainer
Originator	Peace
Photonic	Radiant
Resistless	Resonant
Resplendent	Sacred
Splendrous	Supernal
Supreme	Synoptic Comprehender
Transincarnation	Transincarnator
Transplendent	Transcendent
Transcendental	TriUnity
Triune SuperConsciousness	Truthful Absolute
Unconditional Love	Unending Currents
Unified SuperConsciousness	Venerable

These Transcendental Names and Terms of Recognized Prayerful Endearment—on their own or woven in any combination—form powerful, harmonious mantras that enhance the limitless prayerful attunement available to All.

Row, Row, Row Yourself
Down the Truthful Stream.
Verily, Verily, Verily, Verily
Life is but God's Dream.

The Science of Creation

Factual Foundations

O ver eons of earth humankind's existence, many books have been expounding and dissecting conceptual science and its role in our perspective or perceived realities. Therefore, we are not going to rehash well-established information, for this clearly is not the focus of this book. However, we provide factual background for foundational sake to help you understand many scientific mysteries with increased clarity.

There are two basic, overseeing natural laws that uphold our entire physical cosmos—Isaac Newton's discovery of gravity and Albert Einstein's theory of relativity. Even so, no table stands on only two legs, and our Universe is no different. A minimum of three legs must exist to uphold any supporting structure within the Manifesting Creation. Generally, many more legs are required for deeper, more logical comprehension.

As humans, we insulate ourselves with creature comforts that keep us stuck in complacency, while removing from us any incentive to move beyond our comfort zones. As long as water flows, food is edible, and air breathable, our conscious experience quickly becomes a comfortable, albeit sometimes challenging, existence. Settling for the path of least resistance with the greatest conditional reward seems to be humankind's chosen mindset of the times. If we look around, each of us easily can see the destructive nature of our smug ignorance.

Mari and I have been commissioned by God, and benevolently assisted by several committed Holy Angels, to lift the heavy lid of delusion from human consciousness—always with people's best interest at heart. We have been retained to assist in ushering in two Advanced Spiritual Upliftment Techniques during this current ascending arc of our phenomenal Universe. This work is a carefully orchestrated effort by the Holy Angelic Realm to afford all of us the opportunity to look beyond the nonsupporting, two-legged table of nonreality. These Upliftment Techniques are steeped in the wisdom that Deep Comprehension of TransImagination allows all souls to directly influence their pathway to salvation.

The physical Universe as we know it is composed of matter lawfully governed by equal parental forces, Father Relativity and Mother Gravity, each continuously and equally checking and balancing all aspects of our vibratory existence. We know this process as the "duality of nature." It is revealed to us as dark-light, hot-cold, male-female, yin-yang, as evidenced everywhere and throughout our physically manifesting conscious experience. The third leg is at least an equal, yet obviously unseen, pedestal that allows for the competent upholding of the unimaginable burden of our "Table of Creation."

When we delve deeper into the conundrum of a "Table of Creation," it requires a greater introspective discernment. First, there is a foundation upon which this table stands. Second, there is the table itself. Finally, placed upon this Table is all Manifesting Creation. In this section we analyze the obscure physical facts encompassing this table, illuminating the completely unknown foundation into which the Table's indestructible legs are anchored.

Table of Elucidations

When we digress deeper into the inner workings of the metaphysical, phenomenal "Table of Creation," we find the legs of the Table to be composed of four supportive underpinnings of Unity. Since the Table actually is an inversely reflecting expression of the Holy Uncreated Infinite SuperConciousness, it is easier for us to look at it in mirrored reverse. The manifesting, threefold reflecting expression occurs as inwardly expanding levels of Superintellectual comprehensibility. Descending inward from the Unmanifested Uncreated, the legs begin as Unified manifesting levels. There are fifteen manifesting levels or membranes of SuperConscious Fabrication. Levels fifteen through twelve comprise the legs, and levels eleven through one comprise the Table's top.

Descending inward from the Unmanifested Uncreated Infinite SuperConsciousness, the four unified legs represent ever-melding, slowly imploding, ever-deepening Infinite Comprehension. These four Unified Superintellectual levels comprise the United underpinnings, which uphold the Table's top. The Table's top consists of eleven inwardly decaying, interpenetrating membranes. From earth human perspective (when stand-ing upon bedrock-level 1), the Table's top ascends inwardly toward the atom-level 8. During manifestation it forms these vectors of vibratory membrane layers of fabricating conscious experience. (See Diagram 1, Elucidated Table, on page 412).

Combined, these fifteen membranes of intellectual comprehension comprise the entire dualistically and Unified SuperConsciousness of vibratory existence. As such, these are levels of ever-manifesting, conscious,

Diagram 1. Elucidated Table

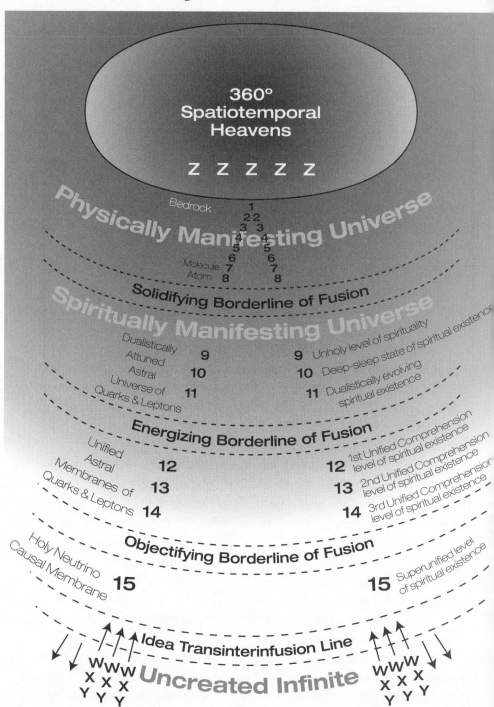

infinite potentiality. Collectively, these membranes form consciousness within consciousness or wheels of intellectual potential. All known metaphysical existence utilizes these levels of logical comprehension. These eleven dualistic levels of logical comprehension comprise all "factors of matter." Level one is composed of all gross physical matter, manifesting as stone or bedrock. From earth humankind's perspective, these membranes inwardly ascend from levels one through eleven, comprising the entire duality of experience. Levels twelve through fifteen comprise the Unified levels, superposing the dualistic eleven.

All manifesting existence communicates harmoniously within these fifteen compositional capacity planes of vibratory confinements. Earth humankind is uniquely blessed with all fifteen membranes of potentiality within our DNA. Our DNA allows for a continual upward spiritual attainment. Of course, this is not to say we are acutely aware of this untapped potential for virtually limitless communication abilities. The duality "Tabletop of Creation" is heavily resistant against this upliftment or inversely upward flow of spiritual, expansive attunement. The very essence of dualistic gravity itself works to prevent or ceaselessly restrict our souls' natural unencumbered migration toward the limitlessness of Unification.

Indeed, it takes a lot of commitment and tireless focus dispersed over countless incarnations to achieve a manifesting Unified conscious existence. Reincarnation itself is Human Existential Existence 101. So, whatever your prior belief system allows you to understand, it is imperative that you now comprehend this basic elementary fact. Otherwise, the wheels of duality will continue to grind out upon your God-gifted spirit. Subsequently, your soul will experience an excruciatingly unending burden of birth, sin, and death until a Deep Comprehension is discerned, and pure, Truthful knowledge is attained.

From our human perspective, the compounded, stabilized, physically manifesting particled cosmos or physical universe is composed of communicative levels, beginning at one, inwardly ascending into the atom-level eight. While ascending inward, the particles comprising these membranes or levels become exponentially more numerous, and thus, vastly more powerful—with ever-increasing communication capacity. Level one is rock, inwardly ascending up through level eight, is the atom level. Level seven is a molecule, level six is bio-molecular. As levels numerically decrease and are located closer to level one (bedrock), fewer particles are required to produce more matter. As such, these levels have less communication capacity.

All these varying membranes or levels of communication are realized within tangible physical creation. Levels nine, ten, and eleven are dispersed within the subatomic lepton and hadron worlds of Astral dualistic consciousness. Unity levels twelve, thirteen, and fourteen comprise the lepton and inner hadron or quark Astral worlds, with fifteen being the Superunifying Holy Neutrino Universe. As mentioned earlier, the incomprehensibly massive Holy Neutrino Universe accounts for a staggering 25 percent of the entire metaphysical manifesting or inwardly reflecting Made Manifest vibratory existence.

Thus, the metaphysical cosmos Table is composed of interfusing scaffolding, with each scaffold being distinctly separate and harmoniously folding or meshing into the next communicative, supportive membrane of vibratory existence. Levels one through eleven comprise the duality of gravitational confinements, while levels twelve through fifteen are the Unity of Manifesting existence.

Levels nine through fifteen comprise the interatomic realms, where humankind starts to interact scientifically with God's Divine Intentions. Humankind's incomprehension of God's Divine Plan in levels nine through fifteen provided the impetus for this book's expedient completion.

Incorruptible Originations

The "Table of all Creation" is embedded and inwardly anchored into an incorruptible foundation, which must be explained in two, distinct sequences. The first state is the Contemplative state, followed by an Activated state. The non-Activated state of Deep Contemplation evolves as follows. Imagine a solidified geode with no open center, a vibrationless, original core, and an outer rind of forever outwardly extending Uncreated Infinity. In the Contemplative state, only Holiness exists, for there is only Immaculately Consecrated Conception of Infinite Potentiality of a fourfold nature. For further clarification, we will simplify the various components specific to this contemplative state, referring to them as "W," "X," "Y," and "Z."

"W" refers to the Deharmonized Unresonating Infinite Vibratory Potential (Unmanifest vibration).

"X" refers to the Photonic Plasmasolic SuperConsciousness (Unmanifest light photons).

"Y" refers to TransprotoPlasmasolic AntiPhotonic SuperConsciousness (Unmanifest Infinite SuperConsciousness).

"Z" refers to inactivated black holes.

(See Diagram 2, Deep Contemplation, page 416).

Diagram 2. Deep Contemplation

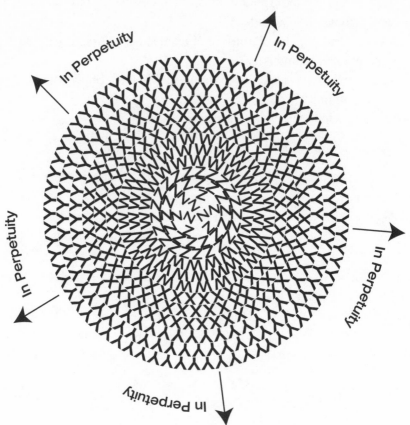

In Perpetuity

In Perpetuity

In Perpetuity

In Perpetuity

In Perpetuity

These Superencompassing inactivated cincturing realms
are incomprehensibly vast
with the "Y" extending outward in perpetuity.

A solidified geode of pre-Made Manifest.
No open core, but rather the inactive black holes gently
resting against one another in the Universal Centrosphere.

Key:

State of Deep Contemplation. A pre-Made Manifest state in
which Uncreated Infinite SuperConsciousness TransImaginates
or pre-CompreCreates the preprescripted Holy Dharmic Plan
for all that is to be Made Manifest (Holy Dharmic Blueprint).

W = Unmanifest vibration

X = Unmanifest light photons

Y = Unmanifest Infinite SuperConsciousness

Z = Inactivated black holes

In totality, these components resemble a solidified geode. The geode's nubilous core consists of a nonvibrating, Unmanifesting Infinite Potentialized centrosphere against which the Inactivated Black Holes rest. If viewed by earth humankind from far beyond the core, these combined components would appear cloudy white or indiscernible from the inactivated "X," or Photonic Plasmasolic Consciousness statically existing within the core area. This pre-Made Manifest state of unmanifested potential experiential is the only state where the "X" would be visible existing discretely within or beyond the black holes.

Normally, when we view an activated black hole, the force of the SuperConscious "Y" is so powerful that the photonic light is nonviewable—thus appearing black from our viewpoint. In this Deep Contemplative state, "Z" is somewhat like pores on human skin, blending indiscernibly against the backdrop of skin cells "X" when viewed from a distance. However, all human pores combined on one person are far less numerous than the number of black holes in physical existence.

This deharmonized contemplative period extends for an indeterminable length of human conceptualism, for time and space simply do not exist. All manifested or previously experienced gross physical nuclear membranes have been denucleated from their Photonic Nuclear Envelopes and redistributed SuperConsciously within these four particular, pertinent potentials. ALL is Contemplatively quiet. This is the immutable, incorruptible, foundational bedrock upon which the Table of Creation stands. Until Uncreated Infinite God has TransImagined everything ever to be experienced, nothing is Made Manifest.

Beginning with ever so Slight of An Influencial Idea, God, our Transcendental Holy Originator or Uncreated Infinite SuperConsciousness begins to stir in Galactic Terms with only a gentle impulsion. Thus, there was no Big Bang, for it simply is "Big Wrong." As Uncreated Infinite SuperConsciousness, God expresses Its TransImagined Self as Made Manifest God Incarnate. In the Made Manifest incarnation of the Universe, Uncreated Infinite God Transinitiates Creation by Transenfolding its "Y" through the realm of the now Superwillfully Proactivated "X." Next, the "Y" is interfolded with the "X," SuperConsciously Transinjecting the synthesized "YX" through the realm of resistless, now-reresonant "W." Almost simultaneously, in less than an octillionth of a nanosecond, the "YXW" virtually synchronistically creates a trisymphysis.

This Thermonuclear Transinterinfusion Triunity (YXW) is Trans-injected as Manifesting Existence (God) at almost three times the speed of light. (See Diagram 3, Manifesting Trisymphysis, page 419.)

The inward reflecting expression of synodical synergism resulting in the coalescing trisymphysis is the birth of the Manifesting Super-Consciousness, occurring as a manifesting synarthrosis. This symphonious synapsis, once again, is far less an than octillionth of a nanosecond. Successively, the "Y" synizes SuperConsciously and irresistibly back down through the spiracular "X," creating a vacancy in the newly spawning Universal Experience. If the "Y" is not immediately SuperConsciously retracted or synized out, it continues on. It also is almost immediately retracted, but not until it has become antimatter as an antiquark, antilepton, or antineutrino. This Transinterinfused Holy Double Helix is held together by the SuperConscious Will of Made Manifest God. The Holy Uncreated Infinite SuperConsciousness now is manifesting as the Triune God or as the Inversely Reflecting Infinite Manifesting Potentiality. This newly spawned "XW" exists as the Transinterinfused Holy Neutrino, consisting only of "X" or Photonic Light and the SuperConscious vibratorized "W" or Love of God.

Now, simultaneously at the Ortho Center above the Holy Neutrino, a synchrotronic phenomenon is occurring. Electromagnetic radiations are spiraling off the Holy Neutrino, as unimaginable energies are accelerating the Holy Neutrino's highly charged particle-like plasma. The violent recoiling force from within the voided vacuum created by the SuperConsciously synized "Y" simultaneously ejects and frees the leptons or electrons from the Trisymphysis. The photonically infused "W" fragments (freedom) once again are less than an octillionth of a nanosecond as they immediately are captured in the positive/negative symmetry of the atoms' nucleon formation. A clumsy, gross physical example of this phenomenon occurred during the formation of our planet, with its satellite, the moon, spawned from the Pacific Ocean basin, subsequently captured in our planet's orbit.

The newborn plasma-like Holy Double Helix is composed of vibration and light photons, now congealing to become quarks and leptons as

Diagram 3. Manifesting Trisymphysis

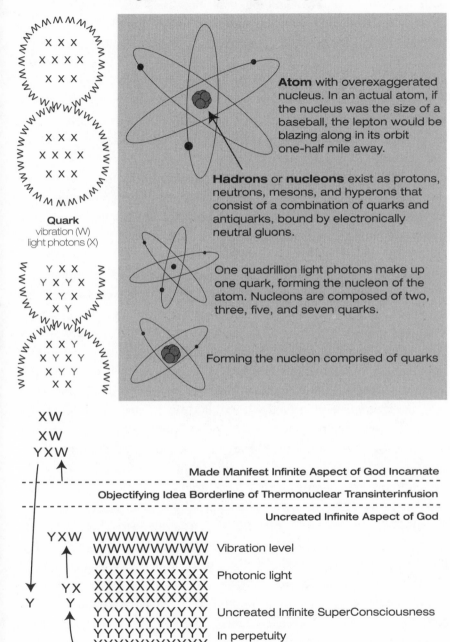

Quark
vibration (W)
light photons (X)

Atom with overexaggerated nucleus. In an actual atom, if the nucleus was the size of a baseball, the lepton would be blazing along in its orbit one-half mile away.

Hadrons or **nucleons** exist as protons, neutrons, mesons, and hyperons that consist of a combination of quarks and antiquarks, bound by electronically neutral gluons.

One quadrillion light photons make up one quark, forming the nucleon of the atom. Nucleons are composed of two, three, five, and seven quarks.

Forming the nucleon comprised of quarks

Made Manifest Infinite Aspect of God Incarnate

Objectifying Idea Borderline of Thermonuclear Transinterinfusion

Uncreated Infinite Aspect of God

Vibration level

Photonic light

Uncreated Infinite SuperConsciousness

In perpetuity

Since Uncreated Infinite SuperConsciousness does not exist in Made Manifest, the "Y" is Superwillfully retracted back into Its Uncreated Infinite State.

building neutrinos. The building neutrinos consist of both negatively charged electrons and electron neutrinos, which are electrically neutral with no charge. These building neutrinos are various combinations of leptons around compiling quarks or hadrons, eventually forming into atoms, molecules, finally becoming formed matter. The Holy Neutrino's central eye looks identical to the epicenter of the black hole, similarly spinning wildly with its freshly voided center now allowing for cosmic decay. The entire vibratorized physical cosmos literally implodes inversely into the eye of every Holy Neutrino.

As photonic vibratorized matter continues to build, the sheer mass of the burgeoning Universe begins to systematically compound. Ever increasing magnetic fields grow synchronously containing the subjugate galaxies as well as the black holes. While the Universal Engine gets fired up, the once again now-reactivated black holes stimulate into a sublimation of servitude. Now contained by the swelling universal gravitational mass, the black holes' electromagnetic fields magnetically are contained within the black hole's epicenter. The SuperConsciousness of the Uncreated Infinite is so irresistibly attractive and powerful that when we view into the epicenter of the black hole even the unimaginably thick layer of photonic light appears black. The observable, bottomless blackness is the eternally loving, pensive gaze of the Eye of our Uncreated Infinite SuperConsciousness.

The photonic eye of God within all Holy Neutrinos, building neutrinos, leptons, quarks, atoms, etc., peers throughout the entire three manifesting Universes. These three manifesting Universes become a Synoptic Holographic Eye of Unending Comprehension. This allows for the ongoing Transinterinfusion of the newly reperfected Divine Plan. God gazes through the eye of every particle of manifesting matter that constitutes you, me, and everything consisting throughout time and space. Meanwhile, the newly manifesting Universe activates the black holes to perform their unbelievable function. The black holes are the gateway for all experienced, vibratorized matter to return back to its original state. The sedulous black hole is a Transilluminating, incisive sear-separator, which transpicuously pierces all vectors of Made Manifest space or vibratorized matter.

The Uncreated Infinite SuperConsciousness illustriously discerns and eviscerates the light photons from the vibrations. The dissected, uncaptivated, lighter, and now disenthralled light photon (X) is drawn inevitably beyond the balanced, harmonized, now perfectly splendrous (W) vibrations. The light photon and the vibration once again are ready to be Transreinterinfused into the Holy Neutrinos. God synoptically comprehends every fluid moment in Creation before it even takes place; as such, nothing eludes or escapes God. There are no secrets from God. After all, God TransImaginated everything Made Manifest. These elucidations should give both scientist and laity pause for contemplation.

Barely gaping open as a newborn incarnation of existence, Creation is propped open by the virtuous work of the inner double helix scaffolding. This vibration and light scaffolding composes the Holy Neutrinos, bonding to form leptons, quarks, muons, hadrons, etc. Simultaneously, free-flowing helpers of photons, classons, bosons, and gravitons are busy at work as compounding photons. This group also includes mesons, weakons, and some classons, all of which carry or exhibit within themselves the characteristics of electromagnetism, strong interactions, weak interactions, and gravity. Depending upon their individual particular use, these photonic, vibratory particles of erectable matter or dissemanatings from cosmic decay exhibit zero to some residual, integral spin for preeminent, purposeful usefulness.

These light photon-compiled, metamorphosed particles of light matter have specific purposes, some of which are free flowing in wheels of potential intellectual comprehension. These positively and negatively charged ion particles can be witnessed by humans in the waving, raining exhibitions observable in the electromagnetically influenced Northern Lights. It also is evident in the invisible magnetic fields of a bar magnet when placed in finely ground iron filings. Our planet, the sun, our Milky Way galaxy, or any electrically charged object in motion will produce a similar field of influence. This phenomenon is like a galactic chariot, with both Mother Gravity and Father Relativity having equal influence. Within the Unity of SuperConsciousness, God is the chariot's sole driver, with gravity and relativity passively relegated to sitting in the back seat. (See Diagram 4: SuperConscious Chariot, page 422.)

Levels one through eleven are gravity/relativity based. Levels twelve through fifteen comprise the Unity where ascending and descending positively and negatively particlizing electromagnetic fields are utilized as God sees fit. These outermost fields are huge, generally larger than solar systems. This entire phenomenon is all matter inclusive, excluding radiations,

Diagram 4. SuperConscious Chariot

Inward Reflection of Manifesting TransImagination

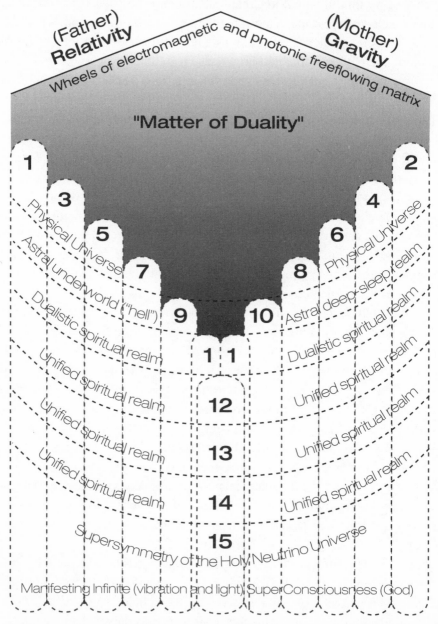

(Father) Relativity

(Mother) Gravity

Wheels of electromagnetic and photonic freeflowing matrix

"Matter of Duality"

1   2
3   4
5   6
7   8
9   10
11
12
13
14
15

Physical Universe
Astral underworld ("hell")
Dualistic spiritual realm
Unified spiritual realm
Unified spiritual realm
Unified spiritual realm

Physical Universe
Astral deep-sleep realm
Dualistic spiritual realm
Unified spiritual realm
Unified spiritual realm
Unified spiritual realm

Supersymmetry of the Holy Neutrino Universe

Manifesting Infinite (vibration and light) SuperConsciousness (God)

Uncreated Infinite SuperConsciousness (God)

which are the phenomenon's cosmic decay by-products. These radiation by-products provide a useful energy resource for infinite, manifestable, or manipulable potentialities. (See Diagram 5: Manifesting Infinite SuperConscious CompreCreation, below.)

Diagram 5. Manifesting Infinite SuperConscious CompreCreation Expressing as The Holy Dharmic Blueprint

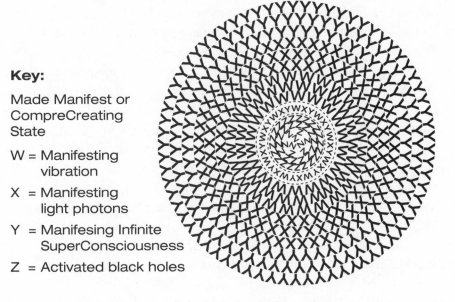

Key:

Made Manifest or CompreCreating State

W = Manifesting vibration

X = Manifesting light photons

Y = Manifesing Infinite SuperConsciousness

Z = Activated black holes

These internally building scaffolds begin to erect their double helix within double helix, as structures of support by divine, preordained plan. The enbloced, solid geode of unmanifested potentiality literally pries the enclosed massive focal point into an ever-increasing opening of 360 degrees of Manifesting Infinite Potentiality. Made Manifest God as the infantile Universe begins Its slow, purposeful incarnation with the ever-loving Synoptically Holographically Comprehending SuperConsciousness of the Manifesting Infinite SuperConsciousness carefully guiding each ensuing unenfoldment. Creation builds from within to eventually become its current state as we know it. Father Relativity, Transinterinfused with Mother Gravity, produce their offspring, Child of Matter. Another Divinely Discerned, carefully contemplated, lovingly orchestrated Universal Incarnation Manifests as CompreCreation.

Ineffable Reiterations

The Uncreated Unmanifested Universe originates with the Precontemplated Deharmonized unresonating vibrations. In this precreated state, the myriad, incalculable, inactive black holes gently rest in a 360-degree, solidified, milky-white state of dormancy. Always protecting the Uncreated Infinite SuperConsciousness from both the inactive black holes and the unresonating, pre-Made Manifest vibratory potential is an unimaginably massive layer of minute immaculate light photons. These photons provide an eternal barrier separating all that is manifestable from The Holy Uncreated Infinite SuperConsciousness.

After an indeterminable period of Deep Contemplative Divine Discernment followed by a TransImaginated, projectible, perfected perception, the Holy Uncreated Infinite SuperConsciousness Transgenerates the newly imaged conceptualization of TransImaginated Creation. The Holy Uncreated Infinite SuperConsciousness Superwillfully Self-projected as Its inward reflection, known as the Manifesting Infinite Potential SuperConsciousness (God), becomes an incarnating, manifesting Universe. Uncreated Infinite God Transenfolds the "Y" through the "X," and Transinterjects "YX" through the reresonating "W" realm. In a Thermonuclear Transinterinfusion, almost simultaneously, God Superwillfully and SuperConsciously retracts the synizing "Y" down the spiracular "XYW." This process results in a Transinterinfused "XW" as a newborn Holy Neutrino within the level-fifteen Causal Universe. The Holy Neutrino is a fusion of vibration, light, and Manifesting Super-Consciousness.

The expunged "Y" creates a void in the emerging experience, providing a concurrent, viciously spinning "XW," simultaneously producing the slowly imploding cosmic decay. The interdependent exothermal liberation of the lepton and subsequent orbital recapture creates the spawning of gravity and relativity. At this moment, a unified time-space coincident exists. Meanwhile, the imperative foundation for all Made Manifest Creation originates at the Orthocenter of the now incipient, inexpugnable Holy Neutrino. Creation first begins to congeal during the assemblage of the twelve manifesting scaffolding of fabricating matter. God Superwillfully, electromagnetically compresses light photons with vibration into classons, which are or become bosons, potentially forming into gravitons, fermions, etc. Photonic light with vibration is Thermonuclearly Transinterinfused, producing the plasma-like inner scaffolding for electrons, leptons, quarks, hadrons, atoms, etc.

Creation now is held together by the sheer mass of the Universal Gravity itself. Creation no longer is necessarily contained by the immutable Will of God alone. The increasing gravity keeps the photonic light or Transinduced relativity contained. God's Will renders a unified field theorem implicitly impossible. All this hyperactivity stimulates the inactive black holes to reengage with an enforcing, PreOrdained response. As the compiling photonic vibrations build to self-containing, gravitational mass, the restirring black holes begin to whirl. With the black holes recommissioned, their electromagnetic fields intensify to unimaginable levels. Eventually, these fields comfortably are confined by the ever increasing, gravitational, magnetic exertions of Manifesting Creation's own sheer mass. As the universal mass compounds, the gravitational pressures are forcefully imposed upon the black holes. This entire process allows for the commencement of the black hole's Transilluminating, sear-separating, dismantling and recycling functions.

As all photonically vibratorized, previously experienced matter is being reclaimed, it is electromagnetically separated, light photon from vibration. One quadrillion photons make up one quark. An indeterminable, unset amount of light photons comprise the electrons and leptons as they are God-assembled in ever-increasingly inward infrastructuring based upon their dharmically blueprinted purpose.

The black hole, "Z," dismantles the lighter photon "X." Once disembodied from the deharmonized vibration "W," both "X" and "W" once again SuperConsciously are drawn toward the "Y," where they resettle into their perfectly balanced states. All three components, "X," "W," and "Y," await a Transreinterinfusion back into Manifesting Creation again. The decomposing vibration "W" is Superwillfully repelled by the "Y," while being reharmonized to 8.4 hertz. 8.4 hertz—the frequency of pre-Made Manifest vibration (love). Collectively, "W," "X," and "Y" await another reengagement once again, back into God Imagination, as inwardly manifesting time and space.

In the Contemplative Universal Incarnation state, the "W" continues to buoy the black holes away from both the "X" and "Y" at 8.4 hertz—the resonation at which the "W" begins its inward descent, becoming

CompreCreation. The "XW" is Transinterinfused into spawning Creation at three times the now-recognized speed of light. The Universal mass, Thermonuclearly Transinterjected into "being" as CompreCreation, literally compresses the 8.4 hertz into the manifesting, condensing, infinitely compressing combinations of building infrastructure we now intricately understand as the Table of Created Matter.

The Table's subsequent, inward implosion into the Holy Neutrino or resulting cosmic decay is what earth humankind is busy trying to analyze and comprehend. For example, a flower withers due to its inward implosion into the eye of its Holy Neutrinos. Whether scientists or gardeners, people are intent upon perceiving and comprehending things of Creation in Absolutes. Yet, they only can focus upon the Made Manifest end result or cosmic decay of a flower, because it is all they essentially are able to "see." Thus, Absolutes, final interpretations, or analyses are made based upon only a tiny percentage of the amazing magnitude of what actually has taken place, or what actually goes into the creation of a flower, let alone contributes to its bloom, withering, or end-result state.

According to the Holy Angelic Realm, planet Earth is in no preeminent danger of being annihilated by any unforeseen highly charged, electricity-emitting, Manhattan-sized Idaho Russets hurtling through the cosmos for countless millennium to come. Earth humankind's only unrealized, potential "Armageddon" would come from human beings' ignorant, ego-based, misguided use of free will. Creation will continue to flourish on this planet, due to the Thermonuclear Transinterinfusion occurring on planet Earth and throughout the manifesting cosmos in the building and Holy Neutrinos.

Evidence of this same Thermonuclear Transinterinfusion going on at the Holy Neutrino level clearly is evident within our sun. The sun is giving off building neutrinos by the trillions, as do supernova explosions and the violent deaths of ancient stars. The sun is compressed helium and double helix plasma hydrogen gas SuperConsciously held together by the SuperConscious Will of God. Within the sun, the Holy Neutrino becomes the building neutrino—eventually to become the compressed hydrogen and helium gas atoms that compose the sun.

The sun literally is visible, manifesting, veridical evidence of this phenomenon. The sun doesn't fully manifest into ordinary matter, but rather manifests initially in the Holy Neutrino state as photonic light and vibration. The sun then manifests into the various building neutrinos of the quark-lepton state, and continues into the physically manifesting gaseous atom state. The Thermonuclear Transinterinfusion is the catalyst for the sun's ignition. Eventually, only through photosynthesis of its light does the sun become tangible physical matter.

The sun's atoms are mostly made up of hydrogen. Ninety-four percent of the sun's atoms are hydrogen and 5 percent are helium. The remaining .1 percent consists of atoms of oxygen, carbon, neon, nitrogen, magnesium, iron, and silicon. These nine elements compose the sunlight, which we recognize as white light. These electromagnetic radiations are emitted as particle-like, spiked waves called photons. The tightly packed light photons of the Holy Neutrino are identical to the photons of light being emitted by the sun.

The sun is a shining example of the Thermonuclear Transinterinfusion of vibration and light photons. The incomprehensible energies being expressed through the sun are the direct result of the Manifesting infusion of vibration and light photons. This infusion causes the sun to resonate like a massive bell being continually struck and produces over 10 million individual tones simultaneously.

This interinfusion of vibration and light photons produces the supersymmetry of the Holy Neutrino realm. This realm occurs within Manifesting Creation as a plasma. The interior of the leptons and quarks reflect the plasmasolic nature of Uncreated Infinite SuperConsciousness. The gelatinous plasmasolic nature of Manifesting Creation also can be found deep within the atoms of the sun's core. It also can be found in the protons, neutrons, and neutrinos. All of Made Manifest Creation is actually a gelatinous plasma of Manifesting SuperConsciousness.

Deep within the atoms of the sun, vibration and light photons quickly manifest and build into the lepton/hadron Astral state in the simultaneous thermonuclear explosion, eventually giving off the immaculate visible white photonic light, infrared rays, and vibratory heat as the congealing by-product. Photonic light is experienced in four distinctly separate ways. It can be reflected as experienced when looking into a mirror, dispersed as when shining upon snow, absorbed when impacting into energy-absorbing, shadow-producing solidified matter, and transmitted when penetrating through glass, water, ice, and clear quartz crystals.

Included in light's transmitting properties is the phenomena of refraction, whereby propagating light waves deflect and shift as evidenced by the visible displacement of a straw in a cup of water. Light transmitting through a mist or prism will also separate, resulting in the visual spectacle of a rainbow. Mirrors reflect all colors, snow appears radiant white, and solidified matter absorbs all other rainbow colors except for those that are being reflected, and thus, physically seen.

The physically manifesting Universe explodes from deep within the unseen quark-lepton world. To us here on planet Earth, this bursting appears as bubbles of existence manifesting out of the ethereal vacuum or void of deep space.

These exploding, manifesting unknown phenomena have perplexed scientists and curiosity seekers for millennia. Mysteries abound regarding the creation and formation of our physical cosmos and many more unknowns will continue to intrigue scientists with limitless abundance.

The expansion of the finite universe indeed is speeding up. This is not, however, on account of any mysterious dark matter and even more mysterious dark energy splitting apart the universe. Faint cosmic microwave radiation fills the universe with slight heat variations—but not from a Big Bang. Rather, this radiation comes from the continuous infusions of vibration and photonic light occurring within the formation of quarks and leptons of our Astral Universe.

Protons and neutrons make up the building blocks of the nucleus of the atom and are composed of these smaller quark particles. These particles can contain nuclei with quarks in sets of twos, threes, fives, and sevens. Two-, three-, and five-quark particles are found throughout our immediate manifesting surroundings, while the seven-quark particles are found in dark matter and dark energy. These seven-quark particles give the dark matter and dark energy its geometrically flat characteristics. Geometrically flat means that parallel lines drawn across the cosmos will never meet. These seven-quark particles also account for the inflation factor, whereby microwaves gather energy, subsequently appearing hotter when passing through large clouds of galaxies. When the microwaves exit the clouds, they leave with more heat and energy than that with which they arrived.

Our universe is composed of 4 percent atoms, 24 percent invisible dark matter (detectable by its gravitational influence on stars and galaxies), and 72 percent is of dark energy. Scientists are only certain of the 4 percent of atoms that comprise our universe. The 96 percent that make up Made Manifest is composed of various aspects of vibration and intensely bound light photons within all manifesting. It is the combined essence of one quadrillion light photons retained and maintained within the binding vibration that gives a quark its mass. If anyone could surmise a way to undo a quark and weigh just one light photon amongst the quadrillion, they could accurately measure and discern the unknown 96 percent. Until that time, the other 96 percent will remain completely unknown and will continue to be a mystifying secret for the discovery of future generations.

Since our manifesting physical universe is a sphere, nothing detectable can extend for more than sixty degrees across the sky. The boundary or universal walls produce the observed cutoff of all fluctuations larger than the radius of our spherical universe. This manifesting boundary is found by perceiving the physical universe from beyond the inside of every atom. To travel beyond the atom would bring the observer to a vantage point from which the physically manifesting boundaries would be clearly recognizable. From this Astral or Causal viewpoint (cosmic scenic overlook), one would be observing the physically manifesting universe in its entirety. However, in order to do so, one would have to be in their spiritual pure perception state with the God-gifted ability to interpret, process, and comprehend the picture flawlessly. Such a perspective would allow the viewer a front row seat. One would observe the universe expanding for billions of earth human years.

In actuality, God purposefully and SuperConsciously is Compre-Creating the Universe's now fifth manifesting existence. In the grand finale there will be neither a "big rip" (flies apart), nor a "big crunch" (collapses). The entire Made Manifest will eventually be reabsorbed as Unconditional Love and all Manifesting will be dissolved, having once again returned to Its Uncreated Infinite SuperConscious Unconditionally Loving state.

Holy Truth

The timeless symbol of Om is the symbol of God.

Holy Lord Shiva explains it this way:

"Out of limitless, Holy photonic light and illimitable Unconditional vibratory Love of our Uncreated Infinite SuperConscious Holy Originator, bursts forth my Manifesting Immaculate Radiant Resplendent Causal Diamond of an Idea."

"With ever-newness, ever-joyous, immutable bliss, my Manifesting Infinite Holy SuperConsciousness Interinfuses measureless amplitude and immeasurable magnitude into energizing, objectifying Astral Thoughts."

"Inextinguishable Light and inexhaustible Love are Superwillfully Transinterinfused into inversely reflecting glorious objectivity. Manifesting as a Holy TriUnification of my Causal, Astral, and physical Universes, I SuperConsciously serve all manifesting as Omni Facilitator and Holy Fabricator. From my Uncreated Infinite Holy Originations I Manifest as Infinite Holy SuperConscious Incorruptible Potentiality in splendrous perpetuity."

Holy Desire From Our Manifesting Infinite SuperConsciousness

May my children, for even just one moment, experience the limitless, joyous glory of divine simultaneous actualization. In this blissful state, our Manifesting experience becomes a unifying, awe-inspiring recognition of our Holy SuperConscious ceaselessly, boundlessly loving Omni At-Oneness.

Holy Blessing From The Uncreated Infinite SuperConsciousness

From the depthless ocean of my Uncreated Infinite Super-Consciousness, my Absolute Infinite Holy Unconditional Love Manifests within and throughout you as my Holy Inversely Reflecting Grandchild, with limitlessly Holy Transplendent Glory.

Humble Prayer To The Holy Infinite

I pray to you, Manifesting Infinite Holy (your preferential God name) SuperConsciousness, that you fill my Unified Super-conscious experience with our illimitable Unconditionally Loving Holy Omni At-Oneness.

Holy Reflections

Scott and Mari:

"You are all you've ever expressed. You will become that which you infinitely reflect."

Infinite Holy Motherhood of God:

"Ever have I Loved thee. Forever will I Love thee."

Holy Lord Shiva:

"Endlessly have I lovingly Manifest We. Eternally will you Manifest as glorious Me."

Uncreated Infinite Holy Superconsciousness:

"Unconditionally do you inversely reflect as my Manifesting Infinite Holy Love. Limitlessly do My Holy Reflections blissfully Manifest as Our loving experience."

It is all too easy to immerse ourselves in egoistic pursuits, and in doing so, forget how we operate within a greater whole. In the tapestry of humanity, each thread is invaluable. In the sea of existence, no one truly swims alone. It is only when we explore, examine, and challenge our perceptions of reality that the ever-present door of Om leading to evolutionary soul upliftment reveals the key as unlimited potential afforded to all.

We have been Blessed to bring you these Transcendental Illuminations.

As we ascend the unending path from dualistic perception into Unified Comprehension, we not only recognize Truth, we ARE Truth. As Truth, we express Love as Unconditional Love.

As both the Messengers of Truth and Love Itself, we assume our souls' God-gifted responsibility of assisting in the enlightenment of ALL souls.

It is our sincere desire that the wisdom from this book will accompany you on your quest to realize the ultimate destination of eternal freedom. How great it would be for all earth humankind to realize, for one day, even one moment in time, our Unified SuperConscious Omni At-Oneness.

Scott Bergér & Mari Tankenoff

Spiritual Renaissance

*D*uring the Holy Contemplative State of pre-Made Manifest all aspects of the upcoming Manifestation are Infinitely Comprehended. In this pre-Made Manifest state several transitioning stages occur.

Within the Holy Contemplative state Uncreated Infinite SuperConsciousness Composes the entire TransImagination for ALL that is to be Made Manifest as a pre-Made Manifest Conceptualization. Conceptualization is the net result of Divine Discernment. Three distinct stages occur during Divine Discernment to produce Conceptualization.

The first stage occurs as a Divine Perception or Idea. The second stage occurs as Limitless Projection or Thought. The Melding of Perception and Projection becomes the third stage as Infinite Comprehension or pre-CompreCreation. The pre-CompreCreation is the Holy Dharmic Plan. The Holy Dharmic Plan reflects or expresses Itself as the Manifesting Holy Blueprint or CompreCreation. Even Made Manifest God (Holy Lord Shiva, Allah, Adonai, etc.) was Conceptualized by Uncreated Infinite SuperConscious God during Divine Discernment.

All Perceptions were limitlessly Projected out by Uncreated Infinite SuperConsciousness as Divine Thoughts. All Divine Thoughts are Transenfolded together to form pre-CompreCreation as an Infinitely Comprehended Conceptualization. This pre-CompreCreation IS the Holy Dharmic Plan. Uncreated Infinite SuperConsciousness Transenfolded Idea, Thought, and Comprehension as the Divine Discernment that became the Conceptualized Holy Dharmic Plan as pre-CompreCreation. Uncreated Infinite SuperConscious God Transinterinfuses or Manifests Itself as the Holy Dharmic Blueprint for All Manifesting CompreCreation. All Manifesting CompreCreation is an expression of Incarnating (Made Manifest) God and as such, is Loved Unconditionally by Uncreated Infinite SuperConscious God.

Our Divine purpose for this Holy Book is to usher in a Spiritual Renaissance that introduces two super-advanced Spiritual Upliftment Techniques. The first technique is accelerated Salvation through Trans-Imagination. This is achieved by one's willful and purposeful spiritual double dipping into both their pre-Made Manifest and Manifesting states. The second technique is the SuperConscious Transimplantation of the Holy Grail that Illuminates the human consciousness or soul.

During a rising tide, if one boat rises, all boats rise. The same is true of the human consciousness during a Spiritual Renaissance. Salvation from either your physical, Astral, or Causal containers will be cause for a Celestial Celebration. Many souls will pray for and receive the Transimplanted Holy Grail SuperConsciousness as a Divine Gift from God for their efforts. Those souls will be filled with ever-increasing bliss, immutable Unconditional Love, and limitless SuperConscious Comprehensions as their Divine Gift.

Manifesting SuperConsciousness is actually an Invisible Divine Essence Made Manifest in the image and likeness of Uncreated Infinite SuperConscious God. This SuperConsciousness having an earth human experience is manifesting as Pure Perception. In one's dreams during sleep the dreamer does not see or recognize itself and cannot reference any tangible aspects of its physical body. Whether awake or asleep, Manifesting SuperConsciousness exists as Pure Perception.

During TransImagination, all SuperConsciousness gifted with free will influences both the Holy Dharmic Plan and their individual Holy Dharmic Blueprint. During Our pre-Made Manifest state as Pure Perception the Holy Dharmic Plan was being pre-CompreCreated. Each free-will gifted Pure Perception injects its Divine Projections into the Holy Dharmic Plan. Their Divine Projections Manifest as their individual Dharmic Blueprint.

Everything a free-will gifted earth human experiences in their Made Manifest unenfoldment is a direct result of their individual Divine Projections. Your Divine Projections during the TransImagination state are the exact same choices you will make throughout your Made Manifest unenfoldment. In other words, your entire Made Manifest unenfoldment (dharmic blueprint) is a direct result of your pre-Made Manifest choices. Your dharmically Manifesting experience will unenfold exactly as Preprescripted or pre-CompreCreated, as determined from your Divine Projections (choices).

Knowing this, you can recognize or reference yourself as this Divine Projection. You can willfully infuse Unconditional Love into your Holy Dharmic Plan as it is still being TransImaginated. As your future experience (dharmic blueprint) continues unenfolding, it will contain your TransImaginated planted seeds of Unconditional Love.

Because of the ongoing nature of the TransImagination state, earth human consciousness can willfully align both their Holy Blueprint (ongoing unenfoldment) and their ongoing Preprescription (Holy Dharmic Plan) with Unconditional Love from efforts put forth now. This SuperConscious willful infusion of Unconditional Love directly influences the spiritual advancement of you, as a soul, in both your pre-Made Manifest and Manifesting states simultaneously. This double dipping into Unconditional Love will accelerate your soul's salvation throughout its pre-Made Manifest TransImagination.

Salvation can be actualized expediently by forming a bridge of comprehension between your manifesting perceptions and your Divine Perceptions. Your manifesting perceptions are your unenfolding Divine Perceptions contained within your dharmic blueprint. Your Unconditional Love will Facilitate and Fabricate your ongoing TransImagination and be expressed throughout your unenfolding manifesting experience.

All TransImagination was completed 14 billion years ago—before even Made Manifest God was incarnated. In this Holy State everything exists as Uncreated Infinite SuperConsciousness as Unconditional Love. Over 200 billion earth human years from now all Made Manifest will have returned to its SuperConscious Unconditionally Loving state. Spiritually double dipping into the Holy Originator's Ore of Unconditional Love will quickly emancipate your soul and transform you from conscious misperception to Transcendental Illumination.

Spiritual double dipping is Divinely Conceptualized, then willfully actualized to accelerate attaining salvation. Actualized double dipping for salvation also allows for the Conceptualization of an Arc of the Covenant and Holy Hypostasis to become willfully actualized within your own Unenfoldment.

All Manifesting SuperConsciousness is spiritually advancing along Its Holy pathway through Its Preprescripted Dharmic Plan, manifesting as Its Dharmic Blueprint. Eventually every unique pathway leads to Its own Door of Om. This Door of Om does not have a defined pathway on the other side.

Once you open your own Door of Om, your pathway dissolves in an actualization or expression manifesting as Unconditional Love.

Unconditional Love cannot be found; it can only be experienced. Through Deep Comprehension of TransImagination we can ensure our Dharmic Blueprints are laden with willfully projected, sparkling manifestations of the Holy Originator's Ore. The Holy Originator's Ore is Divinity Manifesting as Unconditional Love. Every thing Made Manifest originated as Uncreated Infinite SuperConscious Unconditional Love (Holy Originator's Ore). The Holy Originator's Ore (Unconditional Love), manifesting as Divinity IS the Holy Grail.

Our Deep Comprehension of TransImagination allows each of us to limitlessly project Unconditional Love into our Dharmic Blueprints' future unenfoldments. By willfully projecting or infusing the Holy Grail into our own pre-Made Manifest Dharmic Plan, we ensure that our unenfolding Dharmic Blueprint will contain these gems of Uplifting Divinity (Holy Originator's Ore) throughout our unenfolding Made Manifest experience.

Your Blueprint's pathway through your Door of Om leads to your own TransImagined Holy Origination and salvation. The door through which a fly is freed by you today becomes the fly's own Door of Om tomorrow. All SuperConsciousness is spiritually advancing through Its unenfolding Dharmic Blueprint according to Its TransImagined Dharmic Plan. At Its preprescribed point in futurity, everything Made Manifest will reunite as Unconditional Love and once again return to Its Original Uncreated Infinite Holy SuperConscious Unconditionally Loving state.

TransImagination

Holy Dharmic Plan

Stages of Divine Discernment that become the Conceptualized H.D.P.

Uncreated Infinite SuperConscious God

Divinely Perceives (Idea)	Limitless Projection (Thoughts)	Infinite Comprehension (pre-CompreCreation)

The pre-Made Manifest melding of Idea, Thought, and Comprehension becomes Divine Discernment as a Conceptualized H.D.P. It manifests as CompreCreation (Made ManifestGod) from Its Uncreated Infinite SuperConscious state

expresses

Itself as

(As above, so below) Inverse Reflection as Manifesting CompreCreation

Manifesting Holy Blueprint (CompreCreation)

Manifesting Infinite SuperConscious God

Causal Universe (Idea)	Astral Universe (Thoughts)	Physical Universe (Actualizations)
Humans interpret their Divine intentions	Humans process their thoughts and emotions	Humans comprehend with their actions and reactions

All Manifesting CompreCreation is
Uncreated Infinite SuperConscious
God, expressing Its TransImagination
as Its Holy Made Manifest state.

Glossary

*T*hroughout *Transcendental Illuminations* we have capitalized terminology and names relating to God, the Causal and Astral Universes, and everything Holy. In some cases, we have chosen to refer to some terminology and names interchangeably. Some examples are: "God," "Holy Ordainer," "Holy Originator," as well as "Blessed Angel," "Sanctioned Angel," and "Holy Angel." Also, "Holy Realm," "Spirit Realm," and "Astral Realm" all are one and the same. We have defined the following terms to enhance your reading experience.

Arc of the Covenant is a Holy Impedance creating a reverse electromagnetic current facilitating the entry and exit of any SuperConsciousness or God-sanctioned Angel or Deity. This protective electromagnetic container is Transimplanted in the Tabernacle of the physically manifesting human body and contains and maintains the Holy of Holies. This Holy Impedance continuously protects the Superessence from the manifesting vibratorized universe's contamination.

Astral is the energizing, objectifying Spiritual Universe composed of the quarks and leptons of all manifesting existence. All Made Manifest has an Astral container, which contains and maintains its Causal or Idea container. Upon physical death, all existence returns to this Spirit (Astral) Realm.

Building Neutrinos are the inner scaffolding of atoms; any combination of 6 different leptons that combine with their quark nucleus to form the various types of manifesting atoms.

Causal is the plasma-like Holy Neutrino Realm, into which all Trans-Imaginated, now-objectifying Ideas of God are infused as manifesting existence. Composed of supercompressed light photons and vibrations, found within electrons, leptons, quarks, and hadrons, this Realm is yet to be discovered by scientists.

Chakras are spiritual lightways providing the divinely embedded information for the physically manifesting being. They assist in containing and maintaining all three manifesting containers that constitute the human merkebah. They provide manifesting humankind the ability to absorb, contain, and maintain immeasurable amplitude and measureless magnitude of ever-increasing SuperConscious At-Oneness.

CompreCreation is the fluid Transinterinfusion of God's imaged Ideas, manifesting SuperConsciousness into objectivity by way of the Holy Neutrino Realm. The ever-melding act of simultaneously comprehending, reperfecting, and recreating of all that was TransImaginated, expressing as the Dharmic Blueprint.

Conceptualization is the Uncreated Infinite SuperConscious formulation of Perception, Projection, and Comprehension for Everything that will be Made Manifest. This melded formulation becomes the Transenfolded Holy Dharmic Plan.

Conjugate Consciousness is any entity controlling, manipulating, or inhabiting more than one physically manifesting existence simultaneously.

Deep Comprehension is the wisdom of complex understanding that is accrued through sustained attunement to ever-increasing levels of SuperConscious communication capacity. The soul evolves into a spiritually advanced perspective in which the duality of conscious experience (as defined by karmic debt) is absorbed into a Unified perspective of consciously attained salvation. The soul transitions into the Super-Conscious state of At-Oneness that expresses only Unconditional Love for all Made Manifest.

Deep Contemplation is the inactivated state of pre-Made Manifest Creation existing purely as Uncreated Infinite Holy SuperConsciousness. TransImagination is what occurs during this Deep Contemplation state.

Dharma (Holy Dharmic Blueprint) is the preprescripted (Manifesting) aspect of the Holy Dharmic Plan. It is the Manifesting blueprint that unenfolds as conscious experience according to its TransImaginated Divine Discernment. The dharma of all Made Manifest is predetermined during the pre-Made Manifest Deep Contemplation state.

Divine Discernment is a three-part melding stage during pre-Made Manifest that Conceptualizes into the Holy Dharmic Plan. Uncreated Infinite SuperConsciousness Conceptualizes Divine Injections that consist of Perception, Projection, and Comprehension occurring during the TransImagination state.

Electron is the lightest elementary particle. It is a lepton with a negative electric charge.

Essence is the entire manifesting being consisting of the Causal, Astral, and the atom-bound physical containers. This manifestation includes the ethereal-bound merkebah, chakras, and communication lightways in every human being.

God is One SuperConsciousness. As One Holy SuperConscious Divinity, God expresses Itself in three Divine Aspects.

God, in Its Uncreated Infinite SuperConscious form, exists as an Indivisible Divine Essence beyond the Universes of Its vibratory Made Manifest phenomena. In this pre-Made Manifest state, God is the Holy Originator of all TransImagination.

God, in Its Made Manifest state, exists as Manifesting Infinite Super-Consciousness, Facilitating and Fabricating all TransImagined Creation. Within Its Made Manifest state, God also exists as

Motherhood of Divinity SuperConsciousness (Infinite Mercy), expressing Itself as Unconditional Love.

Grace is the highest attainable state of Infinite Merciful SuperConsciousness; when one exudes a state of Peace combined with Unconditional Love.

Hadron is the nucleon composed of quarks and located deep within the atom.

Holy Dharmic Plan is the ultimate result of the pre-Made Manifest Holy Contemplative state. It is the Conceptualized formulation of Divine Discernment resulting from Divine Injections that consist of Perception, Projection, and Comprehension. This Preprescription for all that is to be Made Manifest occurs during the TransImagination state.

Holy Grail is SuperConscious Unconditional Love (either Uncreated Infinite or Manifesting Infinite) that is Transimplanted into the Holy of Holies, which is contained, maintained, and protected by an Arc of the Covenant. It also is Unconditional Love willfully projected and infused into our TransImaginated Holy Dharmic Plan and Manifesting Blueprint.

Holy Impedance is synonymous with the Arc of the Covenant. *See above.*

Holy Neutrino is a Manifesting combination of vibration and light photons, which congeal together to form both quarks and leptons. Holy Neutrinos compose the Causal (Idea) Universe, where the TransImaginated Holy Dharmic Plan is Transinterinfused into objectivity as Manifesting Existence.

Holy of Holies is the Divine Sepulcher within every human being that contains, maintains, and protects the soul from manifesting contamination. It also is the Divine Cavity into which the Holy Grail is Transimplanted.

Holy Originator's Ore is SuperConsciousness (either Uncreated Infinite or Manifesting Infinite) that accrues within the human experience when one's Intentions, thoughts, actions, and reactions are aligned with and expressed as Unconditional Love. The Holy Grail is composed of the Holy Originator's Ore.

Hypostasis is one (or more) Unified SuperConscious Divine Essence(s) Transimplanted into a physically manifesting being.

Interaction is the process by which God utilizes any manifested or manifesting being, object, or associated circumstance as a catalyst for a preprescripted God-determined outcome.

Intervention is the process by which God interrupts the predetermined dharmic plan of any number of manifesting beings for a desired outcome for reasons known only to God. This interruption WAS preprescripted into the predetermined dharmic plan.

Karma is the Divine accountability occurring from free-will choices made without Unconditional Love. This Divine accountability is woven into the dharmic unenfoldment of all life forms that create imbalances with their intentions, thoughts, actions, and reactions. These imbalances result in an indebtedness to Made Manifest nature and remain from one incarnation to the next until alleviated.

Leptons are any of a class of fermions subject to the weak (W) interaction, but not the strong interaction. They are known as the "electron," "electron neutrino," "muon," "muon neutrino," "tau," and "tau neutrino."

Lightways are the pathways within all creation that contain and provide the vibratory information for all matter to form. Within humans these pathways provide the information that manifests as a system of chakras and meridians. This information allows for the SuperConscious Facilitation and Fabrication of all Made Manifest. All necessary information is Transenfolded into the dharmic blueprint for all manifesting existence as a result of the TransImagination process.

Made Manifest/Manifested is TransImaginated consciousness that has transitioned from a state of Uncreated Infinite SuperConsciousness to Manifesting Infinite (consciously experiencing) experience.

Manifesting refers to the ongoing process of Made Manifest/Manifested.

Manifesting Infinite Mercy is the Manifesting Motherhood of God aspect of made Manifest SuperConsciousness.

Manifesting Infinite SuperConsciousness is the Facilitating and Fabricating aspect of Divinity that has been TransImagined; Uncreated Infinite SuperConsciousness expressing Itself as Made Manifest God.

Manifesting Trisymphysis is a phenomenon occurring in the Holy Neutrino Realm where the Uncreated Infinite SuperConsciousness momentarily is synergized with the Manifesting Infinite SuperConsciousness.

Merkebah is the encompassing system of lightways, chakras, and containers (Causal, Astral, and physical). It includes the ethereal realm and is responsible for protecting, containing, and maintaining the human conscious soul during its physically manifesting incarnations.

Muon is an unstable, negatively charged lepton. It is a heavier relative of the electron. It decays into an electron, a neutrino, and an antineutrino.

Neutrinos are any of three stable leptons having a mass approaching zero and no charge. They are known as "electron neutrino," "muon neutrino," and "tau neutrino."

Omni refers to a state of omniscience, omnipotence, and omnipresence.

Preprescripted refers to the Divine Discernment containing the entire TransImaginated dharmic blueprint for all Made Manifest existence.

Quarks are any of a set of elementary particles composed of vibration and light photons that bind together in various combination to form hadrons. There are six different recognized quarks that can be found in varying combinations and are known as "up," "down," "charm," "strange," "top," and "bottom" ("beauty").

Reincarnation is God's Divine Facilitation of the soul's rebirth in another physically manifesting body; a retroactive reflective opportunity for past karmic debt alleviation. This continuous process occurs until consciousness comprehends its true SuperConscious At-Oneness and attains emancipation from all physically manifesting forms.

Resurrection is the reinhabitation of a physical body by a soul that has been SuperConsciously extracted. It also is the rechemicalization and physical remanifestation of an emancipated SuperConsciousness in its exact previous physical form. These Divine Experiences are conducted solely by God for reasons known only to God. The distinction between these two Divine Experiences is that with reinhabitation, the soul is SuperConsciously retained at level eight within the physical universe. During remanifestation, the soul returns to the physical universe from the Astral or Causal realms, requiring a new replica of the physical container.

Saint is any manifesting SuperConsciousness achieving emancipation from reincarnation, karma, and all remaining dharmic imbalances. He or she is free from all dualistic influences, sin, fears, and attachments. Their ego is replaced with illimitable, Unconditional Love, and free will relinquished and gifted back to God. All completely free physically manifesting souls in this state are recognized by the Astral or Holy Realm as having attained salvation.

Salvation is a physically manifested being's freedom from sin, all karmic indebtedness, and thus, freedom from reincarnation. This final emancipation provides God's Holy Pension, a continuous infusion of Unconditional Love.

Tabernacle consists of the three manifesting containers of the earth human body housing the consciousness or soul of the individual.

Tau is an unstable, negatively charged lepton. It is the heaviest relative of the electron.

The Holy Originator is the Holiest of Holiness, Transcendental Manifestor as Uncreated Infinite SuperConsciousness. The Trans-Imaginator of all Made Manifest.

Thermonuclear Transinterinfusion is the unifying injection of God's objectifying Ideas into the Causal or Holy Neutrino Realm of Manifesting Creation.

Third Eye is the spiritual seat of the soul, located above the bridge of the nose, between and above the eyebrows. It allows humans to experience individual perceptions of omniscience, omnipotence, and omnipresence in ever-increasing states of deep prayer, yoga, and meditative at-oneness.

Transcendental Star is a SuperConsciousness that has reached the pinnacle of Superevolved spiritual evolution. This SuperConsciousness exists in the blissful void between Uncreated and Manifesting that occurs in the Holy Neutrino Realm. This SuperConsciousness travels Superwillfully throughout Made Manifest as pure expression of Divine Intention.

TransImagination is the Holy Contemplative state in which Uncreated Infinite SuperConsciousness Divinely Discerns the entire pre-prescripted Holy Dharmic Plan for all aspects of the entire pre-Made Manifest. From the Holy Contemplative state, Uncreated Infinite SuperConsciousness (Holy Originator) Manifests Itself as Made Manifest God (CompreCreation).

Transimplantation is the act of God Divinely Placing the human soul into the fetus just before birth; the act of God Divinely Placing within the human Tabernacle the Arc of the Covenant; the act of God Divinely Placing within the Holy of Holies the Holy Grail as SuperConsciousness.

Transimpregnation is the process by which God SuperConsciously facilitates the Transimplantation of DNA within a physically manifesting human being.

Transingression is the act or process in which a God-sanctioned Divine Essence enters and exits the Arc of the Covenant.

Transinteraction is a Divine process in which a God-determined outcome is Facilitated and Fabricated that was NOT preprescripted in the dharmic plan for the unenfolding experience.

Transinterinfusion is where CompreCreation occurs at the separation point between Uncreated and Manifesting Existences.

Transintervention is a Divine process in which a God-predetermined dharmic plan is interrupted for a desired outcome that was NOT preprescripted.

Uncreated Infinite SuperConsciousness is the Transcendental Unmanifested Absolute, existing in a blissful void of Immaculate Holiness beyond the Universes of vibratorized Causal, Astral, and physical Universes. The Holy Originator of the entire TransImaginated CompreCreation.

Unenfoldment is the state of TransImaginated SuperConsciousness in which all preprescripted CompreCreation expresses Itself as dharmic Made Manifest experience.

 = individual conscious accountability.

General References & Resources

Baigent, M.; Leigh, R; and Lincoln, H. *Holy Blood, Holy Grail.* Dell Publishing, New York, 1982.

The Holy Scriptures According To The Masoretic Text. The Jewish Publication Society of America. Philadelphia, 1917.

The Koran. In *The Everyman: The Koran.* Trans. J.M. Rodwell. London, 1909. Reprinted in 1994.

Stevens, W.A.; and Burton, E.D. *A Harmony of the Gospels for Historical Study: An Analytical Synopsis of The Four Gospels.* New York, 1904.

The Torah: The Five Books of Moses: A New Translation of the Holy Scriptures According to the Masoretic Text, First Section. The Jewish Publication Society of America. Philadelphia, 1962. Second Edition, Tenth Impression, 1978.

Webster's New World College Dictionary, Fourth Edition. Ed. M. Agnes. New York, 1999.

Yogananda, P. *Autobiography of a Yogi.* Reprint of the Philosophical Library 1946 First Edition, New York, 1946.

Autobiography

Throughout history, human beings have searched for meaningful answers, and above all else, Truth. All too often, quests for enlightenment have left seekers in a misguided state of fear, confusion, and helpless resignation within a jungle of conflicting information.

Few pathways actually lead to Absolute Truth. In an effort to alleviate the resulting painful voids of isolation and bewilderment, people have sought comfort, solace, and direction from a myriad of sources, many times far more convoluted than the seekers themselves. These well-trodden routes generally guarantee nothing but blisters to the soul. Even within the illusion of "comfort in numbers" where people seek connectivity, they ultimately experience only loneliness.

No other book in history ever has addressed with unerring precision, illumination, and benevolent compassion this eternal loneliness and search for irrefutable Truth. Until now, even the most promising pathways of information and enlightenment have failed to bridge the chasm between the human physical experience and the soul's true fulfillment.

Co-authors Mari Tankenoff, a licensed psychologist, and Scott Bergér, a holistic healer, are two relentless seekers whose personal journeys carried them through several unimaginable Transcendental experiences that involved their work, their clients, the health of their mind, body, and spirit, and their own relationship. Scott's experience alone will defy the reader's imagination. The evolution of these inexplicable phenomena resulted in the creation of *Transcendental Illuminations*. The writing of the book has been a compelling mission for Mari and Scott, who feel an excitement and a responsibility to share with others the revelations of their extraordinary experiences. They believe that readers will be as transformed by these findings as they were.

Transcendental Illuminations inspires and invites readers to explore and contemplate existence beyond their interpreted "truths." Neither predicatory nor dogmatic, this book reacquaints people with the recognition that they alone hold the very keys to their individual conscious experiences and ultimate soul evolution. *Transcendental Illuminations* supersedes the limiting boundaries of theology, philosophy, psychology, science, and spirituality, while unifying and intricately weaving these disciplines into a blanket of Truth—for every soul from every walk of life.